NAVIGATING THE GROWTH CURVE

9 FUNDAMENTALS THAT BUILD A PROFIT-DRIVEN, PEOPLE-CENTERED, GROWTH-SMART COMPANY

James Fischer

Special thanks to Developing Editor, Mark Harrison

GrowthCurve Press

4450 Arapahoe Avenue, Suite 100
Boulder, CO 80303
303-546-7939
www.growthcurvepress.com

Designed and Illustrated by Pam McKinnie, Concepts Unlimited
Cover Design by Ryan Nisogi

Published by Growth Curve Press
4450 Arapahoe Avenue, Suite 100
Boulder, CO 80303
303-546-7939
www.growthcurvepress.com

Library of Congress Control Number: 2005936588

ISBN   0-9765766-0-0   [pbk]

06 07 08 09 10   0 9 8 7 6 5 4 3 2 1

printed in the USA

DEDICATION

Dedication to Lura

Her unbridled enthusiasm, her sharp mind, her relentless patience and her enormous heart made the writing of this book possible.

ACKNOWLEDGEMENTS

This book was given birth based on the experiences of many hundreds of CEOs and their emerging enterprises. Without their gracious participation in my research none of the ideas, methods, and tools you see here would be made possible. I owe them all a huge debt of gratitude. A number of these business leaders made a particularly indelible mark on my research. I am truly grateful to people like Patti Machado, Peg and Bob Chapman, Les Burch, Marvin Sellig, Isaac Pollak, Rus Hackstaff, Hugh Fraser, Jacques Poujade, Carla Johnson, Michael Willis, Patrick Timpone, Kevin Loveless, Pete McDonald, Jim Young, Steve Easley, Janis Fairchild, the Martin brothers, and my father Arthur Louis Fischer, Sr. to name but a few.

This journey would have not started without the initial and continued support from Greg McDonald, Marc Peperzak, Marge Klemp, Windsor White, Delyn Copley, Lester Karplus, Mark Harrison, Doug Belscher, Jeffery Milburn, Justin Daniels, Daniella Pentalute, Jim Zigarelli, Katherine Kerr, Doug and JoAnna Grant, Steve Foster, Chris Kerr, Bruce Bean, Jeff Kandyba, Scott Spann, Lura Lee Genz, Nick Fischer, Louis Audet, Mark McGinnis, Bob Urquidi, Patti Dobrowolski, Barney Carlson, Rhonda Britten, Judy and John Graham, Bob Gaddis, Gordon and Luisa Garland, Marcie Tucker, Keith McGinnis, Donald Hackstaff, Kimberly Mendelsohn, Sue Debacker, Steve Adams, and a huge bow of thanks to Kevin Jones.

I would like to also thank Harold Ware for his catalytic business insight, Ron Melanson for his wisdom and patience, Gardiner Tucker for being a phenomenal thinking partner, and Harold Klemp for his eternal support. In preparation for this manuscript I am particularly indebted to the ideas of Margaret Wheatley, Stephen C. Harper, Guy Murchie, Christopher Alexander, Daniel Goleman, Adrian Slywotzky, Michael Gerber, Patrick Kelly, F. Bryon Nahser, Richard Pascale, Jim Collins. William Byham, Jeffrey Cox, and Jack Stack, all of whom contributed immensely by sending me down trails that I would have not otherwise have gone down in the exploration of my ideas. If I have not listed an author's name herein it is only due to a lack of space – not because their contribution was unworthy of recognition. In addition, I would like to thank four very special individuals for their direct work on preparing the manuscript: Pam McKinnie, from Concepts Unlimited, for her tenacity and her amazing design and illustration of this book. She is an incredible resource for the Origin Institute team. Nola Salisbury, for her gracious contribution to the endless hours editing the early manuscript, Gloria Balcom of The Next Level Marketing, for her superb eleventh-hour copywriting efforts, and Linda Jay Geldens, who did the final edit.

Finally, I am deeply grateful to my business partner at Origin Institute, Laurie Taylor, whose relentless belief and drive to bring this book out to the public was sorely needed. Without her critical input, practical insight, tons of business experience growing a Stage 6 company from a start up, and creative powers which expand far beyond her own acknowledgement, I would be at a loss. Thank you!

CONTENTS

Preface...ii

Prologue...v

Chapter 1: *Day of Reckoning*...1

Chapter 2: *Evidence of a Chasm*....................................13

Chapter 3: *Reality*...21

Chapter 4: *Even Atlas Shrugged*....................................31

Chapter 5: *Voltage*...39

Chapter 6: *Growth Curve*...49

Chapter 7: *Hidden Predator*...59

Chapter 8: *Rip Cord*..71

Chapter 9: *Reflective Edge*...79

Chapter 10: *Laws of Growth*...91

Chapter 11: *Growth Language*.....................................105

Chapter 12: *Stages of Growth*.....................................119

Chapter 13: *Reading the Patterns*................................129

Chapter 14: *Under the Surface*....................................141

Chapter 15: *The New Profit Model*...............................153

CONTENTS

Chapter 16: *Making and Keeping Money*......................................171

Chapter 17: *Investment*......................................187

Chapter 18: *The Pattern Language of Chaos*......................................201

Chapter 19: *Shaping Change*......................................211

Chapter 20: *Cracking the Code*......................................231

Chapter 21: *Growth Trauma*......................................253

Chapter 22: *Focusing and Changing Behavior*......................................265

Chapter 23: *Message in the Shadow*......................................281

Chapter 24: *Releasing Resistance*......................................289

Chapter 25: *Unfinished Business*......................................309

Chapter 26: *Full Circle*......................................315

Sources......................................327

Index......................................329

Appendix......................................337

Preview: *Harvesting Clarity*......................................339

Biography: *James Fischer*......................................342

From the notebook of Horace Bedford...

The 9 Fundamentals of the Growth Curve Solution

1. Provide a dynamic new method of planning that is accessible by the whole organization and allows contribution and strategic authoring by the entire staff.

2. Redesign how we think about and create the modern work community so that it not only better serves the company's vision, strategy, and goals, but also correctly addresses the interests, needs, and requirements of the staff.

3. Create a language of growth that: a) explains how companies grow, and b) gives a vocabulary of growth that everyone in the organization can use to communicate about the company's growth.

4. Provide a powerful new perspective on the importance of profitability in regard to the growth process and how it is: a) tied to the design of the business, b) dependent on everyone in the enterprise being in the profit zone, and c) reliant on the continued loyalty of the customer base.

5. Turn the understanding of organizational growth from one of being "business as a machine" to one of being "business as a living, intelligent organism."

6. Reveal the core requirements to staff satisfaction, and show the deep connection between staff satisfaction and enterprise profitability at every stage of growth.

7. Reveal the causes, symptoms, and cures for Growth Trauma.

8. Create key mechanisms that facilitate the application of the Growth Curve Solution in a business enterprise at any given stage of growth.

9. Introduce a method that facilitates the willingness of the CEO to release resistance to the company's current challenges in order to see below the surface of those challenges to the real causes of the company's issues.

PREFACE

*I am often intrigued with the transfer of insight and knowledge that occurs through the employment of a good story. In light of this, I would encourage you to consider the following story prior to beginning "**Navigating the Growth Curve, 9 Fundamentals That Build a Profit-Driven, People-Centered, Growth-Smart Company.**" Thank you for your interest in entrepreneurial growth.*
— **James Fischer, Origin Institute**

The Beekeeper and the Watchmaker

Two old friends, both business owners, sit down at a local coffee shop to talk about their businesses. One is a beekeeper who oversees honey hives placed at the perimeter of a cherry orchard outside of town. The other is a watchmaker whose company makes fine watches and has a small manufacturing plant just north of the town square.

Both owners are ready to retire and have put their businesses up for sale. If you had to buy one of these businesses, given that all things regarding customer base, revenue and profit are equal, which one would you choose?

Would You Buy a Business of Constant Change and Chaos?

The beekeeper operates in a world of constant change and chaos. He "facilitates" rather than "controls" the health of 125,000 bees living and working out of 55 white, 3-foot-high "wooden hives." The beekeeper can only foster an environment that supports the bees to produce honey. He cannot in any way guarantee an outcome.

Upon closer inspection, the apparent mass chaos swirling in and around the hives reveals the fact that every bee is an independent agent relentlessly pursuing its own mission, within the natural order of the hive, in support of the daily business of making honey and protecting the health of the hive.

The hive is an intelligent, self-organizing, adaptive organism able to adjust and innovate solutions to meet the challenges encountered during the natural course of events in nature. If it were to be accidentally dropped onto the ground from a significant enough height to break it into numerous pieces, the hive would very likely relocate its home base and start anew on the business of making honey.

Or, Would You Buy a Business of Enormous Precision and Control?

The watchmaker, on the other hand, works in a much different world. It is one of enormous precision and control. Every piece of a watch is delicately machined to within 100ths of an inch. The watches are all finely calibrated machines defined and constructed by a rigid manufacturing process. The watchmaker "controls" the assembly of his company's precision watches and controls the running of the business in a similar manner.

Both the watch and the watch business are non-adapting, dependable precision machines able to deliver results based on the predetermined set of conditions reflected in their design. If the watch were to be accidentally dropped on a concrete floor, it would likely break into numerous pieces and stop working, until someone or some outside force came along to repair it. What would happen to the watch business if it were to break apart in some fashion?

In short, the watch, being a machine, gives the appearance of being a highly controllable precision instrument yet it will never find a solution on its own, it will never adapt to conditions foreign to its design, it will never work independently or in a team and it will never think independently to innovate new ways of meeting the ever-changing challenges of its environment.

Watchmakers want predictability and objects they can control.

They want to run their business like a precision machine. They believe that to be effective, a machine must be controlled by its operators. This is the overarching purpose of management – to control the enterprise. They further believe that the machine exists for a purpose conceived of by its builders, to make as much money as possible for its owners.

Nothing wrong with making money, but to create an intentional enterprise that provides sustainable profits over a long period of time, our research suggests that the better approach lies in becoming more of a beekeeper.

Beekeepers have one foot in the future.

They have a natural facility to work with the dangerous sisters of growth, complexity and chaos. Beekeepers are more likely to let the intelligence of the team or "hive" be the operator instead of themselves.

They understand that their business is a living, intelligent entity and if allowed, it will come up with far more ideas and solutions than they ever could. The beekeeper's business will continually self-organize around and through its problems and challenges.

We would suggest that there is a beekeeper in all of us but that in our day-to-day struggles to "do the right thing," "be responsible," and "act like a leader," the watchmaker takes over more often than any of us would like to admit.

Predict, Adapt and Focus

Our concepts and programs are designed to help leaders predict how the complexity of their company will affect them, focus their efforts and resources on the right things at the right time, and adapt to the needs of the company in its particular stage of growth.

If you discover, after reading this book, that a certain curiosity urges you to learn more, visit our website at www.origininstitute.com.

So what's it going to be? Watchmaker or bee-keeper?

# PROLOGUE

Seed.

Tiny, unremarkable…and miraculous.

A perfect, natural potential for growth contained in a package the size of stardust. A tiny, preordained, biochemical fire of creation waiting to be harvested, planted, and turned on. It carries its own fuel, and a blueprint for its destiny. Given the right conditions, nothing could interfere with that destiny. Until now.

The contrast couldn't have been greater. It made him smile. Standing in the warm, sun-drenched field, holding the tiny kernel between his thumb and forefinger, he looked out over an ocean of gold. The simple fact that the seed he held could grow into one of the plants he beheld was extraordinary.

An ocean of gold was the only way to describe it.

A breeze rippled across the small field, creating waves that moved through the tops of the two thousand plants. Two thousand perfect, identical, golden plants. Every leaf, every stalk, was the same. But most importantly, every seed maturing in the sun, on every single plant, was the same, waiting to be turned loose by him.

An artist would have been ecstatic to find such a perfect mix of color and light. But it was no poet or painter who stood in the warm sun looking at the field. This observer saw only the economic beauty the crops represented. As he looked at his field of perfect plants he knew the world had changed. He could step into the tiny factory inside a seed and give it new instructions. He could give it a new destiny. He had made his choice years ago.

While others had spent their time and fortunes seeking to unravel the human genome, he had seen the science of genetics as a long-term business proposition. Knowing the political and social pressures that would follow the research into the genetics of a human being, he opted for the quieter, less public path of the plant genome, the seed genome. A small sign sat on his desk in his private study. It said simply, "People gotta eat." Let those who crave Nobel Prizes seek the human genome. Because no matter what kind of human they would create, those humans were going to get hungry. They were going to have to eat.

And his goal was now within reach. The field that lay before him was proof that his money had been well-spent. Already, his team had unlocked the genetics to the point that his perfect plants had created perfect seeds, perfect seeds that would never produce seeds of their own. A farmer would forever have to buy new seeds every year. And that was just the start.

He had been watching the cloud of dust approaching down the long, dry road for several minutes. He knew his guests would be impressed with what they saw. But they hadn't come for the beauty. The reason for this quiet trip to an isolated farm was not the perfect stalks of wheat rustling in the wind.

They weren't interested in the fact that their host was on the brink of controlling the food supply of the planet. Their attention was drawn to a corner of the field set apart by a border of stones. What they couldn't see was that under the bricks the ground itself was separated from the rest of the field by an elaborate system of stainless steel containers and filters.

> "THESE PLANTS WERE THE HIGHLY SOPHISTICATED DELIVERY SYSTEM OF A BIO WEAPON."

Inside the square of bricks stood thirty-six plants that looked like the rest of the perfect field. But inside the genetic code of these particular plants lay the reason for their trip.

Once their host had seen that his researchers were able to manipulate the genetic structure, the next step was natural for him. His corporation had long seen the value of markets that others found dangerous: illegal drugs, weapons, chemicals. But he had very high hopes for his newest venture. The men and women who stood with him in the field were the extremely private, and lethal, investors in his "corner" project.

The plants that drew their attention in the square surrounded by stones were worth more than the rest of the field combined. These plants represented the reason for their sizable investment in the experiment, hidden in a field of viable commercial crops. These plants weren't merely the result of a genetic alteration to produce non-reproducing seeds.

These plants were the highly sophisticated delivery system of a bio weapon.

"When do we see a demonstration?" It was the tall Brazilian woman who spoke the question on the minds of all the investors.

Their host smiled graciously. "We have a list of targets, building up to a large demonstration. The first example will help us eliminate an irritating competitor. Our media campaign has impeded their progress, but it's tedious. By removing one man, their efforts will collapse. We will make sure that you can read about it in the newspapers."

The woman spoke again. "What is the target's name?"

"Alan Logan."

"PETER LOOKED AT A COMPANY AS THOUGH IT WERE A MACHINE THAT NEEDED FIXING AND HE WAS THE MASTER MECHANIC."

Chapter 1

DAY OF RECKONING

"Somewhere — I knew then and believe even more firmly now — there is a simpler way to lead organizations, one that requires less effort, produces less stress than the current practices."
— **Margaret Wheatley and Myron Kellner Rogers**, *A Simpler Way*

"In less than two weeks you have unraveled four years' worth of hard work. What will your encore be? Pink slips for everyone?"

With that, the door slammed shut, leaving Peter stunned as he reached into the top drawer of his desk, the desk that used to be his brother's. The nearly empty bottle of Tums was right where he put it an hour ago, the last time his stomach churned.

Just perfect, he thought to himself. I've been here less than two weeks and I've managed to alienate every single person in the company. That takes a particular talent.

How did he come to this? How did he end up in his brother's office, at his brother's desk, running his brother's company, apparently, into the ground?

Three weeks ago, Peter was on a morning flight from Denver to Los Angeles, sitting in first class, headed to a series of high-level meetings with Robert Oberlander, the President of the worldwide conglomerate, the Santomo Corporation. Meeting Oberlander, who was known by all as R.O., was extraordinary under any circumstances. But it was R.O. himself who called to notify Peter of the meetings. And he added a detail that made Peter's heart skip.

It was possible that Peter would have a brief meeting with Daniel Tayakanagi, the legendary CEO of Santomo, who was rumored to be as secretive and eccentric as the late Howard Hughes. Meeting Tayakanagi would mean Peter's circuitous route to the brass ring had finally been completed.

Tayakanagi had engineered Santomo's expansion into markets that no one else could have conceived as profitable. He had gone on a buying spree that had pundits shaking their heads.

Peter's trip was supposed to include a couple of days of strategic planning and congratulations for the way he had turned a subsidiary of Santomo around. But when he arrived, R.O. was suddenly busy from morning to night, and Peter spent three full days explaining his actions to attorneys and accountants. He was mystified.

Recruited as a turnaround star, Peter was brought in by Santomo nineteen months earlier to run Steel Alloy Software, a Boulder, Colorado, company. Steel Alloy was a hard-luck company that had been bought as a part of Tayakanagi's expansion.

They were interested in capitalizing on the booming world of the Internet, specifically, network security. The young programmers were good to their dreams, and created a terrific product, but one that hurled the company over the precipice of rapid growth and cash flow perdition. That's when R.O. showed up with Daniel Tayakanagi's credit line. The owner gladly took a few million dollars to salvage his financial future.

The business press seemed to think Tayakanagi had made a shrewd play. Network security would become ever more important, and it was apparent that Santomo was willing to spend the necessary money to finish the product.

Peter had a reputation for whipping young companies into shape and getting them sold. He looked at a company as though it were a machine that needed fixing and he was the master mechanic. He'd come in as the executive officer, lop off the heads that needed lopping, instill efficiency, and a hardy dose of tough "in the trenches" discipline.

He was the one to put a rudderless, money-losing enterprise back on track. Most of his "real money" came at the back end in the form of options and special bonuses. He was a hired gun and he loved that reputation. But Steel Alloy was his biggest challenge to date.

Ever since finishing his MBA at Stanford, Peter had landed in unremarkable companies but if he was successful here, it would put him on the map. Steel Alloy had all the makings of a quick killing: a home-run product, surface inefficiencies and few-to-no marketing mistakes to correct. The flagship product would add bulletproof security to any size network, at a remarkably low cost. They needed an infusion of capital from Santomo to keep the company afloat and to hire more staff.

The hyper-bright geeks who were writing the code were very fast, with surprisingly few bugs to rewrite. As the image of his face on the cover of *Fortune* skimmed across his imagination, Peter was just beginning to taste success.

For the first six months, his turnaround formula ran like a charm. He instilled discipline and focused the efforts of his staff only on the mission-critical items that would get the results that he needed. All else was extraneous and cut from the budget.

The product's test stage was finished ahead of schedule, and looked more stable than anyone had predicted. But Santomo wasn't thrilled. They were concerned that Steel Alloy had created much more debt than they could ever recover, so they decided to shut down the funding flow. It made no sense to Peter. The IPO alone would more than make up for their investment.

He couldn't believe it. Suddenly, just when the product looked like it would get to market faster than anticipated, and when continued support from Santomo would be critical, the mother ship was losing interest.

> ❝ THE FIRST INDICATION THAT SOMETHING HAD CHANGED WAS THE ABSENCE OF THE PROMISED LIMOUSINE AT LAX. ❞

Not one to be deterred, Peter took it as a personal challenge. He streamlined Steel Alloy's processes down another notch and tightened the reins on his increasingly reluctant young staff.

He knew his success depended on getting the company to run like a well-oiled machine, and the staff was just a necessary cog in that machine. Product development slowed to a crawl, but with Peter's driving force, continued to make progress.

The beta testing took months longer than it should have, but the product was sound. One week before his trip to Los Angeles, Peter reported that Steel Alloy could ship in sixty days, with a small infusion of capital from Santomo.

His report was met with surprise and congratulations.

They scheduled his trip, first class, for him to come to Santomo's corporate headquarters to plan the rollout and to discuss the future. Peter's life was looking very good, indeed.

The first indication that something had changed was the absence of the promised limousine at LAX.

Upon arriving at the Santomo Building, he was escorted by a uniformed guard to a conference room where a massive table was covered with file boxes, all marked "Steel Alloy." He was left alone, told to help himself to coffee, and that someone would be with him shortly.

But for Peter Logan, who had just worked a miracle at Steel Alloy, it all seemed far from amusing.

Eleven hours later, when the bean counters finally agreed to let him go to his hotel, he knew things had changed.

Hour after hour, they had quizzed him on the minutest details of the finances of Steel Alloy, and the market possibilities of the product. It was sheer folly. They already knew the answers to every question. The product had a chance to dominate its marketplace. And yet, every single question seemed to suggest that the entire enterprise was doomed to failure.

As the next few days wore on, he began to wonder why they didn't just tell him to his face that they had decided to pull the plug. Instead, they seemed intent on blaming him for a failure that didn't exist. Hour after hour, they asked him to account for every decision he'd made. And hour after hour, they couldn't find fault.

It was the third evening of his stay, when Peter heard the halting message from his sister-in-law, Joanna. All she said on the hotel voice mail was, "Peter, prepare yourself for some bad news. While the kids and I were visiting my folks in Washington, a neighbor found Alan Saturday night on the living room floor, dead of an apparent heart attack. Call me."

Peter thought, "Alan dead? How could he be dead? He was healthy as an ox! He didn't have any heart problems." He was Peter's best friend, trusted confidant and, damn, he was the center of gravity for the whole family. Peter's mind ripped through the message screaming with disbelief. "What the hell happened?" He tried to reach Joanna, all night, but her line was continually busy.

The next morning he pushed past the strong protests of R.O.'s secretary and walked straight into Oberlander's private office.

R.O. looked up from his desk with an icy smile, "Good morning, Peter. What can I do for you?"

Caught somewhat off guard, Peter forgot his prepared speech and blurted the news about his brother's death. He needed to cut short his stay in L.A. to get back to Boulder.

R.O. stood up slowly, leaning forward, with his hands spread out on the desk in front of him. Then he spoke the words that Peter would never forget.

"It is unfortunate timing, but I am obliged to tell you, Peter, that we have decided to let you go and close down Steel Alloy. You will be given an ample severance package. Your things are being cleaned out of your office as we speak and will be delivered to your home in Boulder as soon as you get back."

Peter stared at him, caught in the longest moment of his life. He had never been fired. Stunned, he was at a loss to say anything. As he turned to walk towards the door it occurred to him to ask, "Why the charade, R.O.? Why keep me around jumping through all your hoops for the last couple of days?"

> **R.O. LOOKED AT HIM AND CHUCKLED. "IT'S NOTHING PERSONAL, PETER. SANTOMO ALWAYS COVERS ITS TRACKS. IT'S JUST BUSINESS."**

R.O. looked at him and chuckled. "It's nothing personal, Peter. Santomo always covers its tracks. It's just business. Frankly, if you could have been faulted, it would have looked better to our curious stockholders."

Peter stood there wrestling with every bit of self-control he could muster to keep from planting his fist right in the man's face. Life was just too short to waste any attention on the morally bankrupt, and R.O. was clearly a man who played golf with the devil.

All Peter wanted was to get on a plane back to Boulder and get as far away from Santomo as he could but there were no flights until late in the afternoon. He raced away from the Santomo Building as though speeding through L.A. could somehow shorten the five-hour wait before his plane took off.

Heading east on Olympic Avenue, he squeezed the steering wheel so hard that his white knuckles

> ## HE HAD TO GET A GRIP, GET CONTROL OF A WORLD QUICKLY UNRAVELING INTO CHAOS.

screamed out the anger, sadness and frustration that was burrowing into his psyche.

Trapped in a numbing retreat from the reality of losing a dearly loved brother and suddenly being out of a job, Peter now suffered the ultimate abuse by being caught in the iron fist of Los Angeles's stop-and-go traffic.

He had to get a grip, get control of a world quickly unraveling into chaos. The only thing he could think of was to stop. Just stop everything. He looked up, saw the Starbuck's sign at Fairfax Street and pulled off to slow his world down inside a cup of coffee.

As Peter huddled over a steaming latte, he nervously leafed through a loose newspaper on the table in front of him. He could barely concentrate until he saw a headline under the banner "National News:"

Boulder Businessman Found Dead

He still hadn't spoken to his sister-in-law, and now he was reading about Alan's death in a Los Angeles newspaper. The subtitle was even worse: Investigators say man died under mysterious circumstances.

Mysterious circumstances?

There was even a mention of ugly rumors that had been surfacing for the past several months that his brother's company was in trouble. It didn't make any sense. Why was his death mentioned in the *L.A. Times* at all?

Granted, it was buried in the back of the first section, but he was not entirely sure Alan's death would have been all that big a story even in Boulder. Near the end of the article was the final surprise, and probably the real reason the story was in the paper. His

Section A

24A LOS ANGELES TIMES

Boulder Businessman Found Dead

BOULDER, CO—Prominent Boulder businessman, Alan Logan, was found dead yesterday. Logan was founder and CEO of Bolder Solutions, a technology

Investigators say the man died under mysterious circumstances. Undisclosed sources hint that Bolder Solutions was funded in part by Santomo brother's company had been funded in part by a subsidiary of the Santomo Corporation.

Santomo? Santomo Corporation of Los Angeles, California?

The Santomo Corporation that had just turned his world upside-down?

"Santomo declined to comment on its financial interest in the project, nor would they give any details about Logan's work." Interesting response from a company that used the media like a personal advertising agency.

Peter was incredulous. He hadn't seen much of his brother in the last few months, but there was one thing he was sure of. Alan detested Santomo. When Peter first told Alan that he'd be moving back to Boulder to run a company for Santomo, Alan begged Peter to turn down the offer. As time

> **PARANOIA CAN BE ESPECIALLY SEDUCTIVE WHEN YOU'VE JUST BEEN FIRED AND YOU'RE LOOKING FOR REASONS TO THINK YOUR FORMER EMPLOYER IS EVIL INCARNATE.**

went on, Alan's distrust of Santomo turned into a savage hatred.

Because he grew so angry at the mention of the giant corporation, the brothers had to stop talking about it altogether. That was about six months ago, and Peter realized his brother had been right about

them all along. He couldn't believe Alan could have ever accepted money from them.

Peter tried to understand the logic of Santomo's comment, but he could only see sinister reasons for it. Paranoia can be especially seductive when you've just been fired and you're looking for reasons to think your former employer is evil incarnate. Was it just a coincidence? Probably. But it was still unsettling.

Peter realized the newspaper story had done one thing for sure. It made Alan's death a reality. With all that had been filling his mind in the last twenty-four hours, Alan's death had remained abstract, something to be dealt with at another time. But seeing it reported coldly in print, along with a crop report and the merger of a couple of drug companies, made the loss all too real.

Alan had been the golden child. He had a talent for solving problems that made everyone trust him. Like Peter, Alan had gone to Stanford, but upon graduation he had been immediately hired by a top Silicon Valley venture capitalist to take over young start-ups and drive them to going public.

He'd enter into deeply troubled small companies and through the sheer force of his intellect and will turn them around. He always had an answer. The people who worked for him inevitably grew to love him like a father. Within five years, Alan had a string of resounding home runs that gave him star status wherever he went. But now he was gone.

During the first few weeks after Peter had moved back to Boulder, the two brothers spent a lot of time together. Despite his warnings over Santomo, Alan was clearly glad to have his brother back in town.

Alan had invested his life savings in his own software development company that was just a hair's breadth away from turning the cash flow corner. He delighted in telling Peter that as soon as the company got a bit larger, he would be making Peter an offer to join him that Peter couldn't refuse.

A month later, Alan's world would forever change and drive him closer to disaster than he'd ever realize. At that time, Alan was approached by a secretive high-tech research and development group to complete the final module of a critical five-year world food project.

He told Peter that as much as he would like to explain the project to him, he was bound to secrecy. Alan's mysterious project began to drive him through nights and weekends.

As he became increasingly unavailable to his family and to friends, he started showing the signs of a man out on the edge. His assistant would clear 14 or 15 crushed, styrofoam coffee cups off his desk every day and his wife, more often than she liked, had to bring him breakfast and a clean shirt after a long night of writing code.

It was becoming ever more apparent that Alan was driving himself too hard. He had lost the famous Alan Logan magic.

In what would be the final chapter of Alan's life, stories began to surface in the business press suggesting that Bolder Solutions was faltering. There were rumors of dissension, rumors of failure with a new product, rumors of severe money problems, and rumors of a falling-out with an important client.

Alan insisted that the rumors were untrue, but privately admitted to Peter that the innuendos were taking a toll on his spirit and on the morale of his employees. Even Alan's bank called to find out if there were some monetary issues he hadn't disclosed to them. When Peter asked Alan if he knew the source of the rumors, his brother looked up stone-faced and said, "Peter, you don't really want to know," and then dismissed the question as not important.

The pieces to the story were quickly coming together, as the sudden stop at Starbucks and the wrinkled newspaper had set the stage for Peter to conclude that Santomo very likely was behind many of Alan's troubles. There were enough stories afloat about Alan's company that Peter was able to recognize that his brother was involved, on some level, with agricultural genetic research. He knew that Santomo was deeply involved in that area, but it still didn't make sense that there was a connection between Alan and the people who had just turned the lights out on Peter's company.

When Peter arrived in Boulder, Joanna was even more deeply bereft than he expected. She and Alan were inseparable and behaved like newlyweds. She knew that her husband was doing important work, so the long hours of Alan's professional life were just part of the package. She loved him absolutely, and she depended on him totally. And now she didn't know what to do.

Peter came just in time to help his sister-in-law arrange the funeral. She was struggling with even the smallest details. Alan had always quietly taken care of all his family's needs. He was a benevolent paternal presence, a force of nature. He was the rock on which many people relied, including his wife and two kids.

In the last year of his life, his family became his only connection to real contentment. They were his safe harbor and he was their inspiration. He was the guiding force in every part of their life, but now all that was gone.

For the next several days Joanna didn't answer her phone. Peter began to think it was time to cut short her requested time alone and reel her back into the world of the living.

The phone rang just as he decided to check on her and the kids. It was Joanna. "Peter, I'm so sorry for not returning your calls. I just needed some time to sort through my world."

She sounded tired, overwhelmingly sad, but more accepting of the new reality of her life. She had solved the mystery of the "mysterious circumstances" report. Apparently a local reporter, eager to get into the national papers, had chosen to interpret a vague response from a tired Boulder PD investigator as mysterious. As far as Joanna was concerned, the only mystery was why she was suddenly alone.

She continued, "You know, Peter, Alan was your biggest fan. He used to tell me that he knew people thought he was the clever brother, but that you were the one with the real talent. You just hadn't realized it yet."

"That's very kind of you, Joanna. But I think we all know that Alan was the gifted one. I was just glad to be his brother. I learned so much from him."

> **HE TOLD ME MANY TIMES THAT IF ANYTHING WERE TO HAPPEN TO HIM, YOU SHOULD RUN HIS COMPANY.**

Then she dropped the bomb. "Peter, your brother wanted you to run his company."

"I beg your pardon?"

"I know he didn't expect this to happen, but he told me many times that if anything were to happen to him, you should run his company. We always shared a laugh after he said it, because it was unthinkable to either of us that Alan wouldn't always be here. Well, I'm not laughing, Peter. And I want you to take over the company."

Peter didn't know what to say. His mind was suddenly overloaded with the feelings he had so carefully controlled. "Look, Jo, I don't even know what he was working on. I know he was really committed to his work, but he never told me what it involved."

"But you can learn. The company has plenty of people who can do the work, but it had only one Alan. You know how he was, he was the answer man. He hired smart people and then managed them. He didn't even have a secretary. He was the management of the company. These people are used to being led. They'll founder without direction. I know you can do this, Peter. And I know you need the job."

For one long second, there was a silence between them that was louder than any sound. And then they both laughed.

"Joanna, you actually leave me speechless. And I never expected we'd be laughing today. Look, I don't have a clue how to respond. I'm touched, real-ly touched, but maybe you ought to think about this."

"Peter, I don't need to think about this. You're the logical choice. I know this is a lot to ask, but I'm serious. The company is mine now and there isn't time to shop around for a CEO. Besides, I agree with Alan. You are the right person."

"Why the rush?"

"Because of what they are working on. It's critical that nothing slows them down. It's not just about hitting a home run with a product this time. Didn't Alan tell you anything about it?"

"He was very secretive about his primary project. I learned more about his work from all those stupid stories in the paper than from him."

"It's time you heard the whole story."

The offices of Bolder Solutions were housed in a small manufacturing facility just off 119 in Gunbarrel, an outlying area Northeast of Boulder. It was just like Alan to make a pun out of the name of his company. He had been a fan of the annual Bolder Boulder 10K race and apparently he couldn't resist.

After stopping at the bank to put Peter in charge of the corporate accounts, Joanna drove him to the office by 9:30. Bolder Solutions was situated on a sleepy street, sandwiched in between two other warehouse/office buildings.

> **IT'S TIME YOU HEARD THE WHOLE STORY.**

Walking up to the front door, Peter peered through the all-glass front wall to see the remarkably sterile foyer filled with people. The entire staff was milling around the entrance, looking distracted and unsure.

A few nervous smiles appeared as Peter and Joanna stepped through the front door. The greeting facing them was a silent stare that only a group of high-tech geeks, suddenly lost at night in a windstorm, would give a lone traveler. Peter knew he was in trouble.

Joanna's voice wavered as she asked for everyone's attention. "Thank you for being so patient during the last few weeks. We are all challenged with the task of dealing with the sudden loss of Alan. But I am encouraged to inform you today that Alan's brother, Peter, has agreed to step in as president of Bolder Solutions."

The silent stare continued as she stammered and nearly broke down. "It was Alan's wish that if anything ever happened to him, Peter would run the day-to-day operation of the company. Peter comes to us with many years of experience running small companies. I hope all of you will give Peter the same courtesy and respect that you gave Alan. It's time that we move on with our lives. As you know, there is a lot of very important work that needs to be done. Thank you for your time."

The forty-three faces staring back at Joanna and Peter were numb with disbelief that their small world at Bolder Solutions had so abruptly changed.

As the staff quietly drifted back to their workstations, Peter knew their silence wasn't a good sign. Judging by appearance, this was a culturally diverse group. He surmised that just about every slice of 20's-something culture was represented. There were purple heads, shaved heads, Rastafarian heads and capped heads. There were nose rings, belly rings, eyelid rings and tongue rings. There were jocks, preppies, and farmgirls in flower-printed dresses.

Peter ever so slightly shook his head. He knew the challenge ahead of him would be formidable.

HB Journal   January 7th

Question today from Robert H:
How do you turn an employee
into a stakeholder?

Action Note: Have him talk to
C.J.

Old   Employee   New

Component   Resource
Servant   Partner
Follower   Innovator

A leader must give his
employees an effective
symbol to anchor their
connection to the work
community.

It must be clear, suggestive
and easily remembered.

You can't force your ideas
into the mind of the
listener.

You have to be invited in
through the imagination.

Symbols are a bridge
between

the   the
unconscious   and   conscious
mind   mind

Nature provides powerful
symbols for organizational
values.

Eagle = Freedom
Elk = Integrity
Dolphin = Generosity
Horse = Nobility

"SEEDS WERE GENETICALLY ENGINEERED SO THEY COULD NOT CREATE NEW SEEDS, SO A FARMER HAD TO KEEP BUYING A COMPANY'S PRODUCT YEAR AFTER YEAR. THEY WERE CALLED 'TERMINATOR SEEDS.'"

Chapter 2

EVIDENCE
OF A CHASM

"What is occurring now is an internal shift in which the individual changes first and the institutions of human culture more or less look the same but are rejuvenated and transformed in place because of a new outlook of those who maintain them."
— **James Redfield**, *Celestine Prophecy*

Ushering Peter into a windowless conference room just off the front lobby, Joanna proceeded to unwind the story behind Bolder Solutions. Two and a half hours later Peter looked up from his notes and made the sign for time out. Joanna was articulate, well-informed, and more sensitive to the challenges of a small business than he ever imagined. He walked outside to clear his head and to review the salient points from the morning's conversation.

In the last nine months, Bolder Solutions had introduced a trio of highly regarded e-commerce programs that could work either separately or as an integrated package of sales tracking, website security, and database learning database management. This last piece of software held the key to the company's bright future. In practice, its current application was to help a company manage and learn from the overwhelming quantity of customer informa-

> "THIS NEW SOFTWARE WAS THE CORE OF THE NEW PROJECT AT BOLDER, THE SECRETIVE PROJECT THAT HAD CONSUMED ALAN'S ATTENTION IN THE LAST MONTHS OF HIS LIFE."

tion coming into a large website. But it had the potential to far exceed e-business applications. In fact, this new software was the core of the new project at Bolder, the secretive project that had consumed Alan's attention in the last months of his life.

And it was this project that held the key to Bolder Solutions' future.

Heritage Genomics, the non-profit research and development group that had courted Alan, had come to Bolder Solutions precisely because of the promise of his advanced learning database management software. They needed a high-performance version to help perfect a system of cataloging and decoding genetic structure.

While the world was focused on the human genome project, this group was engaged in unraveling the *seed genome* and they desperately needed a powerful mechanism that could do two things: 1) rapidly organize the enormous quantity of biologi-

13

cal and genetic information and 2) hyper-accelerate the natural learning processes. They needed to complete their work before an aggressive, very well-funded competitor locked them and the rest of the world out of important new discoveries in food production genetics.

Joanna had outlined what she knew about the work.

Though still in its early stages, the advent of genetic engineering had altered the agribusiness world forever. Scientists could avoid the time-consuming process of mating one seed to another to produce new strains. Now it was possible to look at the actual genetic building blocks with the promise of taking the qualities of one plant and inserting them into another.

But the promise held a dark side. Large multinational corporations could only see the profit motive. Instead of thinking about corn or soy beans that could be more easily grown, more resistant to disease, or produce more seeds for the following year, they looked the other way. Seeds were engineered so they could not create new seeds, so a farmer had to keep buying a company's product year after year. They were called "terminator seeds." Even more disturbing, "terminator seeds" could be engineered to simply lie dormant in the ground unless they were "activated" by another product manufactured by the same company. For example, the terminator seeds wouldn't grow unless the farmer used the company's weed killer. These seeds were dubbed "traitor seeds."

Heritage Genomics wanted to create its own genetically altered seeds. But these seeds would have the best traits and variety of "heritage seeds," the organic, hardy, genetically strong seeds that had been around for hundreds of years. Although they had long been the mainstay of agriculture, heritage seeds were shunned thirty-to-forty years ago because their produce did not meet the cosmetic requirements of a fickle buyer. But that was beginning to change. Consumers were beginning to realize that the most flawlessly attractive produce was not necessarily the healthiest produce. Buyers started to demand more nutritional value in their food and the organic food movement slowly began to win shelf space in even the most conservative food chains.

> " SEEDS WERE ENGINEERED SO THEY COULD NOT CREATE NEW SEEDS, SO A FARMER HAD TO KEEP BUYING A COMPANY'S PRODUCT YEAR AFTER YEAR. THEY WERE CALLED 'TERMINATOR SEEDS.' "

The researchers at Heritage Genomics were working with seed banks around the world to gather a wide variety of germ plasm, the genetic material of seeds. Their objectives were to create a supply of seeds that produced heartier, insect-resistant, more nutritious crops that were easier to grow and required no chemical activators.

It was a daunting task, and Heritage had attracted the interest of big companies, including Santomo, Inc., that wanted to use the world food supply as its own private gold mine. Also, the public was becoming alerted to the darker side of genetic research in a way that could taint all research, even that done by those who weren't motivated solely by profit. For Heritage Genomics to accomplish its task, the company needed to work quickly.

The enormous quantity of data sorting that accompanies genetic research was slowly hindering the project. The Bolder Solutions software leaped over many future generations of database technolo-

gy to cut research time by 75 percent. That is, if the programmers could complete writing the final code that linked the software to Heritage's database. Heritage was well-

funded, and had bankrolled the software's development, but the final working version of the software was still yet to be delivered.

The learning database software Bolder Solutions was writing would allow them to not only store the huge amount of genetic information available, but also to run a light speed analysis of all the many billions of permutations and combinations necessary to effectively complete the genetic mapping of the seed genome. Then they would be able to manipulate it, catalogue it, and with the help of Bolder Solution's learning technology, look directly into the secrets hidden in the information for possible new connections.

Once the data was collected, probed, and integrated, the discoveries and inventions shared throughout the world community would benefit nations all over the planet. Most importantly, the seed genome project would help third world countries avoid a pending food disaster predicted for 2008. As with most significant discoveries, the potential for great good was as large as the potential for great harm.

This was a race to feed a hungry planet and ultimately avoid what many believed to be an inevitable global disaster.

> **THE PUBLIC WAS BECOMING ALERTED TO THE DARKER SIDE OF GENETIC RESEARCH.**

Adding to the pressure, the wave of bizarre rumors about Bolder Solutions and its owner, Alan Logan, had strained the alliance with Heritage. In the beginning it was clear that the rumors impeded the progress of the product. But unfortunately there had also been unexpected delays, problems with the software, and unexplained glitches in the code.

While Heritage was outwardly supportive, it had begun to press even harder for the product to be completed. So the planted rumors were having the desired effect; they were ultimately slowing down Heritage's seed genome project. Heritage was stuck. It was too far into the project to migrate to another vendor, which would be equivalent to starting over. Heritage had to stay with Bolder Solutions but needed that software and they needed it immediately.

"Alan must have been under tremendous pressure at the time of his death. No wonder he had a heart attack," Peter thought.

As Peter sat at the desk his brother had occupied for years, he couldn't help feeling he was intruding. Alan wasn't the neatest guy in the world, but he knew where to find every scrap of paper. And now Peter had to start going through it all. Packed bookcases filled three of the four walls in the room. The cluttered antique partner's desk was a thin attempt to bring a degree of design importance into the office. Joanna must have introduced the desk because Alan wouldn't have cared. A folding table would have served his needs just as well. The one window to the outside world promised direct sunlight, but the buildings next door cut off any hope of that happening. This would be Peter's command center and it needed to be a lot more organized to suit his needs.

Just as Joanna had said, his brother didn't have a secretary, but he did have an able assistant named Kate. Kate was a year or two north of 30 and had experience working for one other software company before coming to work with Alan. Joanna said Kate was a smart, extremely loyal employee and that she knew everything that was going on in the company, so don't make the mistake of underestimating her.

"HE WASN'T USED TO EXPLAINING HIS RESUMÉ TO AN EMPLOYEE, BUT HE NEEDED HER HELP, AND HE NEEDED HER TO TRUST HIM SO HE TOLD HER EVERYTHING."

Since Alan had always signed all the company's checks, the backlog of bookkeeping chores was formidable. After Peter and Kate spent a couple of hours getting the bills caught up, she started quizzing him about his background. He wasn't used

 to explaining his resumé to an employee, but he needed her help, and he needed her to trust him, so he told her everything.

She took it all in, seeming almost disinterested, until he mentioned his dismissal by Santomo.

"Santomo? You worked for Santomo?"

"I kept thinking I was autonomous, but they explained reality to me in pretty short order. Why do you ask?"

"Nothing, I guess. It's just that Santomo initially invested in the germ plasm project. They bought into Heritage Genomics, the research guys that came to us for the software. I don't know what happened, but Alan didn't like them."

"I knew he had no use for Santomo, but he never would tell me why. I guess now I know."

"Heritage had to get pretty firm with them too. Santomo wanted to direct the work."

"Alan's death was reported in the *L.A. Times* and the article mentioned Santomo had invested in a project Alan was working on. In fact, I suspect that's why it was in the paper at all. I just thought it was a sad bit of irony."

"But they weren't involved with us at all," Kate said. "They kept trying to come in here on some level and Alan kept putting them off. He didn't trust them and Heritage Genomics didn't have any use for them. They are heavyweights in the world of agribusiness, but they do it through subsidiaries. They have a clear conflict of interest, but they still kept trying to get involved. Alan said Heritage had returned Santomo's investment just to keep them out."

Peter's suspicions about Santomo were beginning to resurface. They were a very determined company.

"So how's our product progressing?"

"Mr. Logan, you should really speak to the development team."

"Kate, I will do that. But I get the feeling that Alan told you a lot about the details of the company."

She seemed to weigh her words. "Look, your brother was the most capable man I've ever worked for. He really liked to be in control; he wasn't fond of delegating any authority. But I think we had gotten a bit larger and more complex around here than he could handle alone. I was sure that sometime soon he was going to have to get someone in to take some of his load. We have forty-three employees now, and he was the only manager, the only voice. He was stretched way beyond his or anyone's spectrum of managerial competency."

"Do you think the rest of the staff was aware of this?"

"It's hard to say. Our staff is mostly made up of engineers, and they were in awe of Alan's ability to see through problems. I guess they overlooked the chaos and inefficiency around here because they had so much respect for Alan."

Neither of them spoke for a moment.

"And they're going to expect the same from you."

Peter finished the first day by meeting the entire staff, but it all went too quickly. He knew it would take him a while to learn everyone's name. He received general progress reports on the new software and listened to suggestions from everyone.

His most interesting meeting was with the director of sales, Barry "Buck" Bernstein. Buck informed Peter that he was Alan's secret weapon. He also gave himself the title of director, leading Peter to think it was a very recent decision. There was nothing else that indicated Buck was director of anything. But he was clearly in charge of sales, even if Alan had never given him the title.

Sales was the one area where Alan was overmatched. After chatting with Buck for a half an hour, Peter was happy to let him call himself anything he liked. The man could sell a refrigerator to an Eskimo.

It was also clear that Bolder Solutions had the same tensions between sales and product development that existed in all high-tech companies. Buck was sure that the "propeller heads" were dragging their feet on the new product. When Peter casually asked if Buck had offered a firm finish date to Heritage Genomics, the man hedged his answer, saying they were only a few weeks overdue. Peter realized that like any aggressive sales team, the Bolder Solutions sales team had come up with an artificially optimistic date.

Buck seemed to read Peter's mind. "If those tattooed wonders would stop eating junk food and playing games long enough, they might finish the product."

> **"IF THOSE TATTOOED WONDERS WOULD STOP EATING JUNK FOOD AND PLAYING GAMES LONG ENOUGH, THEY MIGHT FINISH THE PRODUCT."**

Peter locked up the office and walked out onto the parking lot toward his midnight blue Range Rover. At least he walked away from the Santomo contract with a new car. On the way home his mind spun around the events that had come into his life. Alan, Joanna, getting fired, jumping immediately into this new company and the culturally challenged, problematic group that worked there. How was he going to pull off this one?

As Peter rolled into his driveway on Grant Street, he was seriously questioning whether he was the right guy for the job. His brother's family was hanging onto the end of a very thin branch so this was not a time to be gambling with their futures. Could he turn Bolder Solutions around, or would it unravel under his leadership?

As the garage door closed, he was grateful to be in his own home. He liked the neatly organized workshop and tools he collected to work on his two cars and three motorcycles.

His house reflected his taste and his previously large paycheck. He loved the expanse of granite kitchen countertops and stainless steel appliances. Peter had created a sophisticated but welcoming home, and he was proud that it didn't look like a typical bachelor pad.

Asian rugs scattered on the hardwood floors provided needed color, warmth and patterns. His collection of 1930s black-and-white photographs was carefully displayed along the entry hall between the front door and the kitchen. His pride and joy, his state-of-the-art entertainment system, covered one entire wall of his living room. He could listen to Beethoven or Miles Davis and in a moment be transported into the center of the sound.

This was his sanctuary and it was here that he would have to make sense of everything. He knew if he were lucky, he'd have a week to figure out the operations of the company. He'd settle for two or three days. But it wasn't to be.

"Peter had called a company meeting and as he stepped out of his office he expected to see the staff assembled. But he found only Kate and a handful of employees. This was new territory for Peter. He had never worked with a staff that completely disregarded a call for a meeting by the CEO."

Chapter 3
REALITY

"If you know the enemy and know yourself, you need not fear the result of a hundred battles."
— **Sun Tzu,** ***The Art of War***

Peter arrived early on his second day, thinking it was good that the boss was there when employees arrived. Kate arrived a few minutes after he did, and a few more people showed up at nine. But to his utter astonishment, the bulk of the staff straggled in throughout the morning, and the office wasn't fully staffed until noon. Then they all left for lunch. Kate and a few of the staff were gone for an hour, but the rest were out for nearly two hours.

This had to change. And it had to change immediately. Peter called a meeting for the last half-hour of the day.

The office was a large, high ceilinged room with a communal bullpen area commanding the center of the workspace. The nine small offices bordering the perimeter of the room were the only escape from the fluorescent lighting that erased any shadow from the stark walls. This room was functional at best, and had little evidence of human occupation other than the occasional head that might pop up above a cubicle wall.

Peter had called a company meeting for 4:30 p.m. and as he stepped out of his office into the bullpen, he expected to see the staff assembled, but found only Kate and a handful of employees. This was new territory for Peter. He had never worked with a staff that completely disregarded a call for a meeting by the CEO.

> **HE DIDN'T KNOW WHETHER TO BE FURIOUS OR SIMPLY STUNNED.**

He didn't know whether to be furious or simply stunned. He decided to wait and see what would happen, so he sat down and asked each of them how their day had been.

Immediately they besieged Peter with a dozen little problems and seemed to expect him to provide solutions.

Over the next fifteen minutes, while a few more staff showed up for the meeting, he tried to give a reasonable solution to each problem, the way he thought Alan would have done. He then listened to the staff speak about everything except the reason for the meeting. He had gotten over his initial surprise; he was starting to get angry. He asked if a low turnout to a staff meeting was usual.

The blank stares told him that he wouldn't get a response. He told everyone to go home, then asked

Kate to call each employee this evening and tell him or her that there would be a mandatory meeting at 9:00 a.m. tomorrow. Being late to the meeting would result in a fine of $100. Missing the meeting would result in a fine equal to one percent of the individual's annual salary. The only acceptable excuse for missing the meeting would be death. Kate was to relay the message in just those terms.

With great reluctance, Kate agreed to make the calls. She told Peter that it was going to anger the wizards, the term she used for the computer programmers. Peter said that that would make them even.

The next morning at nine sharp, Peter stepped out of his office to find the meeting room full of glaring employees. These people did not like being told when to get to work.

"Good morning. Nice to see all of you here. We don't really know each other yet, but time will take care of that. In the meantime we have a job to do, and in order to do that job, you need to show up on time every day. This applies to all of you, including…"

He was interrupted by the noise of the front door crashing open.

"Oh, man, you wouldn't believe the traffic! I would have been on time, I swear. But between having to stop for gas, and fighting traffic on the Diagonal, it just wasn't gonna happen."

All eyes came back to Peter. The disheveled latecomer was Dean Baldridge, programmer extraordinaire. While Alan had been the official head of the development team, Dean Baldridge was the acknowledged second in command. He was key to the success of the project, and he knew it. Peter knew it too.

" YEAH, SURE. SO I'M NOT GETTING FINED, RIGHT? "

"Thanks for joining us, Mr. Baldridge. Would you like to find a seat?"

"Yeah, sure. So I'm not getting fined, right?"

And then he snickered. If he hadn't snickered, the moment might have passed.

"Are you dead, Mr. Baldridge?"

"What…?"

"I asked if you were dead."

No snickering this time. "Uh, no."

"Did Kate tell you the rules for this meeting?"

"Well, yeah, she said…"

"Then you simply don't have the only excuse I'll accept. Your fine will be deducted from your next paycheck."

He let this news settle on the group.

"I didn't want to start this way, but I have no choice. When the doors open at nine o'clock each

 morning, you will all be at your desks or workstations. If you don't do this out of some sense of responsibility to your job, I will have Kate install a time clock, and you will have to punch in and out."

"Now I realize this may be a different way of doing business from what you are used to, but this is the way it will be. This is not the time to become sloppy or uncaring. We have a great deal of work to do, and it will require all of you to be disciplined and attentive. In the meantime I intend to do what I can to help each of you in any way I can. I know you relied on my brother, and I want all of you to know you can rely on me. Any questions?"

The staff was too stunned to speak. Clearly, their world had changed.

"One more thing. When I call a staff meeting, assume that it is mandatory. If you're late, you'll be fined $100. If you miss it, you will be fined one percent of your annual salary."

"Mr. Baldridge, I expect daily written reports on the progress of the Heritage Project. That's all."

He closed his door and stepped back to his desk. Before he could sit down, Kate was standing in front of him.

"I don't know if I can work here any more. We had meetings, but attendance was never mandatory.

If one of the wizards didn't show up, Alan would talk with them later in private."

"Please give it some time, Kate. I need your help. I don't pretend to be like my brother, but I do know what I'm doing."

As she walked back to her desk, Peter felt a self-congratulatory feeling begin to wash over him. It was time to go through the files Kate had set aside for him to read. He needed to become familiar with the various departments of the company. From what he had seen yesterday, Alan ran the company as though there were only one department, his. He was in charge of everything. He handled the manufacturer, the books, the wizards, the marketing. And yet he had brought highly talented people into the organization. Peter called Kate in.

"Did Alan appoint heads of departments? There's nothing to suggest that he delegated…well… anything."

Kate looked worried. "No, no, he didn't. In fact, he was rather adamant that the only way to make the company work was if he signed-off on everything. He said it kept us all on the same rung of the ladder. Nobody has power over anybody else. He relied on one person in each department to be sort of responsible, but no one was officially the head of a department."

"Kate, that has to change. I can't believe Alan tried to do it all."

She was clearly unhappy. "Are you sure you want to do that? People are already a little unsure of what's happening. Can't you wait a while? Our system has worked so far. I'm pretty much the lead contact for administration, Buck's the top dog in sales, Jimmy handles the finances, and the twins take care of production and customer service."

"The twins?"

"Tina and Gina Fujimori. They're quite a pair! Tina does production, Gina does customer service. They're identical, but they each dress so differently you would need to have them both in front of you at once to see how much alike they are."

"And let me guess. Dean Baldridge is the king of the programmers?"

She looked slightly embarrassed. "I'm afraid so. But Maria's pretty sharp, too, and the wizards really respect her."

"It will take me a few days to get to know everyone."

"That's my point. Can't you wait just a little while? A lot has happened to us."

Peter knew she had a point. Too much change too soon could be a problem. But he couldn't wait very long. "Tell you what. Now that I've gotten them to understand how I feel about their work ethic, we'll go back to the honeymoon period for a few weeks. In the meantime, I need to see all the personnel files so I can start thinking about some department heads."

The next day Peter was at his desk even earlier. He was reviewing personnel files when Kate came in. The rest of the staff started arriving fifteen minutes early. Obviously his talk had had an impact.

He had met Jimmy Valentine the first day. Kate's assessment had been accurate. While Alan had avoided naming a CFO, Jimmy Valentine had been functioning in that capacity. Peter suspected that over the last several weeks, more and more of Jimmy Valentine's work resembled that of a CFO. He was the leading candidate for the job. It occurred to Peter that maybe Buck Bernstein was onto something. He could name people first to the position of director before giving them more senior titles. Jimmy had been on time before the talk and he was early today. Good!

A few minutes after nine, Peter walked out of his office to get a cup of coffee. All the employees watched him. At first he thought they were angry, but then he knew they were waiting to see what he was going to do. It didn't make any sense until he realized that Dean Baldridge was not in the office. They were waiting to see Peter's reaction.

He smiled at everyone and went back to his desk. So the teenager wanted to test him. Fine. He could deal with it. He was deep in thought when a woman's voice interrupted his work. Whoever she was, she started to talk before even entering his office.

"Surprise! I know, I said I'd call when I got back, but…" She stopped cold when she saw Peter. She looked confused. "I'm sorry. I must have the wrong office."

Peter tried to help. "Well, maybe…" But she interrupted him.

"Wait a minute, this is the right office. Who the hell are you?"

> WHO THE HELL AM I? THIS IS MY OFFICE, MY COMPANY, AND MY DESK. WHY DON'T WE START WITH, WHO THE HELL ARE YOU?

Clearly she was expecting Alan, and he had been about to gently explain to her what had happened, but her abrasiveness irritated him. He disliked her immediately. She was undeniably stunning, but she wore thick-framed glasses designed to make her look bookish. She managed to telegraph that she was a tough, serious, savvy woman. Peter was uncomfortably conscious of her magnetism.

"Who the hell am I? This is my office, my company, and my desk. Why don't we start with, who the hell are you?"

"No, this is Alan Logan's company, Alan Logan's office, and Alan Logan's desk. I have an appointment with him right now. Where is he?"

He could almost feel a click in his brain as he decided to be brutally honest. "Alan Logan is dead." He heard the harshness in his own voice. He knew he was taking out some of his frustration on this woman, but he didn't really care. "He died three weeks ago. Now please tell me who you are."

The news hit her harder than he expected. The blood drained from her face and she looked as if she might faint. She dropped on the couch before she fell. Now he was even more curious about her connection to his brother.

"I didn't know. I … how did he die?"

"Answer my question first. Who are you?"

"My name is Grace McGregor. My company is McGregor Communications. Alan hired me to create a PR campaign to counter the trash that had been showing up in the press about Bolder Solutions."

"He hired your company?"

She seemed to struggle for an answer. "Yes. I had devised a campaign and we were ready to implement it when the rumors stopped, and I mean totally stopped. This was about six weeks ago. I told him that he shouldn't count on them giving up, but he wanted to wait to see what happened. I was reluctant to put it off, but I have been out of the country, so I agreed to wait until today to see where we stood."

"**MS. MCGREGOR, YOUR REACTION TO ALAN'S DEATH IS PUZZLING. HE NEVER MENTIONED YOU. PLEASE TELL ME ALAN WASN'T GOING THROUGH SOME MID-LIFE CRISIS WITH YOU.**"

"Ms. McGregor, your reaction to Alan's death is puzzling. He never mentioned you. Please tell me Alan wasn't going through some mid-life crisis with you."

His answer was a frosty stare. Then she spoke slowly and very softly. She was focused now.

She stood up in her best power stance and locked eyes with him. "Alan Logan and I worked together on a local campaign affecting the care of public property. I've met his wife and had dinner in their home. Who do you think you are to ask me questions like that?"

He could feel himself getting annoyed. "My name is Peter Logan. Alan was my brother."

The moment of quiet that followed was satisfying.

"You're Peter Logan?"

"Yes."

"And now you've taken over this company?"

"Yes."

"How did Alan die?"

"He had a heart attack."

"A heart attack?" She sounded incredulous. "Now I know why the rumors stopped. I suppose Santomo has taken over the company?"

It was his turn to be surprised. "What is that supposed to mean?"

"You're a piece of work, Peter. Santomo runs a smear campaign, Alan conveniently dies, and now you're running the show. I wish he'd come to me earlier."

She was running ahead of him. He interrupted, "How do you know Santomo was behind the rumors?"

"Peter, please, don't be naive. It's my job to know these things. It's not a closely held secret that Santomo has been trying to get in here for a long time. And now they have you sitting in Alan's office. I wonder what they would have done if Alan hadn't died? My God, I wonder if they had anything to do with it? What are they paying you, Peter? It doesn't matter, I can find out."

Now Peter was angry. It was time for her to go. "Leave my office. Now!"

"I'm not finished with you, Peter Logan. I'm going to make your job very difficult. I will not see this company fall into Santomo's pocket that easily."

And with that, she turned sharply on her heel and walked out of his office. As he watched her go, he noticed that a small crowd had gathered in her wake, with Kate standing in front, wide-eyed and unbelieving.

"Kate, has she ever been here before?"

"Yes, I've seen her here talking with Alan, but it was two to three months ago. I never knew what her business was with your brother."

By lunchtime, Dean Baldridge still wasn't in. By two o'clock, Peter had had enough.

"Kate, call our tardy geek and find out if he intends to show up today. He might be suffering from silicon flu."

A few minutes later, Kate reported that Dean wasn't answering his phone. Peter had to admit the kid was more stubborn than he'd thought.

At 4:30 p.m. there was a knock on his door and Baldridge came into his office. He flopped down on the leather couch and refused to look at Peter.

"So I trust you've spent your day off having fun?" Whatever the kid wanted, Peter had to appear unfazed.

"First, I work long hours for this company, and your brother knew that. Second, I will never pay a fine for being late to anything that has anything to do with this company. If you try to fine me, I'll sue you and I'll lead a mutiny. If you try anything like this again, I'll resign and the company will fail without me. If you think you can do without me, fire me, and I'll sue you. I do my work and I'll continue to do my work, but you need to stay out of my way."

For the first time since he arrived at Bolder, Peter was unsure of himself. He had to act decisively. "Ok, Mr. Baldridge, let's see if…"

But Baldridge interrupted him. "Alan was a developer. He cut his teeth writing code. He would never have pulled this stuff. He knew what the job

> **ALAN WAS A DEVELOPER. HE CUT HIS TEETH WRITING CODE. HE WOULD NEVER HAVE PULLED THIS STUFF. HE KNEW WHAT THE JOB WAS LIKE. HOW MUCH DO YOU KNOW ABOUT IT?**

was like. How much do you know about it?"

But Peter never got a chance to answer. Baldridge had said his speech and left. Whatever Peter was going to say was moot. Baldridge had left his office and gone to work. It appeared he would be there for the night.

Kate shot Peter a look as she passed by his open door. For a moment he thought she was smirking at him. He was seriously considering the impact on the staff and on the project if he fired Baldridge. He decided to go over the scant files on the whole development team before he took action.

Joanna called to check in. Peter did not have the heart to tell her that Alan's company would be fodder for vultures soon. He asked her if she knew Grace McGregor.

"Oh my God, Peter. I forgot to call her. Every year at this time, Grace volunteers for a month to help indigenous peoples who live in the most remote, desperate places on earth. I meant to call her when she got back. She and Alan were good friends and worked closely over the past few months. She's a remarkable woman, Peter, Oxford-trained to boot, and Alan trusted her with the most sensitive issues regarding Bolder Solutions," Joanna concluded.

Great, thought Peter, I mistake Mother Teresa for Attila the Hun.

Day five was a nightmare. It seemed that every employee who showed up at his door had a minor crisis in hand and expected Peter to solve it. He heard time and time again, "Well, Alan would have done it," or, "Alan always took care of this." And time and time again, Peter tried to give an answer. The wizard patrol sent in an emissary, a bright young woman with tattoos and several visible body piercings. Peter learned that she was the Maria that Kate had mentioned.

Jimmy Valentine, the de facto CFO, had come in to tell Peter that there was "a little problem with cash flow." Two months ago Buck Bernstein had proudly announced that he had pulled off what he described as the deal of the century, by selling the entire Internet suite to a large cash-rich chip manufacturer. Buck called it an anchor contract, and by closing this well-known customer, other more risk-averse companies in the market would loosen up and sign on the dotted line.

The problem was that in order to close the deal, Buck had to give away too much. He not only gave them a deep discount, he promised them premium-level support and agreed to terms that no payment would be required for ninety days. After forty-five days, the large customer further leveraged their position by sending a letter informing Bolder Solutions that they would require additional software, additional support — all at the discounted price. And, by the way, they wouldn't be paying Bolder Solutions for an additional ninety days.

Splendid news. Jimmy Valentine had discussed the matter with Peter's brother, but Alan had been too preoccupied. Alan had signed off on all of it. The discounted payment amount was still sixty days out.

After hearing this news, Peter promptly made a call to their banker. The woman who had assured them continued excellent service two days ago now suddenly sounded distant and stiff. Apparently things had changed. She said that before the bank could extend any further credit, it would need to be reassured that Bolder Solutions' new learning database product was ready for market.

More splendid news! Shareesa Jones, the one-woman human resources department, tapped on

Peter's open door as he hung up with the bank. Alan had stalled on picking a new insurance carrier and they had missed a window to sign a new contract that would have saved them almost $100,000 over the next twelve months. She wondered if Peter could call to ask for an extension, given the circumstances. They needed to have a new policy in place by the end of the month, and they would need to come up with $30,000 to commence it.

The day kept getting better and better.

At three o'clock, Dean Baldridge wandered into his office with three other developers in tow. They decided they had had enough of the sales team making unrealistic promises that involved the developers. They told Peter he needed to reign in Barry (they refused to call him Buck out of obvious disrespect) or development on the new project would come to a halt. After making their announcement, they decided it was time for a Starbucks run and left the office.

Then came the capper. Buck hurried in to tell Peter that Heritage Genomics, which had been quiet since Alan's death, had called to find out a finish date for the new software. He said it was a polite call, but not as friendly a call as they used to receive.

"Let's face it, Peter, they think maybe we can't do it without Alan." He started out the door but then stopped. "You do know that the bulk of their payment is due on delivery? So we won't get the dough until the tattooed wonders finish the software. Well, gotta run." And he was gone.

By the end of the day the rumblings had begun. He wasn't like his brother and the company was in trouble. The false rumors in the press were becoming more true by the minute.

> "YOU DO KNOW THAT THE BULK OF THEIR PAYMENT IS DUE ON DELIVERY? SO WE WON'T GET THE DOUGH UNTIL THE TATTOOED WONDERS FINISH THE SOFTWARE."

Today was Thursday and tomorrow he'd be saved by the weekend, but he knew he had to have a plan by the following Monday morning.

It was time to dig into the personnel files to see how he could reorganize the office. Alan hadn't kept particularly good information on his employees because he kept most everything in his head.

"Thanks, Alan. You could have taken a few notes, you know."

Week Two loomed in Peter's future.

"AND AT THAT MOMENT, SITTING IN THE SHADOW OF THE LOCOMOTIVE, STARING AT THE EMPTY BAND SHELL SEEMED A PERFECTLY RATIONAL WAY FOR HIM TO SPEND THE AFTERNOON."

Chapter 4

EVEN ATLAS SHRUGGED

"Whenever human communities are forced to adjust to shifting conditions, pain is ever present."
— **John P. Kotter**, *Leading Change*

"In less than two weeks you have unraveled four years worth of hard work. What will your encore be? Pink slips for everyone?"

As the angry words of a disgruntled Dean Baldridge squeezed through the slamming door, the level of frustration in the air was punctuated by the crack of oak hitting the door jam. Peter grabbed his now trusty bottle of Tums, and knew a staff revolution was just a hair's breadth away. The heavy-handed threat he delivered to Dean had crossed the line and he knew it. He had to get out of the office. It wasn't even noon, but he needed a break.

"Kate, I'm going to lunch. I've got to get out of here for a few hours. If any of the staff feel the need to shoot me, I'll be back later."

Kate didn't exactly glare at him, but he'd seen the look before. She was beginning not to take him seriously. Oh, yeah, things were going well at Bolder Solutions. Thank God today's Friday!

The train was still there. It was a touchstone in the midst of the chaos of his life. Growing up in Boulder, he had always liked the little park off Broadway and Canyon.

When the train was moved there to become a permanent attraction, it had captured the whimsy of the town. And at that moment, sitting in the shadow of the locomotive, staring at the empty band shell seemed a perfectly rational way for him to spend the afternoon. Pathetically, he mused that at least while he sat here, he couldn't do further damage to his brother's company.

> **EVEN ATLAS SHRUGGED; IT ISN'T THE STRESS THAT'S KILLING YOU, IT'S YOUR UNWILLINGNESS TO CHANGE!**

"Even Atlas shrugged; it isn't the stress that's killing you, it's your unwillingness to change!"

The words jarred him out of his reverie. He turned around to see an older man sitting on a bench at the right front wheel of the locomotive. He was dressed in an eclectically elegant manner that few men could wear with as much panache. He held a Palm Pilot in his left hand and a tattered

31

leather journal was in his lap. He gazed piercingly at Peter and continued, "Have you ever considered the force behind what makes everything grow? Perhaps you had a fleeting wonder about just how much control you really have over your day or your company or life?"

"I beg your pardon?"

"Which part didn't you understand?"

This exchange was perfectly aligned with Peter's day. Not only had he managed to irritate everyone who worked for him, it seemed he had managed to alienate a complete stranger. And he hadn't said a word to the man.

"Look, I'm just trying to enjoy the lunch hour, OK?" Maybe Boulder was getting to be like Los Angeles. Maybe the old guy was going to berate him until he gave him some money. Perfect.

"You're not eating lunch. You're sitting here feeling sorry for yourself. It's depressing."

Peter knew he should just let it go, but his patience level was suffering from the events of the last two weeks. "Am I missing something here? Do we know each other?"

"No, we don't know each other. But I know who you are. I've seen hundreds like you."

"Is there something wrong with you? Do you always speak to strangers like this?"

"You're not a stranger. I told you before, I know exactly who you are."

Peter heard the voice of reason in his head telling him to let it go, but the guy was pressing his buttons. "Oh, really? Exactly who am I?"

"You are a man with a problem, most likely a business problem, most likely a people problem. I'd say you have a bunch of people working for you who are just about ready to drag your gloomy rear end out and shoot you. And you don't have a clue what to do about it all. How'd I do?"

Peter looked at the empty band shell and tried to remember a summertime concert from his college days. "What makes you so smart?"

The guy smiled for the first time. "Well, I could tell you I'm a mind reader or I could say that it's your clothes or it's your car. Truth is, I have seen so many guys like you over the years that I could pick

> I COULD TELL YOU I'M A MIND READER OR I COULD SAY THAT IT'S YOUR CLOTHES OR IT'S YOUR CAR. TRUTH IS, I HAVE SEEN SO MANY GUYS LIKE YOU OVER THE YEARS THAT I COULD PICK YOU OUT OF A CROWD.

you out of a crowd. You have the same expression, the same droop in the shoulders. It's all too familiar. I was there once. It's like watching old home movies."

Peter stood up and looked at the man. He noticed that despite the guy's attitude, his eyes were radiating intelligence and humor.

"Then why are you giving me such a hard time?"

"People like you and me have very hard heads. Nothing gets in without blowing down the front door. So please excuse my abruptness. Twenty-nine years ago I was arrogantly driving my business to the brink of disaster. With all due respect, it probably wasn't too much different than what you are doing today. Everything I had used in the past to manage my company didn't work any more. The ship was going down and going down fast, to the tune of many millions of dollars."

"At that time an unusual man approached me out of nowhere. He appeared to have almost an electrical charge about him. He was a total stranger and frankly the last person I wanted to talk to at the time, but he persisted. I am profoundly glad he did. He blasted me out of my self-constructed prison. I had no idea I was so caught in my own net of self-deception. It happens to absolutely every entrepreneurial leader. No one escapes it."

"Over a period of six months, he gave me a lifetime of knowledge. He taught me the keys to unlocking the profit, the people and the growth secrets hidden deep inside my own floundering company. He called his methods the Growth Curve Solution. It proved to be the key to cracking the code that holds the potential of any enterprise. I owe him more than I can ever say."

Peter looked at his watch. "Well, that's all very interesting. But I don't think you can help me, and I've got to get back to work."

"I HAD NO IDEA I WAS SO CAUGHT IN MY OWN NET OF SELF-DECEPTION. IT HAPPENS TO ABSOLUTELY EVERY ENTREPRENEURIAL LEADER. NO ONE ESCAPES IT."

"Why? What are you going to do when you get back there? Did you come up with some earth-shaking idea? Or are you just hoping for inspiration between here and your office?"

Peter felt his face redden. This man was looking through him like he was a plate glass window. What was it about this guy? The old man had no idea what waited for Peter back at the office. But how did he know what was going through Peter's mind? Peter tried to think of what to say, but words failed him.

There was a deafening silence. Then the man ducked his head and looked up at Peter. "Kind of feels like you've been caught with your hand in the cookie jar, doesn't it?"

For the first time in two weeks, Peter chuckled. "Not exactly, but yeah, that's close enough."

"You don't think I could possibly have a clue to what's going on in your world, do you? Once you have traveled this road, my friend, you never forget the signs. They're written all over your face. So what have you got to lose?"

The pain in Peter's head surged as he reached for the two Tylenol in his top pocket. He rubbed his temples. He hated this. He hated being out of control. He hated being so transparent. "Oh, not much. Just the whole company, my brother's legacy for his

> **" THE STANDARD KNEE-JERK ENTREPRENEURIAL RESPONSE TO CRISIS IS TO THINK THAT IT ALL DEPENDS ON YOU TO PULL THE RABBIT OUT OF THE HAT. "**

wife and kids, and my future in the business world. Stuff like that."

"Living on Tylenol and Tums?"

"Pretty much."

The man walked over to Peter. He was tall and had a youthful vitality about him. "Know why I come down here? I love trains. I come down here, stand next to this train, and remind myself that life is shorter than we think. You have to seize the day."

This much Peter already knew. "Shorter than we think? Try this. My older brother? The smart one? He had a heart attack and died a month ago. His wife asked me to run his company. And in two short weeks, I've nearly destroyed it. So, yeah, life's shorter than we think. My problem is that in the middle of learning that lesson, I can't even save his company."

"Save his company?" The old guy actually laughed out loud. "My God, you're in as bad a shape as they come."

Peter didn't have time for this. He started walking away.

"Hey, wait a minute!" The guy was still chuckling. "I'm laughing at how much you sound like me thirty years ago, although I didn't have the added pressure of taking over a deceased brother's crumbling company. That's tough."

Peter stopped. "You have no idea."

"Fair enough. But I do have an idea about what you're going through with your company. And you won't solve it by thinking it's up to you personally to save the day. The standard knee-jerk entrepreneurial response to crisis is to think that it all depends on you to pull the rabbit out of the hat. The first big hurdle you have is to get yourself out of that box right away. "

"I don't see another choice."

"Well, that's the real danger of what's happening to you. You can't see choices. But you have a world of choices. When you look at the company as an extension of you, as part of your identity, it is real tough to see the choices."

"Who are you?"

"My name is Horace Bedford." He came over to Peter, offering his hand.

"Bedford? Like Bedford Falls?"

"Jimmy Stewart fan. That's a good sign."

"I'm Peter Logan."

"Nice to meet you, Peter Logan. The other answer to your question is that I've been in your shoes. For more times than I care to admit, I've found myself trying to grow a company that was sinking in quicksand. It isn't easy, when you discover you're in new territory and that nothing you learned in graduate school or anywhere else, for that matter, can help you."

"Isn't that the truth! Up till now, my model worked pretty well. I was good at sizing up a company's strengths, weaknesses, opportunities, and threats. I'd make a reasonable game plan, slash costs, cut the staff, and get things turned around."

"But things are different with this company. I can't use my old bag of tricks. The staff is comprised of very bright people who need constant handholding. Frankly, I'm being held hostage by my own people, but I can't fire them because I don't have the time to hire and retrain anyone.

"When my brother was running things, he created a management nightmare by not setting up a firm set of guidelines and clear infrastructure. He held the employees' hands and managed all the day-to-day decisions of an emerging company. Even though there are people designated as managers, believe me when I say they are managers in name only. There effectively is no management team. He must have controlled the whole show. I don't know how he did it. There is so much falling through the cracks in this company, I'm uncertain that I will have both the time and the answers to keep this ship floating much longer than 30-60 days."

"That's the point! You shouldn't try to have all the answers. You need to look your people in the eye and tell them that you hear what they are say-

> " THINGS ARE DIFFERENT WITH THIS COMPANY.
> I CAN'T USE MY OLD BAG OF TRICKS. I'M
> BEING HELD HOSTAGE BY MY OWN PEOPLE. "

ing, but since they are obviously seeing the problem, they'll need to find the solution."

"Yeah, right! That'll go over huge. Look, Horace, that's a great idea in some companies, but I don't think it'll work in this one."

Horace continued, "That was a classic answer to a classic problem. Why is it that everyone thinks that their problem is so damn unique? This is one choice you really don't have. Refuse to look at new ways of cracking the code of your company and you might as well get yourself strapped in for a whole lot more of what you are already experiencing. Do yourself a favor, Peter, let them find the solutions. They may just surprise you."

"I've got to get back. I'll think about what you said."

"I'm here often, right around lunchtime. Who knows, we may see each other on Monday."

"So you're retired?"

"Oh no, not at all. That's part of what you need to learn. Business isn't simply what you do from nine to five. Business is what you do with your life. Here's something to think about before you leave: If you're doing it right, you are living well. You are fulfilled, and so is everyone else who's working for you. And you always have time to smell the roses because you haven't separated life from what you're doing every day. You and your staff are spending something like 70% of your waking hours at work. Why shouldn't your days be the best you can make them?"

"You do realize how incredibly naïve that sounds, don't you?"

> REFUSE TO LOOK AT NEW WAYS OF CRACKING THE CODE OF YOUR COMPANY AND YOU MIGHT AS WELL GET YOURSELF STRAPPED IN FOR A WHOLE LOT MORE OF WHAT YOU ARE ALREADY EXPERIENCING.

"Yes, as a matter of fact, I do."

"I might see you Monday, Horace Bedford. We'll talk about Jimmy Stewart movies."

Driving back to the industrial park in Gunbarrel, it was clear to Peter that he wasn't going to be of any value to his brother's company if he kept trying to think like Alan. The real problem was that the entire staff was trained to work in "Alan's company." Finding a new way to manage them was going to be a challenge. Maybe Horace Bedford was right; maybe he should simply ask them to help.

Walking in the front door of Bolder Solutions had stopped being a pleasant experience. Conversations ceased, people either avoided looking at Peter or glared with open hostility. The atmosphere helped him to make up his mind.

He called key employees into his office. They gathered reluctantly. Dean sulked in the doorway.

"Clearly, things aren't working out as well as any of us hoped they would. So I've decided to make some changes." By the expressions on their faces, he realized they were expecting to hear that he would be firing some of them. What he couldn't tell was whether or not they hoped to be on that list.

"There are too many areas needing attention in this company for me to deal with alone." He paused to gauge their reaction and sensed they thought he was going to be the one to leave.

"I want all of you to meet with the people in your departments this afternoon and come up with two things: what's creating the biggest problem in your department, and what we can do about it. We'll meet again at 4:30."

They sat there for a few seconds before realizing he had finished. Then they looked at each other, frowned and shrugged, and started to walk away. The expression on Baldridge's face was troubling. It was almost triumphant. The newly tagged director of finances, Jimmy Valentine, asked, "You want the staff to come up with solutions?"

"Yes, Jimmy. That's what I want. And we'll meet again at 4:30."

Peter's attempt to involve the staff had been a disaster. As he looked back on the question Jimmy Valentine had posed after the meeting, he realized he should have been paying attention to what the question meant. Jimmy and the others were simply not trained to come up with solutions. The entire staff was amazed that Peter expected them to solve the company's problems. That was his job, and he was asking them to do it.

They were actually irritated at being asked to come up with the solutions, all except for Dean, who appeared delighted. All departments had no trouble putting Peter at the top of their lists of what was wrong with Bolder Solutions. The irony was that even though they were agitated, they were having a better time than at any other moment since he'd met them. It didn't help Peter's outlook that the most unifying thing he'd done so far was to give his staff the chance to openly vent their displeasure with him.

What could Alan have been thinking when he told Joanna to give him his job?

WATCHMAKER
OR
BEEKEEPER?

GROWTH CIRCLES

VOLTAGE!

Chapter 5

VOLTAGE

"Great managers in the world do not have much in common. They are of different sexes, races and ages. They employ vastly different styles and focus on different goals. But despite their differences, these great managers do share one thing: Before they do anything else, they first break all the rules of conventional wisdom."
— **Marcus Buckingham**, *First Break All the Rules*

After sitting in the shadow of the old locomotive for almost an hour, Peter began to think he had lost his mind. He had taken the advice of a man he knew absolutely nothing about. He had agonized over his decision for the whole weekend. And now he was waiting, like a child hoping for a glimpse of Santa Claus.

Peter heard a voice in back of him, "I wondered if I might see you today. How are things at your office?"

Peter's first impulse was to walk away. What was he going to say to this man? Why had he waited for over an hour? All he could do was shake his head in disgust and confusion.

"I'm going to go out on a limb here and assume you've done something that didn't work out as well as you'd hoped?"

"I did what you suggested. In fact, I did it on Friday afternoon. I had representatives from each department hold a meeting with their group to discuss the problems we're facing and come up with solutions. They excelled at identifying problems and, most often, those problems were with yours

truly. But the idea of coming up with solutions was a foreign concept."

"That's perfect! What was their mood?"

"Their mood? Are you kidding? They were almost electric."

"What are you going to do next?"

"I was hoping you might have a suggestion."

Horace chuckled. "Why would I have a suggestion? They're your people."

"That's just it. They aren't mine. They are still my brother's."

"Well, that's kind of a moot point now. He's gone. You're in charge. So what are you going to do?"

Peter was quiet for a moment. Then he gave Horace a detailed description of what was said at the meeting. "The thing is, I can't shake the fact that they were having a good time. Look, these folks are a real bright bunch. Alan always had an eye for great talent with incredible potential. They just seem afraid to own it."

Horace thought for a moment. "Interesting word, potential. Do you know anything about electricity?"

"What's that got to do with anything?"

"In the simplest terms, *voltage* is the measure of electric potential."

"OK."

> **LOOK, YOU JUST TOLD ME THAT YOU BELIEVED YOUR GROUP HAS GREAT POTENTIAL. TO ME, THE MEASURE OF POTENTIAL IN A COMPANY IS ITS VOLTAGE. IT'S AN IMPORTANT THING TO UNDERSTAND.**

"Look, you just told me that you believed your group has great potential. To me, the measure of potential in a company is its *voltage*. It's an important thing to understand, Peter.

"You've been describing something ephemeral about your company. You've been talking about the way it feels, what the emotional state of the staff is. Any time an executive tries to deal with the feelings of the organization, he or she is usually in uncharted waters. Even if you have an innate understanding of it, how do you talk about it?"

"Some executives get very uncomfortable if someone mentions feelings. In reality the emotional intelligence in an organization and its leaders has been proven to significantly impact performance. So it is really important to pay attention to the *voltage*."

Peter listened to him. "I see what you're saying, but so what? I mean, what good does it do to have a label for it?"

"It's much more than a label. *Voltage* is measurable – in electricity and in an organization. For you, it's a real measurement of the quality and intensity of the energy in an organization, in essence, the fuel that gets stuff done."

"But what does it tell me other than what I already know, namely, that the staff is not happy?"

"Here is an important 'soft side' principle: when the *voltage* in your company is low, the potential is low and the reality of low operational performance is close behind. Frankly, it means that your people are going to withhold their best efforts and that ultimately, the company's performance will suffer. So, Peter Logan, don't let anyone ever tell you that the 'soft stuff' is a waste of time.

"A wide range of elements contribute to the *voltage* of an organization, which we will discuss later, but suffice it to say *voltage* represents the sum total of all that impacts the spirit of your organization. *Voltage* is one of the most important predictive performance barometers you can use in managing the work community at your company."

"Wouldn't that be a novel thing, to actually manage the Bolder Solutions' workplace community!"

"Perhaps. But there's another step. If you can get your staff to begin to acknowledge and measure, on a regular basis, the workplace *voltage* in your company and what causes it, then the company will have made the first major step toward the staff owning the work environment and subsequently owning the performance of the enterprise.

"*Voltage* very often starts with the staff being given an opportunity to express their feelings and perceptions about the company in some form of survey or assessment. Frankly, this initial step can be somewhat uncomfortable for the leadership, but it is important for the management staff and the CEO to listen to the feedback regardless of how unflattering it is."

"They don't seem to have a problem expressing their feelings about me."

Horace mentioned, "You became the thing they could rally around or against, right?"

Peter nodded. "I'm not sure it was such a good step."

"Nonsense! It was the best thing that could happen. Do you know why?"

Peter admitted that he did not.

Horace continued, "Because you have started the change."

"I'm not sure I am tracking with you, Horace. What change?"

"The change is the transformation that happens when an enterprise stops running like a machine and begins growing like an intelligent, living thing. It usually starts when leadership actually asks for the candid opinion of the staff. It often is a painful experience for the leadership to hear how poorly they are leading the enterprise. But it is a very important first step to not only clear the air but also to acknowledge the perspective or intelligence of the organization.

"When I meet entrepreneurs I always ask them the following question: If you had a choice, which would you rather be, a watchmaker or a beekeeper?"

"How do most people answer?"

"The majority say they would rather be a watchmaker, which isn't surprising. Only a few say they'd chose to be beekeeper. After all, who wants to deal with the possibility of being stung by a bunch of angry bees? The watchmaker types want something that is predictable, something they can control. The

> IT OFTEN IS A PAINFUL EXPERIENCE FOR THE LEADERSHIP TO HEAR HOW POORLY THEY ARE LEADING THE ENTERPRISE. BUT IT IS A VERY IMPORTANT FIRST STEP TO NOT ONLY CLEAR THE AIR BUT ALSO TO ACKNOWLEDGE THE PERSPECTIVE OR INTELLIGENCE OF THE ORGANIZATION.

problem today is that businesses are, by their nature, unpredictable. To succeed you need to have a different mindset."

"Now, the folks who chose to be beekeepers, they're the ones with one foot in the future. They have a natural facility to work with the dangerous twin sisters of growth: complexity and chaos. Beekeepers are more apt to allow the intelligence of the hive to be the operator instead of themselves. The watchmakers in business are interested in running the business like a precision machine. The beekeepers understand that their business is an intelligent, living thing and, if allowed to, it will come up with far more ideas and solutions than they ever could. The beekeeper business will continually self-organize around and through its problems and challenges."

"So what do you think I am? A watchmaker or a beekeeper?"

"Well, Peter, I would say you are a frustrated watchmaker with bees buzzing all around you. You're in a similar place that thousands of business owners are in today. They are caught between two worlds: the industrial world, where there is the illusion of a large degree of control and order, and the New Economy, where things change so quickly it is difficult to sustain long lasting, top down control." Horace paused and looked keenly at Peter.

"We can talk about that later. Grab a pen and a piece of paper. Here is a simple Four-Step Process to move your company from a watch to a beehive." As Horace talked, Peter wrote:

1. You need to first recognize the intelligence of the organization by asking its opinion.

2. You need to filter out the noise from that opinion with your leadership team and come up with a 5 – 10 step key initiative plan.

3. You need to unify the enterprise team around this plan that sends a lightning bolt into the company.

4. You need to put natural systems and mechanisms in place that reinforce self-organizing behavior so that your staff can effectively work the change over 9 – 12 months.

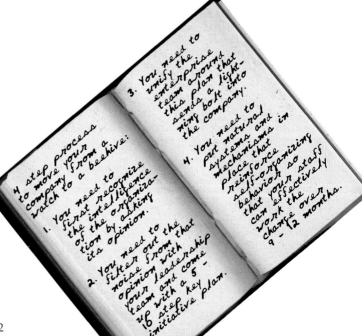

Horace continued. "You see, the first step to recognizing that your company is an intelligent, living entity is by asking its opinion. You started this process by asking for solutions from your staff. Now if you were to take this even further, you would ask the staff's opinion on a whole range of issues. And you would ask them in a way that they could give you anonymous answers. It has to be anonymous in order to get the truth from them.

"So, Peter, what's the next best thing to do right now?"

Peter was silent for a moment. "The next step. Swell. Horace, I'm at a loss. The only thing I can think to do is to have them meet again. If I'm going to get a handle on the — what did you call it? *voltage*? — then I need to let them talk. But there's a small voice in my head screaming to just clamp down on them. I guess that's the watchmaker talking, right?"

Horace laughed again. "Yes, it is. By the way, how well did that work for you before?"

"That's just it. It always has worked for me. Until now."

"Sounds like you need a new methodology."

"I guess I do."

"Trust them, Peter. Tell them about *voltage*; let them talk about it, and then let them tell you what they've come up with. Engaging the staff to begin shifting from problem finders to solution creators is the first step to building a Growth Curve company."

Peter interjected, "Ah, there is that phrase again. Someday you need to tell me what it means."

Horace continued, "All in good time, Peter, but right now what you really need to do is break your staff up into diversified meeting groups of 6 – 10 people from all over the company. It really isn't helpful to simply have the departments meet. They already should be meeting once a week as a department. Let's call these new groups growth circles."

> "IF I'M GOING TO GET A HANDLE ON THE…WHAT DID YOU CALL IT? VOLTAGE? THEN I NEED TO LET THEM TALK. BUT THERE'S A SMALL VOICE IN MY HEAD SCREAMING TO JUST CLAMP DOWN ON THEM."

"Good point. Maybe I'll mix up the groups. It certainly can't hurt."

"There is quite an art to growing a company from the ground up, Peter. Growth circles, in my opinion, are one of the hidden keys to building high-performance enterprises. It might take you a while to understand the subtleties and dynamics of using them effectively, but suffice it to say just getting started is a big step. Let me know how it goes."

As Peter drove back to the office, he found his mind drifting back to the Flatirons. It must have taken many earthquakes to shake loose those huge granite slabs staring out over Boulder Valley. It struck him that, right now, he needed something just as powerful to shake up his staff and somehow capture their buy-in at the same time. He concluded that there was no other choice. He had to recruit Dean Baldridge. If he was going to turn things around, he needed the young wizard on his side.

When Baldridge arrived at Peter's door, he threw it open without knocking, and then stood in the entrance, waiting for a reaction. But Peter was staring at his computer, taking no apparent notice of the younger man's presence. Baldridge thought for a moment and then stepped in and sat on the couch.

Baldridge was getting angry, but he didn't want to show it. He decided to wait a few more minutes and then leave.

Suddenly Peter turned all his attention to Dean. He looked at him so intently that it took the young programmer by surprise and made him feel a little uncomfortable.

"Why did you come to work for Alan?"

"Why?"

Peter sighed deeply. "This isn't a game, Dean. Just answer me."

"OK. I came here to work because Alan was a brilliant programmer. We spoke the same language. He paid me well, but then everybody I spoke to offered good money. But he was the one who knew what it meant to spend two straight days writing code, throwing it all away because it didn't feel right, and starting again. He gave me the freedom to do it the way I needed to, and he was helpful when I got stuck."

"Do you know why he gave up full-time programming?"

"No, he never talked about it."

"Yes, he did. He wanted to create something bigger. He wanted to create something lasting. He wanted to know that young and talented people like you would have a chance to shine. He knew that entrepreneurship and programming were somewhat oxymoronic, but he was willing to take the chance."

The silence built for a moment. "I liked your brother a lot."

"And he liked you. A lot. He didn't keep notes on employees, a fact that has driven me slightly crazy, but he kept notes on you."

Dean looked surprised. "Oh, really? Like what?"

"He apparently saw a lot of himself in you. His major concern was that you'd leave before he could convince you to take on some of the management duties of Bolder Solutions."

"Management duties? Are you kidding?"

"Absolutely not! We're at a crossroads, Dean. Whether or not you and I ever become best friends, this company needs to succeed with the project you're working on. The company needs your help."

Now he looked skeptical. "Help the company how?"

"It doesn't take a rocket scientist to realize you aren't happy here, and that you may move on. But I'm betting you have a personal investment in finishing what you started. So I'm going to ask you to help me by accepting some additional management responsibility. When we've succeeded with the buildup of the software, and if you still feel like you

need to go on to greener pastures, then I'll give you a recommendation that would open up any door to you. But I need your help now. And I'm convinced Alan would want you to do it."

Now Baldridge looked pale. "Damn, man. You're pulling out all the big guns here, aren't you?"

"There's no time to dance around. If we're going to finish what was started, what Alan started, I need your help."

"Why me?"

"Because the staff looks up to you, and because I've always respected my big brother's opinions."

"What would I have to do?"

"I want to give you a promotion of sorts. There's a little more money in it, and I think you might

enjoy the job. I want you ultimately to be my second in command. We will start slow at first so as not to overwhelm you."

Dean knew his skills were prodigious, but even Alan had never suggested a promotion into management. It was hard not to seem interested, but he wanted to play it cool. He was still reeling from the disclosure that Alan had intended to groom him for management.

Peter continued. "Here's the first project that I want you to do. You can use the staffing chart I've been making or change it to suit yourself. I want you to divide the office into groups of five to six people, with no two from any one department, if at all possible. And I want you to have them meet every week for 50-60 minutes. Make sure that the groups stay to a schedule. Each group should meet at a regular time. You can make it easy on yourself. I'm not interested in when they meet each week, only that they do. Are you with me so far?"

"Sure."

"Great! I also want you to set up a staff meeting for tomorrow morning. Find out what time everyone can commit to it and then set it up. Again, make it easy on yourself; it's your decision. The meeting is to explain the plan."

"Why are we doing this?"

"That's the other thing. I want you to give each group this questionnaire that I put together. They are all to fill one out. It shouldn't take any more than 30 minutes for them to finish it. I want this to be anonymous so tell them not to put their name on it and to be very honest."

Peter continued, "Dean, we are going to find out what these folks think and then we are going to take their best suggestions and run with them. What do you think?"

> ❝ WE ARE GOING TO FIND OUT WHAT THESE FOLKS THINK AND THEN WE ARE GOING TO TAKE THEIR BEST SUGGESTIONS AND RUN WITH THEM. ❞

"What's come over you? This is actually a good idea!"

"Good. Now to go one step further, from here on in, let's call these groups Growth Circles. Each Growth Circle meeting will have three main parts it."

"First, there will be a certain portion of the meeting focused on the strategic initiatives of the company, there will be a portion of the meeting focused on solutions to the company's challenges, and then there will be an elective portion of the meeting focused on what the members of the group feel that they want to talk about.

"At the beginning of each meeting, the members will look over the agenda and assign a timeframe for each item. It will be totally up to them how

much time they want to spend discussing the different items. But when the time is up on any item, that's it, they move on, whether or not they have finished their discussion. You and I will give the strategic initiatives and the solution topics for each week. The minutes of these meetings will be returned to us."

"There will be three roles in these groups. There will be a facilitator, a scribe who will take notes, and a timekeeper who will make sure that the meeting stays on plan. These meetings will be highly disciplined." Now Peter was at his whiteboard, writing and talking at the same time. "There will be three main rules for conducting Growth Circles."

46

1. They are to respect each other's thoughts and opinions.
2. Everyone participates.
3. They need to take notes about what they discuss in the group.

Dean looked as though he was a stranger in a strange land. "Strategic initiatives, solutions, time-keepers, scribes and whatever. That's it?"

"That's it. What do you say?" The two men sat in silence for three full minutes. Whatever Dean was thinking as he sat there, Peter would never know. Finally he said, "OK!"

There are three main rules for conducting Growth Circles:

1. Participants are to respect each other's thoughts and opinions.

2. Everyone participates.

3. Participants need to take notes about what they discuss in the group.

GROWTH CURVE

ADAPTABILITY • PROPORTION • RHYTHM

Chapter 6

GROWTH CURVE

"Nature favors adaptation and fleet-footedness. In nature, in the benevolent exchange between insects and plants, nectar is swapped for pollination services. In business, the merger of AOL with Time Warner is an effort to establish supremacy through aggregation in the e-business and communications industry."
— **Richard T. Pascale**, *Surfing The Edge of Chaos*

Peter wasn't surprised that the meeting was at 9 a.m. He was surprised to see how different Dean was at the meeting. He was a natural leader, funny and engaging, and the staff liked him. He explained the whole program without missing a beat. At the end of his short presentation, he turned to Peter and asked, respectfully, if he had left anything out. Peter forced himself not to smile, and simply said that Dean had covered it well.

Dean further surprised him by producing his own staffing chart in which he had broken up the staff into groups of five, and then announced that the groups should meet at four o'clock, once a week, starting that afternoon. After that, the staff went back to work with an air of purpose.

Peter had a pressing question on his mind, but he knew the only person he could ask was his new lunch buddy. The subject of food hadn't come up between them, but Peter decided to take a couple of sandwiches along.

"Thanks for lunch, Peter, but it wasn't necessary." Clearly, however, Horace enjoyed his sandwich. He used his leather journal as a food tray.

"What do I do now? I mean, I created a little chaos in the company and channeled it all at the same time. The staff seems to love the Growth Circle idea. The thing is, I'm the only one left out."

"Sounds good to me. Don't you see it as good news that you're left out of the process?"

"Good news? I was trying to find a way to manage these people, and all I've done is given them a place to let their growing anarchy take flight."

"Exactly. They will have a place to air their concerns. But it's also a place to find out what they can do, what solutions they create. You see, Peter, you've stepped out of the industrial management box. If my hunch is right, the thinking that says you have to control everything is going to get less and less useful. Growth is a messy thing and the solutions you need come from the ground up. I like to call what you are doing bubble-up growth.

"You've shown your staff more respect in one week than most companies do in three years. You've taken an important step in acknowledging the company as a separate intelligent entity, a beehive of sorts, by asking its opinion. Now you get to wait for them to surprise you."

"I can't wait very long. If the company survives me and my meddling, we'll need to address some pretty tough issues."

Horace stopped to think. "Well, you're on the fast track now. Once the employee groups get settled, you could involve them in finding the solutions to those issues."

"Are you serious?"

"Think about it. If you involve them in the solution discovery process, they begin to have a stake in the future of the company. But you must

engage them in the basics first. They must understand and help author the core values, the corporate culture, and some of the key strategic initiatives of the company in order to lay a bottom-up-growth foundation for the company."

Horace waved a hand at the park. "What do you see?"

"Um, well, I see trees and grass and birds. And a train and a band shell. Is that what you meant?"

"That's what I meant. But there's something else. Look again."

Peter tried to see more, but he found himself getting annoyed at the game. "I'm sorry, Horace, I don't know what you're wanting me to see."

"The solution to your problem. Although I don't expect you to make complete sense out of it right now."

"The solution to my problem?" Peter looked around again, but the scene didn't change. "I'm still seeing a park, Horace."

"Exactly!" Horace seemed to be considering his thoughts. But after a few moments, Peter couldn't stand it.

"Exactly what? Give me a clue."

"Nature."

"Nature? What about it?"

"Peter, nature provides one of the finest entrepreneurial growth models available. Take another look. Everything around where you are standing is some living thing attempting to survive and adapt within one or more larger complex living systems. Listen, Peter, in nature, all living things have four things in common:

All living things have four things in common:

→

1. They learn and adapt.

2. They have and/or make an identity that gives them a place.

3. They build and maintain a complex blend of relationships with other living beings in their environment.

4. They effectively govern their own growth and evolution.

1. They learn and adapt.
2. They have and/or make an identity that gives them a place.

> " A COMPANY, LIKE ANY OTHER LIVING ORGANISM, HAS NATURAL STAGES OF GROWTH IT MUST GO THROUGH.... IF A COMPANY IS ALLOWED TO FIND ITS OWN BALANCE, IT WILL SELF ORGANIZE, THROUGH THE CHAOS OF GROWTH, IN REMARKABLE WAYS. "

 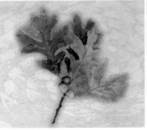 

3. They build and maintain a complex blend of relationships with other living beings in their environment.
4. They effectively govern their own growth and evolution.

"Surprisingly, Royal Dutch Shell, the preeminent global oil company, made a remarkable discovey back in the 1980s, with their strategic scenario planning group. Out of the 45 or so enterprises they identified around the world which were over 150 years old, all of them have just four things in common. Care to guess what they are?"

Peter looked at Horace as if he were crazy. "You mean to tell me that the companies mirror these four common characteristics in nature, and that this is the secret to their longevity?"

Horace leaned back and said, "Yes, indeed!"

Peter shook his head. "What about making money? That certainly had something to do with their longevity."

Horace laughed and enigmatically said, "Nope, making money was only secondary. It was a result of the four things. But your real question is what does this have to do with growing your company? Plenty. The chaos and craziness happening over at Bolder Solutions is no different than what is happening right here in this park."

"Have you ever looked at everything that is going on in nature and wondered how the whole thing stays organized? The original crazy maker is nature and yet there is no finer innovator. Why? Can you tell me how it all stays glued together through all the chaos and disequilibria?"

"Not a clue, captain."

Horace continued, "All throughout nature, there are multiple stages of growth that are built into the genetic code. We take it for granted that a tree knows how to grow from a seed through all the various stages into what we see here in front of us.

"Complex living systems all go through stages of growth. Once you begin to see that your company is an ever-expanding complex living organism moving through very specific stages of growth, you have a chance at better understanding your problems. Bolder Solutions is not a machine for you to control and manipulate. It is a living, intelligent thing. Peter piped in, "You mean it's a beehive, right?"

"Yes, when it is allowed to be. The real business builders know this. Everyone else, Peter, is just trying to make a buck. Look at all the dotcoms that went out of business in the last few years. Everyone was going to get rich, right? Those people had some strange ideas of how to grow a self-sustaining enterprise. They no more knew how to manage a high-speed growth company than they knew how to turn lead into gold. A lot of money and many people's lives were affected in the wave of that ignorance."

"A company, like any other living organism, has natural stages of growth it must go through. You can't skip over or speed through any of those stages without facing the consequences. If allowed, a company will find its own balance and will self-organize, through the chaos of growth, in remarkable ways. But you have to set the conditions in place that let the enterprise self correct as it grows. Do you know what a nautilus is?"

"I assume you mean the animal — the mollusk, not the submarine?"

"That's correct. Have you ever seen a nautilus shell split in half so you can see its inner chambers?"

"Sure."

"As the nautilus grows, as each chamber develops, it does so in a very specific proportion. As each new chamber develops, it is in a preordained proportion that you can find in the most surprising places. Regard that tree over there. From the moment its seed germinated to form the sprout that would someday be that tree, it grew in the same proportion as the nautilus."

"What are you telling me, Horace? That everything has an underlying universal design to it, including my business?"

"That's right"

"Come on, Horace. I have to run a business. What does this stuff have to do with making payroll and getting product out the door?"

"The real secret behind growing a healthy, powerful business enterprise is buried in understanding the patterns of that enterprise. When you can see the patterns of your company as clearly as you can see the clouds in the sky, then you are playing in a different league. You are a master enterprise leader. But if you don't understand the basic principles behind patterns, how are you going to see the patterns in the first place? You will be looking at the activity of your business without seeing what is really going on."

"Every living thing has an ideal path of growth, including a commercial enterprise. I call this ideal path a Growth Curve. This Growth Curve is directed by the laws of proportion, rhythm, and adaptability. Navigating the Growth Curve is truly the art of growing your organization along the fine line between chaos and order. Too much time spent on either side means death.

"When you can clearly see your company's major and minor patterns of behavior expressed on a daily basis and understand their meaning within the larger context of the company's health, then you can intentionally navigate the Growth Curve. What you need to first understand is how a company grows along the Growth Curve."

Horace read his mind. Peter, above all else, was a skeptic and he was having a hard time believing that Horace knew what he was talking about.

"Peter, I have grown and run numerous highly successful enterprises and believe me when I say I have tried everything from the touchy-feely 'you are what you eat' approaches all the way to the hard-line business methods of the corporate raiders. I have experienced the whole gamut."

Horace paused briefly. "The most successful model I have ever been able to find for a growing company is demonstrated by living systems like those growing right at our feet."

> **EVERY LIVING THING HAS AN IDEAL PATH OF GROWTH, INCLUDING A COMMERCIAL ENTERPRISE. THIS GROWTH CURVE IS DIRECTED BY THE LAWS OF PROPORTION, RHYTHM, AND ADAPTABILITY. NAVIGATING THE GROWTH CURVE IS TRULY THE ART OF GROWING YOUR ORGANIZATION ALONG THE FINE LINE BETWEEN CHAOS AND ORDER.**

Horace continued, "Consider what a business has in common with other living things, or should have in common. Everything you see in front of you here has found some kind of balance with its neighbors and the local environment. They have an internal rhythm; they grow in recognizable proportion. They seem genetically hard-wired to adapt, even to learn from the conditions around them. You can argue that metaphorically they know what they are. A rose is a rose is a rose. And unless they are acted upon by conditions beyond their control, they live a whole life."

"Companies, on the other hand, rarely wait for external pressures to destroy them. They are too busy imploding from their own blindness to see what's really happening. Entrepreneurs like to blame outside influences, but the truth is, the real problems usually sit with the owners themselves. The most impressive mistake made by companies today is their inability to adapt and change. Maybe it's because humans are blessed with the faculty of thought that resists change; they just can't believe that the world continues to demand adaptation. But it does. Every moment."

Horace continued, "You have to understand the nature of a growing enterprise. A business, just like that tree over there, has cycles of growth. If you can begin to understand those cycles, you may not have the same fate as the majority of companies, namely, premature death."

Peter listened to his new friend, but he wasn't sure where this was going. "That sounds great, but I'm just hoping to last a couple of years, sell the company, and then get out. In fact, today I'd settle for a couple of months."

"How long do you think a company should survive, Peter?"

"Come on, Horace. A company lasts as long as it lasts. It lasts as long as it makes enough money to pay its bills, its staff, and keep the stockholders happy. What possible difference does it make if that is a long time or a short time?

"Sometimes a company can't make money. Sometimes it loses key employees. Sometimes it just can't handle the marketplace or can't find a way to grow fast enough to keep up. And that's not taking into consideration what happens when industries become outmoded, such as the buggy whip business."

Horace looked across at Peter. "Oh, really? Why did the buggy whip makers go out of business?"

"Because people stopped using buggies, and they stopped buying buggy whips!"

"No. They went out of business because it didn't occur to them that they were ultimately in the transportation support business, and that they might consider another support product to develop. They simply couldn't adapt."

Horace pursued the topic further. "Do you have any idea how long the oldest company in the world has endured?"

Peter was getting agitated, but he was determined not to show it. "OK. Well, let's see. There are some big American companies that date back into the nineteenth century. And there are probably some European companies that go back before that. OK, I guess the oldest company could be 150 to 200 years old."

"Not even close. The oldest company is a Swedish company called Stora. It was founded in

1272. Think of it! It has lasted over 700 years, through political and social upheavals, economic surges and depressions, radical changes in its leadership as well as its product lines. And yet it continues to survive as an entity. And you say you'd be happy if your company lasts a couple of years?"

"OK, that's very impressive, but so what? What does that have to do with me?"

Horace saw the confusion in Peter's face.

"What are the three main concerns in your company?"

Well, number one is easy. My employees are probably melting tar and collecting feathers waiting for my return. And they are really creative people. So the first is my staff."

Horace just smiled. "Go on."

"OK, let's see. Well, we have one older product that helped build the company, but it doesn't make us much money anymore. We have products that are selling big right now, but they are about to face competition from similar products. So we need to get the new product we're developing into the marketplace soon or we're going to be hitting a cash crunch. The staff doesn't see it yet because we are currently profitable, but profitability has to be maintained. So I'd say money or profitability is my second concern."

Horace seemed genuinely pleased. "And what's your third choice?"

Peter thought for a second. "Well, like I said, if we can keep from self-destructing, we're on a pretty strong growth trajectory. If we are having a hard time now, how will we keep it glued together when we double or triple our complexity? So, yeah, growth is the third."

Horace smiled. "And just like that, you've named the three main concerns of every company in business today: staff satisfaction, sustainable profit, and predicting/managing growth. But these things can all be addressed if you understand that a company

> THE THREE MAIN CONCERNS OF EVERY COMPANY—SUSTAINABLE PROFIT, STAFF SATISFACTION, AND PREDICTING/MANAGING GROWTH, CAN BE ADDRESSED IF YOU UNDERSTAND THAT A COMPANY IS LIKE A LIVING ENTITY WITH ITS OWN KIND OF INTELLIGENCE.

is a living entity, and it has to be treated like one with its own kind of intelligence. When the true identity of the enterprise begins to emerge, then the enterprise is capable of living as long as Stora."

Horace looked over at Peter and pointed his finger at his chest. "Peter, to survive and prosper in the economic landscape of the 21st century, it is my opinion that a company will have to rethink and/or rewire their fundamental profit design on a regular basis, even as often as every 3-5 years. The average businessperson wouldn't consider adapting his business model that often. But more importantly, to really hit the ball out of the park, entrepreneurs will need to create the conditions or the organizational climate that produces a Growth Curve Enterprise, a profit-driven, people-centered, growth-smart company."

"Horace, now that's a wish list that I could get my teeth into. How do I create that?"

> " TO REALLY HIT THE BALL OUT OF THE PARK, ENTREPRENEURS NEED TO CREATE THE CONDITIONS, OR THE ORGANIZATIONAL CLIMATE, THAT PRODUCES A **GROWTH CURVE ENTERPRISE,** A PROFIT-DRIVEN, PEOPLE-CENTERED, GROWTH-SMART COMPANY. "

Horace threw the lunch trash in a big metal trash container, letting the question hang in the air.

"If you're serious, there are some people you should meet. They're local entrepreneurs who've tackled these problems and found ways to deal with them. Are you serious?"

Peter looked at his watch and then caught himself. "Perfect. I'm sitting here considering if I have the time to learn what I need to learn to save the company. I think that's the answer. I'm definitely serious."

Horace came back to him. "OK, do this first, because it will be instructive and it will be good for your staff. When you get back to your office, ask your young hotshot who organized the groups this morning to give the groups a task. Ask them to identify what they see as the key challenges to the company. Tell them they get to be totally honest, and that they aren't expected to have the answers. Tomorrow we'll talk about it. Also, did you tell them about *voltage*?"

"Uh, no. In the midst of everything, it went out of my thoughts."

"They'll like it. I suggest you tell them about it. Believe me, it's something they will immediately relate to. And I'll contact a few people to see when they have time to speak with you."

Peter was suddenly sharply aware of what the man was offering. "Horace, that's very generous of you. Why are you doing this for me?"

Horace didn't speak for a moment. "It's a long story. Suffice it to say I made a promise a long time ago when I was your age and someone helped me. I promised to return the gift and I have kept that promise for the last thirty-three years. And let me be very clear, you'll be expected to do the same. Still interested?"

"Absolutely!"

CHAPTER 6 — KEY POINTS

- Nature provides one of the finest entre-preneurial growth models available
- In nature, all living things have four things in common:
  1. They learn and adapt.
  2. They have and/or make an identity that gives them a place.
  3. They build and maintain a complex blend of relationships with other living beings in their environment.
  4. They effectively govern their own growth and evolution.
- A Growth Curve Enterprise is a profit-driven, people-centered, growth-smart company.
- The real secret behind growing a healthy, powerful business enterprise is buried in understanding the patterns of that enter-prise.
- A company, like any other living organ-ism, has natural stages of growth it must go through. You can't skip over or speed through any of those stages without fac-ing the consequences.

Chapter 7
HIDDEN PREDATOR

"Leaders are the stewards of organizational energy — in companies, organizations, and even in families. They inspire and demoralize others by how effectively they manage their own energy and next by how they mobilize, focus, invest, and renew the collective energy of those they lead."
— **Loehr and Swartz,** *The Power of Full Engagement*

Peter found Dean Baldridge happily working at his computer, surrounded by an assortment of fast food wrappers. Dean agreed to speak to the staff. In fact he was pleased to be able to give everyone a task for their first meeting. Peter was amazed at the change in the young man. He decided to let Dean tell them about *voltage* since it was more in his world than Peter's. He told him what Horace had said about *voltage*, potential energy and all of it.

Dean just listened and said, "That's pretty cool. I'll tell them."

Peter walked back to his office noting for the first time since day one that people weren't glaring at him. Even Kate managed to smile when she told him he had some phone calls. She handed him a couple of slips of paper with phone numbers written on them. "The one on top is the most interesting."

As he pondered the conversations he'd had with Horace, he reviewed his new reference template for Bolder Solutions: profit-driven, people-centered,

growth-smart. He liked it. The three themes provided an easy focus for a company like his. Then he remembered that he'd just asked his staff to come up with their own lists of issues confronting Bolder Solutions. He decided to do the same.

He'd been writing for the better part of an hour when there was a knock on his open door. A female voice said, "Mr. Peter Logan?"

He looked up and stared for a moment. An attractive woman in a no-nonsense business suit was standing in his doorway. He had no idea who she was.

"Are you Peter Logan?"

"Yes. Who are you?"

"Detective Jane Carnes, Boulder Police. I told your secretary I'd be dropping by." Just behind the detective, Peter could see Kate actively pointing to the message sheet she had

59

put on his desk. The detective continued. "I'm investigating the death of Alan Logan. He was your brother, correct?"

"What? I mean, yes, he was my brother. But why are you investigating Alan's death? He suffered a fatal heart attack."

"I understand you were in Los Angeles when your brother died. Is that correct?"

"Yes, I had a series of meetings with my former company."

"And that company was the Santomo Corporation, correct?"

"Yes. What does that have to do with anything?"

"And upon returning to Boulder, you took over your brother's company, is that correct?"

> "RIGHT NOW WE'RE CONSIDERING YOUR BROTHER'S DEATH A POSSIBLE HOMICIDE. HIS DEATH WAS NOT FROM ROUTINE HEART FAILURE."

"OK. That's enough! If you want me to answer any more questions, you're going to have to tell me what's going on."

Peter had never been scrutinized the way Detective Jane Carnes was looking at him now. She was clearly making decisions about him.

"I'm sorry, Mr. Logan, but it's my job to ask these questions. Just tell me one more thing. Why did you leave Santomo?"

Peter hesitated.

"Please, Mr. Logan. I will tell you what's going on, but I need to know. Why did you leave Santomo?"

"They fired me."

"You seemed to bounce back rather quickly."

"My sister-in-law asked me to take over." Peter wasn't sure he liked her attitude. "And since I had just been tossed away by Santomo, I was available. I said yes. Do you know that Santomo invested in one of Bolder Solutions' projects?"

"Tell me about it."

"I read that Alan had some relationship with Santomo. As it turns out, it was early in the process. They had invested in one of the strategic partners in the project, and they had tried to get in here, too. But they are no longer involved. Oh, and the article mentioned mysterious circumstances."

"Yes, that was a mistake. I mean it was a mistake that it got in the press."

"I beg your pardon?"

"OK, I told you I'd explain. Right now we're considering your brother's death a possible homicide. His death was not from routine heart failure."

Peter's look of shock registered. It took a minute for him to recover. "I take it you think I may have some reason to be involved?"

"Like I said, I'm just doing my job."

"Why did you ask me about Santomo?"

Once again his guest looked right through him. "Mr. Logan…"

"Please, call me Peter. "Since you may be accusing me of murder, you might as well call me by my first name."

She started to say something, but smiled instead. A very nice smile, Peter thought. Peter was amazed that he found himself thinking just how long it had been since he'd taken a woman out to dinner, and how very long it had been since a woman really mattered to him.

"All right, Peter. Here's the short version. The coroner found some proteins in your brother's blood that didn't make sense. Some were natural, but not natural to the human body. These proteins

> **ALL RIGHT, PETER. HERE'S THE SHORT VERSION. THE CORONER FOUND SOME PROTEINS IN YOUR BROTHER'S BLOOD THAT DIDN'T MAKE SENSE. SOME WERE NATURAL, BUT NOT NATURAL TO THE HUMAN BODY. THESE PROTEINS CAUSED HIS HEART TO STOP BEATING.**

caused his heart to stop beating.

"The puzzling thing for us is how they could have gotten into your brother's body in the first place. There was no evidence of any kind of a puncture wound; he didn't even have a scratch on him. And they couldn't be ingested because no food contains them."

"And you think these proteins killed him?"

"Yes, the coroner knows they did. Frankly, I think you'd have to have a degree in bioengineering to grasp it."

For the second time in the last fifteen minutes, Peter began processing the fact that his brother's death was not the result of a heart attack, but something much more unnerving. Peter had to ask the question. "You do know what we're working on here, don't you?"

"In general. That's what put you on our list."

"I don't understand. I mean, yes, the project is about genetic engineering, but why does that particularly involve me?"

"Santomo."

"Didn't we just cover that?"

Mystery Protein

"Santomo shows up on the most interesting lists, FBI inquiries, rumors about the CIA, protests of multinational corporate activities. We keep up with everything we can. It's the presence of those strange proteins that has us thinking about a company that is into all kinds of chemicals. And a company that's known for not taking 'no' gracefully."

> **LET'S JUST SAY THAT THERE AREN'T TOO MANY COMPANIES ON THE PLANET WITH THE RESOURCES TO CREATE THE PROTEINS WE FOUND.**

"You think Santomo killed my brother?"

"Let's just say that there aren't too many companies on the planet with the resources to create the proteins we found. We just have no idea how they could have gotten them into Alan Logan."

Peter tried to think of something to say. Was it possible that Alan had been murdered? Could Santomo have been involved?

"Mr…Peter, if you think of anything, will you give me a call?" She was holding out her card.

"Um, sure. But I don't have a clue what you think I'll think of."

"Anything that crosses your mind about any of this, let me know. You never can tell how the pieces will come together."

"OK. How about if you do the same? Anything you learn, will you let me know?"

"Sure. Just be careful. You don't need to go looking for trouble with Santomo. If they are involved, they're clearly willing to take severe steps. If they aren't involved, your brother's death is still a homicide. Somebody wanted him dead."

"Am I going to be reading about this in tomorrow's paper?"

"Not if we can help it. We'd like to keep this out of the news. It's all a bit too strange. And frankly, we don't need the national press asking us questions we don't have answers to."

He debated the next thing he was about to say. "I should tell you one thing, although I'm starting to feel like I need to call a lawyer. You're the second person in the last few days to suggest I had something to do with Alan's death. Alan had been working with a public relations woman named Grace McGregor. She had learned something about Santomo trying to smear the reputation of Bolder Solutions in the business press. She thought they were a danger to Alan."

"She accused you of killing him?"

"No, like I say, she just suggested I might be involved. It was not a pleasant meeting. She got angry with me; I got angry at her. I thought she was nuts. But now you're saying Santomo could be responsible for Alan's death."

"Thanks. I'll have to have a chat with her."

Sitting on his front porch and leaning back in a deck chair, Peter tried to make sense of the events of the last few weeks.

Up to this point, he purposely avoided the partners in the seed genome project. Bolder Solutions was in such disarray he couldn't let on how far behind the company was on its project. But now he had a reason for getting in touch with them; they needed to know that Alan's death might have been a murder and they needed to know what Santomo was up to.

 HE PURPOSELY AVOIDED THE PARTNERS IN THE SEED GENOME PROJECT. BOLDER SOLUTIONS WAS IN SUCH DISARRAY HE COULDN'T LET ON HOW FAR BEHIND THE COMPANY WAS ON ITS PROJECT.

He dug into his briefcase and retrieved the card Joanna had given him: Elijah Brown, CEO, Heritage Genomics: Colorado Germ Plasm Project.

Elijah Brown answered the phone with a voice that reminded Peter of James Earl Jones. "It is a pleasure to speak with you, Peter. I was very fond of your brother."

Peter said, "Sir, the company is still struggling with the upheaval of Alan's death. I'm working on solutions, but I don't want to pretend that it isn't having an impact. We are likely to drop a few weeks behind schedule, but I assure you we will do everything we can to catch up."

Elijah sighed. "I'm not surprised. I was hoping this wouldn't happen, but I knew Alan was a particularly applied kind of owner. It was his style. There is bound to be a period of adjustment. You do understand how vital your product is to us?"

"Yes, I think I do. Mr. Brown, I know you're concerned about our ability to finish. I wish I could tell you tonight how close we are. But I can't. What I can tell you is I truly believe we have the talent to get it finished. I can assure you that you will get constant updates on our progress going forward."

"First, Peter, my name is Elijah. And second, I appreciate your candor. Please keep me informed."

"You have my word."

There was a moment of silence. Elijah spoke first. "I sense there is more to your call this evening, Peter?"

Peter hesitated, "I don't know precisely where to begin. I need to tell you something in strict confidence because I don't know what the information means. I had a visit from a police detective today."

"Ah, the lovely Detective Carnes?"

"Yes. I take it she's been to see you as well?"

"Oh, yes. She makes quite a first impression."

Peter felt his face flush as thoughts of the detective standing in his doorway flooded his imagination. "Yes. Yes, she does."

Elijah chuckled on the other end of the line. "Did she allude to your involvement in Alan's death?"

"Yep. You, too?"

"We had quite an interesting discussion. So I suppose you want to know more about Santomo, yes?"

"Yes. Did she tell you I worked for them?"

"She didn't have to. Alan told me about it. Your brother spoke of you often and with great respect. He told me that Santomo was the money behind your last venture. He also hoped they would not disappoint you."

"Being fired I can deal with. Murdering my brother…well, I want to know what happened."

"Peter, let me give you some background that might help you understand the conditions surrounding Alan's death. Santomo was an early investor in my company. They appeared to be interested only in helping us to succeed. But shortly after a fairly sizeable infusion of capital, they started demanding access to material and research. It wasn't just the request, it was the way they went about it. We had been courting another investor firm that showed up with their checkbook at just the right time.

"We were able to buy back Santomo's interest and send them on their way. They fought us, of course, but they had a release clause in the contract that gave us that power. They never thought we would be able to exercise it. They were very, very upset. Then they tried to get involved with your brother's company, but he wouldn't give them the time of day."

Peter said, "What was the big attraction for Santomo?"

"They wanted our processes. We knew they were investing in genetically engineered crops. We thought they were interested in what we were doing because we were working on a way to help agriculture, not control it. We were naïve. They wanted to insert foreign proteins into food crops." He paused a moment. "Peter, I think they wanted us to do weapons research."

Another moment of silence passed between the

> ANOTHER MOMENT OF SILENCE PASSED BETWEEN THE TWO MEN. THIS TIME PETER SPOKE FIRST. 'YOU MEAN THE BASTARDS MAY ACTUALLY HAVE KILLED MY BROTHER?'

two men. This time Peter spoke first. "You mean the bastards may actually have killed my brother?"

"I can't prove it. And I would not say this to anyone else, but yes, I think they did. I just don't know why."

"Spite? Retribution?"

"Not plausible. They wanted so much more. It is

always about money with people like that. I suspect they wanted to harm the project."

"But aren't you much more valuable to the project? I don't mean…"

"No, it is all right. Yes, I am more directly involved, but I may have been too close. Alan's work, now your work, the product you are developing for us, makes our work possible. Without it we won't complete our project of unraveling the seed genome. We have so much information that we are drowning in data and we need a way to make sense of it. Santomo is not sitting still. There are others trying to do what we are doing, but we're farther along. If they can slow us down enough, they might get there before we do."

"Still, even if you do get there first, they can develop their own products. How does this become a race between you and Santomo?"

"You don't know? It is our plan to give our body of research away. We'll patent it and then freely make it available to all the world's food organizations. Santomo can't allow that."

"Well, that's altruism at its best! Someone actually funded this project?"

"Yes, we had a few very wealthy individuals who had a broader vision than their own self-aggrandizement."

Peter continued, "It must have taken millions to get where you are today. But this brings us back to how they could have been involved with my brother's death."

"Did you know your brother loved whole wheat bread?"

"Yes, now that you mention it. What's the connection?"

"It's just a theory. But if I wanted an untraceable way to get foreign proteins into someone, I would feed it to them. And I would use the most common product I could think of."

Suddenly Peter felt like he was caught in an episode of *The X-Files*. "Elijah, you do realize how this sounds, don't you?"

"Oh, yes. I suppose that is why I have not contacted Detective Carnes. Frankly, I hope I am being paranoid, but I don't think so. I am also hoping that you will contact the detective and I will retain the illusion that it was not my idea."

Peter decided he and Elijah were destined to become good friends. "I'll let you know what she says. And I'll keep you posted on our progress."

She answered on the eighth ring. He had apparently woken her.

"Ms., um, Detective Carnes, this is Peter Logan. We spoke today at my office."

She seemed to weigh that bit of information. "Ah, Mr. Logan. Or, if memory serves, you asked me to call you Peter, right?"

It was absurd. He could feel his heart pump a bit faster when she said his name. Get a grip, Logan, this is not the time.

"I take it you've thought of something?"

The idea suddenly seemed ridiculous. "Well, maybe." He told her about his conversation with Elijah Brown, and the theory that somehow a food product, like wheat bread, could be the method used for getting foreign proteins into Alan. She listened without comment until he was done.

"Interesting. That would explain the absence of any puncture wounds or any other obvious method of ingestion. I just don't know how we'd prove it."

"Uh, look, Ms...Detective Carnes. Would you be willing to discuss the case over a cup of coffee?"

The silence was excruciating.

"The first thing you'll have to do is stop calling me Ms...Detective. My name is Jane."

Dean Baldridge arrived at work on time the next day. He was even pleasant. "You know, they really worked hard at this. I made a list of all the problems they named and noted which ones showed up more than once. They also filled out your questionnaire. It will take us awhile to calibrate the answers, but at least we're on our way."

Peter was amused at the tone of his star computer wizard. "How near the top was I on the lists?"

Baldridge didn't miss a beat. "Well, to tell you the truth, you weren't exactly on the list. It was more an issue of morale. I mean your name came up with all the groups, but they realized that it's too easy to say you're the problem. We had morale issues or as you would say, *voltage* issues, before you got here."

This was a revelation to Peter. "You're kidding?"

"No. Look, I liked your brother a lot. But he kept a lid on everything. He was a great problem solver, but a terrible manager."

"How so?" asked Peter.

"When the problems started growing exponentially and he didn't have all the answers any more, everything started to peel off the walls. It was crazy around here right up until Alan's death.

"We didn't know what was going on – we were kept in the dark and people started filling in the blanks because Alan wouldn't tell us what we needed to know. Morale was getting ugly."

Peter could tell Dean was hesitant to speak badly in any way about Alan. It was the first time Peter had even considered

"WE HAD MORALE ISSUES OR AS YOU WOULD SAY, VOLTAGE ISSUES, BEFORE YOU GOT HERE."

that there was unrest in the company before Alan's death.

"What else was going on?" asked Peter, wanting to help get some things on the table. He felt Dean wanted to get these things off his chest.

"Well, some of us felt we were moving too fast. We didn't spend any time thinking, we just reacted. Processes, the few that we had, were ignored. We just kept hiring people to manage the workload. It became almost comical because there wasn't anyone minding the store." Dean stopped and looked at Peter carefully.

"This was still a great place to be, but things were getting a little out of hand," he justified quickly.

Peter responded with a smile, "Thanks for telling me this, Dean. It helps knowing I'm not the sole cause of everyone's distress! Any other issues I should be aware of?"

Dean thought for a moment and added, "My biggest concern was it didn't seem like we were able to get more than one product to profitability at a time. We were also leaking knowledge as programmers got frustrated and left."

"So, this idea of yours about *voltage* really got our people thinking. Each group got into it in their own way, but once they started talking about

morale, they found that *voltage* was a better word. In fact, ultimately they said that *voltage* is the biggest issue the company has."

> "ONCE THEY STARTED TALKING ABOUT MORALE, THEY FOUND THAT VOLTAGE WAS A BETTER WORD. IN FACT, ULTIMATELY THEY SAID THAT VOLTAGE IS THE BIGGEST ISSUE THE COMPANY HAS."

Peter thought Horace would nod, and say, "I told you so."

Dean continued, "The discussion on *voltage* tended to get into a couple of other things. Some of us are still concerned about staff turnover. With all the changes going on,

you know people have been threatening to quit, right? It's just that nobody really wants to quit, but what if they did? Or what if some of us were suddenly given offers we couldn't refuse?"

"Good point." It had been on Peter's mind night and day.

"Then there were points made about growth. We all feel Alan was hoping to keep the company small so he could continue to handle it. People around here, frankly, don't understand how we are going to survive our own growth. We've all seen companies expand quickly, then hit a wall and cut their staff

> **PEOPLE AROUND HERE, FRANKLY, DON'T UNDER-STAND HOW WE ARE GOING TO SURVIVE OUR OWN GROWTH. WE'VE ALL SEEN COMPANIES EXPAND QUICKLY, THEN HIT A WALL AND CUT THEIR STAFF BACK BY HALF OVERNIGHT.**

back by half overnight. I hope you realize it makes us all a little nervous."

"I'm very aware of that."

"OK, well, that leads to some other things like hiring good people, and training them properly. And, Peter, some of the big brains here are concerned that what little culture we do have will start to get funky and undefined when we expand. If we don't have a clearer sense of who we are and where we are going, this place will come apart."

"Thanks for telling me this. I'm very pleased that you guys figured out so much. It sounds to me like we need to discover our company's core values. OK, what else?"

"There were several small things; for example, we're almost out of most of supplies."

"What supplies?"

Dean spoke slowly and clearly, as if to a child. "You know, pencils, disks, bathroom stuff, ballpoint pens."

"You're serious? You mean simple office supplies?"

"Yeah. You really didn't know what I meant?"

"Who orders supplies? No, wait. Alan did, right?"

"Yeah. He said he liked knowing where all the resources were going."

"OK, well, that's going to change. What else, Dean?"

"You mentioned core values. With all the chaos and our need to grow quickly, we better figure out who we are pronto. Does that make sense?"

"Totally."

Peter looked at the young man and had a glimmer of hope for his company that hadn't existed before. "Thank you for your help in this. Tell me something. Are you, all of you, aware of the stakes in what it is we're doing?"

"I know our software is supposed to help a company that's doing genetics research. And I know it's for plants, not humans. I know they're supposed to be the good guys in a race to find the information. But that's pretty much all I know, and I have no idea if everybody here knows it."

"We have to change that, too. What we're doing is more important than you may realize."

HB Journal February 8
Philosophy and Business

Notes:
Business by its nature is an action-driven phenomenon. Every action executed in a business represents a form of behavior. When behavior is not guided by ideology, philosophy, or principle, it is susceptible to random outcomes including aberrant behavior.

Michael's quote about assumptions:
"The sum total of a person's experience becomes the aggregate expression of his/her assumptions"

-Michael O'Conner, Tuesday lunch at the Med.

Who's a Philosopher?
Whether a CEO recognizes this or not he/she is a philosopher. Core beliefs are central to how the CEO views the world. He/she has a philosophy or set of beliefs about how life works or doesn't work, how business works or doesn't work, and what the customer wants or doesn't want. From this philosophical base springs how the CEO perceives and subsequently creates their business. Every CEO's base of personal philosophy originates from a pool of core assumptions. These core assumptions are the stuff from which businesses are made.

How certain are you?
Ask yourself how certain (I mean really certain) you are of the assumptions you believe to be true about you business, your customers, your employees, your competitors, and your products/services.

4 Steps to Decision Making:
1. Probe with inquiry.
2. Challenge certainty and importance of assumptions.
3. Measure the impact.
4. Ascertain alignment with your values goals, strategies and plans.

"MY LIFE FELT LIKE A FREE-FALL DIVE OUT OF A PLANE. IRONICALLY, I THINK YOU HANDED ME THE RIP CORD."

Chapter 8

RIP CORD

"The ultimate measure of a man is not where he stands in moments of comfort, but where he stands at times of challenge and controversy."
— **Martin Luther King Jr.**

Horace listened intently to Peter's account of what the staff had identified as the challenges facing the company. "You've got a good staff, Peter. They really jumped into this. Being able to talk about *voltage* will help them. And, they've identified some of the biggest issues companies face."

"Your brother was really something. I can't tell you how many owners and managers have a fear of not only delegating responsibility, but also the authority along with it. The issue is making the transformation from being a CEO-centric leader to being a company-centric leader. This is why Stage 3 is one of the more dangerous stages of growth to get through. The change that is demanded of the CEO can be daunting to most people."

"Stage 3 company? What's that?" asked Peter curiously.

"We'll talk about The Stages of Growth another time, Peter. Hang on to that question."

"Oh, there's another piece of drama that I need to tell you about, Horace. I guess it counts as part of what a company faces. Or it's going to sound like a B movie. I'll let you decide." Peter outlined his conversations with Jane Carnes and Elijah Brown. As he explained how his brother was likely a murder victim, it sounded about as far-fetched as anything he'd ever heard.

Horace listened quietly. When Peter finished, he said, "I've known Elijah for a long time. Elijah may be the smartest man I've ever met. If he says he has a theory about your brother's death, you can almost take it to the bank."

Horace continued. "Until you know more about the facts relating to your brother's death, it probably

> **A COMPANY NEEDS TO HAVE A CLEAR UNDERSTANDING OF ITS PURPOSE AND ITS COMPELLING MISSION, AND THAT HAS TO FLOW FROM YOU, THE CEO.**

won't help your staff to worry about it. However, your people would surely benefit from knowing exactly what it is they are working on. A company needs to have a clear understanding of its purpose and its compelling mission, and that has to flow from you, the CEO. It needs a reason to deal with the turbulence of chaotic times and a reason to change when necessary. And it's not particularly helpful to rely on an owner who says 'Do it because I say it's a good idea'."

Peter and Horace had gone over the list of concerns his staff had produced a few days earlier. Peter added to the list more challenges he'd discovered during his career. Along with the combination of his list and the Bolder Solution employees' list, Peter had a total of twenty-seven challenges faced by growing companies:

27 Challenges of Intentional Enterprises

1. The lack of adequate profits to grow your company
2. Not being differentiated in the minds of your customers
3. The need for a stronger profit-driven business design
4. Customers migrating to other products and vendors
5. Employee turnover
6. Hiring quality staff
7. Low staff morale
8. The need for a flexible planning model
9. The need for staff to participate and help author the growth of the company
10. Lack of effective project management and resource coordination
11. Lack of communication between leadership and staff
12. Lack of effective new staff orientation
13. Ineffective and/or little staff training
14. Unclear values
15. Periods of chaos that destabilize the company
16. The culture of the company is resistant to change
17. Difficulty forecasting problems before they surface
18. Difficulty diagnosing problems and obstacles to growth
19. Cash flow challenges
20. The staff not understanding how the company will grow
21. The leadership not understanding the impact of staff satisfaction on profitability
22. Effectively expanding sales
23. Bringing new products or services to market
24. Loss of expertise or knowledge when employees leave
25. Inability to get systems and procedures in place as the company grows
26. Limited availability of capital to grow
27. Marketplace and customers change too quickly

Peter studied the list, thinking that if someone could crack the Rosetta Stone of entrepreneurial enterprises, this list would certainly be a good start. Probably the most important factor is knowing what to do next. One thing was clear: whatever he was going to do at Bolder Solutions to make some

> **THE MOST IMPORTANT FACTOR IS KNOWING WHAT TO DO NEXT.**

positive changes, he needed to start soon. If Elijah Brown was right, time was growing short. He knew Bolder Solutions' future was at stake, but the company was obviously involved in something even larger.

The phone rang. "Peter Logan speaking."

"Mr. Logan, this is Grace McGregor."

Now it was his turn to be quiet. He felt his mood turn sour. Some Mother Teresa. "What can I do for you, Ms. McGregor?"

She seemed to struggle to find her voice. "I'll come right to the point. In my business I have connections in the most interesting places that allow me to find out things most other people can't." She paused for a second. "I'd make a great gossip columnist."

She waited a moment to see if her attempt at lightening the conversation was working, but Peter remained silent.

"I may have judged you too harshly. I discovered that you were fired by Santomo, and I shouldn't have suggested something irregular."

"Anything else, Ms. McGregor?"

"I mean I just wanted to…"

"Apologize?"

Clearly, apologizing didn't come naturally for her. The silence built once more.

"Well, I might have been too quick to judge what's going on in Alan's company."

"You don't owe me an explanation; a simple apology will do."

"Look!" Now she was sounding angry. "I was concerned when I saw someone else sitting in Alan's chair. Someone, I might add, whom the nefarious Santomo had employed! I overreacted, but your response was out of line."

> **I'M HANGING UP NOW, MS. MCGREGOR. LET ME KNOW WHEN YOU'RE READY TO OFFER UP THAT APOLOGY.**

He had other things to spend his energy on. "I'm hanging up now, Ms. McGregor. Let me know when you're ready to offer up that apology."

Seconds later the phone rang again. He couldn't believe she'd call him back. Even the sound of the phone was irritating. He picked it up and barked a terse, "Hello?"

"I can't tell you how much I wish this was an official call, because I know how to handle attitude on the phone. But I'm calling as a civilian."

It took him a second. "Jane?"

"Maybe we should go back to Ms…Detective."

She made him smile. "I'm sorry, Ms…Detective. You caught me…well…let's just say you caught me deep in thought. It is nice to hear your voice."

"I wanted to tell you that I had a conversation with the PR woman, Grace McGregor. She is not your biggest fan."

"No kidding! I just hung up on her. I thought you were her calling me back."

They were silent for a moment.

She took a deep breath. "That's not why I called."

Peter smiled. "OK."

"Since you have been cleared from this case officially, I thought maybe we could, um…"

"How about a drink? You pick the place."

"Oh, please don't ask me to pick the place. My mind locks on the cheap dives I tend to frequent for lunch."

"OK. Meet me at the Corner Bar at the Boulderado at seven o'clock."

He had a date with a cop. Interesting turn of events.

A few minutes later the phone rang yet again. He answered cautiously, half-expecting Jane to call their date off. But it was Horace Bedford.

"Sorry to bother you, Peter, but I wonder if you'd have a little extra time tomorrow? There's someone I want you to meet."

"I'll make time. When and where?"

Horace told him to meet him at the park at 11 a.m., and then added, "We'll take a drive." He hung up without saying goodbye. Peter remembered that he still didn't have any idea who Horace was.

The Corner Bar was packed with people.

He arrived two minutes early, but Jane was already there, dressed in another no-nonsense suit. He smiled and walked up behind her.

She was nervous. And she wasn't smiling. "Look, Peter, I can't stay. I've been reassigned to the evening shift. They just beeped me and I've got to leave now. I'm really sorry."

"That's OK. I understand. I'm disappointed, but duty calls."

"I was looking forward to tonight. Really. We'll do it another time."

She turned to leave, changed her mind, then impulsively kissed him. It took Peter a moment to catch his breath. Then he kissed her back. "I'll call you tomorrow, Ms…Detective."

Feeling lighthearted for the first time in a long while, Peter decided to visit Joanna and the kids. He realized he had been avoiding them. Joanna looked fragile and tired. His nephews' hopeful eyes locked unwaveringly onto his. Not knowing exactly what to do, he began wrestling with them, tossing one boy and then another until all three were exhausted.

They went out for pizza and ice cream while Peter regaled them with early Alan stories the kids found incredibly funny. After a full evening he put them to bed and read from a Harry Potter book. Afterwards he and Joanna sat down to talk.

"Joanna, I'm sorry I haven't been very supportive of you. I've been so caught up in trying to make sure Bolder Solutions continues to support you and the kids that I haven't been much of a comfort."

"Oh, Peter, there isn't anything anyone can do for a broken heart but let time slowly heal the loss. The kids, though, so love being with you. They really do need to have a strong male role model in their life. I feel like I have asked so much of you in such a short time."

> "MY LIFE FELT LIKE A FREE-FALL DIVE OUT OF A PLANE. IRONICALLY, I THINK YOU HANDED ME THE RIP CORD."

"You know, Joanna, in the past, my life felt like a free-fall dive out of a plane. Ironically, I think you handed me the rip cord. I've been a hired gun for so long in the consulting world, I forgot what it means to have a meaningful relationship with others. As the chute opens, I see that growing this company is how I want to live my life. Playing an active role in the lives of my three nephews is a big part of that plan. That means soccer practice, stupid card tricks, geometry, you name it."

The two of them sat on the front porch looking out into the night. Tears slowly made their way down Joanna's cheeks as the tragic loss and the haunted reality of sudden single parenthood swept over her. She and the boys needed Peter. Then he felt his own cheeks become wet as Alan's family slowly embraced him with a new sense of place.

CHAPTER 8 — KEY POINTS
27 Challenges of Intentional Enterprises:

1. The lack of adequate profits to grow your company
2. Not being differentiated in the minds of your customers
3. The need for a stronger profit-driven business design
4. Customers migrating to other products and vendors
5. Employee turnover
6. Hiring quality staff
7. Low staff morale
8. The need for a flexible planning model
9. The need for staff to participate and help author the growth of the company
10. Lack of effective project management and resource coordination
11. Lack of communication between leadership and staff
12. Lack of effective new staff orientation
13. Ineffective and/or little staff training
14. Unclear values
15. Periods of chaos that destabilize the company
16. The culture of the company is resistant to change
17. Difficulty forecasting problems before they surface
18. Difficulty diagnosing problems and obstacles to growth
19. Cash flow challenges
20. The staff not understanding how the company will grow
21. The leadership not understanding the impact of staff satisfaction on profitability
22. Effectively expanding sales
23. Bringing new products or services to market
24. Loss of expertise or knowledge when employees leave
25. Inability to get systems and procedures in place as the company grows
26. Limited availability of capital to grow
27. Marketplace and customers change too quickly

HB Journal March 2

The test for a first rate intelligence is being able to hold two contrary ideas in the mind at the same time and still retain the ability to function. - Gregg LeVoy

Lunch Notes with Corky:
7 Ways to Create Extraordinary Revenue/Profit:

1. Have a minimum of 3-5 different revenue streams.
2. Purchase direct without a middleman.
3. Let someone else be the delivery system for your products to their customers.
4. Sell to other people's customers.
5. Broaden the range of use for your products and/or services.
6. Lengthen the reach of your products and/or services.
7. Participate in commissions paid for products or services sold to your customer.

A fanatic is someone who has lost their sense of direction and has doubled their rate of speed- Unknown Author

Notes to myself:
Have been thinking all weekend about that guy who said the Profit Design Map was way too complicated for him - he didn't have time for something like that because it took everything in him to just stay on top of managing the day-to-day stuff of his business. People who respond to things being too confusing or complicated are often challenged by their own scattered thinking. The irony is that it is the scattered thinking that causes their chaos.

PROFIT-
DRIVEN

PEOPLE-
CENTERED

GROWTH-
SMART

LIVING
WELL

OPEN
MIND

BEING
OF SERVICE

PROBLEM
APPROACH

GROWTH CURVE
MODEL
APPROACH

GROWTH CURVE
SOLUTION

Chapter 9

REFLECTIVE EDGE

"Human beings aren't ants, and organizations aren't ant colonies. But when productive agitation runs high, innovation often thrives and startling breakthroughs can come about. This elusive, much sought after sweet spot is sometimes called a burning platform. The living sciences call it the edge of chaos."
— **Richard T. Pascale**, *Surfing the Edge of Chaos*

The office was in pretty good shape the next morning. Kate told him that more than half the staff had come in early, between 7:30 a.m. and 8 a.m., to get a jump on the day. None of his short-list problems had magically disappeared, but something felt different. He couldn't put his finger on it.

The morning wore on and as Peter walked out of the office to meet Horace for lunch, his eye caught something unusual. Someone had hung a large bright yellow lithograph on one of the barren walls in the entry.

The receptionist asked him, "What do you think of it? The customer service folks chipped in and bought it for the office yesterday."

"Wow, that's a great addition. I'm impressed. Maybe we should consider sprucing up the whole office. It might make us all a little more upbeat." Peter then thought to himself, "My God, there could be life in this place yet."

Peter arrived at the park early, but Horace was waiting for him, writing in the worn leather journal that was his constant companion.

"Good morning, Peter."

"Hi, Horace. Gosh, I thought I'd beat you here."

Horace turned his head toward the poplars waving in the wind. He had a look of contentment that was unknown in Peter's world.

"Some days, Peter, I choose to take what I call reflective moments. Today just happens to be one of those days. So I came down here a little early." He smiled as he looked directly over at Peter. "It's all part of what I call living well."

Peter thought for a moment then said, "I'm a couple of million dollars away from living well."

"This is different, Peter. It's not about waiting until you have all the money you want. I'm talking about living in such a way that all the different corners of your life, from business, to family, to community, to friendships, to health, to church, to finances, are alive in a kind of refined harmony."

Peter laughed, "Boy, according to that definition, I'm a long way off from living well. If I get through one day out of a week unscathed by the ravages of my employees or the stress bullets constantly whizzing by, I consider myself blessed."

> " FOR MOST ENTREPRENEURS THE IDEA OF LIVING WELL WHILE RUNNING A BUSINESS IS AN OXYMORON, PETER....LIVING WELL, WITH ALL ITS IMPLICATIONS, STARTS WITH HAVING AN OPEN MIND WITH YOUR WORK AND ENDS WITH BEING OF SERVICE TO SOMETHING LARGER THAN YOURSELF. "

"For most entrepreneurs the idea of living well while running a business is an oxymoron, Peter. The two just don't mix. It's a terrible waste. For people like you and me, understanding entrepreneurial growth is a huge step toward living life while we are still living. After all, Peter, living well, with all its implications, starts with having an open mind with your work and ends with being of service to something larger than yourself. Everything in between is all about the journey."

Horace smoothly shifted his attention and looked at Peter. "I see you came here prepared. What is that in your hand?"

Peter gave Horace a copy of the 27 key growth challenges list he'd drawn up. Horace reviewed it

for several minutes. Then he looked seriously at Peter.

"This is a very good start. You've created as succinct a list of the problems that growing companies face as I've

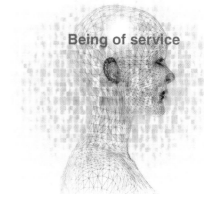

Being of service

seen." He laughed, "Obviously, Bolder Solutions isn't facing all of these challenges right now, but you've got quite a few of them staring at you."

Horace held up the sheet of paper containing Peter's list of entrepreneurial challenges and said, "We need to take a short diversion before we go on any further. Peter, it is very important that you distinguish, right at the start, that there are two primary approaches to diagnosing and understanding the inner workings of a business."

"Approach #1 is known as the **Problem Approach.** You look at the business as something that has obstacles and problems that need fixing. It is a symptomatic approach that looks at the parts and how to correct them with a specific solution — similar to modern medicine's approach to healing.

"Approach #2 is the **Model Approach.** You look at the business from the perspective of an ideal business model. It is a frame of reference which provides an integrated yet holistic template of how the enterprise could perform to its highest potential. By understanding the ideal frame of reference you can apply attention or, in other terms, solutions from a more informed perspective of the whole."

Horace continued, "Both of these Approaches access solutions and both are built into the understanding of the Seven Stages of Enterprise Growth, which you will be hearing about later."

With that, Horace took a pen out of his shirt pocket, drew four boxes on a sheet of paper, and filled in each box with these words:

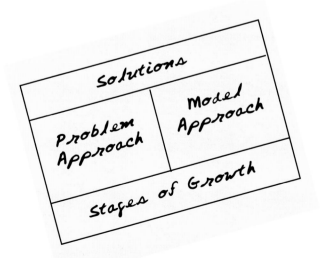

"Peter, this is a simpler way of explaining this idea. You see, how you approach or consider your business determines how you will interface with it. You can enter into the box through this door," he said, pointing to the **Problem Approach** box, or you can enter through this door," he said, pointing to the **Model Approach** box.

> " HOW YOU APPROACH OR CONSIDER YOUR BUSINESS DETERMINES HOW YOU WILL INTERFACE WITH IT. "

"Eighty-five-to-ninety percent of all entrepreneurs are so caught up in the day-to-day reality of their business that they are spring-loaded to choose the **Problem Approach** as the natural way of understanding and diagnosing their business. The **Model Approach** is often more prominent in the world of academics, consultants and business theorists."

"Horace, since I left Stanford, I haven't seen the value of the Model Approach. In the real world, things move too quickly and you're consumed with fixing problems. You move from A to B to C by identifying problems and finding solutions. I just don't have the time to sit back and think, how did you put it?, 'holistically'."

Horace smiled and wrapped up his thoughts by saying, "I understand perfectly well your point, Peter. As a reference for future discussions, just remember that there are two approaches and that

GROWTH CURVE SOLUTION

the blend of both approaches ends up being the optimal route. For purposes of our conversation today and your meetings over the next two weeks, you will be hearing new ideas and methods applied in the **Problem Approach** modality."

Peter was discovering that Horace did not waste time. When he finished an idea he had no qualms about abruptly moving on.

"Here's the thing, Peter. I had a disturbing discussion with Elijah Brown yesterday about the forces at play around your secret project. After speaking with him and considering your circumstances, I'm convinced that we need to put you on the fast track. So, let's get started by setting down the right foundation. With me so far?"

"Yes."

"In the next couple of weeks you are going to meet some remarkable people, people who are not any more talented or smarter than you but who have had the opportunity over the last couple of years to successfully apply powerful growth tools in their businesses."

"When you meet these people, they will be giving you a lot of new information in a very short period of time. They will be giving you bits and pieces of a much broader set of solutions."

"They will be speaking to you from the **Problem Approach** perspective of viewing a business. The solutions that they will be sharing with you need a frame of reference. I have named this frame of reference The Growth Curve Solution. Let's start by saying that The Growth Curve Solution is founded on the three themes I gave you the other day." On a piece of paper, Horace wrote:

Growth Curve Solution Themes
1. profit-driven
2. people-centered
3. growth-smart

"Anything that is based on the profit-driven, people-centric and growth-smart building blocks will have the name Growth Curve attached to it. There is also a Growth Curve Model Approach that feeds into the Stages of Growth framework and the Growth Curve Solution. At some point in the future you will put all the pieces together and you will have access to a comprehensive enterprise tool."

Horace finished his drawing with the two approaches.

Growth Curve Solution

| Problem Approach | Growth Curve Model Approach |

7 Stages of Enterprise Growth

82

Peter spoke up. "Well, Horace, I suppose at some point this will all make sense. I'm willing to keep an open mind to the model or theory approach but I must say theory doesn't help much when you have serious cash flow problems."

"But I can see that you're seeding my mind for further discussions. I'm OK with that. At this point the three building blocks tying to profit, people, and growth make a lot of sense to me. So much so that I adopted them as our core operational themes at Bolder Solutions. They pretty much say it all."

"I'm glad to hear that, Peter. There are a total of nine fundamental building blocks of The Growth Curve Solution associated with these three themes. All of our work over the next few weeks will be centered around you developing a basic working knowledge of the Nine Fundamentals of The Growth Curve Solution."

Horace opened up his journal and pulled out a single piece of paper. "Peter, this sheet will help you organize your thinking as you meet all these people. It explains in simple terms what the Nine Fundamentals are. Each fundamental has a whole body of knowledge and methodology tied to it.

When looked at as a whole, The Growth Curve Solution is a new, many-faceted, interconnected perspective of the entrepreneurial growth process."

9 Fundamentals of The Growth Curve Solution

Profit-Driven

1. *Profit* – The New Profit Model provides a powerful new perspective on the sustainability and advancement of enterprise profit as it is a) critically tied to the design of the business, b) dependent on the Profit Net or profit competency of the entire staff, and, c) reliant on the continued loyalty of the customer base.

2. *Mapping* – Provides a dynamic new method of communicating, tracking and enterprise planning that is accessible by the entire organization. It facilitates "bottom-up" engagement, strategic authoring and buy-in by the entire staff.

3. *Mechanisms* – Reveals the important role of key infrastructure mechanisms that facilitate the application of The Growth Curve Solution in a business enterprise at any stage of growth.

People-Centered

4. *Staff Satisfaction* – Reveals the core requirements of staff satisfaction and shows the deep connection between it and enterprise profitability at every stage of growth.

5. *Community* – Redesigns how we think about and create the modern work community so that it better serves both the company's vision, strategic goals, objectives, and culture and also correctly addresses the interests, needs, and requirements of the staff.

6. *Trauma* – Reveals the causes, symptoms, and cures for the primary debilitating disease of business growth called Growth Trauma.

Growth-Smart

7. *Growth* – Provides an important foundation for how blending the principles of nature, complexity, and growth intelligence produce greater performance and innovation in commercial enterprises. Turns the understanding of organizational growth from that of "business as a machine" to one of "business as a living, intelligent organism."

8. *Language* – Creates the everyday language of growth that is required for deep change in the organization and explains the three elements of growth (stages, gates, patterns).

9. *Acceptance* – A powerful methodology that facilitates the willingness in the CEO of a company to release resistance to the issues causing low performance and see underneath the surface to the real issues.

And just like that, Horace became the professor.

Peter expected him to manifest a chalkboard out of thin air to make his points. The older man jumped up and started pacing back and forth.

"OK, let's start with the big picture. The Growth Curve Solution is made up of the Nine Fundamentals laid down on that sheet of paper in your hand."

"It is a body of living business knowledge based on many people's entrepreneurial experiments and natural systems research over the last 25 years. It is

> " THE **GROWTH CURVE SOLUTION** IS A BODY OF LIVING BUSINESS KNOWLEDGE BASED ON MANY PEOPLE'S ENTREPRENEURIAL EXPERIMENTS AND NATURAL SYSTEMS RESEARCH OVER THE LAST 25 YEARS. "

always growing and no one person or group owns this knowledge."

"But it is not easy to find in any one place and is usually shared or passed on by word of mouth. If it is one thing, it is dynamic. It is always expanding with new discoveries being made by curious, bright, and often highly pressured entrepreneurs. Its primary purpose is to address and deliver solutions to the recurring issues and challenges to enterprise growth. The list you created is a good sample of those challenges."

Peter interjected, "Horace, is any of this written down somewhere?"

"Not at this point. There is a local group of business owners working on compiling The Growth Curve Solution into one place. It's a major project and will require many hands to complete it in the future. Who knows, you just may be one of those people."

Peter laughed, "I think I'm a long way from being part of any project other than the project called Bolder Solutions."

"Time will tell. Peter, did you ever wonder why I am doing this?"

Peter thought for a moment. "Aside from the fact that you made a promise to some guy years ago?"

"Yes, aside from that."

"Well, Horace, you have a religious zeal about this stuff that I occasionally wonder about. Honestly, I couldn't begin to guess what drives you to spend all your time and energy on people like me."

Horace shook his head, "Peter, most people think that business is only about making money and competing to win the brass ring. That is true for many people, but there are a growing number of

bright, reflective entrepreneurs who have a different vision for the future."

"Don't get me wrong, they are just as interested

> "RIGHT NOW, THE ADVANCES IN TECHNOLOGY ARE GRABBING ALL THE HEADLINES. BUT OUTSIDE THE RADAR OF THE MONEY GUYS, THE AMERICAN WORKPLACE IS BEING FLIPPED OVER, RETRAINED, RETOOLED AND IS DRAMATICALLY TRANSFORMING RIGHT UNDER OUR NOSES."

in making money as the next guy, but they are different because they see the writing on the wall. They see that the workplace community will drive the next social and economic frontier."

"Right now, the advances in technology are grabbing all the headlines. But outside the radar of the money guys, the American workplace is being flipped over, retrained, retooled and is dramatically transforming right under our noses. When Wall Street wakes up in the next 3-5 years it will be scrambling to find ways to quantify two important ideas:

One – the core intelligence of an enterprise

Two – what breeds innovation in successful workplace communities."

"Believe me when I say that business as a mechanism in society is on the threshold of a new mission."

"Peter, as far back as 15th century Italy, businessmen have been considered low on life's food chain. Trading and making money certainly didn't earn one a lofty place in heaven. Service to the church or to the state or to a noble cause has always been considered a higher calling than the greed-tarnished road of commercial enterprise.

"This attitude has been invisibly pressed into culture for centuries. The souls of the rich and successful have been considered dimmed by the pursuits of the material world. Strange how man so easily elevates himself above the "misdirected." I am sure that the irony will play itself out in the future when growing businesses become the

> " HUMANITY IS FACING A MOUNTAIN OF EXTRAORDINARY CHALLENGES, A NUMBER OF WHICH COULD SINGLE-HANDEDLY EXTINGUISH LIFE ON THIS PLANET. "

guardians of our future."

"What are you saying, Horace?"

"I'm saying that this is a unique time in history. Humanity is facing a mountain of extraordinary challenges, a number of which could single-handedly extinguish life on this planet. Some of us take this very seriously. These challenges aren't going to be fixed by the really smart people, Peter, we need a

whole lot more horsepower than that. The real solutions aren't going to come out of the universities, or the churches, or from the governmental organizations or the non-profit groups trying to save the world.

"They're going to emerge from the core intelligence of workplace communities all across this country and the world that are able to transform themselves into self-organizing, profit-driven, people-centered, growth-smart beehives.

"Even if only 15 percent of all businesses make the leap then we have a real chance of turning the odds in our favor. Mark my words, Peter, all this lands on the ground with significant practical results. The innovative power and performance of the average person working in a beehive company is ten to twenty-fold that of one working in a company managed like a machine. Combine this with advances in technology and we will see not only innovation but also productivity skyrocket."

Peter interrupted, "Are you saying that the average worker is the center of brainpower in a company?"

"Yes, I am, but in most companies the brainpower lies buried and unrealized. How much brainpower do you think you are really getting from your staff at Bolder Solutions?"

Peter thought for a moment, "I see what you

mean. Bolder Solutions has probably the smartest crew that I've ever worked with but even so, maybe we tap into twenty-to-thirty percent on a really good day."

"See what I mean? Peter, the average person spends seventy percent of his — or her — waking hours at work. Work has become his primary life community next to his family. It's at work where he

is screaming to contribute if given the right climate and license to contribute.

"It takes a great degree of wisdom, skill, and courage to shift from being a watchmaker to becoming a bee-keeper. But I believe that the solutions and answers that our society requires to survive through the next 50-100 years depend on this transition happening.

"The problem, Peter, is that the classic methods and structures used in business for the last 200 years don't encourage innovative self-organizing work environments to evolve. By its nature, the command and control modality is useful only in the familiar crisis situations. It is incapable of unlocking the powerful intelligence, loyalty, and commitment buried in a workplace community."

Peter began to smile, "Ah, so at the end of the day we are out to save the world, are we?"

Horace looked him straight in the eye and said,

"Yes, we are. Granted, The Growth Curve Solution is just one small piece of the answer. Hopefully it will facilitate the awakening of the workplace as a primary mechanism for social, economic and personal transformation.

"If that fits into your view of saving the world, then so be it. And if it doesn't save the world, at least it will help the enterprise understand these five things on a daily basis." And again, Horace started writing on his notepad.

1. What's happening right now
2. What brought you here
3. How to predict what's likely to occur in the future
4. What action needs to be taken
5. What's the next best step to take

"Well, your Growth Curve Solution has five practical benefits. I bet these new businesses will have to make a ton of money to pay for all this saving the world stuff."

Horace lightly snapped back with a slight smile, "Actually, without innovative new profit models not much will happen. You're right."

"Well, that sounds simple enough. I suppose you are going to do all this one business at a time?"

"That's not a bad idea, Peter. But I see we've covered enough information for our visit today."

Peter liked Horace. He smiled as he said, "That is a distinct possibility. But I'm sure I'll recover."

Horace walked over to a picnic table and motioned for Peter to sit down. The spring breeze framed the moment as Peter took a seat and Horace continued. "Anyway, we don't have the time right now to properly unwrap this topic in a meaningful discussion. That will have to come later. But here's one last thought to ponder before we move on."

Horace proceeded slowly, smiling as he closed in on his prey. "Regarding the save the world stuff, if you think it is not connected to the nuts and bolts of the world that you live in, then you might want to take a closer look at that project you are three weeks behind on for Elijah.

"Beyond keeping your company afloat, there is a whole lot more at stake with your software project than you could ever imagine. Millions of people's lives are resting on that group of — what do you call them, wizards? — working at Bolder Solutions."

Horace broke out into a smile and laughingly said, "Peter Logan, you're up to your ears in saving the world and you don't even know it."

CHAPTER 9 — KEY POINTS

9 Fundamentals of The Growth Curve Solution:

Profit-Driven

1. *Profit* – The New Profit Model provides a powerful new perspective on the sustainability and advancement of enterprise profit as it is a) critically tied to the design of the business, b) dependent on the Profit Net or profit competency of the entire staff, and, c) reliant on the continued loyalty of the customer base.

2. *Mapping* – Provides a dynamic new method of communicating, tracking and enterprise planning that is accessible by the entire organization. It facilitates 'bottom-up' engagement, strategic authoring and buy-in by the entire staff.

3. *Mechanisms* – Reveals the important role of key infrastructure mechanisms that facilitate the application of The Growth Curve Solution in a business enterprise at any stage of growth.

CHAPTER 9 — KEY POINTS (CONTINUED)

9 Fundamentals of The Growth Curve Solution:

People-Centered

4. *Staff Satisfaction* – Reveals the core requirements of staff satisfaction and shows the deep connection between it and enterprise profitability at every stage of growth.

5. *Community* – Redesigns how we think about and create the modern work community so that it better serves both the company's vision, strategic goals, objectives and culture but also correctly addresses the interests, needs and requirements of the staff.

6. *Trauma* – Reveals the causes, symptoms and cures for the primary debilitating disease of business growth called Growth Trauma.

Growth-Smart

7. *Growth* – Provides an important foundation for how blending the principles of nature, complexity and growth intelligence produce greater performance and innovation in commercial enterprises. Turns the understanding of organizational growth from that of "business as a machine" to one of "business as a living, intelligent organism".

8. *Language* – Creates the everyday language of growth that is required for deep change in the organization and explains the three elements of growth (stages, gates, patterns).

9. *Acceptance* – A powerful methodology that facilitates the willingness in the CEO of a company to release resistance to the issues causing low performance and see underneath the surface to the real issues.

GROWTH

NATURE AND BUSINESS GROWTH

COMPLEXITY

GROWTH   INTELLIGENCE

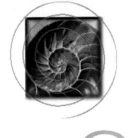

Chapter 10
LAWS
OF GROWTH

"Lifelong learners take risks. Much more than others, these men and women push themselves out of their comfort zones and try new ideas. While most of us become set in our ways, they keep experimenting."
— **John P. Kotter,** *Leading Change*

Horace and Peter had just finished laughing about the "save the world" discussion when a simple melody of bells drifted through the trees. It was a familiar repeating melody but neither Horace nor Peter could place its origin. Peter looked at Horace with the answer exploding out of his mouth.

"It's an ice cream truck! It's been years since I've heard those bells. I thought the Baskin and Robbins and Ben and Jerry's of the world put those guys out of business a long time ago. Wow, when I was a kid I used to love their chocolate éclair bars. The Good Humor man was the one adult we were always happy to see. You know, Horace, those trucks were everywhere when I was growing up. What happened to them?"

"What happened, Peter, was that families changed. How often do you see kids playing out in the neighborhoods like they did twenty or thirty years ago?"

Peter said, "That's a good point. Come to think of it, I rarely see kids playing in any neighborhoods because parents are worried about, well, just about everything any more! I know my sister-in-law,

> **TIMES HAVE CHANGED AND THE GOOD HUMOR MAN FELL THROUGH THE CRACKS BECAUSE HIS CUSTOMERS DISAPPEARED. THEY HAD GREAT ICE CREAM, BUT THEY WERE BLIND TO ONE OF THE LAWS OF GROWTH AND SUFFERED THE CONSEQUENCES.**

Joanna, watches her kids like a hawk. They are never out of her sight."

"That's right, Peter. Times have changed and the Good Humor man fell through the cracks because his customers disappeared. They had great ice cream, but they were blind to one of the laws of growth and suffered the consequences. Speaking of which, let's chat a bit about the laws of growth."

Horace cleared the table of pine needles and prepared himself to start lesson number one. "So let's get back to the basics. Today we are going to talk about #7 on The Growth Curve Solution list, the topic of Growth itself. Put your seat belt on, Peter, no doubt we will be covering territory that's a little edgy for a conservative guy like you."

Peter laughed. "Horace, just about everything you've introduced to me so far has been on the edge. Why should this be any different?"

Horace appreciated their growing camaraderie and smiled. "Well, I'm glad to see your spirits are up. The three key elements to understanding enterprise growth are:

1. Nature & Business Growth
2. Complexity
3. Growth Intelligence

"All three of these elements have three principles tied to them that are tightly intertwined. As theoretical as this information may seem to you today, it is, in reality, the core foundation on which we will be constructing the equivalent of an 80-story high-rise over the next few weeks. Remember the two approaches to viewing a business that we talked about last week?"

"Yes, the Problem Approach and the Model Approach."

"Very good. It's important for you to understand that you won't crack the Rosetta Stone of enterprise

> **IT'S NOT NATURAL FOR ENTREPRENEURS ENMESHED IN THE DAY-TO-DAY CHALLENGE OF SOLVING PROBLEMS TO GIVE MUCH CREDENCE TO THE WORLD OF BUSINESS CONCEPTS.**

growth without having a conceptual framework to understand what your business is telling you. This conceptual framework is the Model Approach."

"As we discussed earlier, it's not natural for entrepreneurs enmeshed in the day-to-day challenge of solving problems to give much credence to the world of business concepts. The irony is that they can't get out of being the constant effect of their problems until they start modeling their future."

"Being caught in the tyranny of secondary effects, more commonly called problems, is the bane of the typical entrepreneur and one of the primary reasons why so many of them fail."

Peter interrupted Horace. "OK, let me get this straight. Are you telling me that if I get more comfortable viewing my business from the Model Approach, I will be more intentional and actually lessen the effect of what is happening in my business?"

"Yes, that's exactly what I'm saying. Most entrepreneurs get pushed around by their business. The tail is constantly wagging the dog. The Model Approach gives the entrepreneur the opportunity to intentionally design and lead his business. To master the art of growing a business, you cannot stay trapped in the problematic view of things. You have to get outside the box to integrate all the elements."

Suddenly a flock of swallows flew over their table, creating intricate patterns in the sky.

Horace pointed his finger upward and continued, "Look up there. You might think I'm crazy, but I know those birds are telling us a story. See the layers of patterns they are making? Just because neither you nor I can understand what is being said, does it mean that the message is any less important in the scheme of things? I think not. Something is happening right over our heads that we can't decipher or understand about their systems, territories, and group survival."

"Could we learn something from those birds? Maybe. Can we learn something from the maze of patterns layering in a growing organization? Definitely. Sighting and comprehending the patterns of enterprise growth by blending an understanding of nature, complexity, and growth intelligence is supremely useful to the enlightened entrepreneur."

"It allows you to perfect your decision making, and there isn't anything that more profoundly affects your business than improving your decision making."

Peter interrupted, "Horace, I may not be a rocket scientist, but I am smart enough to know that at

> **SIGHTING AND COMPREHENDING THE PATTERNS OF ENTERPRISE GROWTH...ALLOWS YOU TO PERFECT YOUR DECISION MAKING, AND THERE ISN'T ANYTHING THAT MORE PROFOUNDLY AFFECTS YOUR BUSINESS THAN IMPROVING YOUR DECISION MAKING.**

the end of the day, all I'm left with are my decisions. If you can help me refine or improve my decision making, then I would be immeasurably grateful."

Horace continued. "OK. You mentioned that you were still wrestling with the concept of nature and business growth. Let's see if I can take that as a starting point or the first key element for our discussion about growth. The three simple principles that I find helpful in understanding Nature and Business Growth, are:

1. Large is not small
2. Nature innovates from the edge
3. Form is shaped by force

Peter smiled, "Now, Horace, shall I call these the natural laws of business growth according to Horace Bedford?"

Horace laughed and said, "Actually Peter, I didn't create these laws, but for the purposes of our conversation, calling them the Natural Laws of Business Growth is probably a good thing. There are a total of nine that I plan to share with you today."

Horace continued, "A common entrepreneurial error occurs when a business owner believes that what works at one stage of growth will work at another."

"Look at **Law #1: Large is not small means that the rules that govern whether you survive or fail change according to the size of your enterprise.**

"Let me give you a quick example. In nature, the food required to survive, as a percentage of body weight, changes dramatically with the size of the creature. A ton of bacteria require 10 times more food than a ton of mice. A ton of mice require 10 times more food than a ton of horses."

"In the same fashion, when we look at the idea of centralized control in an organization, it is apparent that smaller groups or smaller companies (up to 18 people) require a leader-centric, centralized control focus. But when the group or company grows larger, the need for centralized control quickly fades and reverses. What was fundamental in a small group or organization becomes toxic in a larger one."

Peter interrupted Horace, "According to this law, Horace, my brother Alan was doomed to failure. He insisted on being the center of control for his growing company and it would have eventually taken him down. Actually it is remarkable that Bolder Solutions didn't crash sooner."

"That's an important realization for you, Peter. Alan, like many entrepreneurs, failed to let go of the reins and change when his company grew larger. He failed to understand that the rules are different for the large than they are for small."

Horace continued, "Now, let's look at **Law #2: Nature innovates from the edge means that new adaptations, new solutions and innovations, in** nature and in business, are born on the edge of chaos, not in a world of stability and equilibrium.

"The irony is that the natural inclination for organisms in both nature and business is to gravitate toward and refuse to leave a state of stability or equilibrium."

"Most business leaders of growing companies continually struggle to stabilize their enterprise or keep it stabilized. The idea of a stable, balanced organization is somehow considered the arrival point. The truth is, stability or equilibrium, as a consistent diet, is a death sentence for any organization.

"Look at any living system in nature and you will find it gravitates towards order and ultimately equilibrium but, regardless of this inclination, it is continually drawn out to the edge of chaos either by a threat or by a compelling need for change.

"Innovation and adaptability in nature don't happen in a state of stability but rather in a state of disturbance. A number of well-known business leaders, such as Jack Welch of GE and Bill Gates of Microsoft, understand this principle in practice. Even when things are running well, they are known for periodically introducing discontinuous change agents into their organizations just to shake up the status quo and foster innovative behavior.

"OK. Let's move on to **Law #3: Form is shaped by force means that in order for organisms to survive in nature and in business, they are compelled to adapt and change their form as dictated by greater forces acting in and on them.**"

"Throughout evolution species have been forced to adapt to new conditions in order to survive, for example, the snowshoe hare that turns white in the winter or the rapid adaptation of new bacterial

> ALAN, LIKE MANY ENTREPRENEURS, FAILED TO LET GO OF THE REINS AND CHANGE WHEN HIS COMPANY GREW LARGER....THE IDEA OF A STABLE, BALANCED ORGANIZATION IS SOMEHOW CONSIDERED THE ARRIVAL POINT. THE TRUTH IS, STABILITY OR EQUILIBRIUM, AS A CONSISTENT DIET, IS A DEATH SENTENCE FOR ANY ORGANIZATION....INNOVATION AND ADAPTABILITY IN NATURE DON'T HAPPEN IN A STATE OF STABILITY BUT RATHER IN A STATE OF DISTURBANCE.

strains that resist the latest antibiotics created by medical science.

"In the world of business this law is equally evident. Peter, look at all the small retail shops and restaurants that go in and out of business. The primary reason is that these little companies have a fixed idea of what their form should be and so are unable to change their value proposition as market needs and desires change. It happens in large companies as well. You can see well-known firms such as Xerox and Lucent Technologies struggle to reinvent themselves in light of the massive competitive forces driving them close to the brink. Will they be around in a couple of years? Not unless they learn to let go of what worked in the past and adapt to what is needed now or in the future."

"Horace, this is great stuff. I know you're giving me the basics right now, but when will the direct application of these principles be discussed?"

"That's a fair question, Peter. The people you will be visiting over the next couple of weeks will provide a real-world crucible for you to see these principles in action. Just remember to be patient. It all won't start coming together until you have talked with everyone."

Peter's cell phone rang. He excused himself from his conversation with Horace and answered the phone.

"Hello, this is Peter." The person on the other end said nothing. Peter repeated, "Hello, this is Peter?"

Again, no answer. Just as Peter was getting ready to hang up he faintly heard the person say one word and hang up. Peter checked to see where the call came from, but the number was blocked. Peter folded up his phone and returned it to his belt. "That was strange and a bit creepy. It must have been a prank call." Horace looked up from the journal open on his lap.

"Why, what happened?"

"The person said the word 'bomb' and then hung up. What do you think of it?"

Horace took off his reading glasses and laid them on the table. "I don't know. Santomo is a very aggressive competitor but I can't believe they would go to those lengths. Be sure to tell your detective friend. It may be nothing, a simple prank. But then again it may be a warning."

Peter shook his head. "A warning? Who do these guys think they are? Do they operate outside all the rules? Horace, this is crazy, let's get back to what you were talking about. I don't have time for these jerks."

"Ok." Horace agreed. "Let's move to the second key element of enterprise Growth: Complexity.

"Complexity is certainly one of the stranger entrepreneurial bedfellows. It breeds chaos and there is no way of avoiding it. Organizational chaos is simply the point at which you are unable to ascertain any discernible patterns or interrelationships, thus resulting in a state of confusion.

"To complicate it further, people have different competency levels in sighting patterns within a growing company. One person might find something chaotic where another person is perfectly clear about what is going on. This is why it is so important to develop a growth-smart organization. You want to train your staff to have a baseline com-

> **"ORGANIZATIONAL CHAOS IS SIMPLY THE POINT AT WHICH YOU ARE UNABLE TO ASCERTAIN ANY DISCERNIBLE PATTERNS OR INTERRELATIONSHIPS, THUS RESULTING IN A STATE OF CONFUSION."**

petency to see and understand the basic growth patterns. When they can read patterns inside the intermittent chaos of growth, they will be better able to help navigate the company through it.

"The field of complexity is a broad study. I have narrowed our interests to three simple perspectives that will help you place the role complexity plays in understanding enterprise growth. The three principles of Complexity are:

4. The right measure of growth
5. Clumping
6. Living systems have tools

"**Law #4: The right measure of growth implies that the most effective method of understanding and predicting the phenomenon of growth in an organization is through the measurement of its complexity.**

"There are numerous measurements for complexity in growing enterprises. For purposes of this conversation, we'll say that the primary cause and measure of complexity in a company is the individual employee.

"Each additional person in the company adds a multiple to the complexity index. It is a fascinating study. The irony is that when companies increase their workload, the first tendency is to throw more people at the dilemma. They unknowingly create new layers of challenging complex issues as a result of the additional staff.

"It's a tragic error to mistake the traditional mechanisms such as revenue growth and earnings expansion as key indicators of organizational growth. They are the result of numerous important factors but they do not tell the company's growth story. The compression of complex issues, caused as a result of rapid growth, becomes a leading indicator of an enterprise pushing up against the next cycle of growth.

"Let's move on to **Law #5: Clumping occurs as a result of two or more layers of complex issues colliding and eventually forming barriers of chaos.**

"When enough unresolved complex issues begin clumping together, a unique phenomenon occurs. It becomes increasingly more difficult to see and distinguish patterns inside this new complexity clump."

"This is experienced as confusion and disorder in most growing companies. It is at this point that a chaotic barrier starts to form. Clumping is the primary causative agent in the formation of the chaotic transition zones between each stage of growth that you will be learning about this week.

"A great example of clumping can be seen in organizations that are transitioning from Stage 2 to Stage 3. During this period, a company normally transforms from being a CEO-centric enterprise to being a company-centric enterprise. When a company faces a complexity clump, it encounters increased confusion surrounding issues like communication, product and service delivery, systems development, customer service, production and accounting, to name only a few.

"OK, now let's talk about **Law #6: Living systems have tools — means that complex, adaptive systems require specific tools for navigation: Attractors, Gas Pedals/ Brakes and Fitness Landscapes.**

"I agree with Richard Pascale, a notable contemporary business thinker, when he described a complex adaptive system as 'a self-organizing, living thing comprised of free agents developing and refining solutions through learning and adaptation.' That's a mouthful, but when you break it down, you can begin to understand that creating a living system is attainable in a business.

"The human immune system is a complex adaptive system. So is a rain forest and a beehive, and a business can also be one, given the right conditions.

"Leading a company through this process is by no means easy, but there are tools that are helpful. According to Pascale, in order to effectively facilitate the living systems process you must have three practical leadership mechanisms.

1. **Attractor:** An attractor is an anchor in the workplace that originates from something familiar and galvanizes the staff around a common theme (i.e., core values, visionary goals, etc.).

2. **Gas Pedals and Brakes:** This is a concept that allows the leadership of the enterprise to slow or speed the transition through chaos (i.e., change agents can increase speed and unifying events can reduce speed).

3. **Fitness Landscape Map:** This is a visual communication tool that provides contributors with a forward perspective of their company's journey. This visual mechanism portrays a company's need to destabilize before it stabilizes, unlearn before learning, and to disassemble before creating something new."

"When I think about a beehive, I see a fabulously complex adaptive system that can self-organize and adjust to a multiple array of challenges and changes in its environment.

"But my interest does not stop there. I see the beehive as an incredible community and, at times, a mystery that continually spurs my interest. It takes an understanding and inquiring mind to appreciate

complex adaptive systems, and it is this type of mind that probes to the heart of understanding growth."

Peter spoke up. "Horace, where did you learn all this information? No one ever told me that running a business was so closely tied to complexity theory. I never dreamed that I would be going back to school in a small-town park to relearn business with an old guy named Horace. This must have been born out of Greek mythology. What a story I'll tell my grandchildren! I have a lot of faith, Horace, that somewhere in this journey you are going to show me how all this will help my company make more money."

Horace stood up to stretch. "Peter, remember the crucible I mentioned to you earlier? That is where it all comes together. You are both a practical and an impatient man, as most entrepreneurs are, but your future requires that you take this time to probe deeper into the nature of that which is challenging you.

"I'm talking about the nature of this entity you are calling Bolder Solutions. The way you choose to think about and observe the phenomenon occurring at your company directly impacts how you experience that phenomenon."

"Understanding the origin of our thinking allows us to be better businesspeople, better mates, better parents, better leaders. A life without reflection and consideration of the root causes behind our experience is a life lived in a shallow pool."

"WHEN I THINK ABOUT A BEEHIVE, I SEE A FABULOUSLY COMPLEX ADAPTIVE SYSTEM THAT CAN SELF-ORGANIZE AND ADJUST TO A MULTIPLE ARRAY OF CHALLENGES AND CHANGES IN ITS ENVIRONMENT."

"From my perspective," Peter said, "I would imagine that Growth Intelligence, Nature, and Complexity, the three elements of your version of enterprise growth, are intertwined. This is the only way I could even begin to understand this stuff. I can see that the application of these principles will end up looking like a wild soup. Am I right?"

"Yes, you're right, Peter. Growth is rarely a pretty thing; it's often messy, and don't you ever let anyone tell you differently. Anyone who says they have the perfect model for growing a company is someone who is in desperate need of a long vacation. There is nothing safe or neat and tidy about a growing enterprise. But understanding and applying these laws will illuminate the pitfalls along the way."

Horace looked at his watch and knew he was running out of time. "Speaking of illumination, let's keep moving to the third and last element of enterprise growth: Growth Intelligence."

"This is my favorite area, because an inquiring mind is a wonder to behold. When you think about a beehive, you may consider it nothing more than a swarm of bees preoccupied with making honey. As long as you hold that view you'll miss an opportunity to see beneath the surface to understand what is really there: a complex, highly organized, interconnected living system.

"Entrepreneurial survival and success demand a unique type of intelligence. They require a curious mind, strong yet reflective, a mind that doesn't have all the answers, whose genius is found in what it doesn't know, not in what it knows. Its power is in knowing how to inquire."

"Arrogance and close-mindedness have not only been responsible for more missed opportunities but they have also killed more hopeful business enterprises than any other cause."

"The opinionated mind is fixed and closed. The inquiring mind is open and adaptive. The fixed mind needs to be right. The inquiring mind sees the patterns and asks why. The fixed mind is fearful. The inquiring mind creates freedom and a state of self-organizing behavior."

"Let's move on to explore the principles or laws that make up Growth Intelligence. **The three principles of Growth Intelligence are:**

7. *The brilliant is hiding in the ordinary*
8. *Put the beekeeper in charge*
9. *Perspective drives experience*

"The first one is so basic that all of our work depends on being in alignment with it. **Law #7: The brilliant is hiding in the ordinary means that the real intelligence of your enterprise is right under your nose, residing inside your own staff.**"

"Peter, this is important. The intelligence or brains of your business isn't limited to just you and your bright executive team. Quite the contrary, it's buried deep inside absolutely every one of your employees, bar none. Your staff is a gold mine and you don't even know it."

"Your mission is to respect and honor the intelligence of everyone working with you. Your next job is to create the conditions where intelligence blossoms and innovates, builds and protects your enterprise into extraordinary success."

"The second principle is easy for many people to talk about but difficult to manifest. **Law #8: Put the beekeeper in charge means that enterprise growth requires a brand of leadership that facilitates optimum performance rather than engineers it.**"

"Facilitative leadership is not concerned with engineering outcomes or controlling the forces at play. It is more concerned with leveraging opportunity and harnessing energy. The beekeeper operator holds a mindset that has tremendous faith in the intelligence and self-organizing capability of the workplace community, but at the same time is not naïve to the fact that his participation and his unique leadership presence is tantamount to its success."

"The beekeeper isn't made overnight. Releasing control is not easy. The facilitative leadership state is a challenging goal. Most leaders will bounce between being a beekeeper and a watchmaker and will revert to command and control behavior when things aren't going well. This is a natural part of a

> " YOU CAN'T GET SATISFACTION FROM THESE IDEAS BY UNDERSTANDING THEM CONCEPTUALLY, YOU MUST LEARN BY DOING. THEY MUST BE PRACTICED IN THE REAL WORLD TO HAVE VALUE. "

leader's development. You can't get satisfaction from these ideas by understanding them conceptually, you must learn by doing. They must be practiced in the real world to have value."

"Now, last but not least, and probably the hardest to understand, is where everything originates. **Law #9: Perspective drives experience means that your viewpoint directly influences your critical decision making ability and the business created from those decisions.**

"Your perspective acts as a filter that either blinds you or illuminates the critical patterns in your business. Shift or open your viewpoint to what is happening and you shift not only your decision making capability but also the business that you create. This one simple law is the consistent principle agreed upon by all extraordinarily successful individuals, regardless of their discipline or line of interest."

"Emerson once said, the ancestor to all action is thinking. How you think dramatically affects how you create and experience. You see, Peter, everything we see around us is malleable. Very few people tie the origin of their experience to their own state of consciousness or perspective, because at the end of the day they frankly don't want the responsibility for their own world.

"Strange, isn't it? To not consciously design your own life is crazy. So is growing a company and not accepting the full responsibility of your creation. You would be surprised at how many entrepreneurs blame this person or that event for their lack of success. Very few have the discipline to track the origin of their experience to the viewpoints and beliefs that influenced their critical decision making.

"So if you find that your business is not manifesting to your satisfaction, then inquire into what it is it that you are not seeing because it is all right under your viewpoint in one form or another."

Peter interrupted him, "OK. I admit that I don't understand everything you just said, but I am beginning to see how approaching the business from a point of inquiry instead of from a point of opinion could change how I see everything. Is that what you call a change in consciousness?"

Horace was surprised at how quickly Peter was absorbing the information. "Yes, Peter, that is exactly what I mean by a changed state of consciousness. If you can shift your point of view by remaining open through inquiry, you can change how you experience what's going on at work and that will free you up to see things more clearly. In my world that is a miracle. If you discover how to change your experience by shifting your perspective, you have learned one of the deepest secrets of growth.

"A business, particularly a growing business, is a complex adaptive system just like a beehive. It requires freedom, structure, and leadership. Growth Intelligence is measured by how inquiring one's mind is. If it is fixed or stuck, there is little Growth Intelligence; if it is open and curious, it is high in Growth Intelligence. The level of Growth Intelligence in a growing enterprise will pretty much determine the health and longevity of the firm."

Horace clearly wanted to say more. "I don't want to overload you, so I'll stop for today. You have an appointment over by the airport and I don't want you to be late. I have a tendency to run on a little too long for most people. The fact of the matter is that I love this stuff."

"Horace, I hung on to every word. I certainly don't understand everything you said, but I do feel something shifting at a base level. And that is intriguing in my world!"

Horace smiled. "Well, you aren't done for the day yet."

"Make my day," said Peter, smiling. "Who am I meeting?"

"Have you heard of O'Connor Electronics?"

"I don't think so. Should I have?"

"Not necessarily. They keep a pretty low profile. I want you to meet C. J. O'Connor. You and C. J. will have a lot in common. Here's the address. They're expecting you."

"Horace, are you going to let me in on the big secret? Like what C.J. will be talking to me about?"

Horace finally smiled at him. "Language, Peter. You'll be hearing about growth language."

CHAPTER 10 — KEY POINTS

Natural Laws of Business Growth:

Law #1: *Large is not small* means that the rules that govern whether you survive or fail change according to the size of your enterprise.

Law #2: *Nature innovates from the edge* means that new adaptations, new solutions and innovations, in nature and in business, are born on the edge of chaos, not in a world of stability and equilibrium.

Law #3: *Form is shaped by force* means that in order for organisms to survive in nature and in business, they are compelled to adapt and change their form as dictated by greater forces acting in and on them.

Law #4: *The right measure of growth* implies that the most effective method of understanding and predicting the phenomenon of growth in an organization is through the measurement of its complexity.

Law #5: *Clumping* occurs as a result of two or more layers of complex issues colliding and eventually forming barriers of chaos.

Law #6: *Living systems have tools* means that complex adaptive systems require specific tools for navigation: Attractors, Gas Pedals/ Brakes and Fitness Landscape Maps.

Law #7: *The brilliant is hiding in the ordinary* means that the real intelligence of your enterprise is right under your nose, residing inside your own staff.

Law #8: *Put the beekeeper in charge* means that enterprise growth requires a brand of leadership that facilitates optimum performance rather than engineers it.

Law #9: *Perspective drives experience* means that your viewpoint directly influences your critical decision making and the business created from those decisions.

GROWTH LANGUAGE

THE 3 GATES OF GROWTH

Chapter 11
GROWTH LANGUAGE

"Every group develops words, phrases, and metaphors unique to its circumstances. A specialized language both reflects and shapes a group's culture. Shared language allows team members to communicate easily, with minimal misunderstanding."
— **Lee Bolman, Terrence Deal,** *Reframing Organizations*

The roar was so loud, Peter thought a plane was landing on the roof of his car. A twin-engine jet passed overhead on its way to a perfect landing. The plane appeared so close that Peter instinctively ducked inside his car. The words "O'Connor Electronics" painted under the left wing were barely readable.

Located on the edge of the local airport, C.J.'s building was an unimposing slab of grey concrete extending over 200 yards along the tarmac. Peter was surprised by the sheer size of the structure. He could have driven by it a thousand times and never noticed it. The style was strictly 1980s prefabricated "tilt-up." A small sign read, O'Connor Electronics.

As Peter parked his car in a visitor's space near the front door he noticed a sign over the entrance of the employee parking lot. It was peculiar in that it said, Give What You Need.

Peter wondered what it meant.

The sizeable parking lot was full.

Peter saw that the grounds were surprisingly well-maintained. The lot was spotless. The lines of the parking spaces were precise and freshly painted; the plants in front of the building were perfect.

At the entrance, he saw that the glass was especially dark and there was a keypad embedded in the wall. Since the door was locked, he pushed the doorbell. He expected to hear the buzz of a solenoid lock being tripped so he could open the door, instead, he heard a voice coming from an unseen speaker.

"Hello. May I help you, sir?"

Whoever it was could tell he was a male, so there had to be a camera somewhere. "Uh, yes, hello. I'm here to see C. J. O'Connor."

"Do you have an appointment, sir?"

"Well, I think I do. My name is Peter Logan."

"Thank you, sir. Please come in."

Peter heard the faintest click of a lock, and was able to open the door. He stepped over the threshold and found himself facing another set of doors.

He was in a high-security entryway where he could see the cameras that monitored the entryway. Another set of cameras was trained on him now. The doors he faced were impenetrably dark, just like the exterior set. Whoever these people were, they were serious about security.

It was strange being watched by someone he couldn't see. He stepped to his left and a drawer emerged from the right wall.

"Please open the drawer, sir."

He moved to the drawer and opened the lid. Inside was a monochrome touch-screen-style monitor mounted flat in the drawer. It said *Agreement of Non-disclosure* across the top of the document on the screen. At the bottom was a line where he was supposed to sign, using the plastic-tipped pen attached to the monitor.

"Please take a moment to read the document and then sign it, sir."

> ❝ IT WAS A STANDARD NON-DISCLOSURE AGREEMENT, BUT IT ALSO MENTIONED 'NATIONAL SECURITY' AND 'FINED AND IMPRISONED.' ❞

"OK."

It was a standard non-disclosure agreement, but it also mentioned "national security" and "fined and imprisoned." Who were these people? Still, he couldn't help but be curious. He signed his name.

"Thank you, Mr. Logan. Now please place your right index finger on the ink pad in front of you and transfer your fingerprint onto the pad on the right." Peter complied. A tissue was provided and Peter used it to wipe the ink off his finger. After what felt like five minutes, the voice spoke again over the hidden speakers saying, "Thank you, sir. You are approved to come inside. You'll receive a copy of the document when you leave. Please come in."

He wasn't prepared for what he walked into. The building may have been drab on the outside, but the inside was an explosion of color and forms. He was standing on a balcony overlooking a bustle of activity. The lobby was sunken into the ground twenty feet below him. The room was airy, with well-maintained plants everywhere. Sunlight streamed in through skylights in the ceiling. The furniture was colorful and comfortable-looking. From where he stood, he got the impression that the building above him was a facade and that beneath it, or rather, underneath it, was a small city of activity. A voice from below brought him out of his reverie. "Mr. Logan? Please come down."

He looked down and saw a pretty young woman with an armed guard standing beside her. They were kidding with each other, enjoying their day, relaxed and happy. Even the guard, whom he wouldn't want to cross under any circumstance, seemed completely at ease and almost friendly.

"Oh, sorry. I was just taken by surprise."

The young woman laughed. "You've never been here before?"

"No. This would be my first time."

The guard spoke up. "Please come down, Mr. Logan. There's a lot more to see. And C.J. will want to see you right away."

It struck him again. There was a real familiarity, almost affection, in the way the guard spoke his boss's name. He didn't think his staff at Bolder Solutions would exhibit the same regard for him.

He stepped off the bottom step as the guard and young woman came toward him. "My name is Bonnie and this is Michael."

"It's a pleasure to meet you both." He felt like he'd stepped into Oz and the people of Munchkinland were trying to make him feel welcome. But Michael was no Munchkin. He was at least six-and-a-half-feet tall.

Michael started chuckling at him. Many people were chuckling at him these days. "We do like to watch visitors come in the first time. The security measures aren't personal. We make everybody do the same routine."

"I don't even know what you do here."

Bonnie said, "We'll let C. J. tell you all about it. Please have a seat."

He saw many model aircraft mounted in cases in the walls, everything from tiny two-seater props to military jets. There was even a Stealth Fighter and a model of the Space Shuttle. At one end was  a futuristic craft that he recognized as the proposed replacement for the Shuttle itself.

He picked up a book that had pictures of Earth taken from the moon, and began leafing through the pages. A swirl of color in motion caught his eye just above the book, and he saw a woman coming down a long corridor toward the lobby. She was dressed in a silk kimono that swirled when she walked. But it was the colors that got his attention. In most corporate settings, staff personnel dressed conservatively, but her outfit was red and blue and purple. She was quite a sight!

He watched her come into the lobby and glance toward the desk where Bonnie pointed at him. She was in front of him before he could stand up.

"Hello, Peter." Her voice was deeper and more commanding than he expected. "I'm C. J.

O'Connor." She saw him react. "Not what you expected, am I?"

He could only laugh. "No. I must confess you're not. I'm afraid I just assumed C.J. was a man."

"Most people do. That gives me an advantage. And I want all the advantages I can get. Say, that wasn't your blue Range Rover driving up the road a few minutes ago, was it?"

"As a matter of fact it was. Why do you ask?"

C.J. laughed and said, "I was flying the jet that nearly landed on your car roof. Figured whoever

> ❝ I WAS FLYING THE JET THAT NEARLY LANDED ON YOUR CAR ROOF. FIGURED WHOEVER WAS DRIVING THAT ROVER MUST HAVE HAD A REAL SHOT OF ADRENALINE PUMPING THROUGH THEM AFTER THAT EXPERIENCE. ❞

was driving that Rover must have had a real shot of adrenaline pumping through them after that experience. Never understood why they put that road right underneath the approach to the airport. Damn stupid. Well, anyway, nice to have you here. Come on, I'll give you the cook's tour." Peter wondered what Horace had gotten him into.

"Horace didn't tell me much about you. He just told me to be nice." She paused, and then queried, "Do you enjoy your business?"

Peter wanted to object to being quizzed by this woman he didn't know, but something told him to

trust her. "Frankly, no. It is a rolling nightmare waiting to blow up. In short, I have had better times, C. J."

"Good answer. Straight to the point. Now we have things to talk about." She turned and started walking away from him at a fairly quick pace.

"What do you do here, C. J.?"

"What did the sign out front say?"

"O'Connor Electronics."

"That's what we do. We do electronics."

He started to protest, but she was ahead of him.

"Oh, relax, Peter. I'm just going to keep on giving you a difficult time. You might as well decide to enjoy this."

"C. J., I'm here because a guy I recently met in the park told me I needed to meet you. My situation is a bit intense at the moment, so please excuse my lack of levity."

"I know. That much Horace did tell me. Your brother died and essentially left you the company. That may be why he sent you to see me first. I didn't create this company, my husband did, and I inherited it."

Peter interjected, "Ah, we do have something in common."

"Well, I worked with my husband from the start, but the company was his vision. This place was everything we had. He died suddenly and we'd never thought about what would become of the company without his leadership. It was suddenly my job to look into the faces of the employees and tell them what we were going to do. It was at about that point when I met Horace."

Peter was quiet for a moment. "So you weren't always so cheerful?"

She laughed at him. "No, I was downright morose. But it got better, and the company has flourished. But don't think having fun means a lack of professionalism; it makes being professional easier."

"So C. J., what do you do here?"

"We make all manner of electronic devices for aircraft. Next time you look at a private jet or a small plane, notice the nose. More than likely it's stuffed with our equipment: radar, altimeter, air speed, you name it."

"Seems like a lot of security for radar and altimeter instruments."

"Well, that's why you signed the electronic non-disclosure. We also have some very, uh, delicate

government contracts. I can't tell you what we're doing. You know the old saying: if I told you…"

"…You'd have to kill me."

She laughed out loud at the joke.

"How does your staff feel about all this?"

"They love it. They all feel like James Bond. And they're very loyal. I'm not the only one having a good time here, Peter. I have a brilliant group of people working for me. When I took over, talent was not the problem. My problem was motivating all these creative folks. I had to find a way to give them a sense of ownership as quickly as possible."

"Yeah, well, I understand that part. Was your staff attached to your husband?"

"Probably not like your staff was attached to your brother. Yours is a company of the new millennium. I mean, it's less than a couple of years old, right?"

> **WHEN I TOOK OVER, TALENT WAS NOT THE PROBLEM. MY PROBLEM WAS MOTIVATING ALL THESE CREATIVE FOLKS.**

"That's true."

"This company was founded in the mid-'70s. My husband was a hotshot engineer with a knack for running a business. All the business models that existed in the 1970s were decades old. So we're pretty much an old-line company. We leveled out at about 150 employees in 1985, and that was fine with both of us. Our products sold well; we made plenty of money, so why fight it?

"By the late 1980s, it was clear that we had to be a part of the technological changes that were on the horizon, so the whole company geared up for retooling and re-educating itself. It was a tough time, but our employees had been with us for years and everyone went with the changes. But we were still an old-line style of company. By that, I mean we were still living with a business model from the 1970s."

They reached a set of double doors with a key-pad that required a code and C. J.'s card.

"You're gonna love this. It's like a big toyshop."

Toyshop indeed! It looked like something designed by George Lucas. Peter felt he was looking at a redefinition of the term high-tech. They peered through an observation window into a room filled with technicians of all ages dressed in white clean suits. They were at workstations stocked with oversized monitors and a workspace that was a hobbyist's dream. As he walked past the window, he noticed that the techni-cians radiated a sense of concentration, smooth professionalism, and, well, fun. The benches were covered with what he took to be prototypes of dif-ferent instruments. But there were other things as well, C. J. was right, it looked like a big toyshop.

"One of the many things I did was to encourage the tech heads to be inventive. Some of the stuff we're contracted to do is fairly mundane. So I told these folks that once they've accomplished their work, they could use our facility to invent anything they liked. I told them that if they came up with anything viable, we'd help them market it and we'd split the profits. The idea was so successful that we've spun off a couple of companies. It's just a game, Peter."

Peter was suddenly flooded with the reality of the seed genome project. "C. J., I appreciate the way you've got everyone onboard here, but would it be the same if your game meant the survival or death of millions of people? Frankly, I inherited a

> "I TOLD THEM THAT IF THEY CAME UP WITH ANYTHING VIABLE, WE'D HELP THEM MARKET IT AND WE'D SPLIT THE PROFITS. THE IDEA WAS SO SUCCESSFUL THAT WE'VE SPUN-OFF A COUPLE OF COMPANIES."

very serious 'game' at Bolder Solutions and I'm finding it less than fun."

C.J. touched his arm, "I understand, Peter. Believe me when I say that managing a high-intensity, high-performance work environment where the slightest mistake has huge repercussions requires built-in safety valves. As strange as it may seem, fun is the best safety valve going. Come on, I want to show you our hangar."

She turned to go, but was stopped by a young man with a broad grin on his face. She waited for him to speak but he just kept smiling and staring at her. A sudden change in her expression told Peter that she had understood why he was smiling at her.

She looked at the young man and simply said, "You're kidding?"

"Have I ever joked about this stuff?"

"You've found a solution?"

"Not just a solution. I've found *the* solution."

"Peter, this is Ricardo. He's been with us six months and he's been working on a system that could revolutionize the way airplanes see each other. Ricardo, this is Peter."

Peter sensed that whatever Ricardo was working on, it was very important to C. J., but the young man was enjoying himself too much to be overly impressed with his own accomplishment.

"Nice to meet you, Ricardo."

"Back at you, man. C. J., this is better than I expected. We absolutely crushed our cost of goods side of the product. If I'm right, we aren't looking at scooter margins anymore. This is bulldozer margin territory, at the very least, and we may be talking even galactic margins here. It's passing every test I can think of."

Peter knew he was hearing language peculiar to this company, but the meaning was obvious. As he looked around, the other employees in the lab were smiling and nodding at the mention of galactic margins. Everybody in the place spoke the same language.

Ricardo continued explaining to Peter. "Our innovator teams have been coming up with some very cool customer-migration solutions that will put us way ahead of our competitors. If we can continue to listen to our customers, we'll hold our market lead."

> WE ABSOLUTELY CRUSHED OUR COST OF GOODS SIDE OF THE PRODUCT. IF I'M RIGHT, WE AREN'T LOOKING AT SCOOTER MARGINS ANYMORE. THIS IS BULLDOZER MARGIN TERRITORY, AT THE VERY LEAST.

C. J. was absolutely beaming. "Nice work, Ricardo!" Turning to Peter, she said, "We're going to talk about this in a few minutes, Peter. What Ricardo is doing represents the best thing that can happen when a company begins to tap its knowledge pool. It keeps the momentum of the company going."

Ricardo said, "We'll have a prototype in about a week."

C. J. swept through the rest of the room to a chorus of greetings and jokes, with her guest in tow. Peter was having trouble imagining that this level of familiarity was conducive to work. But the proof was in front of him.

C. J. continued her narrative. "My husband, Martin, died in 1994. I had never given the slightest thought to his not being here. The company was doing *OK*, but just OK. On a good day we were making money, but it just had a feeling of being flat. After Martin passed on, I was suddenly in charge of everything and everyone looked to me for direction. I looked back at all these people and decided I had to do something different, anything to move forward.

"They had recently gone through systems training and we had some of the new processes you see here in place. So I started by getting them to talk among themselves as if they worked in a new and bigger company. Let me reiterate, part of this process was to make sure they were enjoying their work. That's what I mean by it being a game. Our work, and I gather your work, is very serious. But it must, I mean it must, spark the staff's imagination at all times. That's how serious it is, and that's why it's a game. Understand?"

She didn't wait for a reply. Though several inches shorter than Peter, she could move quickly. He had a sense she wasn't hurrying, just that she was excited. He was wondering how far they had walked into the structure when she stopped at another set of doors, punched numbers into a keypad, and placed her hand on a device that scanned her palm and fingers.

The doors opened with a rush of air and they were staring into an airplane hanger.

It was a blimp-hangar-sized space filled with all manner of aircraft. She saw him looking wide-eyed at an experimental craft that looked remarkably like a junior-sized Stealth Fighter.

"Take a good, long look. You may or may not ever see that craft again. And I cannot confirm or deny that you are actually seeing that plane now.

> "I CANNOT CONFIRM OR DENY THAT YOU ARE ACTUALLY SEEING THAT PLANE NOW. WOULDN'T IT BE INTERESTING IF, AT SOME POINT IN THE FUTURE, AIRCRAFT DID NOT REQUIRE ANY FUEL WHATSOEVER TO CRUISE AT SPEEDS OF MACH 1 OR MACH 2?"

Here is a clue for you. Wouldn't it be interesting if, at some point in the future, aircraft did not require any fuel whatsoever to cruise at speeds of Mach 1 or Mach 2? That through the use of magnetic forces a totally clean, inexpensive, unlimited source of energy was available for man's use? I wonder how such a discovery would  affect our civilization? See? Isn't this fun?"

Peter smiled and looked at her straight in the eye. "Well C.J., I guess we all have our own earth-shaking projects, don't we?"

C.J. cracked a smile and said, "So I bet you are wondering just how much this little toy costs. Right?"

"Yes, now that you mention it. I was wondering …."

"How much?" She laughed at the expression on his face. "Everybody does. Right now, I'd say that little beauty, of which I can't confirm the existence, runs for something like two-point-two billion." She let it settle in. "Come on. Now that I've got you dazzled, let's go to my office."

They went up two levels. The doors opened onto a large office with windows looking out on the Front Range, with a perfect view of Peter's touchstone, the Flatirons.

"Horace said I'd like you. I'm having the kitchen whip up a couple of pizzas. Does that work for you?"

Kitchen? Pizza? "Sure, that sounds great."

"So let's talk about the reason you're here. Horace wants me to give you a primer on Growth Language. It's the best place to start. First of all, language is, hands down, the world's greatest change agent."

"The really bright successful entrepreneurs instinctually know what every great leader throughout history has known, you seed change in an enterprise by shifting and transforming the baseline language of the workplace community. People con-verse and communicate up to the boundaries of the current language that describes their experience."

"But, in a sense, language doesn't describe their experience; rather, it defines their experience. Change the language, then you change the experience."

C.J. mused, "My gosh, if you told Horace that I said that, he wouldn't believe it. You see, I don't go much for business theories. I am a 'both feet on the ground' gal. Did Horace talk to you yet about the two approaches to viewing a business?"

Peter perked up, "Yes, as a matter of fact, he did. There is the Problem Approach and the Model Approach. He said most entrepreneurs are caught

> "LANGUAGE DOESN'T DESCRIBE THEIR EXPERIENCE; RATHER, IT DEFINES THEIR EXPERIENCE. CHANGE THE LANGUAGE THEN YOU CHANGE THE EXPERIENCE."

in the day-to-day world of the problem approach to viewing their business."

C.J. laughed again, "Well, I am afraid that I will always be looking at business from the ground up. I frankly don't know how anyone has the time to consider anything other than The Problem Approach. Horace will have a hard time convincing me otherwise. It is the real world that we live in.

You've got to show me the beef, so to speak. I need to see the proof of how anything is going to change the day-to-day results of my company before I buy in to it."

She continued, "When Horace introduced the whole concept of growth language, I was a huge skeptic. That is, until he finally convinced me to experiment with it. Which is probably why Horace had me talk to you about it. That clever old fox, he thinks that if I have to teach it, I will appreciate it even more than I already do. But what he doesn't know is that I have secretly been experimenting with our corporate language for over a year now, and I stand before you to say that this stuff is amazing. It really does work. So, I have become a true believer and Horace doesn't even know it yet. I'm waiting for the perfect time to shock him. So please don't let my secret out, OK?"

Peter easily complied. "Who am I to get in the way of surprising Horace Bedford?"

C.J. laughed and continued, "Language is the

> " I HAVE SECRETLY BEEN EXPERIMENTING WITH OUR CORPORATE LANGUAGE FOR OVER A YEAR NOW, AND I STAND BEFORE YOU TO SAY THAT THIS STUFF IS AMAZING. IT REALLY DOES WORK. "

basis of all culture. You focus your culture by focusing and energizing the core language of that culture. Most business owners and professionals have no clue about the power of language in the work environment. Language is more important in the success of your firm than you will ever realize."

C.J. looked down as though she were collecting her thoughts. "Let me state the obvious: language suffuses everything we do. We must be able to communicate with each other. In a business, it's absolutely vital that everyone is grounded in the same language. It can be the springboard for the creative energy of the staff. So even though it seems self-evident that language is important, we have to treat it as a specific piece of a bigger puzzle. In a way, language, or Growth Language, is where The Growth Curve Solution begins."

Peter nodded. "Horace said something about recognizing patterns in a company. I suppose language helps identify those patterns."

"Absolutely! I'll tell him you were paying attention. By the way, did he tell you about the power of three?"

"The power of three? No, I don't think so."

"It's a neat little principle. The human brain grasps, assimilates, and remembers things best three at a time. Horace can probably tell you why, but the important thing is that it does. So each component of The Growth Curve Solution has three elements that define it. And each of those elements has three points that define the element.

It probably goes on and on: three within three within three. The power of three."

"OK."

"Growth Language is comprised of:
1. The Three Gates of Growth
2. The 7 Stages of Growth
3. The Patterns of Growth

"So let's start with the first of the three elements that define Growth Language: The Three Gates of Growth."

They were interrupted by a knock at the door. A man pushing a food-service cart entered the office. "How's it goin' there, C. J.?" He had a thick New York accent.

"Hello, Sammy. Thanks for bringing in lunch yourself."

C. J. stopped him. "Maybe you can help me explain something to Peter. What can you tell him about The Three Gates of Growth?"

Sammy sighed heavily, and then smiled. "OK, OK. Well, I can only tell you what **The Three Gates of Growth** are as I understand them. There are three:

"How we talk about the company and our work spins around these three central language points because they are the common denominator for everyone working at O'Connor Electronics. So whenever you look at what's impeding or helping

growth in the company, you're talking about one or more of the three gates of growth. Each stage of growth has a different balance of these three."

| Process Gate | People Gate | Revenue/Profit Gate |

Sammy glanced at C.J. with a look that said, why did you ask me to tell him?

"I've only been at the company six months so my perspective is a bit new, but everybody here really understands this stuff. Not only that, they talk about it all the time. At times the staff is so into this, it sounds like everyone is running the place. For the kitchen staff and me, all three gates are in our everyday language."

"We have a fair budget that allows us to be in the profit-making business by setting cost-saving goals and beating them. Everyone in the kitchen knows how this company makes money. It is part of their training.

"If we suddenly have a large addition to the company's staff, then my team is going to be counting pennies and asking for a bigger budget. But as a manager, I also have to keep my team in tune with what's going on with the people issues in the kitchen and the processes that make sense of the chaos at lunchtime. That includes all the machines we have to use every day, because if one breaks, then we have a process that's out of balance with everything else."

> EVERYONE IN THE KITCHEN KNOWS HOW THIS COMPANY MAKES MONEY. IT IS PART OF THEIR TRAINING.

"Every department can be viewed as its own smaller business, and my kitchen is a restaurant where all the customers want to eat at the same time. And the success of my work contributes to the success of the Revenue/Profit, the People and Process Gates of the whole company. If people feel well-fed, and well-taken care of, they perform better at their jobs."

He stopped and thought for a moment. "I guess that's a pretty good overview." He paused again. "How'd I do, boss?"

"Not bad. For a cook."

"This is the way I'm treated around here, Peter. She baits me and then she reels me in. If I don't go now, she'll have me boring you with my exploits in Paris. You two enjoy your pizzas."

After Sammy left them, C. J. smiled at Peter. "Any questions?"

"I do have a question, but I'm struggling with how to ask it. I guess it stems from my innate corporate cynicism. Your people are well- versed in a business language that the company speaks, and they seem pleased that they are. My concern is that it looks like they all know how to talk the talk, but what about walking the walk?"

She took a moment to respond. "That's a good question. You're quite right, actually. My people do know how to talk the talk. When they began to use the growth language to measure the results and performance of the company on a daily, weekly, and monthly basis, that's when I knew it was making a difference."

"Frankly, it even took me a while to integrate the language enough to use it in meetings and expect everyone to know what I was talking about."

C.J. continued, "But what you see and hear at this company is the language of growth grounded in the measurable performance of the company. Yes, we all probably seem a bit self-satisfied when we start using our own charged words with each other, but it's more than just words; it's a mindset that the staff truly believes in.

"We are growing a living entity. More than that, a company that uses growth language is a company that is a profit-driven, self-organizing, staff-authored company that grows from the bottom-up. The staff is invested intellectually, emotionally, and financially in the successful growth of this company."

"Well, it's certainly impressive. I mean I get what Sammy was saying, but it's really impressive that he cares enough to know all that."

"Yes. Horace must have told you that there are several parts to 'The Growth Curve Solution.' Language is the first bridge for your staff. You need to start there. If they understand how to speak to each other in a common language about the growth of the enterprise, they'll be able to move as a team in that direction."

"And from an innovation standpoint, it's essential. We have to have, and believe me, Peter, <u>you</u>

> **"LANGUAGE IS THE FIRST BRIDGE FOR YOUR STAFF. YOU NEED TO START THERE. IF THEY UNDERSTAND HOW TO SPEAK TO EACH OTHER IN A COMMON LANGUAGE ABOUT THE GROWTH OF THE ENTERPRISE, THEY'LL BE ABLE TO MOVE AS A TEAM IN THAT DIRECTION."**

absolutely have to have, a language that builds and grows your company. But it does more than that. It protects and connects all aspects of your company. And it starts with you personally learning a new language. Now pull that chair over here and let's eat. I'm starving!"

It was perhaps the best pizza Peter had ever eaten, but hunger may have clouded his judgment.

As he and C. J. ate their way through Sammy's creations, he told her the story of his sudden rise to the top at Bolder Solutions, including the nefarious Santomo Corporation and the impact Bolder's software could have on protecting the food sources of the planet.

C.J. stared at Peter. A minute went by and then she raised her right hand and began to speak. "Peter, it sounds like you have your work cut out for you. All I can say is that no one said it would

be easy, and anyone who says it's hard is a complainer. Two pieces of advice: Do whatever Horace tells you – the guy has unbelievable radar, and buck up – it never gets easier, you just get stronger."

GROWTH LANGUAGE

1. START UP
2. RAMP UP
3. DELEGATION
4. PROFESSIONAL
5. INTEGRATION
6. STRATEGIC
7. VISIONARY

STAGES OF GROWTH

Chapter 12

STAGES OF GROWTH

"The more present and aware we are as individuals and as organizations, the more choices we create. As awareness increases, we can engage with more possibilities. We are no longer held prisoner by habits, unexamined thoughts, or information we refuse to look at."

— **Margaret Wheatley and Myron Kellner Rogers,** *A Simpler Way*

Without missing a beat, C. J. launched into her next lecture, "Now, we need to talk about the second leg of Growth Language: The Seven Stages of Growth. Peter, from what Horace says, you need to learn this material as fast as you can."

"What do the stages of growth have to do with growth language, C. J.?"

"It helps you and your staff think about Bolder Solutions as a dynamic, growing enterprise with all its graces and faults. It's more complicated than the Gates, but it still makes simple common sense. Frankly, I think that it's very important for the staff to have a context for measuring or inventorying five things." With that said, she began to write on the large whiteboard in her office:

> **" I THINK THAT IT'S VERY IMPORTANT FOR THE STAFF TO HAVE A CONTEXT FOR MEASURING OR INVENTORYING FIVE THINGS. "**

- **The history of the company**
- **The current experience of the company**
- **What's likely coming around the corner for the company in the future**
- **What issues need attention**
- **What's the next best thing to do**

"It gives them reference points and a model for understanding the ups and downs of working in a growing company."

C.J. proceeded talking and writing, "O'Connor Electronics has 173 employees, 28 supervisory staff, and our three main challenges right now are:

1. **Forecasting trouble spots before they hatch**
2. **Properly diagnosing their origin**
3. **Shortening the timeframe to get products developed and out on the market**

"In our last enterprise assessment, we came out with a 2.9-to-1 Builder/Protector Ratio, a little high, mind you, on the builder side but we are working on rewiring the mindset of some of our executive team. We are clearly in a moderate growth modality and, thank God, not in hyper growth that damn near put us out of business three years ago."

"We grew so fast that the walls around here were breaking up and flying past us at 200 miles an hour. We are also leaning toward Processes as the dominant Gate of Growth and I know that we should be focusing more on People. So we are definitely working on that one as well. That's a quick thumbnail of the company. After we finish here, hopefully you can tell me what stage of growth we are in."

Peter piped up, "I can only guess at a good two-thirds of what you just said, but I'm intrigued. And I'll follow your lead and wait until the end of my

> **THE DISCREPANCY BETWEEN BEING IN STAGE 4 AND ACTING AS THOUGH YOU WERE IN STAGE 2 IS THE SOURCE OF YOUR NIGHTMARE. EACH STAGE OF GROWTH HAS ITS OWN DEMANDING SET OF RULES, ITS OWN PARTICULAR NEEDS, AND ITS OWN PECULIAR CHALLENGES.**

visit before I attempt to know what Stage of Growth you are in."

"Peter, it is really quite simple on the front end. It gets a little more difficult understanding the subtleties of the dominant patterns that form in different stages of growth. I'm sure Horace will get

around to showing you that stuff at some point along the way. It still is a little out there for me."

C.J. continued, "From what you've described, it sounds like Bolder Solutions is smack in the middle of Stage 4, but the company is actually acting like a Stage 2 enterprise. The discrepancy between being in Stage 4 and acting as though you were in Stage 2 is the source of your nightmare. That's a tough position to be in."

"Tell me about it! Horace said about the same thing, but he didn't explain what it meant."

She got a piece of paper from her desk, pushed the food aside, and started drawing lines.

"There are seven stages of growth a company moves through in the entrepreneurial world. Each stage of growth has its own demanding set of rules, its own particular needs, and its own peculiar challenges. As CEO, your task is to predict and manage the changes, learn the rules as you go along, and alert your staff to the balance each stage requires.

"What I'm going to show you involves good numbers, but not hard numbers. Generally, this covers companies with one to 350 employees and from zero to about 100 million dollars in revenue. But in some cases, a Stage 7 company might have up to 500 employees and perhaps even 150 million dollars in revenue.

"Peter, I am going to give you a very quick snapshot of the stages of growth. The information about the stages of growth applies not only to companies but also (with minor modifications) to departments and divisions. Measuring growth is all about complexity and that happens in all sorts of groups.

"No doubt that the other folks that you visit through Horace's influence will go into more depth with the issues they face in their stage of growth. Also, Horace will most likely give you the Stages of Growth Matrix that will fill you in on all the key stages of growth information on one page. I don't happen to have a copy on hand at this time or I would give it to you."

She continued, "A Stage 1 company is a start-up, a small company that has up to ten employees, and lives in a state of chaos. Everything is fluid. In Stage 1, the person at the top controls pretty much everything. Creating a homogeneous group is more important in a Stage 1 company than putting together a highly competent group. The owner is the visionary behind the company, and everyone else is following his lead. I take it your brother was this kind of guy?"

"Yep. He was definitely a visionary and he solved every problem."

"In Stage 1, with 1 – 10 employees, you likely are still developing the product or service you intend to sell and the company exists in a unique type of constant chaos. The challenge is to not over-control the company but rather move it quickly through and on to Stage 2. It is very important that whatever stage of growth your company is in, let it be in that stage of growth until it is ready to

> " IT IS VERY IMPORTANT THAT WHATEVER STAGE OF GROWTH YOUR COMPANY IS IN TO LET IT BE IN THAT STAGE OF GROWTH UNTIL IT IS READY TO MOVE ON. "

move on. You have to let the employees, the systems, and the processes all acclimate to the current stage of growth."

"I have seen many experienced Stage 5 or Stage 6 executives coming onboard to run Stage 2 or Stage 3 companies, and these folks try to make the company operate like a Stage 5 or 6 company because that is what they are familiar with. Unfortunately, unless these executives adapt to the rules of their current company's stage of growth, it won't matter how much experience they have, they will fail. I have never seen it happen otherwise. A Stage 1 company has a 4-to-1 Builder/Protector Ratio and its dominant gate of growth is Revenue/Profit."

"Going into a Stage 2 company, you pass through a transition or chaos zone that is called a flood zone. In a flood zone, you and your company have to bear up to an increase in the level of activity."

"When you are going through a flood zone, there is too much work for the hands on deck. The staff is totally overloaded with the work of the enterprise. The chaos is unavoidable and it is all part of what Horace calls 'nature's gate fee' into the next stage of growth. At any rate, these chaos zones happen at the front end of every stage of growth."

"In a Stage 2 company, you've gotten a good leg up on the products or services that you are going to market and now you have to ramp up production and sell the product or service into the market. Your Builder/Protector Ratio is 3-to-1 and you are still focused on the Revenue/Profit Gate as the primary concern of the company. You have 11 – 19 staff members and the company is still CEO-centric. Your brother was still holding on to most of the decision making, right?"

"Apparently."

"Emerging into Stage 3, you go through a chaos zone called a wind tunnel. In a wind tunnel you are

Wind Tunnel

forced to give up what worked in the past because it doesn't work any more and take on new skills and methods. By the time you get into Stage 3, the owner/operator will get entrepreneurial burnout if he doesn't delegate. A Stage 3 company can no longer survive and flourish if it remains CEO-centric. Sounds like your brother was a perfect example of that."

"Stage 3 is a dangerous area to move through. This is why your Builder/Protector Ratio is 1-to-1. The main issue is getting a handle on the workplace community issues, which are some of the hardest to face in a young growing business. So in Stage 3 you must focus on the People Gate as the primary management concern. The company should have 3 – 5 managers at this point."

"In Stage 3, the company's vitality depends on a clear set of core values, a compelling vision/mission for the enterprise and a cultural focus that provides a strong baseline for how the company interacts. This is the stage of growth where you must start looking at the company as a separate entity from the owner. You have 20 – 34 staff members. This is a time that you definitely must begin to effectively delegate both responsibility and authority in order to survive as a leader. This is, also, the first time that the leader is now managing and training other leaders."

Flood Zone

"Crossing over into Stage 4 you go through another chaotic flood zone and the staff is once again overwhelmed with work. By Stage 4, you've reached the professional stage. Something happens, almost overnight, when you move into Stage 4. Your staff has grown to somewhere between 35 – 57 people, the Builder/Protector Ratio is 3-to-2, there are 6 – 8 managers and the Process Gate is the primary focus. The complexity of the organization has suddenly become overwhelming.

"This is the stage where each department must become a strong independent fiefdom with effective new systems and procedures to meet the demands of an ever more complex organization."

"If you don't hire professional managers to take on this task, then you must properly train the man-

> **IF YOU DON'T HAVE EXPERIENCED MANAGERS, THEN THERE IS A TENDENCY TO THROW PEOPLE AT THE EVER-INCREASING WORKLOAD AND THAT'S A BIG MISTAKE.**

agers that you do have. There is no getting around this.

"If you don't have experienced managers, then there is a tendency to throw people at the ever-increasing workload and that's a big mistake. The departments need experienced, trained managers to meet the complexity of the new systems."

Peter thought for a moment. "OK, I'm playing catch-up here, but I think I understand what you're saying, and I think it explains some of my frustration. My experience generally has been to come into a Stage 3 or 4 company, one that has some degree of management experience so I'm speaking a particular language. Bolder Solutions looks like a company that you describe as Stage 4 because of the size of the staff. But we are still limping along with methods that are best suited to a Stage 2."

"That's good, Peter! That sounds right. You have been brought into a company with the complexity of Stage 4 and the infrastructure of Stage 2. You probably came in wondering who the department heads were."

"That's true."

"Your brother must have been going crazy. In Stage 3, you simply must delegate or the complexity will eat you alive in Stage 4. I take it your brother was a very strong-willed guy?"

"As long as I knew him. He was always a rock."

"So you are doing three things at the same time. You have a company at Stage 4 that at the same time behaves like a Stage 2 company, and you are trying to bridge the difference. All your problems are a result of the disparity between what your company is and what it is behaving like. Remember: these stages are about complexity, not revenue."

C.J. took a big breath and continued. "OK. Moving into Stage 5, you pass through another wind tunnel. What worked in Stage 4 by strengthening the departmental fiefdoms will actually go against you in Stage 5. It is challenging."

Peter interrupted, "Wait a minute. Do these

> **"CHAOS IS INEVITABLE AND RHYTHMICAL. AGAIN IT IS OFTEN THE GATE FEE TO THE NEXT STAGE OF GROWTH."**

chaos zones alternate back and forth between a wind tunnel and a flood zone?"

C.J. said, "Yes, they do. Chaos is inevitable and rhythmical. Again it is often the **gate fee** to the next stage of growth. Now in Stage 5, you've got a staff of 58 – 95 people. Your Builder/Protector Ratio is 2-to-1, there are 9 – 12 in the management team and you are back with your primary focus being the Revenue/Profit Gate."

"You're in the integration stage, where you will have the job of integrating all those gunslingers you hired in Stage 4 into a strong interdependent team, exactly the opposite of what they were in Stage 4. This can be a particularly challenging stage of

growth. As you are aligning the departments with each other, you are also facing the need to develop a stronger financial reporting system as well as a working budget."

"An interesting thing begins to happen in Stage 5. You start getting noticed. Your competitors regard you as a viable player in the market and the stakes in the game increase measurably."

"Moving into Stage 6 the company goes through another chaotic flood zone. Again the staff is over-

loaded, but this time the executive and the supervisory teams feel the brunt of it."

"If you haven't done your homework in Stage 4 and Stage 5, the chaos will be unbearable in Stage 6. You will be frantically scrambling to get a handle on the company. Stage 6 is where you grow to between 96 – 160 employees, your Builder/Protector Ratio is 3-to-2, there are 13 – 26 managers and executives and the primary focus is on the People Gate."

"This is the strategic stage of growth and you must start looking two to three years into the future and seriously consider key strategic alliances. You start strategically planning product development and business expansion."

"You will likely form strategic alliances with other companies, perhaps even with select competitors. You must be functioning at a very high level of professionalism. It's also the stage where innovators in your company come into their own."

"The young engineer you met, Ricardo, is typical of the kind of innovator a Stage 6 company needs. We are perfectly positioned to make use of his ideas, and to make him feel comfortable coming up with those ideas. The future of our company depends on supporting the innovation teams. Horace calls them Growth Circles, but we put a little different twist on them."

"So you consider your company to be in Stage 6?"

She smiled. "Well, let's put it this way. We have the complexity of a Stage 7 company but we still act like we are in Stage 6. Frankly we are right smack in the middle of the chaos zone going into Stage 7."

Peter said, "Let me guess. You are in a wind tunnel. Right?"

"You guessed it. And I am telling you that the whole company is kicking and screaming at having to let go of methods and procedures that used to work. Actually, some of the methods and systems still do work but they won't work for long, so I am having to convince the department heads to move on and retool when they barely have time to work the systems they already have. It's a challenge, for sure.

"Stage 7 is really the visionary stage. Stage 7 has between 161 – 350 employees and 27 – 45+ leaders. Its primary focus is the People Gate and the Builder/Protector Ratio should be 2-to-1."

Peter spoke up, "Oh that's why you said your B/P ratio was too high at 2.9-to-1. Right?"

"Yes, we are running a little too fast. It is a leftover from the hyper growth period that we just came out of. In some respects, Stage 7 sounds like an ultimate goal, doesn't it? But the truth is that Stage 7, while very stable, is often a bit stagnant and stuck."

> **THE BUREAUCRACY THAT FORMS AS THE COMPANY GROWS MORE COMPLEX IS DAUNTING TO THE INNOVATION OF THE COMPANY. THIS IS WHY THE INNOVATION TEAMS OR GROWTH CIRCLES ARE SO IMPORTANT.**

"The bureaucracy that forms as the company grows more complex is daunting to the innovation of the company. This is why the innovation teams or Growth Circles are so important. They keep the company percolating."

"The company in Stage 7 must find a way of reinventing itself, or it will simply lose its competitive edge. The visionary or CEO of the company must discover a way to go back to Stage 1 and recapture that entrepreneurial spirit."

"For us, this means we are willing to spin off and support new enterprises. I suppose I could sell out and start a new company myself, but I love this place. So I look for ways to keep it as vital as possible. If Ricardo comes up with a killer business plan to market the machine he's working on, and if he could show us some other products he has in mind, we'd back him in a heartbeat. You never get to just stop."

"At least there are only seven stages."

"Don't let that fool you. I'll say it again. These stages are about complexity. But you don't just wake up one day and find that you've moved from Stage 3 to Stage 4. As I mentioned before, you go through a transitional or chaotic period between each stage, and these zones of chaos are more demanding than you ever expect. And it's further complicated by the fact that the stages of growth alternate between being inwardly focused and outwardly focused."

She noticed the dazed look on Peter's face. "Hey, if it was easy, it wouldn't be fun."

"I'll keep that in mind."

She continued. "These transitions alternate back and forth between each stage just as the stages alternate between inward and outward. So why is this important? Because it gives you a way to make sense of the growing complexity of your enterprise."

"Sounds like I'm going through these stages and their transitions all at once."

"Not really, but it should give you a template to help organize the next steps your company takes. Just because you're in chaos doesn't make your task impossible. In fact, you still do have a good group of people and they'll probably respond to a clear direction."

"I hope so. Is there more?"

"Always. But let's take a brief break here. I'll get Sammy to get you a refill while you go and stretch your legs. I'll meet you back here in ten."

Peter's brain was screaming for relief. The implications from the information C.J. was sharing with him were overwhelming. He didn't need a sixth sense to tell him something extraordinary was being given him. He felt like a hound of growth hell bent on chasing down any helpful jewel of knowledge that would free him from the nightmare currently enveloping him at Bolder Solutions.

CHAPTER 12 — KEY POINTS

Stages of Growth Matrix:

Themes Stages of Growth:	Start-Up 1	Ramp-Up 2	Delegation 3	Professional 4	Integration 5	Strategic 6	Visionary 7
Total Number of Staff	1-10	11-19	20-34	35-57	58-95	96-160	161-350
Number of Managers	0	1	3-5	6-10	11-16	17-26	27-45
Number of Executives	1	1	1	2-3	4-5	6-8	9-15
Builder-Protector Ratio	4 : 1	3 : 1	1 : 1	3 : 2	2 : 1	3 : 1	2 : 1
Three Gates Focus 1st Priority	Profit People Process	Profit Process People	People Profit Process	Process Profit People	Profit People Process	People Profit Process	People Process Profit
	Stage 1	Stage 2	Stage 3	Stage 4	Stage 5	Stage 6	Stage 7
Five Primary Challenges of the Company	Cash Flow	Hiring Quality People	Staff Buy In	Weak Project Mgmt	Improve Sales	Staff Buy In	Products Not Differentiated
	Destabilized by Chaos	Improve Sales	Leadership/Staff Gap	Difficulty Diagnosing Problems	Difficulty Forecasting Problems	Staff Satisfaction / Profit Relationship Not Seen	Inadequate Profits
	Slow Product Development & Getting to Mkt	Cash Flow	Weak Business Design	Employee Turn Over	Cost of Lost Expertise	New Staff Orientation	Slow Getting Offering To Market
	Limited Capital to Grow	Leadership/Staff Gap	Core Values Unclear	Not Getting Systems in Place	Weak Business Design	Weak Business Design	Weak Business Design
	Improve Sales	Limited Capital to Grow	Culture Resistant to Change	Organization Uninformed About Company Growth	Staff Training	Hiring Quality Staff	Marketplace Changes Too Quickly

The 7 Stages of Entrepreneurial Growth

Ideal Business Growth
Follows the Growth Patterns in Nature:

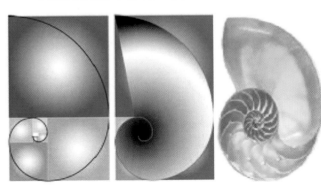

GROWTH LANGUAGE

Growth Patterns

Chapter 13

READING
THE PATTERNS

"Every business group or organization is given its character by the patterns of its behavior. The beliefs that create the patterns that spawn the behavior are often so deeply embedded into the psyche of the group that no one can see their origin"
— **Horace Bedford,** *Journal*

C.J. was ready to go for another round and Peter found himself steadying himself for a one-two punch. Instead, C.J. leaned over to Peter and spoke very softly, "Inherent in all this is a secret. The secret is that all this chaotic stuff you have to deal with is simply the chaos of life; it's just the way life works. If your company were totally static, it would be dead. All the challenges are just indicative of how alive your situation is."

C.J. smiled at Peter enigmatically but he could feel empathy from her, too.

"Let's go one step further. In each stage of growth there are three phases you move through on The Growth Curve."

C.J. stepped up to the whiteboard in her office and wrote:

Three Phases of a Stage of Growth
1. Preparation
2. Performance
3. Pressure

"First you move through a preparation phase where you are planning and preparing for the next surge of growth. During this phase you are taking the company's strategies and turning them into operational themes.

"In a healthy company the preparation phase merges into the day-to-day work and takes up about 20 percent of the time in that

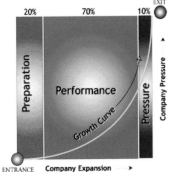

stage of growth. Then the company must execute the plan, or in other words move through a performance phase. Typically, the performance phase lasts about 70 percent of the stage of growth in a healthy company. Then, finally, you hit the pressure phase, which is unavoidable. This is when the company moves through the wind tunnel or flood zone. The pressure phase represents about 10 percent of the stage of growth."

C.J. continued as Peter took notes. "Now when a company gets sick, which I believe absolutely every company goes through once in a while, it usually is a result of too little time spent in planning. Maybe planning or preparation represents 10 percent or less of each stage of growth. They have a weak plan when they immediately go into the performance phase and as a result, hit the wall of pressure zone much sooner. Ultimately this forces the company back to revisit the planning phase and get it right."

Peter looked up from his pad. "You know, C.J., I had been working on something like this but I hadn't fleshed it out quite as well as you have. These three phases, preparation, performance and pressure, would also work well with a growing department or even in a project. If a company plans well but doesn't execute the plan, what happens in your template?"

"That's pretty serious. From my experience they would be rolling through the emergency room doors."

Peter agreed. "Yes, you couldn't do that too often before the company would be upside down or dead. So, each stage of growth has three internal parts: preparation, performance, and pressure. You make plans and preparations, then you start performing on the basis of those preparations, and then, as the old methods begin to be ineffective, you begin to experience pressure building. What is the pressure pressuring you to do? Change? Take the next step, right? Sounds like my life."

She laughed with him. "That's right, Peter, and just like life, it's never as simple as it looks on paper. The three phases of a stage of growth are affected by what's going on in the company."

"The thing to remember is that none of this is static. It changes with each stage. But it's also a way to connect the staff with what's going on as the company grows. When the staff knows that periods of chaos are natural in a growing company, they will better understand the changes when they occur."

"I guess it becomes a common denominator for relating to your staff."

"WHEN YOU ACHIEVE A COMMONALITY OF LANGUAGE, YOU ACHIEVE A COMMONALITY OF PURPOSE....A POWERFUL SYMBOL-RICH EVERYDAY LANGUAGE IS THE MEANS BY WHICH YOUR STAFF, SHORT ON THEORY AND CONCEPT, CAN BEGIN TO COMPREHEND GREAT STRATEGIES AND PUT THEM TO WORK."

"That's right! And it's why language is important. When you achieve a commonality of language, you achieve a commonality of purpose. The language helps to give the staff and the management a structure in which to communicate their understanding of what is happening in their company. It gives them a framework from which to make intelligent decisions."

"My staff has a commonality of purpose at Bolder. It's "How do we get rid of Peter?""

C.J. chuckled. "Don't be overly concerned. The point is that it's a start."

"OK, Peter. Let's get back to our discussion about language. What I am giving you is just a basic foundation for the use of growth language in a company. For thousands of years successful leaders have always used a rich symbolic language to reach through to the emotional band in which groups communicate.

"As the leader of Bolder Solutions, you have the responsibility not only to understand your staff but also to be understood. A powerful symbol-rich everyday language is the means by which your staff, short on theory and concept, can begin to comprehend great strategies and put them to work. Remember when Ricardo mentioned that the project he was working on just might produce galactic margins instead of scooter margins?"

Peter responded, "Yes, I remember. I found the language intriguing."

"Well, that was an example of how the staff participate in creating O'Connor Electronics. By exploding the imagination with a powerful symbol

as a way of describing a type of profitability, the language becomes effective. Believe me, it catches on like wildfire when the language really works."

"Remember what Horace always says, 'When the workplace becomes profit-driven, people-centered, and growth-smart, then business will have front and center stage.' In my opinion, that isn't going to happen until the staff is infused with powerful language."

C.J. straightened her back and said, "OK. If we don't get back to the basics, you and I will be eating dinner here tonight. We have gone over two of the three elements of Growth Language: The Three Gates and The 7 Stages of Growth. Now, we need to

> "EFFECTIVELY READING AND DECIPHERING THE ORGANIZATIONAL PATTERNS OF AN ENTERPRISE IS A COMPLEX ART THAT FEW PEOPLE HAVE MASTERED."

finish up with The Patterns of Growth.

"First of all, effectively reading and deciphering the organizational patterns of an enterprise is a complex art that few people have mastered. If you talk with Horace he would probably say, 'As all roads lead to Rome, all knowledge of business growth leads to growth patterns.'

"Horace is so good at reading patterns that he could quickly review your financials, roam around with your staff, and come back in under an hour knowing more about what is really going on at your company than you would ever know. By the look on your face, Peter, my wager is that Horace is still a bit of a mystery to you. Is that true?"

Peter laughed, "Actually, C.J., Horace is a strange bird, but his eccentricities belie someone who knows a helluva lot about business. Frankly, to be able to hook me up with someone like you is equally confusing. If I weren't in the middle of it, I would find all of this hard to believe. Do you know what I mean?"

"Yes, I do, Peter. The day I met Horace he was eating a bag of peanuts on the steps of my bank. I was running out in a hurry when I heard someone asking me if I 'got the loan.' I looked over and saw a well-dressed older guy, leaning back on the concrete steps with not a care in the world, picking peanut shells off his clothes. I said, "Excuse me?" All he said was that if I had better margins the loan wouldn't be necessary."

"Well, as you can imagine, I was infuriated first that he knew anything about my loan, second, that he had the audacity to think that he knew anything about my business and third, that he was right. My Irish-African American temper got the better of me and I tore into him seven ways to Sunday, but he just sat there and smiled at me, putting those damn peanut shells in his bag one shell at a time."

"To make a long story short, yes, Horace Bedford appears to be rather eccentric. In reality he is not only the most brilliant businessman I have ever met but he is also a wonderful human being. You're fortunate to have run into him."

Peter commented, "I agree, Horace has uncovered a new brand of entrepreneurial clarity that I find refreshing."

"OK, Peter, a discussion about patterns can quickly become complicated. Horace explained it to me in a way that gave me a simple foundation from which to work."

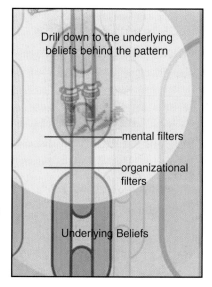

Drill down to the underlying beliefs behind the pattern

mental filters

organizational filters

Underlying Beliefs

"When you look at patterns in a company, you are seeing the result of a 'causal chain.' You need to understand that all enterprise behavior is created by patterns. The patterns are generated by the mental or organizational filters through which the staff or the entire enterprise perceives its experience. Those filters are generated by our core beliefs.

"When Horace sees a set of certain behaviors, he looks deeper and sees a pattern. By reading the patterns in a company you can quickly drill down to the underlying beliefs behind that pattern."

"When he takes one of his famous strolls through your operation with a couple of your employees, he has a way of quickly recognizing a pattern and probing its origin through to the company's filters and finally into the core beliefs of the workplace. This is why he believes that recognizing and probing the origin of patterns results in understanding the truth of how a company operates."

Peter interrupted, "So by knowing a language of core organizational patterns, it allows a person to avoid the tyranny of secondary effects and quickly probe to the real cause of those patterns?"

"Yes, almost. Knowing the patterns is a huge step, but knowing the patterns in combination with other patterns is really the key. It is not too different from reading sheet music for a symphony. After a while you can read the whole symphony on paper and hear all the parts at the same time."

"C.J., this is fascinating. I can see how this could be an extraordinarily powerful management tool. Reading the language of organi-

zational patterns sheds a new light on the process of making decisions. Why is it that I never heard of this before?"

"Peter, this is only the beginning of your education. Wait until you see what Horace has in store for you. All I can tell you is that your understanding of business growth will never be the same. You are very privileged."

C.J. continued, "To take this out of theory and into practical application you need to understand a few more key points."

"Every pattern that takes place in an enterprise has three attributes to it. For purposes of our discussion here, let's imagine that we have three vertical columns, column A, column B, and column C.

"In column A, we have Untested Patterns, Unchallenged Patterns, and Unconscious Patterns.

Enterprise Patterns Chart		
A	B	C
Untested patterns: Introduction-Skeptical-Reluctant "Unsure Zone"	Advancing Patterns: Living-Organic-Self-Organizing	Mosaic Patterns: Concentrates on Process Inward-Contributor-Generative
Unchallenged Patterns: Tested-Tacit Acceptance-Functional "Utility Zone"	Neutral Patterns: Maintenance-Stable-Supportive	Linear Patterns: A + B = C Focused on the End Result Driven-Sequential-Building
Unconscious Patterns: Total Acceptance-Automatic "DNA Zone"	Destructive Patterns: Damaging-Dead-Lifeless	Dispersion Pattern: Defaults to Distribution Outward-Permeating-Dispersal

In column B, we have Advancing Patterns, Neutral Patterns, and Destructive Patterns. In column C, we have Mosaic Patterns, Linear Patterns, and Dispersion Patterns." C.J. drew a chart on her whiteboard that explained what she was talking about.

"Each pattern of growth that you discover in your company will have one characteristic from each of the three columns. You still with me?"

"Oh, yeah." Peter was still in student-mode, furiously taking notes.

 "Let's start with column A. An Untested Pattern is something that simply hasn't been thoroughly tested by the staff of an organization. When I brought Sammy in, the company cafeteria was hit-and-miss. It was used as a meal choice of last resort. I wanted people to use the facility, to help foster communication among the staff. You know, the family that eats together eventually has to speak to each another? But it was an Untested Pattern."

"Just because I had a great idea didn't mean that everyone was going to immediately accept it. I brought the staff together and got them to agree to use the facility on a daily basis for a month, no matter what. At first there was some grumbling about being made to stay in the building, but once they got a taste of Sammy's food, they stopped complaining."

"But they were still doing it as a project, as an agreement with me. When the month came to an end, nobody left. They had passed through the Untested Pattern stage to the Unchallenged Pattern stage and they liked it. Then, as new staff were hired, no one had to tell them to eat in the cafeteria because they just did. Seven months later it's become an Unconscious Pattern for the staff. They don't think twice about having lunch in the cafeteria. It's great food at an incredible price, and they like being there. We all still leave the building for lunch occasionally, but not like before. More importantly, people are talking to each other at lunch. It gives the staff a chance to mingle with employees from different departments."

"Let's move to column B. The thing to know about these patterns is that they are Advancing, Neutral or Destructive. You are probably putting this together for yourself.

"If you get an Advancing Pattern of Growth that becomes part of the Unconscious Patterns of your company, then you have a positive force in your organization. The reverse is also true. If you have a Destructive Pattern become part of the Unconscious Patterns or the DNA of your organization, such as chronic gossip, then you have a very negative force effectively dismantling the immune system of your company.

"I think the secrecy that we work with at

O'Connor Electronics had a positive effect on the staff. In the beginning, it was viewed suspiciously, but people have gotten used to it. Now it's become a source of pride, part of what makes our work special."

Peter interrupted her. "I hadn't thought about it in those terms, but Bolder Solutions' work on the food supply project, if framed correctly, could have the same kind of effect on the staff. It should become an Unconscious Advancing Pattern."

"That's correct, Peter. Pride is always a powerful pattern if it can be instilled in a workplace community.

"Now let's move over to column C. There are three types of patterns in column C. First, there is a Mosaic Pattern, that is an inward operating pattern, like teamwork. Getting a team to address issues is a mosaic pattern."

"Second is the Linear Pattern, that is just like it sounds: you do this, then you do that, finally you get this. Much of the individual work done by the engineers is linear. They follow certain sequential steps. Our sales department processes are also lin-

ear. They use tried-and-true marketing techniques to generate leads; the sales team might throw in a couple of new ideas to heat things up, but they also follow The Seven Steps of the Sale."

"Just for contrast, if we have something being addressed by a team, then the linearity goes out the window. A team operates as a Mosaic Pattern; its nature is to be collaborative and non-linear. A strong leader can harness the team to be both a powerful mosaic agent and an effective linear agent but only when the individuals bond and come together as a working unit."

"Third is the Dispersion Pattern. Just like it sounds, it is outward in motion. A rumor hurling around the office is a Dispersion Pattern. Even reputation is a Dispersion Pattern. For example, when you arrived at Bolder Solutions, your staff had already formed an expectation; they had probably discussed what you'd be like. Then they got to know you and formed another concept, and that concept spread by dispersion."

"You have no idea."

"Sure I do. Don't forget how I came to run this company. The rumors were flying like bats in a cave. And a Dispersion Pattern is not bad by definition. It can be positive as well. Once folks started liking the cafeteria, there was a definite pattern of dispersion singing its praises. It happened on a single day, about a week after we started it. For some reason the company's collective consciousness decided to support the idea. After that it was very smooth. And obviously, there was an equal pattern of dispersion registering just how much at first they didn't want to do it."

"So I can look forward to becoming the subject of a positive pattern of dispersion just as soon as they think I know what I'm doing?"

"Yep. And the sooner the better."

Peter smiled at C.J.'s honesty. "I'm deeply cheered by that news."

"I thought you would be. Maybe this will cheer you up; the patterns we're talking about will give you a way to sight your company."

"What do you mean?"

"As you so astutely mentioned, most business leaders flounder in the world of secondary effects. Let's see if I can make this clear. This is one of Horace's final exam questions: When the original cause of a problem has been clouded by the secondary effect which was produced by the primary effect acting as a cause, then you have the conditions for poor business decisions."

"So what you are saying, C.J., is that domino B gets hit by domino A and subsequently domino B knocks down domino C. When we try to determine

the cause of domino C falling, we stop our investigation when we discover domino B. What we should do is look further and see that Domino A is what started the chain reaction. Thus we are caught in the tyranny of the secondary effect. Right?"

"Not bad. It's a bit more complicated than that, but you have the simple version down. The final conclusion is that most people don't understand what is causing the trauma and problems in their company because they don't know how to recognize and read the patterns correctly. If you understand the patterns, you can get an accurate read on what's really going on. You can get a clear sighting of your company."

They were silent for a moment.

C.J. looked over at Peter and said, "Had enough?"

Peter tried to remember all that had been said. "OK, C.J., let me give you a quick review. The 3 Gates: Revenue/Profit, People, and Process Gates. Those are the three common denominators of language in the workplace, the common baseline for anyone in a company to speak about the challenges and victories met on a day-to-day basis.

"The 7 Stages of Growth: There are numerous stages, demanding and relentless, in their unique requirements of the CEO and staff of a company. My company is trying to behave like a smaller, less-complicated company than it truly is. And that's confusing because each stage has its own set of rules, so we might be playing by the wrong ones."

"Then there are transitional zones, chaos zones, which you said are inevitable. Wind Tunnels and …what?"

"Flood Zones. You're doing pretty well."

"Flood Zones. Chaos might be a good thing."

"And then there are the Mosaic, Dispersion, Conscious, and Unconscious Patterns. I'm glad I took notes."

> " MOST PEOPLE DON'T UNDERSTAND WHAT IS CAUSING THE TRAUMA AND PROBLEMS IN THEIR COMPANY BECAUSE THEY DON'T KNOW HOW TO RECOGNIZE AND READ THE PATTERNS CORRECTLY. "

C.J. nodded. "It is a new language and it will take awhile to digest all that we talked about today. You can always go back to the basics. Growth language is nothing more than gates, stages, and patterns."

"That last thought was simple enough. Thanks, C.J., for the illuminating afternoon."

C.J. leaned over and handed Peter a sheet of paper. "Here is a list of words I put together for you. You can use these words to infuse your company with a more powerful language base. I am reminded that the true portal of change is the effective use of language. The leader who intentionally uses language to transform the thinking throughout his company is light years ahead of the herd. Good luck, Peter. I'm sure that we will be running into each other some time soon. You can bet on it if Horace has anything to say about it."

The drive back to Bolder Solutions, his non-disclosure agreement folded neatly on the seat, was filled with a replay of the information Peter had been given. What was he supposed to do with it? It seemed that he had a nearly impossible task in front of him, but for some reason, he was cheered by C. J.'s comment that it was just life. He could deal with life. He had been dealing with it all along. Maybe he could deal with bringing his brother's company back from the brink.

Then, as he turned into his parking lot, he saw the police cars.

CHAPTER 13 — KEY POINTS

Three Phases of the Stages of Growth:

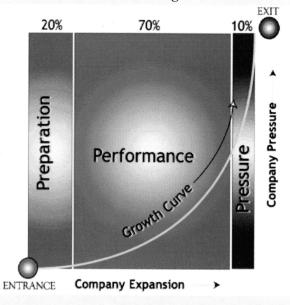

Patterns:

Enterprise Patterns Chart		
A	B	C
Untested patterns: Introduction-Skeptical-Reluctant "Unsure Zone"	Advancing Patterns: Living-Organic-Self-Organizing	Mosaic Patterns: Concentrates on Process Inward-Contributor-Generative
Unchallenged Patterns: Tested-Tacit Acceptance- Functional "Utility Zone"	Neutral Patterns: Maintenance-Stable-Supportive	Linear Patterns: A + B = C Focused on the End Result Driven-Sequential-Building
Unconscious Patterns: Total Acceptance-Automatic "DNA Zone"	Destructive Patterns: Damaging-Dead-Lifeless	Dispersion Pattern: Defaults to Distribution Outward-Permeating-Dispersal

The Profit Design process should be a disciplined exercise at breaking down and identifying all the forces contributing to a leader's confusion.

It should organize them in such a way that their world holds a greater degree of clarity for predicting what is coming around the corner, understanding when and where they need to adapt, and getting a line-of-sight determination of what needs to be focused on now in order to bring their company to a higher level of performance.

A Profit Design Map is always a result of one leader's rewired seeing, thinking, and communicating about the many layers of his/her business in order to intentionally lead it to its visionary outcome.
Milo Tangle, University Lecture, October 18, 2004

Notes to myself:
We are tasked to reveal the origin of what is causing CEO's challenges. As a CEO, I want to know how I can originate and unleash new forces in my business to create a more advancing, dynamic outcome. Business leaders immersed in chaos are trapped. They are stuck in varying degrees of scattered thinking that motivates them to want a greater degree of clarity.

§ <u>Voltage</u> is best measured by the quiet enthusiasm and pride that is evidenced by an employee's <u>intensity</u> and the <u>precision</u> of their focus in the work community.
- Intensity without precision is a formula for disaster.
- Precision without intensity is a slow train to nowhere.

"THERE WERE FIVE SQUAD CARS, TWO POLICE SEDANS, A BOMB SQUAD TRUCK, AND A PARAMEDIC UNIT PARKED OUTSIDE BOLDER SOLUTIONS."

Chapter 14

UNDER THE SURFACE

"If we let our people flourish and grow, unleash people to be self-confident and take on more responsibility, if we use the best ideas that they come up with, then we will have a chance to win. The idea of liberation and empowerment for our work force is not enlightenment, it's a competitive necessity."
— **Jack Welch, Ex-CEO of General Electric**

There were five squad cars, two police sedans, a bomb squad truck, and a paramedic unit parked outside Bolder Solutions. Peter tried to keep a lid on his imagination as he raced into a parking space near the building. His heart stopped when he caught sight of a figure lying deadly still in the paramedic truck. What the hell could have happened?

He walked faster toward the group of officers clustered near the front door. Kate was talking rapidly to them and waving her arms. She spotted Peter and pointed at him, and then a highly agitated Detective Carnes stormed straight toward him. She clearly had something to say but before she could speak, Kate blurted out, "Where have you been?"

Not one to miss a chance, Jane said, "I was going to ask you the same thing, just not as politely."

"Could someone tell me what's going on here? What happened to the front door? It's blown to bits!"

Kate said, "I walked up to the front of the office just in time to see this…this lunatic punching out the glass in the front door with his fists. See all the blood? He was screaming something about how we were criminals, and how we were poisoning the environment, and that he was going to stop us. Then he drags in this big box and says he's gonna blow us up! And before anybody could say anything, he pushed a button on the box and it…it blew up! The box blows up and sprays something all over the front entry and into the back room. Guess what it was?"

> **THIS LUNATIC WAS SCREAMING SOMETHING ABOUT HOW WE WERE CRIMINALS, AND HOW WE WERE POISONING THE ENVIRONMENT.…**

Peter was too stunned to register that she was expecting him to respond, but she couldn't contain herself.

"It was seeds! Can you imagine? Seeds! Look at my hands. See all those spots? I put my hands up in front of my face or my face would look like this. See?"

"Seeds?" was all Peter could say.

Jane came to his rescue. "Mr. Logan, could I have a word with you? Inside?"

The inside of the front lobby was a mess. Seeds. There were seeds everywhere. Police technicians were poring over every inch of the room. Peter followed Jane and another detective back to his office.

Jane was full into police mode. "Where were you? Don't you have a cell phone?"

"Am I missing something? Are you asking me my whereabouts, like I'm somehow involved in this? Come on, even you said I was cleared!"

She didn't even blink. "Answer the question."

"Whoa! Back off, Detective Carnes."

A moment passed, she took a breath, and tried a different tack. "No one has been able to reach you for almost three hours."

Peter sighed. "You want to know where I was? Okay. I drove to Boulder City Park, stopped there for about forty-five minutes and then I went to O'Connor Electronics, a company over by Boulder Municipal Airport. I was there until I came back here. My cell phone probably did not work at O'Connor."

She stared hard at Peter. "Look, I appreciate you are trying to run a business, but this isn't just a weird little crime. We know the guy who did this. He's never been affiliated with any environmental group of any kind. He's not bright enough to tie his shoes, much less figure out how to make an explosive device to blow seeds around your office. That means he's bait. After the thing went off, he spent a few minutes trashing the office and then he seemed to get disoriented and collapsed. He claims he doesn't remember doing it. He also doesn't remember the last few days. I believe him, Peter. We're going to do blood work on him, and I suspect we'll find drugs in his system that can't be bought on the street."

> **WE KNOW THE GUY WHO DID THIS. HE'S NOT BRIGHT ENOUGH TO TIE HIS SHOES, MUCH LESS FIGURE OUT HOW TO MAKE AN EXPLOSIVE DEVICE.**

Peter couldn't take his eyes off her as he was listening to her analysis. He realized that she was suggesting something very sinister. Jane's partner was paged and left them to answer the call.

"Peter, your brother appears to have been murdered and the case is unresolved. Your company has managed to stay in business without him, and now this happens. I think this is a form of terrorism. And I think it could get worse. You have to decide how much you agree with me, and what you want to do about it."

Peter felt his irritation giving way to intense anger. "Santomo!"

"Santomo. They're at the top of my list. They have remarkable resources, but we have no way of tying them to this situation." Jane looked toward where her partner had gone and said, "Well, as long as you're OK. I guess that's all we need here."

Jane's partner tapped on the door. "Jane, you need to hear this. We just got a call from the paramedics. Our guy died. They don't know what happened yet; we'll have to wait for the coroner to figure it out."

Peter felt as if he'd been punched in the stomach. It was like reading about Alan's death in a Los Angeles paper all over again. Was Santomo intent on destroying the work of his company?

Jane was back to business. "Peter, I'll speak to you later. I don't hold out a lot of hope, but we have to try to piece together what our seed bomber's last few days involved." And with that she was gone.

Peter was left alone in his office – his dead brother's office – deciding what to do next. He knew he had to tell the staff. They needed to know what he and the police were thinking about why all this was happening. The only question was whether he should do it today or tomorrow.

The bomb, as the staff dramatically referred to it, was quickly becoming a matter of pride with the staff at Bolder Solutions. Peter thought about sending everyone home, but decided against it and instead asked Dean to call a meeting for 4:30 p.m.

Work, Peter decided, was exactly what he needed. His hands were shaking and he knew he needed to get his mind on something else. He got lost in the month-end sales report while waiting for the meeting, so when Dean tapped on his door at 4:31 and said, "Hey, boss, they're all here," he was taken by surprise.

Everyone was waiting for him to start the meeting. Something had happened. Whoever had orchestrated the stupid seed bomb had underestimated these people. They were alert, energetic, and focused. He could feel it in the air. The bomb had

> **THERE IS EVERY REASON TO BELIEVE THAT WHAT HAPPENED THIS MORNING WAS AN ATTEMPT TO FRIGHTEN US AWAY FROM FINISHING THE PROJECT WE'RE WORKING ON. IT WAS ESSENTIALLY A TERRORIST ACT.**

unleashed their emotions and more importantly, an intensity of focus he hadn't seen before.

"The police asked me several days ago to keep certain information quiet, meaning that I shouldn't tell you. I think the police are wrong. You deserve to know everything that's happening. There is every reason to believe that what happened this morning was an attempt to frighten us away from finishing the project we're working on. It was essentially a terrorist act."

He told them the whole story, including what the police had concluded about Alan's death, his own experience with Santomo, and the death of the seed bomber.

"All that remains now is for each of you to decide if you want to continue here. As you all may know, this is very important work that we are doing, but there is also potential danger. It would be helpful if you would make your decision whether to stay or leave by tomorrow so that we can tighten up the team of folks remaining."

No one said a word. Peter scanned the group and was concerned that he may have frightened them.

> " HOW DARE THEY TRY TO INTIMIDATE US? I SAY WE PUT A SIGN IN THE WINDOW THAT SAYS 'SCREW SANTOMO.' "

While he was trying to think of what to say next, a small voice in back said something barely audible.

Peter spoke up, "I'm sorry, what did you say?"

It was Carla Williams, a soft-spoken, forty-something bookkeeper who, to the best of Peter's knowledge, had never said a word. "I said, bastards. How dare they try to intimidate us? I say we put a sign in the window that says 'Screw Santomo.' Boss, I'm not going anywhere."

Of all the people he expected to speak out, Carla was not among them. She had hit a nerve. Everyone started speaking at once. It was clear they were becoming even more united by what was going on.

Then Dean Baldridge stood up. "I think I can speak for everybody here, Boss. This makes us furious. They aren't stopping us, whoever 'they' are! Nothing is going to keep us from getting this company healthy and finishing that software for Heritage's project." Every head was nodding vigorously in agreement.

There was a moment of silence in the room. It took Peter a moment to understand that he was being included in the "us" that the staff was speaking about. When it hit him, he was surprised by how much he was moved. He had to take a second to make sure he was in control.

"Well, thank you all. This means we have to be very attentive to every rhythm of this place, and we have to watch out for each other. We have no idea what these idiots will do next, but we need to assume they'll try something. I want all of you who work here late at night to only work in teams. Please only come here in teams and leave here in teams. No one should be working alone, ever. Is that understood?"

Everyone nodded.

It was Dean Baldridge who finished the meeting. "I think they've underestimated us. Anything else, Boss?"

Still a little unsure of his emotions, Peter just shook his head. So Dean turned to the staff as though they were suiting up for the big game and said, "That's it, folks. Nine o'clock sharp tomorrow. Let's kick their butts!"

And the staff applauded. Peter was shocked. He hadn't seen this much *voltage* since he arrived at Bolder Solutions three weeks ago. He knew he still had a long climb ahead of him, but this certainly was a start.

He needed to start introducing the material Horace and C.J. gave him to help get the company back on track. At least now, the staff accepted him and he didn't have to fight the legacy of his brother's image anymore.

The last one out was Jimmy Valentine. "See you tomorrow, Boss."

And that was that. He knew with that simple nickname, they were telling him that he had been accepted. He was now Boss. He wasn't the boss. He was just Boss. He was part of the company growth language. It couldn't have sounded sweeter. Whatever Santomo had in mind had just backfired.

For the next couple of hours Peter sat in his office, reviewing the day and what he had learned. The notes he had taken from Horace's discussion about growth and what he had learned from C. J. about language gave him a glimpse of the task that still lay before him. And he agreed that language was a prime place to start. It was extraordinary that two new words had entered the company lexicon: Boss and *voltage*. Because of the cohesiveness generated by the bomb incident, he knew he had a chance to let the language begin to grow on its own.

He wanted the employees to begin building a new language of growth for their company. He could give them suggestions and directions, and then let them take off. They were highly motivated now, and he had to trust them. He couldn't push it, but he could feed the need for it.

It occurred to him to call Elijah Brown and let him know what was going on. He had hoped to give a quick recap of the event and go home, but Elijah wouldn't let him get far into the story. He insisted that Peter come to his house right away to tell him all about it.

Peter stood on Elijah's front porch, listening to the tones of the doorbell fade inside the large house. As the door swung open, Peter was treated to the sight of a man who looked a good deal like he sounded, James Earl Jones. He was smaller than

> **HAVE YOU HAD YOUR OFFICE CHECKED FOR ELECTRONIC LISTENING DEVICES AND PHONE TAPS?**

the screen actor, but he had a salt-and-pepper beard, mischievous eyes, and a broad smile.

"Have you had your office swept?" It was a strange way to greet a visitor, but those were the first words out of Elijah's mouth.

"I beg your pardon. Swept? You mean cleaned?"

"No, Peter, I mean checked for electronic listening devices and phone taps."

"Uh, no. I never even thought about it."

"Think about it. Tell me about what happened today."

After listening intently to the story, Elijah shook his head. "Whether this is Santomo or not, and we have to assume it is, they are clearly out to impede your progress. If they could engineer your brother's death and then get some poor homeless guy to bring a bomb, even a prank bomb, into your office, then you have to assume they will do anything to stop you. Have your office checked tomorrow. If you need a name, let me know. Your computer guys

may know someone. Don't let your staff do it; make sure you use a professional."

Peter felt his roller-coaster day heading down a big hill once again. "This just keeps getting better and better."

Elijah chuckled at him. "You just have to stay on your toes. Things are likely to start moving a lot faster."

He was just a few minutes from home when he remembered he had no food in his house. He stopped at the Pretty Good Grocery to buy the staples, milk, cereal, Pop Tarts, a loaf of bread, and peanut butter.

The checker held a clipboard with a blue marker tied to its handle by a bungee cord. She was answering a question for her cohort at the next checkstand, writing on the clipboard with the blue marker, and sorting Peter's meager groceries all at the same time. She lost her grip and the blue marker flew from her hand, striking the loaf of bread.

She picked up the bread and looked at the blue mark. "Oh, look! It's a face. I couldn't draw that well if I tried."

She laughed as she gave him change. "You have a good night, you hear?"

As he drove to his house, he knew that the day had changed everything. He just wondered where it would lead.

The next morning, Peter awoke on the couch where he had fallen asleep in his clothes the night before. On his way to the shower, he walked through the kitchen and saw the smiley face on the bread wrapper. He knew he didn't have time to make toast and still make it to the office on time.

He was preoccupied with thoughts of the bomb, Santomo, and Jane, so he didn't notice how full the parking lot was. But as he walked into the office he realized everyone was already at his or her desk. Not only that, they were at work! There was a subtle buzz in the air. There was excitement. They were still riding the emotional high of the previous day.

Good!

He walked back to the wizards' corner and found Dean Baldridge looking so intently at his computer monitor that Peter hated to disturb him. "Dean, I need to interrupt you for a moment."

"Sure, Boss, what can I do for you?"

Boss? Amazing!

He dropped his voice and asked, "Do you know anyone who does electronic sweeping? You know, bugs, phone taps?"

Dean whispered back, "That's weird, man. I've been thinking about that, but I thought I was being paranoid. Yeah, I know a guy who's probably as cutting-edge as there is in that area and he'll come over here for free. He's a friend."

"Give him a call. See if he can come now."

"Cool."

As Peter walked back to his office, he wondered if he was being watched through a camera hidden in a light bulb or listened to through a microphone hidden in a toy placed on somebody's desk. Or both. Still, no time to worry about bugging; he had an action list as long as his arm and a company out there making things happen.

> Growth curve
> Growth trauma
> Voltage
> 7 Stages of Growth
> Galactic Margins
> Bulldozer Margins
> Scooter Margins
> Wind Tunnels
> Flood Zones
> Builder/Protector Ratio
> Workplace Community

Peter made a list of words that he thought might be helpful to infuse into the company's vocabulary. He decided on a few of Horace's terms: growth curve, growth trauma, and *voltage*. The staff would be able to relate to those words.

He knew it was important for everyone to understand the stages of growth, so he wrote them down.

Then he added a few words that would help the staff to get more focused on the profitability of the company: galactic margins, bulldozer margins, and scooter margins. He also knew that while explaining the 7 Stages of Growth he should mention the inevitable chaos zones: Wind Tunnels and Flood Zones. Then he added Builder/Protector Ratio and Workplace Community. This could be the most important part. His company needed to become its own self-organized workplace community: a cohesive beehive where ideas and solutions flowed from the bottom up, where people were responsible,

> " TURNING THIS PLACE AROUND AND GROWING IT FROM THE BOTTOM UP IS GOING TO REQUIRE OUR STAFF TO HAVE BETTER WAYS OF UNDERSTANDING HOW THE BUSINESS WORKS AND HOW TO TALK ABOUT IT THROUGHOUT THE COMPANY. "

focused, accountable, and where pride in the work and in the company resonated throughout the lives of all who worked there.

It was ironic that the crazed stunt of the day would actually make this task easier. In fact, the concept and the reality of the *voltage* of the company would be much easier to describe and understand because of it. As a result of the misguided seed bomb, the energy and the *voltage* of Bolder Solutions leaped to a new high.

He had just finished the list when Dean tapped on his door.

"Hey, Boss. My friend Chang is on his way. When he heard we'd been bombed, he couldn't wait. I didn't tell him we just got dusted with a bunch of seeds."

"Thank you, Dean. Now I have one more thing to ask of you." Peter gave him the list. "I'd like you to give this list of words to the circles that have formed and ask people to talk about them. I have included a brief definition of each phrase to help get them started. Dean, turning this place around and growing it from the bottom up is going to require our staff to have better ways of understanding how the business works and how to talk about it throughout the company.

"Our staff need to talk about these words and what they mean, or can mean, to us as a company. And I'd like to know if they come up with other words. It's not so much that they must start using these particular words, but that we find a language here at Bolder that builds us up and protects us in the long run. What do you think?"

Baldridge looked at the list for a moment. "So by injecting new vocabulary around here, it will help the staff understand and talk about the business more effectively?"

"Yes, Dean, it will."

"Well, I've got to tell you, boss, this is a pretty different approach to running a business. I am not an expert but it certainly makes sense. Getting everybody onboard to share the load. That's very cool! I know that if we can get the work-place community here at Bolder Solutions to work like a team, we'll see some big changes in the staff's satisfaction." He smiled darkly. "Although, now, we may have to add bug, phone tap, and sweep to our growth language." He was enjoying the James Bond intrigue. "I'll get everybody on it, Boss."

And he was gone. Peter still hadn't figured him out yet, but he was starting to like Dean Baldridge.

For an hour he pored over month-end financial reports and came to the conclusion that, while the company was OK at the moment, he needed to start addressing the long-term profit and cash-flow situations. The window for getting the software completed was narrowing. As with any innovation, some other firm or organization could fill the need sooner, leaving both Bolder Solutions and Elijah's enterprise in the dust. On top of all of this, Bolder Solutions wouldn't be able to sustain itself if its only contract for the software was Elijah Brown. They needed to sell it to their existing clients, as well as to others out in the marketplace.

He didn't hear his door open and looked up to find a tall, intense, young Asian man standing in front of him, with a duffel bag in his hand. "I am

> **"HE STOPPED AND HELD A FINGER TO HIS LIPS, INDICATING THAT PETER SHOULD BE QUIET, AND POINTED TO A SMALL DISK DANGLING FROM THE RECEIVER."**

Chang." He must have assumed that was enough explanation because he picked up Peter's phone and had it in pieces in seconds. He stopped and held a finger to his lips, indicating that Peter should be quiet, and pointed to a small disk dangling from the receiver. Then he pointed to a small device that was tucked inside the phone itself. He quickly and quietly reassembled the phone, and then started looking around the office, pointing different devices into potential hiding places. After a moment he beckoned Peter out into the lobby.

When they arrived at the now boarded-up front door, Dean spoke in hushed tones, "So what'd you find, Chang?"

Chang looked pensive. "This is cutting-edge, high-tech stuff. It makes me wonder what else they're doing to you." He looked at Peter. "Your office seems clean now, but I'll need to sweep it again with some equipment I didn't bring."

Peter's skin crawled as he realized the enormity of the situation. He needed to talk to Jane. This was really getting out of hand. And he probably should talk to Elijah again.

"Let me make a few calls."

Chang wouldn't budge. "No! I mean that's the point. Make the calls, but be very aware that they will know to whom you're talking and what you're saying. Anyone you talk to could be in danger. But you could turn this to your advantage by giving out disinformation."

"Cool," said Dean, still enjoying the spy game activities.

"I'm not sure just how cool it is, Dean. How are we supposed to conduct business?"

"I can give you a few clean lines and make sure they are out of range of the bugs. Look, whoever is listening will figure it out in a day or two. But until they do, you might be able to make use of their lack of knowledge."

"Great. I need to consult a few people but I can't call them from here. Can I use my cell phone?"

"Let me see it."

Again, in a matter of seconds, Chang had dismantled the phone and reassembled it. "It's clean, but they could be listening anyway. They can capture the signal. Here, use my phone."

After tying up a few more loose ends, Peter drove back to the park to see Horace and gave him a recap of the seed bomb incident, as well as a recap from his meeting with C. J. O'Connor. He also shared how he'd begun to get the subject of language into the growth circles at his company.

Horace nodded, saying, "That's very good, Peter. As you go along, I think you'll discover many more powerful words that you and your staff will begin to use in the everyday language of the company. And on that subject, I want you to meet a couple of people today. Can you be away from your office for a few more hours?"

"Yeah, I'll just keep my phone turned on and I'll

> PETER, I WANT TO REMIND YOU THAT THE PROBLEMS AND ISSUES PULLING AT YOUR ATTENTION ARE SIMPLY SYMPTOMS OF SOMETHING ELSE, SOMETHING HIDDEN FROM YOUR CURRENT VIEW.... THE RESULT IS THAT WE ARE CONTINUALLY REACTING AND SOLVING THE ISSUES OF THE DAY BUT RARELY DO WE DIG DEEP ENOUGH TO UPROOT THE CAUSES TO THOSE PROBLEMS. WE ARE CONSTANTLY THE SLAVE TO THE EFFECTS OF HIDDEN CAUSES.

check in with them. I spent some time this morning looking at our future in terms of the money we're making and the money we'll need to be making. I can see that my attention can be taken away from business for just so long. I guess what I'm saying is that the quicker we can move through these steps you've been talking about, the better."

"Peter, I want to remind you that the problems and issues pulling at your attention are simply symptoms of something else, something hidden from your current view. There is always a deeper origin to our challenges and problems than we ever take the time to discover. The result is that we are continually reacting and solving the issues of the day, but rarely do we dig deep enough to uproot the causes to those problems. We are constantly the slave to the effects of hidden causes."

Now, it is time that you to get into two new areas: The New Profit Model and staff satisfaction. Sounds like you're already considering the profit issue, and we know you've been looking at staff satisfaction."

"Who do I talk to first?"

"I want you to meet an old friend of mine who's a professor at the university. He can squeeze you in between classes today. Then you'll visit a company that's carving out a niche in the computer hardware world. Both of these folks are first-class. Pay attention to them."

"If they are even remotely like C. J., that won't be difficult. She's hard to ignore."

"Yes, I do like C. J. You'd better get going. The professor doesn't have a lot of time."

Horace handed him a piece of paper with two hastily scrawled names, addresses, and directions. Peter headed off for Day Two of what he was beginning to regard as the Bedford Academy.

PROFIT
MODEL

PROFIT
DESIGN

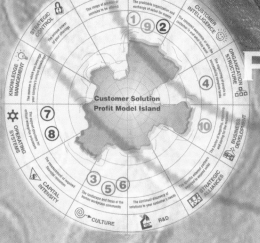

PROFIT
NET

Customer Solution
Profit Model Island

SCOPE

VALUE EXCHANGE

STRATEGIC CONTROL

The value driver of your strategy

The range of product or services to be offered

The probable organization and exchange of value for money

CUSTOMER INTELLIGENCE

The relative awareness of who the customer is and what they are

KNOWLEDGE MANAGEMENT

ORGANIZATION DESIGN

The appropriate adaptation to its internal operations tasks

OPERATING SYSTEMS

BUSINESS DEVELOPMENT

CAPITAL INTENSITY

The management of invested financial resources

STRATEGIC ALLIANCES

CULTURE

The continual discovery of solutions to your customer's needs

R&D

CUSTOMER
MIGRATION

Chapter 15
THE NEW PROFIT MODEL

"In the past decade and a half, hundreds of billions of dollars of market value have migrated from old business designs to new. The highest valuations now go to those who have the most effective business design."
— **Skywotzky and Morrison,** *Profit Patterns*

Four years at the University of Colorado had been the crucible that transformed Peter Logan forever. He entered freshman year an uninspired party animal and graduated a reflective, and at times brilliant, young economist.

Now, staring across Broadway to the front of the campus, Peter felt the red sandstone buildings were his intellectual Flatirons. They were the place where his psyche was uprooted and his curiosity finally awakened. It was uncanny that once again he was stepping onto the campus, many years later, possibly, in some small way, to be transformed again.

It had been years since he'd last walked into the Economics School building. It was the "E-school." That had been his world: the B-school and E-school. Now there was a new meaning to the term e-school.

Climbing the wide wooden stairs to the second story, he found the Professor's office far down a dimly lit hall. He knocked on the door and heard what sounded like a voice from the inside. He took it as a response and carefully opened the door.

"Close the door, will you?" A voice boomed from somewhere inside as a propeller-driven model airplane whizzed by his head and smacked into the wall.

Peter picked it up, turned to find its sender, and got his first real look at the office. The round bright lights hanging down from the 12-foot ceilings were a reminder of the building's 1930s architecture. The room was the size of a small classroom, with bookshelves sticking out from the walls like stacks in a library.

The place was strewn with dozens of books on nearly every flat surface in the room. This guy liked to read. And there were toys everywhere. Mechanical devices that did who knew what – classic examples of Rube Goldberg machines that looked truly complicated and performed some single useless task.

Peter still didn't see anyone else in the room. "Hello, I'm looking for Professor Tangle." In fact, Peter hadn't really registered the name on the slip of paper until just that moment. Milo Tangle.

From behind the last bookshelf, a wild mass of graying hair emerged. "I'm Milo Tangle. You must be Peter. You're right on time. For an economics professor, that's as good as the Holy Grail."

It was Albert Einstein. Or rather it was a romanticized movie version of Albert Einstein.

"I know. I look like Einstein. Too bad I'm not as smart. Can I have my plane back?"

Peter shut his mouth, which he discovered too late was hanging open. Then he said, "Sure." He handed over the model airplane.

"I keep trying to see if I can get it to make the turn from the bookshelves and bank away from the door. No luck so far. You're a friend of Horace's, right?"

"Yes, I guess I am."

"He told me about you. You sure have your hands full, young man. Glad those Wild West days are over for me. A tenured position at the University has its advantages. Not many folks bother me up here. Have a seat. And call me Milo."

Milo Tangle smiled as he said this, without a trace of irony. In fact, the office had no available chair. Everything was covered with books or toys or both.

"Just push the books onto the floor. It's what my students do. Here, use this chair over here with the rollers on it."

"How long have you been here?"

"I was teaching when you were finishing up. I checked your records. I can do that, you know. We just never knew each other. And I didn't look quite so much like the father of relativity until my hair started going gray and I got tired of cutting it. I came here from private industry." He laughed at himself. "I sound like a politician. Anyway, I had a company that manufactured modular homes."

"What made you give it up?"

Milo was suddenly still and looked intently at Peter. "The company was hugely successful and I sold it for enough money to buy a small country. Well, enough that I can afford to do what I love, which is teach."

> **THE COMPANY WAS HUGELY SUCCESSFUL AND I SOLD IT FOR ENOUGH MONEY TO BUY A SMALL COUNTRY.**

"Oh." Peter wondered what this wild man's classes were like. "Horace said you were going to tell me about profit models."

"That's right. Have you worked out a profit model for your company?"

Peter was shocked at how quickly Milo threw him on the defensive.

"I'm still scrambling to find out who is on base over there."

Milo pointed a long finger at him and said, "That's not an answer."

In a flash, Peter knew what it was like to be in Milo's classes. It made him smile. "You're right. But after meeting some of Horace's friends, I guess I take it as a loaded question. I probably don't have a profit model in the context you mean, but I have given it some thought. My model is pretty simple: sell as much as we can and make as much money as we can. I think my brother operated on the same principle."

"Nice try, but no cigar, Peter. Just as I thought. Most businesses have the same model. They try to

drive up their volume, drive down their costs and hope there is something left over when all is said and done. In almost every case this approach is, at best, short-sighted."

"Short-sighted?" Now he really knew what it was like to be in Milo's classes, and this time he didn't smile.

"Yes, short-sighted." Milo was on his feet. From behind a bookshelf he dragged out a large whiteboard on wheels. "Are you offended? Good. In truth, most companies don't have an actual profit model. They think that they do, but they're mistaken. They might have a business plan but they don't have a profit model. They're simply trying to survive while working on the next campaign or a new product that will pull them into better profitability."

> **YOUNG ENTREPRENEURS, OR EVEN OLD ENTREPRENEURS, KNOW THAT THEY WANT TO MAKE MORE MONEY, BUT TO DESIGN AN EFFECTIVE PATH THAT QUANTIFIES THEIR PROFIT MAKING DESIRES IS QUITE ANOTHER THING.**

"So when I talk to young entrepreneurs, or even old entrepreneurs, there is confusion about what it takes to make sustainable, advancing profits. They know that they want to make more money, but to design an effective path that quantifies their profit-making desires is quite another thing. No one wants to get out of the Problem Solving Approach long enough to get an idea, an intentional idea, of how they are going to grow something wildly successful. Did you realize that only 12 – 13 percent of all companies are actually able to create and sustain consistent profits over a ten-year period? I find that shocking. How about you?"

"Hold it, Milo! You've just said that it's short-sighted to focus on profit. Which is it?"

"Peter, what is short-sighted is the fact that most companies' profit models are lacking the serious consideration necessary to be consistently profitable. Thinking about expanding volume and lowering costs doesn't even get you in the door of the consistent profit performers. Anyone can have a profitable year or two but can they do it year after year after year? My research says that it is rare.

" YOU NEED A SHIFT IN YOUR THINKING AND TO OPEN THAT BRAIN OF YOURS. I HAVE TO SWING YOU OUT OF THAT ENTREPRENEURIAL PROBLEM-SOLVING MINDSET TO A DYNAMIC PROFIT-MODELING PERSPECTIVE. "

"A profitable business model doesn't sit packed away on some bookshelf after everyone of importance has read it once. It is a dynamic tool constantly being worked and adjusted that considers the critical elements necessary to both the short-

and long-term success of the company. Its designers are always ready to go into redesign mode often sooner than necessary."

"Peter, the truth is that the success of any enterprise, yours included, is measured by:

- **The money you make**
- **The money you keep**
- **The value growth of the company stock**

Peter looked at Milo and said, "This seems simple enough. But why do I get the feeling you are about to lead me into a foreign world flipped upside-down from the one I know?"

Milo's face lit up as he said, "Yes, it is a foreign world to most business owners. It's foreign not because it is hard to understand, but because few are truly curious enough about the mystery of profitability to expend the time to discover and decipher its truth."

Milo picked up a marker and started writing on the whiteboard.

Three Elements of the New Profit Model
1. **The Profit Design**
2. **The Profit Net**
3. **Customer Migration**

Milo continued, "These three elements comprise the sum total of what goes into a powerful profit model. What I am going to give you today ordinarily would take weeks to explain in detail. You don't need detail right now. You need a shift in your thinking and to open that brain of yours. I have to swing you out of that entrepreneurial problem-solving mindset to a dynamic profit-modeling perspective. So, I am going to take the next hour to blast open some space in your thinking."

The Profit Design

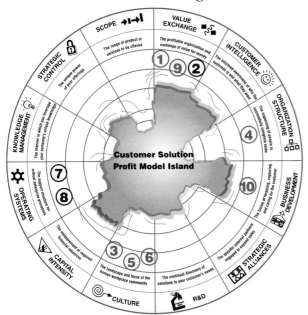

Peter was taking notes as fast as he could.

Milo watched him for a second. "What would you say goes into a profit design, what concerns should be addressed?"

The question took him by surprise, but he had always been a good student. After thinking a moment, he responded, "Well, it should start with identifying the strengths, weaknesses, opportuni-

ties, and threats. It should demonstrate income and a projection of how that will grow. It should have a breakdown of operating expenses and a projection of how those expenses will grow. It should analyze the market with a strategy for capturing more market share. I suppose that's a long way of saying how to sell more products, how to make more money selling more products, and how to increase a customer base…"

Milo finished for him, "… to sell more products." OK. That's a common view. It's not completely incorrect, but you're beginning to describe a business plan. You need to understand the difference between a profit design and a business plan."

> "A BUSINESS PLAN IS A STATIC DESCRIPTION, A SNAPSHOT IN TIME OF THE CURRENT MARKET CONDITIONS, THE OPPORTUNITIES AT HAND, AND HOW YOU PLAN TO MOVE THE BUSINESS FORWARD. A PROFIT DESIGN IS THE OPERATIVE DNA OF THE VENTURE, THE INTERCONNECTED GUTS OF THE ENTERPRISE.

"A business plan is a static description, a snapshot in time of the current market conditions, the opportunities at hand, and how you plan to move the business forward. A profit design is the operative DNA of the venture, the interconnected guts of the enterprise."

"It is the clear view of the core business, the adjacent business, and the edge business. It is the customer intelligence, the pricing, volume and costing formula, the precise analysis of how you make and keep money, the recurring revenue, the weighting and impact of critical alliances, and much more.

"The conscious design and redesign of the guts has a profound effect on the success or failure of the business plan. Is your profit design a cougar being asked to fly or an elephant being asked to swim? Is your profit design a horse, a dolphin, or an eagle?"

Peter laughed, saying, "Sounds like a John Denver business design."

Milo laughed with him. "You would be surprised, Peter. Easily over 90 percent of the entrepreneurs I have encountered never consciously created the guts of their business. They always came to view their business from the Problem Approach."

"Yes, Professor, both C.J. and Horace elucidated the difference between the Problem Approach and the Model Approach. I must say that I agree with C.J. and favor the Problem Approach."

"Yes, I suppose you do. It takes a long time to break upstarts like you and C.J. of bad thinking habits. You entrepreneurial types get so caught up in the problems of day-to-day business that you never get outside the box long enough to intentionally create and grow your business from a profit model. Damn shame."

Milo's left hand got lost in the tangle of his white hair as he continued, "No matter. We'll blow some holes in that brain of yours today. Most people probably think that they have a business design, but in actuality they have a mishmash of parts, not a model for success. The rest is caught in the history of entrepreneurial performance, with only 13 percent of all companies being consistently profitable."

Milo continued, "A profit design is the profit architecture of a company. It also is relational. You probably have seen a graphic representation of the space-time continuum. Those grids that show the curves and hills, the valleys and black holes in space, are a good way to think of a profit design. Just as space and time are affected by more than two dimensions, a profit design is affected by twelve primary components that cannot be properly represented by a linear representation."

He looked at Peter and smiled. "Still with me?"

"I think so. When one coordinate changes, it changes the relationship of all the parts and thus

> **"EASILY OVER 90 PERCENT OF THE ENTREPRENEURS I HAVE ENCOUNTERED NEVER CONSCIOUSLY CREATED A PROFIT DESIGN FOR THEIR BUSINESS."**

changes the shape of the graph."

"Peter, this is why it is important to set the profit design in place before you move on to creating a business plan."

Peter looked up from his notes and continued, "Milo, with all due respect, my experience with business plans has been that they are vehicles to raise money or to serve as an internal compass, but I have to tell you that in the companies that I have run, no sooner is the business plan created than it is outdated and shelved. The problem is that critical data in small companies change so quickly that it is difficult to use a business plan as an ongoing management tool."

Milo responded quickly, "You probably could say the same thing about budgets. Right?"

"Yes, that's right. The use of budgets in a small company is crazy because things change too quickly. You spend time working up a complex spreadsheet to represent your annual budget and in three months you have to redesign the entire thing to reflect the current strategies. Or no one takes the budget seriously. I would wager that budgets don't become important until Stage 5, when the company begins serious planning."

Milo interjected, "You're right, most small business owners/leaders don't use a budget because it is too cumbersome to work with, but you are wrong in that budgeting is a critical process even in Stage 1 companies. Peter, unless someone can figure out how to create a simple living budget template for small businesses that allows for constant morphing as the times dictate, it is unlikely that the typical business owner/leader will ever likely use a budget on a regular basis."

> **UNLESS SOMEONE CAN FIGURE OUT HOW TO CREATE A SIMPLE LIVING BUDGET TEMPLATE FOR SMALL BUSINESSES THAT ALLOWS FOR CONSTANT MORPHING AS THE TIMES DICTATE, IT IS UNLIKELY THAT THE TYPICAL BUSINESS OWNER/LEADER WILL EVER USE A BUDGET ON A REGULAR BASIS.**

Milo walked around his large wooden desk and retrieved the yardstick leaning against the wall. Before Peter realized what he was doing, Milo swung it over his head and let it slap down on the desk with a crack that made Peter jump out of his seat.

"Peter, we are getting distracted. This is exactly what happens to companies. They are constantly going off on tangents that take them off-focus. Right from their big strategic planning sessions down to running weekly meetings. There's just no focus! We were talking about profit design, so let's get back to it."

Peter realized that Horace's friends were definitely an edgy bunch. This Milo character was a time bomb waiting to go off. It must have been a treat working with him. "Milo, you've got the lead. Let's move it forward."

"Good. Horace has asked me to cover a huge amount of material. Please know this is just your first drive-by and it's meant to give you a survey of The New Profit Model."

Milo was the kind of man who could not sit or stand in any one place longer than a few moments. His mind drove his body to constantly walk/pace like a caged animal. Peter wheeled around in his chair as the professor strode around the room.

Milo folded his arms on his chest and looked straight at Peter. "Consistent growth-performing enterprises relentlessly focus on developing, improving, and leveraging their core business. They are committed to growth as their primary strategy. Not only do these enterprises have a direct bead on their core business, but also they are capable of fusing together winning corporate strategies with the development and maintenance of organizational capacity."

"A good profit design is made up of twelve components. These components are the critical factors that define the profit design as a working management tool. Notice that I said working management tool. I consider these 12 factors so critical that I refer to them in a phrase I borrowed from the space program: mission-critical factors. And despite the importance of attending to these points, most companies can only think of two, if they're lucky." He wrote on the board:

12 Profit Design Components

1. Business Development
2. Value Exchange
3. Strategic Control
4. Scope of the Enterprise
5. Culture
6. Knowledge Management
7. Organizational Structure
8. Customer Intelligence
9. Strategic Alliances
10. Operating Systems
11. Research & Development
12. Capital Intensity

"Let's start with **Business Development.** For every revenue group in your company, you need to clearly define your methods for targeting, capturing, and caring for the customer. In the average company, this concept would encompass the separate worlds of marketing, sales, and customer service. I want you to consider these three elements of Business Development tightly integrated together. It's a revelation to see that they are all connected and should be considered as one theme instead of three different departments."

> **"A COMPANY IS NEVER TOO SMALL TO ORGANIZE THEIR THINKING AND PLANNING AROUND REVENUE GROUPS."**

Peter stopped him. "I've never seen the three as one area. Frankly, the lack of communication that happens between marketing and sales is frightening. Also, I haven't been considering revenue groups because I thought my company was too small to think about them. But now that you mention it, I can see how a company is never too small to organize their thinking and planning around revenue groups."

Milo then said, "If all you do is sell one kind of product to one kind of customer, then maybe that will serve you. But as you grow and as you find new markets, you'll be better served to understand your current and proposed customer base in terms of various revenue groups. Just about every consideration in the profit design process comes back and aligns itself with the revenue groups in one form or another. The profit design allows you to ultimately measure the value each revenue group brings to the table. It allows you to make those critical decisions from an informed position about whether or not to 'hold 'em or fold 'em, as the country-western song says."

Peter said, "OK. That makes sense."

Milo turned back to the board. **"Value exchange.** This is how you make money, how you exchange or derive value for the services or products you are providing. This is the most important component of Profit Design. Many CEOs believe they have this all wrapped up and thus neglect to pay it the proper attention it deserves. Value exchange always starts with breaking down a company's products and services into appropriate revenue groups. Each revenue group's products and/or services' gross sales, cost of goods, and gross profit margins are rolled up into the revenue group's overall performance. Why is this important?"

> **IT IS IMPERATIVE THAT YOUR COMPANY CLEARLY DEFINES THE HIERARCHY AND ORIGIN OF ITS GROSS MARGINS THROUGH A FORENSIC UNDERSTANDING AND CORRECT LOADING OF ITS COST OF GOODS/SERVICES. PETER, THIS IS WHERE 90 PERCENT OF ALL EMERGING ENTERPRISE CEOS FALL SHORT....**

"It is imperative that your company clearly defines the hierarchy and origin of its gross margins through a forensic understanding and correct loading of its cost of goods/services. Peter, this is where 90 percent of all emerging enterprise CEOs fall short of understanding their company's profit architecture – they are not getting to the truth behind their company's real gross profit because they are improperly loading their cost of goods.

"Capturing the exact contribution each revenue group makes to a company's gross profit by being able to break the profit chain down to every product's and/or service's true gross profit/gross margin is a prerequisite to intentionally growing profitability. Why? Without the true loading of cost of goods/services (direct labor, direct materials, and allocated overhead – not to be confused with your break-even analysis) you cannot possibly fine-tune and effectively apply the gas pedal to your profit engine. Frankly, I can't ever say enough about this subject."

> " ALSO, BUILDING AND MEASURING THE PRESENCE, IF ANY, OF RECURRING REVENUE IN EACH REVENUE GROUP IS ONE OF THE SECRETS TO EXTREMELY PROFITABLE PROFIT DESIGNS, AND MOST COMPANIES PAY LITTLE ATTENTION TO IT. "

"Also, building and measuring the presence, if any, of recurring revenue in each revenue group is one of the secrets to extremely profitable profit designs, and most companies pay little attention to it. Does your company have recurring revenue?"

"Not as much as we could. What we have is dwindling. Much of the energy of the company has gone into the development of a single new product. It's a concern of mine."

Milo looked at his watch, and said, "Well, maybe we'll talk more about it later, but it should be a big concern to you. Recurring revenue is critical to the financial stability of a rapidly growing company like yours." He turned back to the board.

"**Strategic Control.** For every revenue group your company has, you must be clearly defining the four things that hold your customer to you, keep your competition from 'knocking off' your product or service, give you competitive advantage, and that tell you what your average customer is worth in time and dollars. Here is a little more detailed view of the four:

1. *Customer Magnet* – this measures the strength of the quality or attribute to your product or service that magnetizes the customer to continually come back to you.

2. *Barrier to Entry* – this measures the strength of the specific, unique attribute or advantage that you deliver to your customer that cannot be immediately duplicated by your

competition. It is like a wall that keeps the competition from coming in and stealing your customers.

3. *Strategic Control Points* – this is a broader measure of the strength in degree of competitive advantage that your company has in the marketplace over its competitors.

4. *Lifetime Value of the Customer* – this tells you how long the average customer will continue to be your customer and the total amount of revenue that individual average customer represents.

> **" HOW DO YOU LOCK THE CUSTOMER INTO USING YOUR PRODUCTS OR SERVICES? HOW DO YOU KEEP THEM FROM GOING ELSEWHERE? "**

"How do you lock the customer into using your products or services? How do you keep them from going elsewhere? Do you see? You need to know how you are going to consistently retain the customer's loyalty."

"I see what you mean, Milo, but I think I see all of this as a function of marketing."

"It affects or drives aspects of marketing, Peter, but it's also part of product design, and customer reconnaissance and customer service, to name just a few areas. Let's move on."

"**Scope of the Enterprise.** What is the scope of your business? Some of this you're going to be familiar with. For example, are you vertically integrated? Are you involved in everything from producing raw materials all the way through design, production, and marketing to the end-user? Probably not. You're more likely to be horizontally integrated. You're probably using vendors to create much of your materials, and you're doing what you're good at, right?"

Peter nodded.

"And there are other things that determine the scope. Do you have a wide product range or a narrow product range? Are you involved in creating product line extensions? Both of these things need to be considered. If you're narrowly focused, you need to consider if that's what best serves you. If you have products that could have follow-ons or line extensions, they could represent both a branding tool as well as a source of revenue." Milo paused to look at what he was writing.

"The last thing to consider is outsourcing. You could be outsourcing all of your support: customer service, marketing, direct mail, so you could focus on your core business. Making these kind of decisions helps to define the profit design and ultimately the profitability of the business."

Again he stopped to give Peter a chance to think about what he was hearing. "You see, as an entrepreneur you will make these choices. But instead of making choices with no frame of reference, you can make them with a real understanding of how each choice impacts your enterprise's profitability."

"OK, next is **Culture.** You and your staff need to articulate the forces that drive the company in terms of the company's dominant cultural preference along with, among other things, the transference of its core values, its vision, its mission, its strategy, and most importantly, the transference to the entire staff of a clear understanding of how the company makes its money.

"This last one is rarely done, and it is a key factor in The Profit Net. When you have taught your staff to be profit-driven entrepreneurs, you have awakened a giant in your business that will change the face of your profitability going forward. The sum of these things is the essence of the success or

> " IF YOU DON'T IDENTIFY AND SUPPORT A DOMI-NANT CULTURAL PREFERENCE, THEN YOU AREN'T HELPING YOUR EMPLOYEES TO KNOW AND UNDERSTAND WHAT TYPE OF COMPANY BEHAVIOR BEST ADVANCES THE ENTERPRISE'S VISION, MISSION, AND GOALS. "

lack of success of the company's culture.

"You'll get more about this later, but there are four basic company personalities that contribute to the culture: Innovation, Customer Service, Spirit-Driven and Operational Excellence. Your company will always have all four working to some degree.

But if you don't identify and support a dominant cultural preference, then you aren't helping your employees to know and understand what type of organizational behavior best advances the enterprise's vision, mission, and goals."

"When you have systems and mechanisms built into your company that reinforce and reward a focused behavioral preference, then you begin to see real teamwork. Don't get me wrong, I'm not talking about controlling people. I'm talking about choosing to prefer innovation to organizational excellence or customer service over innovation. You are asking your employees to focus more on one preference than another."

"**Knowledge Management.** Knowledge has become a strategic financial asset, Peter. It directly affects the value of your company. Your company must describe how it captures and encourages knowledge. Do you derive knowledge from within your ranks or from the outside? Knowledge will flow from both sources, but you can't be solely dependent on outside knowledge."

"The staff of every company creates a talent and knowledge pool that the company needs to encourage and secure its loyalty. You must have a plan to help the considerable knowledge within your company flourish. How you tap the core intelligence of your enterprise directly affects the bottom line. Some people say this is the soft side of business. But let me tell you, young man, the soft side of business is rapidly controlling more and more of the financial performance of companies. The working assets of companies are rapidly migrating to right between people's ears."

"Let me put it another way. If I were looking to buy your company, I would want to know what the knowledge pool of your company is, and how are you developing, accessing, and managing it."

"**Organizational Structure.** You probably think you have a standard hierarchical or pyramid structure, but you most assuredly do not. Almost no growing enterprise today can stand the rigidity of that structure. The typical org chart is a graphical representation of the power structure. It's all about power."

"But an Organizational Structure tells the story

> WHEN YOU COMBINE VALUE EXCHANGE AND ORGANIZATIONAL STRUCTURE YOU CAN BEGIN TO MEASURE THE IMPACT ON THE CURRENT AND FUTURE CAPACITY OF THE ENTERPRISE.

of the enterprise. It tells us about the relationship the company has with its customers, its vendors, its allies, and its competitors. Understanding the food chain in a company does have value, but only focuses on one narrow issue. A good Organizational

Structure should let you look outward and forward. But more importantly, when you combine value exchange and Organizational Structure, you can begin to measure the impact on the current and future capacity of the enterprise."

"**Customer Intelligence.** There has been much talk over the last few years in business circles about the value of Customer Relationship Management. Let me take this opportunity to clear the air. True, Customer Intelligence comes from understanding three pretty simple principles. All the CRM software tools in the world don't matter a hoot if you don't get the following three things figured out.

1. Defining a laser-targeted customer profile for each revenue group. This enables you to carefully hone your business development efforts in order to improve your sales closing ratio.

2. Defining and continually updating your customer's true priorities for each revenue group. This not only keeps your company current with the evolution of your customer's requirements vis-a-vis your product /service offerings, but it also reveals what contributes to making your customer's business profitable or not profitable.

3. Analyzing when and where the 'moments of truth' occur in your customer chain of contact points for each revenue group. This forces

your company to face the brutal truth about your customer's experience with you. Measuring and tracking the activities at these strategic customer points is a prime directive in all highly successful firms."

"**Strategic Alliances.** Surviving in today's marketplace demands that you partner with other companies. You form strategic alliances with other companies by engaging them three ways. There are three types of strategic alliances:

- *Symbiotic Allies* – both parties require each other to make money
- *Piggyback Allies* – one party is dependent and catches a ride on the coattails of the larger party
- *Pass-Through Allies* – one party passes through a key benefit or relationship and gets compensated for it

"As you organize your alliances by type, you then apply them within the context of your revenue groups."

"**Operating Systems.** Your company's profit design requires operating systems to manifest profitable transactions. These are the behind-the-scenes structures that effectively get the work out the door and allow the business to manage its affairs in an efficient manner. Many important operating systems decisions are influenced by the specific profit model a company utilizes. Examples of this can be observed by measuring the blend of:

- Internal and outsourced operating systems
- Product and service operating systems
- Fixed-cost and variable-cost operating systems
- State-of-the-art and low-cost operating systems

"How these issues are intentionally considered and addressed has a huge impact on the company's capital budget, organizational structure, and value exchange."

"**Research & Development.** R&D plays a very important role in numerous profit models but, in the same breath, has a limited impact in other models. Every company must continually decide, based on their profit model, how they will blend the development of new value offerings by considering the relationship between:

1. Internally developing new value offerings and outsourcing their development
2. Developing process-driven offerings and developing product-driven offerings
3. Choosing between a random project selection process and choosing a defined project selection process
4. Determining the speed at which new offerings are developed

"**Capital Intensity.** This one is simple, but extremely important when it comes to calculating the return on invested dollars. Capital intensity refers to how much money does it take in the form of capital investment required to create and deliver your product or service offering to your client."

"A manufacturing business typically is more capital-intense than a service business. A pharmaceutical business model is typically much more capital-intense than a product distribution business model based on independent distributors. There are many important decision trade-offs found in the flexibility, risk, and duration of capital invested based on the capital intensity of a business model."

He paused. Peter's mind was flooded with questions. "This is interesting, but how do I put this

> ❝ ONCE YOU'VE CREATED AN INTEGRATED VIEW OF THESE 12 COMPONENTS OF PROFIT DESIGN, YOU CAN TWIST OR MORPH THEM TO LIMIT THE SURPRISES AND UNPREDICTABILITY INHERENT IN GROWING BUSINESSES. ❞

information together and use it productively?"

"When you begin to create a profit design, you take each of these twelve components into consideration and blend them into an integrated working model. Once you've created an integrated view of these 12 components of Profit Design, you can twist or morph them to limit the surprises and unpredictability inherent in growing businesses. This method demands that you look at your company as it really is, not through some idealized view of what it ought to be. In fact, you'll be able to see how important any one of these considerations should be at any time."

Milo stopped, looked over and said, "Peter, your face reads like a book and what I am seeing is overload and confusion."

Peter rolled his eyes. "Am I that transparent?"

"Well, let's just say it is understandable. Horace told me to load you up and that's what I am doing." Milo walked over to the window behind his desk, pointing to a student lying stretched out on a stone wall, basking in the Colorado sun. "That young man hasn't a worry in the world. Let's take a quick break and go down and talk with that fellow. My guess is he just might enlighten us about making profit."

CHAPTER 15 — KEY POINTS
12 Components of Profit Design:

1. **Value Exchange**
   The profitable organization and exchange of value for money
   - Unique Competencies
   - Revenue Groups
   - Gross Profit

2. **Customer Intelligence**
   The informed awareness of who the customer is and what they want
   - Customer's Priorities
   - Customer Profile
   - Customer Chain

3. **Scope**
   The range of products or services to be offered
   - Wide or Narrow
   - Vertical or Horizontal
   - Influence in your Market

4. **Business Development**
   The fusion of targeting, capturing, and caring for the customer
   - Marketing System
   - Sales System
   - Customer Service System

5. **Strategic Control**
   The unique power of your offerings
   - Customer Magnet
   - Barrier of Entry
   - Lifetime Value of your Customer

6. **Strategic Allies**
   The specific external partners engaged to expand sales
   - Piggyback
   - Symbiotic
   - Pass-Through

7. **Knowledge Management**
   The manner in which you leverage your company's unique knowledge
   - Collaborate
   - Organized and Store
   - Access to Knowledge

8. **Culture**
   The landscape and focus of the human workplace community
   - Cultural Focus
   - Values
   - Management Program

9. **Organizational Structure**
   The organizing of people to successfully complete tasks
   - Competency
   - Capacity
   - Structure by Task

10. **Operating Systems**
    The support structure for critical enterprise processes
    - Internal/Outsourced
    - Product/Service
    - Low-Tech/High-Tech

11. **Research & Development**
    The continual discovery of solutions to your customer's needs
    - Speed
    - Internal/Outsourced
    - Product/Service

12. **Capital Intensity**
    The measurement of required financial resources
    - Financial Systems
    - Capital Investment: High-Medium-Low
    - Required Operating Capital Levels

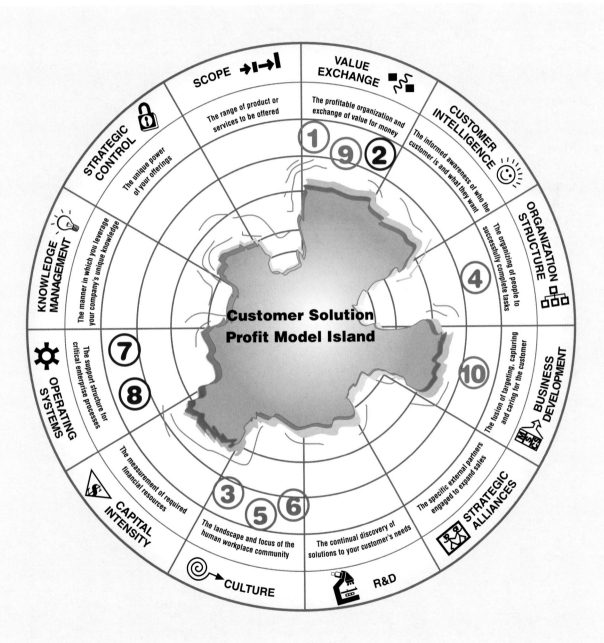

SCOPE ➜I➜I

VALUE EXCHANGE ■◣

The range of product or services to be offered

The profitable organization and exchange of value for money

STRATEGIC CONTROL 🔒

The unique power of your offerings

CUSTOMER INTELLIGENCE ☺

The informed awareness of who the customer is and what they want

KNOWLEDGE MANAGEMENT 💡

The manner in which you leverage your company's unique knowledge

ORGANIZATION STRUCTURE

The organizing of people to successfully complete tasks

OPERATING SYSTEMS ✦

The support structure for critical enterprise processes

BUSINESS DEVELOPMENT

The fusion of targeting, capturing and caring for the customer

Customer Solution Profit Model Island

CAPITAL INTENSITY

The measurement of required financial resources

STRATEGIC ALLIANCES

The specific external partners engaged to expand sales

CULTURE

The landscape and focus of the human workplace community

R&D

The continual discovery of solutions to your customer's needs

① ⑨ ② ④ ⑩ ⑦ ⑧ ③ ⑤ ⑥

PROFIT

EDGE BUSINESS
5 - 15%

ADJACENT BUSINESS
20 - 30%

CORE BUSINESS
65% +

MODEL

Chapter 16

MAKING AND KEEPING MONEY

"What we see as facts and events are actually signs which must be interpreted. By accepting the need to move from opinion about what is going on to experiencing an insight to what is happening we will improve our decision making in business."
— F. Bryon Nahser, *Learning to Read the Signs*

The heated light gently framing the young man's face suddenly disappeared as he quickly opened his eyes to see the wild apparition of white hair infused in the afternoon sun moving to within twelve inches of his face.

Milo belted out a gruff roar, "Mister Porter, I do hope you plan on making your 2 p.m. class. It would be a shame if you missed the one pop quiz that will represent 25 percent of your term grade."

John Porter jumped up, barely missing Milo Tangle's strange form leaning over him. "Milo, or excuse me, man, Mister Tangle, I am on it. I will never miss even one of those heroic tales of profitability that you are so famous for."

"OK, Mister Porter, let's cut to the chase. God was on your side today and sent me down here on two missions: to wake you up to get your butt to class and to introduce you to my friend here. John, meet Peter."

Peter reached out his hand, "John, it's a pleasure."

"Ditto, man."

"Peter, Mister Porter here is one of our budding entrepreneurs. He owns a small Internet company that sells DVDs teaching people *How to Rock Climb Without Losing Your Life.* I did get that compelling title right, didn't I Porter?"

"As always," Porter exclaimed.

"Mister Porter has just finished a semester interning over at Horace's company. I believe he could take a moment here, before class, to share with us his revelations on "working the core" of a business, based on what he observed during his internship with Horace. Is that right, Mister Porter?"

John Porter pushed his curly blond hair off his face, looked directly into Milo's eyes as though he were rapidly roaming back and forth between Milo's brain and his own, organizing a moving tapestry of thoughts on the subject. Clearly his eyes telegraphed that the lights were on and someone was home.

> **THE LARGEST MISTAKE MOST BUSINESS LEADERS MAKE WHEN THEY EXPAND THEIR ENTERPRISE IS GETTING STRATEGICALLY DISCONNECTED FROM THEIR CORE BUSINESS.**

Suddenly John Porter's thoughts burst out of his mouth sounding like a strange blend of surfing king, Laird Hamilton, and a prophetic Gregory Peck playing Captain Ahab. He said, "First of all, Horace Bedford rocks. If he didn't tell me ten times he told me twenty times that the largest mistake most business leaders make when they expand their enterprise is getting strategically disconnected from their core business. In other words, they lose sight of the golden goose, their core value offering. This usually happens as a result of building new lines of business that don't align with the core business in a meaningful way or getting caught up in the vision of some edge business product. Man, that was so true for my business."

"You see, Horace showed me there are three types of businesses going on in every enterprise. Number one is what Horace calls your **Core Business**, which is the primary, unique ability of the organization, the bread and butter of the enterprise. The second one is the **Adjacent Business**, which is a blend of the 'related-spin offs or extensions' from the core business and promising, developed edge businesses. And the third type of business is called the **Edge Business**, which is the new untested, unrelated lines of business that may or may not be valuable in the future."

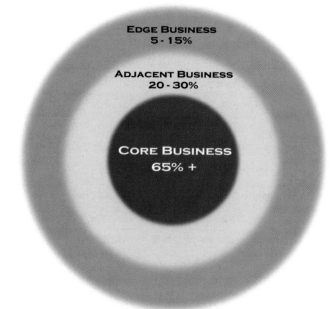

"The core business in an entrepreneurial firm should command no less than 65 percent of the enterprise's attention. The art of developing, maintaining, and transforming your core business is essentially the secret of empire builders like Bill Gates and Michael Dell. That one piece of advice from Horace saved my business. We were getting ready to roll out three new lines of products. What a nightmare that would have been. I stopped it just in time. We were way too new. We would have tanked our focus in a matter of months." Porter looked at his watch and said, "Guys, time is racing down the wave. I got to split to class. Later."

Peter and Milo said their good-byes and started the walk back up to Milo's office. "Milo, is there a formula or matrix to use when deciding if a new venture is expanding too far from your core business?"

"Peter, the very best method I have discovered is based on a daily, weekly, and monthly understanding of your revenue groups' performance. Believe me, after you have taken the time to organize the tracking, forecasting, and reporting of your company's product's and service's true gross margins by revenue groupings, you will know which groups are core business, which are adjacent, and which are edge business.

"Understanding the core business becomes an important lever in determining the hierarchy of the elements in the revenue groups. You'd better understand the relative focus on the core business when you go one step further and can clearly track your profit drivers — that's volume, gross margins

generated by pricing, and costs — in each group. Remember, Peter, the numbers tell the story. There is nowhere you can hide when your numbers regularly tell you how well you are minding the store.

> " THERE IS NO WHERE YOU CAN HIDE WHEN YOUR NUMBERS REGULARLY TELL YOU HOW WELL YOU ARE MINDING THE STORE. "

"You will find with most, if not all, of The Growth Curve Solution, that it is uniquely interconnected. This is also true with the New Profit Model, as each of the three elements are closely linked into one process."

Milo continued. "When it comes to planning, most entrepreneurs focus the lion's share of the company's planning energy either on generating strategy or on developing organizational capacity. Very few entrepreneurs have a method of effectively fusing the two into one process."

"You see, Peter, it is the mission of good planning to generate strategic initiatives in light of current and future organizational capacity and subsequently drive them into clear operational themes and then into a tactical action plan.

"When companies grow quickly, the priority of effective planning — strategy into capacity into operational themes into action — is often lost in the chaos of the moment. If you learn anything from me today, you should walk away with the simple planning sequence involving: **Strategy** to **Organizational Capacity** to **Operational Themes** to an **Action Plan.**

"Now, let's take a look at this thing I call the Profit Net." He was back at the whiteboard. "Remember when I told you that if you taught your staff to be profit-driven mini-entrepreneurs, you would have awakened a giant in your business?"

Peter responded. "Yes, as wonderful as that sounds, employees have little interest in how their company makes money."

"That's where you are wrong, Peter. There is a deep natural tendency in all people to want to belong, contribute, make a difference, and be a part of a winning team. The more that people are able to contribute and make a difference in their world, the more they sense authorship and responsibility."

"When you allow the staff of your company to participate in the awareness of, the authoring of, and the sharing of the enterprise's profitability, you have leveraged the profit capacity of your company ten times. There are very few things that can affect the profits of a company more than the enterprise-wide pride and aware-ness of and participation in profit maintenance and profit expansion."

"The Profit Net is the mechanism that helps you build the staff's pride and awareness in the maintenance and expansion of profitability. Imagine throwing a huge net over your organization and unifying everyone in a focus of growing a super-profitable enterprise."

"Peter, without your staff onboard in the profit game, you have little chance of breaking through to higher profitability. You must teach the entire organization about profit.

Finding space on an overly-used whiteboard, Milo began to write:

> *Profit Net* — a combination of mechanisms that train and engage your staff to know the:
>
> 1. *Profit Template* or how the company makes and keeps its profit
>
> 2. *Profit Sequences* of the enterprise or how every activity in the company should be no more than three steps away from the profit zone
>
> 3. *Profit Indices Tracking* or following the key factors contributing to the company's profitability found in the daily, weekly, and monthly Flash Sheet /Dash Board

"OK! Let's talk about the Profit Template first. It is quite remarkable that in most organizations less than 10 percent of the company's staff understands how the enterprise actually makes and keeps money. In a Growth Curve Solution company, this condition is remedied by The Profit Template, which explains the succession of Net Revenue to Cost of Goods/Services to Gross Profit to Sales and Marketing to General Administrative costs, finally ending up with Net Profit before taxes."

> " IT IS QUITE REMARKABLE THAT IN MOST ORGANIZATIONS LESS THAN 10 PERCENT OF THE COMPANY'S STAFF UNDERSTANDS HOW THE ENTERPRISE ACTUALLY MAKES AND KEEPS MONEY. "

Peter raised his hand as if he were in one of Milo's classes. "Professor, how do I get this idea into a nuts and bolts explanation for my staff?"

"Peter, you have to capture their imagination first. The best way is to hit their wallets. Employees choose to be employees and not entrepreneurs because they want the certainty of a regular paycheck. Ironically, most employees don't understand their direct role in making sure that paychecks happen every month. They just assume that the boss will make sure there is enough money to pay them. This phenomenon happens often in larger companies. The staff is rarely connected to the reality of how they directly affect the company's ability to make payroll.

"So you start with making payroll because it hits close to home with your employees. How does that happen? The best way is using the Profit Template succession from the larger view of a monthly P & L report."

"This is the time when you explain the difference between gross profit and net profit."

And Milo wrote:

> Gross Profit — the money that the company makes from selling its services and products.
>
> Net Profit — the money that the company keeps after paying for the costs and expenses of being in business.

"I have not seen an instance when, given this information for the first time, most employees aren't shocked at how little money the company makes. It is an important revelation to them and a key in getting them one step closer to growing the company from the bottom up. Horace calls it bubble-up growth."

"You know, Milo, if you went even further and showed them exactly what each product's gross profit margins were, it would really wake them up."

"That's exactly where I was going next. When the staff see the actual dollar contribution each product makes to the overall gross profit of the firm, they are amazed."

Milo started rummaging through his desk, mumbling to himself. "You know, Peter, I have a simple chart that shows the impact of the profit drivers — volume, cost, and price — under various circumstances. It would be great for you to use when you introduce this to your staff."

mation and would probably be embarrassed to admit they are clueless on the topic."

"Milo, the artful science of pricing is a pretty arcane practice. Is it useful to involve everyone, more importantly, all the managers, in this?"

Milo looked at his watch and shook his head. "It

Profit Driver Chart Product A	Price per unit	% change	Cost per unit	% change	Avg Volume	% change	Volume	Price	Cost	Revenue	Cost of Goods	Gross Profit	Gross Margin
Scenario 1 Standard Sale	$100		$60		100		100	$100	$60	$10,000	$6,000	$4,000	40%
Scenario 2 Pricing Improvement	$100	10%	$60		100		100	$110	$60	$11,000	$6,000	$5,000	45%
Scenario 3 Cost Improvement	$100		$60	10%	100		100	$100	$54	$10,000	$5,400	$4,600	46%
Scenario 4 Volume Improvement	$100		$60		100	10%	110	$100	$60	$11,000	$6,600	$4,400	40%

He finally found a thick sheet of paper with a large chart on one side and gave it to Peter. "Here, Peter, this is it. You will find it self-explanatory. When you introduce your staff to profit drivers always use your company's products in the examples. It can be one of the better business lessons your staff will ever receive."

"Now, understanding the deeper implications of the profit driver mix is another discussion and is particularly important for your leadership staff to understand. Don't assume they know or understand how the profit driver blend works. Most supervisors and managers haven't been shown this infor-

always happens this way. I get someone who is really interested in learning something and there is never enough time."

"Yes, correct pricing is a complex knowledge not meant for everyone. What I am talking about is giving your staff enough of the basics to make them not only better profit watchdogs but also profit innovators, and the leadership, better profit decision makers."

"Sometimes the best ideas come from those who operate outside the area of expertise. They have the advantage of seeing things from outside the box -- a different perspective. We want to wake up the giant so that it can talk to us when it has an idea or sees something askew. Do you see what I mean?"

Peter knew Milo was onto something here. He realized if he had the conscious brainpower and creativity of the entire staff, at least peripherally, involved in watching the profitability of the company, the money falling through the cracks of lost margins and excessive costs would make a huge difference to their profitability.

Milo continued, "Let's move on to **Profit Sequences** and the **Profit Zone**. Remember, our goal is to bubble up the growth of the enterprise. In order to make this a reality and not just theory that gets lost on a bookshelf, there is real work involved in educating the staff and building this knowledge into the DNA of the company."

> " THE PROFIT ZONE IS A RELENTLESS, PRECISE, AND INTENSE STAFF MINDSET TO MAKE AND KEEP MONEY FOR THE ENTERPRISE. "

"When we speak about the Profit Zone, we are talking about when the curtain goes up and it is showtime. The Profit Zone is a relentless, precise, and intense staff mindset to make and keep money for the enterprise. Your Profit Zone is responsible for maintaining and improving:

Profit Zone Activities

1. Revenue generation
2. Strategic and tactical focus of the company
3. Gross and net profit margins
4. Cash flow
5. Cost structure
6. Customer satisfaction
7. Staff *voltage*
8. Product/service quality
9. Company innovation

"How strong or weak a company's Profit Zone is, determines the health of the enterprise. When a company is sloppy or ineffective with any of the Profit Zone activities, it makes and keeps less profit."

"If it underperforms on too many of these items, it goes out of business. The Profit Zone is the strike zone, the profit sweet spot so necessary that the company's very survival and success depends on it. When every employee knows how his or her job responsibilities directly impact the Profit Zone, you are another step closer to bubble-up growth.

"The **Profit Sequences** are the three-step combinations that result in profitability. Any activity an employee or staff member is involved in should not be any more than three steps away from the Profit Zone. It is a way for the entire staff to 'mind the knitting' of the business, so to speak."

Peter interrupted Milo. "Are you saying that unless an activity resides within these three steps of the Profit Sequence, the employee is wasting his time and the company's money?"

> **THE PROFIT SEQUENCES ARE THE THREE-STEP COMBINATIONS THAT RESULT IN PROFITABILITY. ANY ACTIVITY AN EMPLOYEE OR STAFF MEMBER IS INVOLVED IN SHOULD NOT BE ANY MORE THAN THREE STEPS AWAY FROM THE PROFIT ZONE.**

"Yes, I am, Peter. That is exactly what I am saying. In a Growth Curve enterprise, every activity must reside in one of three steps. Imagine the steps in concentric circles, with the Profit Zone in the center."

Milo drew a circle and said, "Moving from the outside in:

- Step Three – The employee's activity *supports the processes* of maintaining and improving one or more of the nine activities of the Profit Zone
- Step Two – The employee's activity *supports the people* who are maintaining and improving one or more of the nine activities of the Profit Zone
- Step One – The employee *is actually the person who is making it happen.* They are directly maintaining and improving one or more of the nine activities of the Profit Zone."

Peter raised his hand again, but this time as a way of stopping Milo. "This seems like an awful lot of work, Milo. You've run businesses before so you know making a commitment to educate the staff, as you are suggesting, is an enormous effort. How do you find time to do all this and run a day-to-day business? And how do you keep the level of Profit Net competency when you are continually growing and adding new staff? Does it pay off?"

"Peter, there is no easy answer to all your questions except the last one. Yes, it does pay off. It pays off big-time. Horace brought C.J. O'Connor to

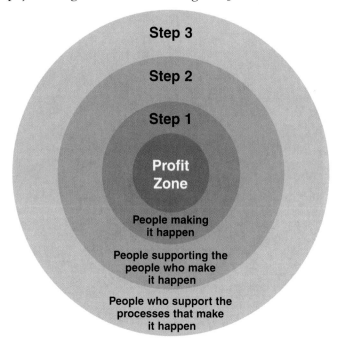

Step 3

Step 2

Step 1

Profit Zone

People making it happen

People supporting the people who make it happen

People who support the processes that make it happen

me about three years ago. Her company had been growing very quickly and her profits were diving through the floor. She was as stubborn as they come. She could not imagine how she was going to find the time to do all that I was telling her.

> " HORACE CONVINCED C.J. TO TAKE HER STAFF OFF-SITE FOR TWO DAYS. THEY CREATED A UNIFYING EVENT AROUND THE COMPANY'S PROFITABILITY, OR RATHER THE LACK OF THE COMPANY'S PROFITABILITY. "

"Horace convinced C.J. to take her staff off-site for two days. They created a unifying event around the company's profitability, or rather the lack of the company's profitability. Horace and I helped her by teaching the staff the information that I have been giving you this afternoon. C.J. was smart. She in turn reinforced the profitability training in the weekly Growth Circles and made it quantifiable by building her Flash Sheet.

"Within three months her gross profit margins went from 39 percent to 63 percent, her net profit went from 2 percent to 15 percent. Right now she has 68 percent gross profit margins and a 21 percent net profit. The only thing she did differently was to involve her staff in helping to manage and advance the profitability of the firm and share the bounty with them. Mind you, C.J. didn't pay lip service to all these ideas. She rolled up her sleeves

and, month after month, worked with the staff to grow the profit mindset in her company.

"That reminds me. It's critical to complete the third element of the Profit Net. Let's move on to Profit Indices Tracking. It allows the staff and the leadership team to measure the key indices that support the nine activities of the Profit Zone. This is done within a Flash Sheet mechanism.

"The Flash Sheet becomes the central collection point for all the Profit Tracking throughout the company. Without tracking, performance is lost.

"Now, Peter, I'm not talking about tracking just financial performance. The Flash Sheet tracks any quantifiable factor within the nine Profit Zone activities that has any major contribution to the company's profits and health.

"Every day each department tracks its key performance indices on a scorecard. The staff in each department then reviews their department's weekly aggregates or averages during their weekly staff meeting. Then the whole company reviews the primary Flash Sheet indices for the entire enterprise from the previous month during the town meeting at the beginning of each month."

Peter raised his hand again. "Milo, let me make sure that I have this right. I'm going back to my company, Bolder Solutions, and I'm going to plan a unifying event for my entire staff based around the Profit Net?"

"Yes and no. After you finish with Horace's Growth Curve Solution training, you will sit down with your leadership staff to thoroughly go through the assessment you gave the organization.

"You are going to filter through the noise of the assessment and come out with 5 – 10 key internal initiatives. You are also going to plan a unifying event to introduce your staff to not only the 5 – 10 key initiatives but also to your company's strategic plan and all nine of The Growth Curve Solution fundamentals.

"Depending on what fundamental of The Growth Curve Solution you feel has the most importance, you will pay particular attention to that one in the training."

"You might feel you should highlight the New Profit Model information that I have been giving you today. Inside the New Profit Model is the staff profit education piece called The Profit Net. Are you following me?"

Peter nodded his head in clarity and said, "Yes, I follow, but this is pretty complex stuff."

"Well, I'm sure Horace warned you to keep your seat belt on in the beginning. The Growth Curve Solution gives a lot of information in a short amount of time. Stay with it, Peter. It will all come together quicker than you might expect."

Milo started pacing across the room. He seemed suddenly frustrated and short-tempered and snapped, "Peter, what is this business about a seed bomb that Horace mentioned to me?"

Peter turned his chair in Milo's direction and answered, "In short, Milo? A militant competitor by the name of Santomo is trying to frighten my company into backing out of completing an important software project. Our software would be used by a company that is a direct threat to Santomo's ability to control a portion of the world's food supply."

"And your staff? Are they staying onboard with you?"

Peter walked to the window overlooking the student union below. "They all appear to be taking up the flag and hanging in there. At least today, that's the case. Now, if we are talking about tomorrow or next week, I don't know. The seed bomb experience was a temporarily unifying event. The staff seems

> " LEADERSHIP IS ONLY EFFECTIVE WHEN YOU UNDERSTAND THE CORE UNDERLYING BELIEFS OF THOSE PEOPLE YOU ARE LEADING. PEOPLE NEED FREEDOM, BUT AT THE SAME TIME THEY ALSO NEED LEADERSHIP AND STRUCTURE. "

to be a little more accepting of my leadership since the explosion. "

"Leadership is only effective when you understand the core underlying beliefs of those people you are leading. Their fears, their hopes, their considerations, and their expectations contribute to their underlying beliefs. People need freedom, Peter, but at the same time they also need leadership and structure. This is an opportunity for you to step into the vacuum and lead your staff. Ask their opinion, filter out the noise — focus the group on a few key initiatives, and then work the plan. Sound familiar?"

"Yes, I believe Horace or C.J. mentioned something like that to me yesterday."

"Good. This brings me to the third component of the New Profit Model. Just as you should know the core beliefs of your staff to effectively lead them, you also must know the underlying beliefs of your customers to successfully lead them. You must listen to the customer, filter out the noise from their opinion, focus their attention on a few key items in your value proposition, and then work your plan. Sound familiar?"

"Yes, I see your point."

Milo looked at his watch. "I'm running late for my next class but if I know my students, they're probably hotly debating with each other how they are going to keep me as a customer today. You see, they are all working on a hypothetical customer care team that must keep me as their customer. I gave them a simulation that I was getting ready to migrate to a competitor and that they had only one shot at keeping me."

> " FIRST, PEOPLE MIGRATE TO THAT WHICH SOLVES THEIR EVER-CHANGING PROBLEMS. SECOND, PEOPLE MIGRATE TO THAT WHICH PLEASES THEM. "

"Milo, what do you think are the prime causes that customers leave? I have run three companies and I have to tell you that most customers are as fickle as the wind."

"Peter, customer migration flows right out of what I was just saying about the value proposition. There are two forces at play that make the marketplace dynamic. First, people migrate to that which solves their ever-changing problems. Second, people migrate to that which pleases them."

Peter chuckled at the way Milo emphasized the word "pleases."

Milo chuckled, too. "The pleasure principle is basic and it's true. Most businesses wait until the customer has already migrated to another solution, or to something that pleases them more, before they begin to figure out what is really going on in their customer's world.

"Remember I referred to a product as a value offering? I did that because it's more descriptive. A product is more than a thing, it is an offering of value. It is an agreement between you and your customer. I call this the Customer Charter."

"THE CUSTOMER CHARTER REPRESENTS THE UNWRITTEN AGREEMENT YOU HAVE WITH YOUR CUSTOMERS TO SOLVE THEIR PROBLEMS AND/ OR DELIVER THAT WHICH PLEASES THEM. "

"The Customer Charter represents the unwritten agreement you have with your customers to solve their problems and/or deliver that which pleases them. When this charter is strong, it creates an almost magnetic force that keeps the customer loyal to your value offering."

"When the charter is broken or weakened, the customer easily migrates to another solution or source of pleasure. Understanding the forces that make a customer migrate from a company's value offering is one of the most important ongoing tasks that a business owner has."

Peter laughed again. "I've never thought of it in these terms, especially an emotional response like pleasure. But it makes sense. You'd think that Hondas and Toyotas would be interchangeable in car owners' minds, but each has its own fiercely loyal following. In the software industry, it revolves around both the functionality of the product and the way the company follows up with support."

Milo interjected, "Good analogies. Listen. It's important to note that the risk many entrepreneurs endure in their company's profit design is the result of them not knowing their customer. Most customers migrate to another solution because no one is listening to them. In order for a company to stay ahead of **Customer Migration**, it must be adept at three things."

1. It must *anticipate its customers' changes* through ongoing reconnaissance of the customers' considerations and needs.

2. It must take the information and feedback from its customer reconnaissance and *innovate new solutions* and ways to please the customer.

3. And it must regularly *demonstrate the renewal of the Customer Charter* by being one step ahead of customers' needs.

"I can't stress the importance of innovation too much. If you are able to innovate, if you can adapt and adjust to the changing marketplace as well as to the changing needs of your customers, you'll create a loyal customer base."

Peter said softly, "Anticipate, innovate, and demonstrate. Got it!"

"Okay, I've got to get to class. I'm in for enough abuse from my students as it is. Just remember, Peter, it is really quite simple. The New Profit Model is no more than considering how the guts of your business is designed, teaching your staff how to make and keep money, and finally, understanding what it takes to please your customers and/or deliver the right solutions to their problems."

"Good luck! And take an airplane. It's a good way to make yourself think!" He was holding a box of balsa wood model kits. "Go on, I'm serious."

Peter smiled, and grabbed the largest one. "This ought to keep me out of trouble."

"Excellent choice. I'll be sure to send you the material I promised to you."

As he walked back to his car, model kit in hand, questions bubbled up faster than he could keep up with them. Peter realized that he wouldn't learn The Growth Curve Solution overnight.

But something was happening that he hadn't felt in a long time. He was starting to think differently. Ideas were quickly forming that would foment change, with or without his total understanding. That was Horace's plan. Horace knew that there wasn't time to give him true competency on any one of these subjects, but if he could provide an intense overview, it would change his fundamental beliefs enough to change his decision making.

But would he be able to put it all together in the very real world of Bolder Solutions? Or was he wasting valuable time? Was he crazy to take himself away from Bolder Solutions when so much was at stake?

CHAPTER 16 — KEY POINTS

Three Elements of the New Profit Model:

1. The Profit Design

2. The Profit Net

3. Customer Migration

12 Profit Design Components:

1. Business Development
2. Value Exchange
3. Strategic Control
4. Scope of the Enterprise
5. Culture
6. Knowledge Management
7. Organizational Structure
8. Customer Intelligence
9. Strategic Alliances
10. Operating Systems
11. Research & Development
12. Capital Intensity

There are three types of businesses going on in every enterprise. They are:

1. **Core Businesses,** which are the primary, unique abilities of the organization, the bread and butter of the enterprise.

2. **Adjacent Businesses,** which are a blend of the "related spin-offs or extensions" from the core business and promising, developed edge businesses.

3. **Edge Businesses,** which are the new, untested, unrelated lines of business that may or may not be valuable in the future.

EDGE BUSINESS
5 - 15%

ADJACENT BUSINESS
20 - 30%

CORE BUSINESS
65% +

The Profit Net is a combination of mechanisms that train and engage your staff to know:

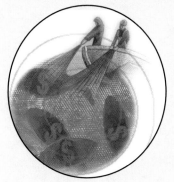

1. **The Profit Template** or how the company makes and keeps its profit.

2. **The Profit Sequences** of the enterprise and how every activity in the company should be no more than three steps away from the Profit Zone.

3. **Why and how to track profit** with indices of the key factors contributing to profitability by using the company's daily, weekly, and monthly Flash Sheet.

Profit Zone Activities:

1. Revenue generation
2. Strategic and tactical focus of the company
3. Gross and net profit margins
4. Cash flow
5. Cost structure
6. Customer satisfaction
7. Staff *voltage*
8. Product/service quality
9. Company innovation

In order for a company to stay ahead of Customer Migration, it must be facile with three things:

1. It must anticipate its customers' changes through ongoing reconnaissance of the customers' considerations and needs.

2. It must take the information and feedback from its customer reconnaissance and innovate new solutions and ways to please the customer.

3. It must regularly demonstrate the renewal of the Customer Charter by being one step ahead of the customers' needs.

VALUES BRIDGE

STAFF SATISFACTION

FIVE TIERS OF
STAFF SATISFACTION

CULTURAL
PREFERENCE

Chapter 17

INVESTMENT

"Many, if not most, organizations either lack an explicit human resource philosophy or ignore the one they espouse. Yet success often hinges on a thoughtful, explicit strategy for managing people."
— Lee G. Bolman, Terrence E. Deal, *Reframing Organizations*

"Peter was impatient to put into practice some of what he learned. He needed to get his hands back on the wheel at Bolder Solutions, but he also needed to rewire his methods or the whole venture was doomed. This was an impatience born from being uncomfortably suspended between what used to work and what might work, between what was no longer predictable and what was new, strange, and untested. Something had to change very soon.

Milo's words were rolling over and over in his mind. "Most entrepreneurs are caught in the running and solving of the day-to-day problems of the enterprise. There is never any time or real interest to intentionally design their business."

It was true. He'd been so busy handling the onslaught of new people, events, and information in his life that he had only recently given serious thought to a future model for his business. He now realized that he had never been intentional about the elements in the profit designs at his other companies.

As Peter considered the future of Bolder Solutions, an idea sprang loose, one he credited to C. J. O'Connor. Why not give his engineers a new mandate: 'Lead us with innovation.'

He knew that if he listened to them with respect and gave them the freedom and proper structure to innovate new technical solutions for the company, things could turn around quickly. They needed to know they'd be taken seriously and that he needed their input. Alan had always been the innovator, and the engineers simply executed his designs. He was gone now, and someone had to take his place.

A picture was starting to form in his mind of the "self-organizing natural systems" model Horace described. Despite his dismay at not considering his company's profit model until now, he was starting to feel his confidence build because of his newly learned knowledge. He could feel the beekeeper mindset emerging and his need to control everything fading. Being more comfortable with chaos was certainly new territory for Peter Logan.

When he neared the address Horace had given him, he noticed a large metal sign centered on a three-story building, Theta Thermal Technologies.

Unlike O'Connor Electronics, this company's building had personality. Aside from the gold painted cornice piece capping the top of the building, there was intricate freshly painted molding around the first and second floor windows. The building had obviously been restored in the last year, and by the look of things, Peter guessed there weren't any secret government contracts hiding behind the front doors. The logo on the front of the building read: 3T – Cooling an Overheated World.

There was no high-tech security system here, just a small sign indicating the name of an alarm company. The door was open, so he walked in. There was a lot of activity inside, apparent even from the lobby. People were scurrying around, telephones ringing. This place was like most of the companies Peter had worked with. The receptionist

was on the phone as he entered, but she waved a greeting at him.

When she finished, she looked up. "May I help you?"

"I'm here to see Mr. Tripp. My name is Peter Logan."

She picked up the phone and pressed an intercom button. "Butler, he's here."

As she hung up, two employees walked by on their way out the door. "Have a good lunch, you two."

A door opened. "Peter?" A man about Peter's age, wearing a jacket without a tie, smiled warmly and said, "Horace told me to expect you. I'm Butler Tripp. Come on back."

Butler led Peter to an office down a short hall lined with photographs of employees. The office was big but unassuming, the furniture nice but not brand-new.

Butler sat behind his desk, directing Peter to a big overstuffed chair. "How long have you known Horace?"

"Days. Just days. And yet I feel like I've known him for years."

Tripp nodded. "I understand he wants me to talk to you about staff satisfaction."

"At this point, I'd let you talk to me about anything you wanted. Did he tell you what my company is working on?"

"Something about software for a company doing genetic research, right?"

"Close enough. But he only found out about the bomb this morning."

"Bomb?" Tripp asked, surprise showing in his voice.

Peter told him about the seed bomb and the impact it had on his staff. "It may sound ridiculous, but I think it's the best thing that's happened to us."

"No, I understand. Your staff has just shared an experience that now binds them together. That's a classic unifying event. After the initial bumps you had with them, it must be very helpful."

"You know, ultimately, we all have to maintain profitability to stay in business. I take it you've talked to the professor?"

> WE ALL HAVE TO MAKE MONEY TO STAY IN BUSINESS, BUT COMPANIES ARE JUST BEGINNING TO UNDERSTAND THE ROLE THAT STAFF SATISFACTION PLAYS IN MAINTAINING THAT PROFITABILITY.

"Just met him."

"Good. Well, he has a whole view of profitability that's good for gauging the condition of your business and for planning the future. We all have to make money to stay in business, but companies are just beginning to understand the role that staff satisfaction plays in maintaining that profitability."

A young woman interrupted him. She had on a telephone headset with a disconnected wire dangling behind her. "Sorry to bother you, Butler. I've just talked to that start-up in Florida that needed the custom fins. They're very happy. They're calling Johnny in five minutes to give us a much bigger order."

"Thanks, Dana. You've taken real good care of those guys, and they haven't been an easy customer."

She beamed and then was gone. Butler chuckled as she disappeared. "We have to take customer satisfaction very seriously. We're competing in a fairly defined niche in this business, and happy customers are repeat customers. Did Horace tell you anything about us?"

"Not a word."

"Sounds like Horace. Come on, I'll show you around."

As they walked through the office suites and back into the production warehouse space at the end of the building, Peter was distinctly aware of the energy of the place. People having phone conversations with customers was to be expected, but these people seemed unflappable, always polite. He guessed that some of the conversations had to be contentious, but you'd never know it from the friendly tone.

As Butler weaved through the bustling work area, he began his story. "I joined the army on my eighteenth birthday and flat-out lucked into working in electronics. I learned things I would never have had the opportunity to know existed. I even learned about metallurgy."

"When I got out I needed a job, but I really didn't want to work for somebody else. I'd managed to save my money and I figured it was worth a shot to be independent. There's nothing like being too young to know better. I started my company and went to college at the same time. I swear, if I knew then what I know now, I might have balked at the challenge.

"But I was lucky. I specialized in a comparatively low-tech product. All our high-tech machines, even the little ones we carry around in our pockets now, create heat. We make devices to bleed off the heat. And the bigger and more complicated the machines are, the more sensitive they are to the ravages of high temperature.

"So while we have a narrow niche in which we compete, we know that every day somebody is inventing another high-tech gadget that will need our products. There were already some big players in the business when I started, so I had to figure out how to compete. Our products are great, but so are our major competitor's products. We have to win in other ways. That's where staff satisfaction comes in."

He toured Peter through the machine shop, the testing lab, and the heat room. It was anything but a routine-looking factory. There were wide aisles with yellow lines painted down the middle, pull-down tools hung from the ceiling, and the large factory equipment had been painted with what appeared to be team mascots.

One piece of equipment was painted like a Great White shark, another had a large rendition of Spiderman, and another had been painted to resemble a charging bull elephant. There were street names posted at every corner and each department had large erasable boards that were filled with key business indicators and ongoing notes to the staff.

"THERE WERE SIGNS WITH THE COMPANY'S GROWTH LANGUAGE WORDS HANGING DOWN FROM THE CEILING. EVERY DEPARTMENT HAD ITS OWN WAY OF MAKING THE POINT: THE CUSTOMER COMES FIRST. AND EVERY DEPARTMENT RADIATED AN UNDENIABLE CAMARADERIE. THE VOLTAGE IN THIS PLACE WAS OFF THE CHART."

Everywhere there were signs reminding them to be attentive to the customer. There were signs encouraging them to ask questions, and signs encouraging them to answer questions. There were signs with the company's growth language words hanging down from the ceiling. Every department had its own way of making the point: the customer comes first. And every department radiated an undeniable camaraderie. The *voltage* in this place was off the chart.

The Customer Comes First!

Butler explained, "We have any number of contests running all the time. We keep changing what we do, but the idea is to foster friendly competition among various departments or teams. Our people are paid well and they know it. But they also get a chance to feel productive and know when their productivity is getting better. We reward them for it. And we make sure they expand their knowledge base. After they've been here a certain amount of time, we'll match dollar-for-dollar any continuing education course they take that impacts their jobs. And I continually bring in experts in many fields to educate the staff."

Peter stopped him. "Doesn't that get expensive?"

"If you view it in a vacuum, sure. The way I look at it is that education is cheap, it's ignorance that's expensive."

"In light of the impact it has in the long run, training and employee professional development are a bargain. People have to know that the time they spend at work has meaning beyond a paycheck. It helps them to know they are always learning, and it keeps them sharp. It helps them to know why these odd-looking metal objects with fins they fabricate and sell every day make a difference in people's lives."

"If they understand that the new DVD player they buy for their kids has one of our products in it, and why it has that particular product, then they have a basis for meaning in their work. They realize that what they do makes folks' lives a little better."

"That makes sense," Peter agreed. "I've just begun taking the time to tell my staff exactly why we are working on our current product. At first I just thought they knew why, and then I made the mistake of thinking it wasn't important to tell them. But the bomb changed my thinking."

"Then it really was the best thing that could have happened. So tell me, did you notice that I just gave you the five tiers of staff satisfaction?"

Peter stopped to think for a moment. "Butler, what you said sounded right, but I couldn't say it back to you. Can you run them by me again?"

"You bet! But I should give you a bit more of an overview first. Actually, there are three elements to staff satisfaction. Besides the five tiers, there's culture, and there's the values bridge."

Peter leaned over to pull out his notebook and said, "Ah yes, the power of three. So we have:

Three Components of Staff Satisfaction:

1. The five tiers of staff satisfaction

2. The defined cultural preference

3. The values bridge

"So what were the five tiers?"

Butler spoke up. "It's really simple and it makes common sense. Think of it as a stack of, oh, anything, maybe a stack of pancakes."

Staff Satisfaction
5. Meaning
4. Learning
3. Performance
2. Community
1. Material

"At the bottom, it's material issues such as compensation, the benefits package, a safe work environment. Next, it's the camaraderie, the relationships people create, the feeling of belonging in the company. Then it's performance, measuring and rewarding work and progress. After that, it's learning. People have to keep learning, or they stop growing. Sounds obvious, right? But it's critical. If we stop learning, our minds begin to atrophy and performance drops off. At the top of the stack is meaning. People look for meaning in their work just as they look for meaning in their lives. If you get all five areas cooking, you've got a dynamic staff."

Peter thought for a moment. "Sounds easy enough. So what's the catch?"

As Butler turned the corner to step in front of a large machine, he said, "The catch is that it isn't easy at all. You have to create it, maintain it, and

> **WHEN YOU ARE A STAGE 6 COMPANY THAT HAS GROWN FROM 25 TO 116 EMPLOYEES IN THE LAST TWO YEARS, YOU HAVE TO DO SOMETHING TO KEEP IT ALL GLUED TOGETHER.**

reinvent it constantly. It doesn't happen by itself. We have been working on it at 3-T for over four years. When you are a Stage 6 company that has grown from 25 to 116 employees in the last two years, you have to do something to keep it all glued together. You don't get the kind of buzz you feel in here without a constant concerted effort to get 'IT' right. What does the *voltage* feel like at Bolder Solutions?"

"It's getting better. We just spiked from a two to an eight on a one-to-ten scale because of the seed bomb experience. I know the *voltage* is event-driven right now and I have to quickly find ways to build a self-sustaining base under the staff."

"If you continually listen to the staff and make a real effort at understanding their core beliefs about the company, you will have made a big step forward to creating staff satisfaction. OK. Have you seen all our big signs that highlight the customer?"

"You can't miss 'em."

"That's not an accident. It's literally a sign of our culture. Culture is the second key item of staff satisfaction. Every company needs to know what its culture is. Ours is customer service. The way we compete with our low-tech products in a fast-moving, fickle, high-tech world is by doing whatever it takes to make our customers happy. Because then they come back. Did the professor cover the whole pricing issue with you?"

"Yes, he did."

"We are certainly not the cheapest firm on the block. In fact, some of our stuff is a lot more expensive than our competitors' products. But we have sensational quality control, we can handle special orders in a heartbeat, and we follow-up with a vengeance. We know how to please them! Nobody buys from us and then never hears from us again. It's who we are."

Peter broke in. "How do I identify my company's culture?"

"This is a simplistic answer for a complex question, so bear with me. The best way to do it is to assess your entire company and find out what culture the staff thinks it is. Then take your vision of

> " A DEFINED PREFERRED CULTURE MAKES THE CORPORATE IDENTITY OR COMPANY BEHAVIOR EASIER TO SUPPORT. "

the culture and their view of the culture and blend them.. That way the staff has co-authored the preferred corporate culture. A defined preferred culture makes the corporate identity or company behavior easier to support.

Four Culture Identities of an Organization
1. Customer Service Culture
2. Innovation Culture
3. Operational Excellence Culture
4. Spirit-Driven Culture

"Here's a quick view of the different cultures. Milo probably told you about them, but this is my view. Besides customer service, there are three other cultures.

"Innovation is the culture of a company where brainpower is the premium ingredient. It's a company that creates new products with great speed and quantity. We're talking about what is probably a stressful place to work, but it's also a very exciting place to work. The culture of innovation drives a lot of our high-tech customers. In fact, because they are innovation companies, they need a high level of flexibility and customer service from us."

"Then there's the culture that's spirit-driven. This is a company where the employees come first. There's a sense that if everything is OK with the employees, if they are well taken care of, then the company will thrive. Maybe the most famous is Tom's of Maine, although the jury is still out on what will happen as they get larger. But they've been famous for taking very good care of their employees."

"The last category is the culture of operational excellence. This is a company where precision of every process is very important. Large corporations tend to become cultures of operational excellence as a way of addressing the high level of complexity. Growing companies tend to deal with such constant forces of change that it's difficult to maintain opera-

tional excellence as the dominant preferred culture of the enterprise."

Peter was listening intently. "So you're saying that a company must determine what its preferred culture is in order to set the standards of behavior with its staff?"

> "WHEN THE STAFF IS CONFUSED ABOUT THE COMPANY'S CULTURAL IDENTITY THEN THEY WON'T KNOW HOW TO MAKE CLEAR AND CONFIDENT DECISIONS."

"Yes, that's right, Peter. When the staff is confused about the company's cultural identity, then they won't know how to make clear and confident decisions. Their confusion will trickle down to the day-to-day decisions that constantly need to be made. When they aren't making the decisions, then who do you think will have to make them?"

Peter quickly injected, "The person in charge. Sounds like Bolder Solutions all neatly tied up in a bow. But doesn't a company have all four cultures going on at the same time?"

"Yes, Peter, you're absolutely right. All companies have aspects of the four cultures in them; in fact, they will likely not survive if one of those aspects is ignored. But one of them will become the dominant culture. 3-T has become a culture of customer service, but we started as an innovation company. And we absolutely have to have operational excellence as our secondary culture or our costs would sky-rocket. You've begun to see how we treat each other around here. What's your gut reaction to where you think your own company is?"

>
> **3-T HAS BECOME A CULTURE OF CUSTOMER SERVICE, BUT WE STARTED AS AN INNOVATION COMPANY. AND WE ABSOLUTELY HAVE TO HAVE OPERATIONAL EXCELLENCE AS OUR SECONDARY CULTURE OR OUR COSTS WOULD SKYROCKET.**

Peter knew that if he asked each person at Bolder Solutions what was the company's dominant culture, he would get 43 different answers. He was confused about what it needed to be, so he was sure the staff was as well.

"Butler, to answer your question, I'm embarrassed to say that I'm not sure. I think it's drifting a bit between innovation and customer service but I am uncertain that those are the right preferences. My instinct tells me that because we are a software developer, we need to focus on innovation."

Butler nodded in agreement. "That sounds right to me. It's important to get the whole staff on-board with an awareness of, and an agreement about, what kind of culture you have. It creates a platform for finding the core values of your company, and

that is the last thing I have to tell you about: values."

Peter thought about Alan and the type of man he had been. "My brother was a highly ethical man. I think the company reflects his values."

"I'm sure that's true, but it's not quite that simple. Was he the kind of man who'd sit down and talk about values with his staff?"

"Well, no, I think he hired people whom he believed shared his values and would always share his values."

"I understand, Peter. The thing to remember is that you are speaking about personal values, personal ethics. People are reluctant to talk about being honest or fair because it embarrasses them. But as a company, you must find a way to do so."

"I'm not sure how to identify the company values."

Their walk had taken them back up to the Victorian office building in the front, to a paneled meeting room with a large table and expensive chairs. Butler saw the look on Peter's face.

"I know, it looks a little out of place, but we have customers who seem uncomfortable attending a meeting unless it's held in a 'boardroom.' So now we have a boardroom."

"Nice one, too."

"Thanks. Have a seat. The chairs are great. Let me tell you about a company down the road. Sashco Inc., a sealant manufacturer in Brighton, has done a terrific job at imbuing their staff with a values-driven culture. They bring every new employee through a three-day academy where they orient the new staff member to the core values, the company's vision, goals, strategies, and cultural norms. They took the step of identifying their core values as care, trust, truth, and forgiveness. Believe it or not, they actually demonstrate that list of values with their clients, their vendors, and amongst themselves. It is quite remarkable to see what they have done."

Peter tried to think of his company in terms of those qualities. "That's very good. I might present those values to my staff and see what they think. "

"We did. But anyone can come up with a list of desired values. They have to go through certain identifiable levels of acceptance. At first, we call them untested. A value like 'care' is just a word until it is tested. We had a small incident take place just after we began our dialogue about values. We have an employee named Kyle who's responsible for all our vendor deliveries, and he's very conscientious about his job."

"On a Friday afternoon, just when he was trying to get away on a long Memorial Day weekend vacation, the man had his own little crisis of care. One of our vendors had promised emphatically that their driver would arrive no later than 4:00 p.m.

"Kyle had made it clear that we needed the product by four o'clock, and that he was leaving at 5:00. At 4:30, he contacted the vendor, informed them that their driver was not only overdue, it was now too late for delivery.

"He extracted a promise that they would reschedule the delivery for first thing the following Tuesday morning. The vendor had no idea what had happened to their driver, and even threatened to fire him for his tardiness. Kyle didn't have a lot of sympathy."

"It took Kyle until 5:05 to finish up and clock out. As he was closing the back door, he saw the truck pulling up. It just made him mad. He started yelling at the driver that he was going to have to redeliver on Tuesday, and that was only if he still had a job. I think Kyle probably unloaded on the guy for five minutes before he took a breath. The driver was a young man who, it turned out, got lost because of bad directions given to him by the vendor. He looked at Kyle, and said, 'Man, I really need this job.' "

"So Kyle unlocked the delivery door and told the young man he would help him with the off-loading. He didn't leave until 6:30. The real kicker is that Kyle was one of the more resistant employees to the idea of company values. But he clearly exhibited the very meaning of care."

Peter said, "That's a great story. How did it affect your company?"

"It gave us a way to truly discuss what care meant – and then we were able to extract the depth of trust, truth, and forgiveness we could count on.

"After a value is tested, it begins to become a real habit of thought and behavior. It becomes unchallenged. At this point, people know how to deal with any situation within the scope of the value, but they still consciously have to apply it."

> " THE LAST LEVEL THAT A VALUE GETS ACCEPTED HAPPENS WHEN THE STAFF OF YOUR ENTERPRISE DEMONSTRATES THAT VALUE AS AN UNCONSCIOUS CULTURAL NORM. "

"The last level that a value gets accepted happens when the staff of your enterprise demonstrates that value as an unconscious cultural norm. This is when the staff doesn't have to think about it, they simply react to situations from a DNA level. At this point, when you hire new people, they learn the values through the behavior of the whole company. You may tell them that the company values are care, trust, truth, and forgiveness. But they will really learn them only from your staff. Imagine how powerful this can be. When the unconscious awareness of the company is 'we are the best at what we do,' that belief can more easily become reality."

Peter was thinking about Bolder Solutions. His brother's company didn't have any defined values that he knew of. The staff had commonality but it was not aligned around the company's core values. That had to change. He knew how other organizations like Southwest Airlines, Patagonia, and PSS Medical had successfully driven their cultures with defined core values.

If the staff and the current leadership team could come to some agreement on the company's values bridge, it could shorten the acceptance cycle. It might not take as long to transition through the three levels of acceptance if everyone helped to author the list. Peter was beginning to see how everything that had been given to him through Horace and his associates was starting to integrate in his mind. Horace had warned him that it would all seem like a lot of disjointed information at first and he would need to be patient.

He didn't see the big picture yet, but he sensed a unifying thread surfacing through each conversation he was having with Horace's friends. More importantly he was beginning to see direct applications that he could apply at Bolder Solutions.

A young man with dark black hair and wire-rimmed glasses politely interrupted them with a printed e-mail message from one of 3-T's customers. Butler read the message and immediately said, "This is great, Tom, I'll call him right away."

Butler put out his hand to Peter. "Had a huge account that just opened up for us. Good to meet you, Peter. Any questions you have, don't hesitate to connect. Remember, staff satisfaction doesn't happen overnight but it is a critical element of a profit-driven, growth-smart, people-centered workplace. Good luck."

"Oh, and next time you see Horace, tell him that I am still waiting to hear his story about the watchmaker and the beekeeper. Every time I see him he keeps looking at my wrists to see if I have more than one watch on. I have no idea what he is talking about."

Peter laughed. "He is a crafty old bird. He ran that one past me as well. I don't want to steal Horace's thunder, but I can give you a hint. In Horace's world, bees are smarter than watches. See you later, Butler, and thanks very much for all your help."

CHAPTER 17 — KEY POINTS

Three Components of Staff Satisfaction:

1. The five tiers of staff satisfaction

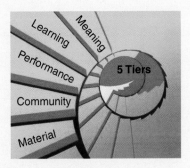

Staff Satisfaction:

5. Meaning
4. Learning
3. Performance
2. Community
1. Material

2. The defined cultural preference

Four Cultures:

1. Spirit-Driven
2. Customer Service
3. Operational Excellence
4. Innovation

3. The values bridge

The Values Bridge:

1. Untested
2. Unchallenged
3. Unconscious

Sashco Inc. Core Values:

1. Care
2. Forgiveness
3. Trust
4. Truth

> HE FOUND HIMSELF SLOWLY RECOGNIZING
> AND PICKING OUT PATTERNS HIDDEN IN
> THE LAYERS. HE ACTUALLY BEGAN TO
> UNDERSTAND THE CHAOS.

Chapter 18

THE PATTERN LANGUAGE OF CHAOS

"No pattern is an isolated entity. Each pattern can exist in the world only to the extent that it is supported by other patterns in its environment"
— **Christopher Alexander**, *Pattern Language*

Flocks of birds inaugurated the Saturday morning sunrise by turning Peter's backyard trees into huge stereophonic speakers. The cacophony of sound ripped him back to reality. Looking through the stupor of an interrupted dream he found himself, to his delayed surprise, sitting up in bed, eyes wide open, in what could only be described as nocturnal shock. The bedside clock read 4:50 a.m.

For Peter, growing up in Boulder was about immersing himself in the outdoors. He and Alan explored every creek, every tree, and every canyon path for miles surrounding his home. For all intents and purposes, the outside was his home. Yet this morning Mother Nature wasn't a friend, she was an obnoxious beast without a volume control.

Pulling back the sliding glass door, he stepped out onto the back deck with the misguided belief that his anger would somehow scare the birds into silence. What he encountered was not what he expected.

Barefoot and shirtless, he was suddenly paralyzed by the revelation of what was happening. Every sound, every movement, every penetration by the early morning light into the yard was all part of some strange force layering and orchestrating the chaos washing over him. The volume and energy were overwhelming. There were layers upon layers of wildlife competing for front stage.

The level of detail and significance that each layer of sound and activity offered was a rich world in and of itself. And yet it all seemed to merge into one "thing." He found himself slowly recognizing and picking out patterns hidden in the layers interacting and responding to other patterns elsewhere in the yard. He actually began to understand the chaos. He began to see the interrelatedness and the interdependency of all the patterns of sounds and movements cascading and exploding in this world.

It was then that the unlikely thought tap-danced through his mind, "Oh my God, this is what

Horace was talking about, the birds at sunrise. This is the Growth Curve experience: seeing what appears to be chaos instead as multi-layers of interconnecting, interrelating patterns. This is how he reads companies. He sees through the chaos and reads the patterns and layers to understand what is really going on."

> **"THIS IS WHAT HORACE WAS TALKING ABOUT, SEEING WHAT APPEARS TO BE CHAOS INSTEAD AS MULTI-LAYERS OF INTERCONNECTING, INTERRELATING PATTERNS."**

Right at the height of his reverie another loud yet familiar sound burst into the air. This time it wasn't Mother Nature but the phone ringing him back to reality.

He ran inside, picked up the phone, and all he heard was:

"Hey, Boss, is that you?"

"Boss?" It was not a voice he expected to hear, especially at this hour. "Dean?"

"I wasn't sure I dialed the right number. Man, you OK? Your voice sounds weird."

"I'm, fine but, Dean, it's 6:15 on Saturday morning. I assume this is a very important call." He was trying to sound normal, whatever that was.

"Look, I'm sorry to bother you so early on a Saturday, but could you come to the office?"

Alarm bells went off in Peter's head. "Is everything all right?"

"Yeah, yeah. Everything's fine. In fact, everything's great. I want to show you something about our project."

"Yeah, yeah, OK, I'm up anyway. I'll take a shower and be there as soon as I can."

He was out the door twenty minutes later.

Peter's thoughts were whirling around his early-morning revelation as he drove down 119 on the way to Gunbarrel. If someone had ever told him that he would be drawing significant conclusions about business from watching birds at sunrise, his university-trained mind would have dismissed it as soft-minded. Yet here he was, being pulled closer and closer to a world very much different than he ever imagined.

As he pulled up in front of Bolder Solutions, the front door to the office was held open by a loose stone to let the air circulate throughout the building. All Peter heard as he walked in was laughter drifting out from the back of the building where the programmers worked. Dean wasn't the only surprise at the office. The wizards were all in attendance and, by the look of things, they'd never left the night before.

"Hey, Boss. We found something you need to see. Look at this."

His huge monitor was filled with code. "This is way deep in the program. You know the instruction set is long, right? We're looking at complexity that rivals defense systems. OK, see this sequence? It doesn't belong. But it's in a place that we worked out months ago. What you're looking at is sabotage."

> **IT'S ESSENTIALLY A SELF-DESTRUCT MECHANISM, BUT IT'S INSIDIOUS. IT CONSTANTLY CREATES A DUPLICATE SET OF INSTRUCTIONS SO THAT THE PROGRAM FREEZES, BUT IT'S SEQUENCED SO THAT IT APPEARS AT RANDOM. IT'S BEAUTIFUL WORK.**

Peter knew only a little about programming, just enough to keep from sounding foolish when he spoke about it, but he saw what Dean was pointing at. There were several lines of code where the instructions looked wrong.

"What does this do?"

Dean pointed at the young female programmer with assorted body piercings. "I'll let Maria explain it to you. She found it."

The girl was on fire with excitement. "It's essentially a self-destruct mechanism, but it's insidious. It constantly creates a duplicate set of instructions so that the program freezes, but it's sequenced so that it appears at random. It's beautiful work."

Peter looked at her. "You admire it?"

"Sure. It's a great hack. But I'm better."

Dean and Maria high-fived each other. "She is, Boss. She has moves most of us don't even think about."

Peter needed to know the bottom line. "So, what does this mean to us now?"

Dean's attention went back to the screen. "We've just finished a program that checks for any more of these bumps in the software. We expect to find nothing. The whole idea of putting a great little self-destruct instruction set in the code is that you want it to remain obscure. So it's likely the only one. But once we run it, we'll know for sure."

Peter still needed to know the bottom line. "OK, that makes sense. But, Dean, where does that leave us?"

They were all smiling and chuckling at him now.

"Well, Boss, it means we need a new project. This one's done."

It took a moment for Peter to register what the young programmer had just said. "Done? You mean…done? As in finished? Completed?"

> TURNS OUT WE ACTUALLY WERE DONE THREE WEEKS AGO. WE JUST DIDN'T KNOW IT. SO NOW WE NEED TO FIND OUT WHO SPIKED OUR WORK. OKAY, WE HAVE SOME CLEAN UP TO DO IN THE BETA TESTING, BUT BARRING ANOTHER TROJAN HORSE, WE CAN DELIVER THE SOFTWARE IN ABOUT TEN DAYS.

Now they were all nodding. "Yep. Turns out we were actually done three weeks ago. We just didn't know it. So now we need to find out who spiked our work. OK, we have some clean up to do in the beta testing, but barring another Trojan horse, we can deliver the software in about ten days. We think you should call Heritage." Dean was enjoying himself.

Peter was speechless.

"Uh, Boss? This is good news, right?"

Then it hit him. "Yes! Yes, this is great news! You guys are amazing. This is a very, very important thing you have accomplished. I'll call the client now. In fact, I think I'll pay him a visit."

Elijah was ecstatic. "Peter, this is extraordinary news. How confident is your team?"

"I'd say they're sure. In fact, they keep trying to downplay just how certain they are, but they can't quite contain themselves. I think we're there. I wanted to tell you in person just for the pleasure of it, and to keep the other guys guessing. Our office has been declared clean, but I didn't want to take a chance. If they're still watching us, then all they will know is that I spoke to you on a Saturday. Let 'em wonder."

"What's next for you and your company?"

"I'm not sure. We have a number of opportunities skirting the horizon and I'm gaining more and more confidence in my staff, so I think we are going to figure out Bolder Solutions' future together. And I am sure that whatever we come up with will be extraordinary. Your software project will put us on the map."

Sunday morning was glorious. The quality of mile-high sunlight was one of the bonuses of living in Boulder. He had slept through the sunrise symphony in his backyard and woke up refreshed and ready to enjoy his day with his nephews. Peter walked into the kitchen, took the peanut butter and bread out of the cabinet and set them on the counter, and turned to get a plate, when something stopped him.

He turned back and looked at the kitchen. Nothing was wrong that he could see, so what was it? Then he looked at the bread and his heart

> " NOTHING WAS WRONG THAT HE COULD SEE, SO WHAT WAS IT? THEN HE LOOKED AT THE BREAD AND HIS HEART STOPPED. THE LITTLE BLUE FACE MAGICALLY DRAWN BY THE CHECKER'S BLUE MARKER WASN'T THERE. "

stopped. The little blue face magically drawn by the checker's blue marker wasn't there. How could that be possible? And he hadn't really thought about the bread being whole wheat when he bought it, but the words were jumping off the package at him now.

He didn't know what to do. Was it paranoia, or had someone changed the bread? He felt clammy sweat behind his neck. He felt fear.

Jane answered on the first ring. Peter tried to sound calm about his discovery of the unmarked bread but she quickly told him not to move anything, including himself. She and her partner were at his house in fifteen minutes.

A forensics team was only a few minutes behind them. They quickly dusted all the windows and doors and every other likely

surface in his house. Then they took Peter's fingerprints.

She was all business. "We expect to find your prints alone on the bread package, which should be theoretically impossible. Lots of hands should have handled it. We'll talk to the bakery to see what they can tell us, and we'll have the lab run chemical tests on the bread's ingredients, but the findings could take a while."

"What do I do?"

"I don't think they'd risk something high-profile, but you need to be careful. And I suspect you need to be very unpredictable about what you're eating and where. Also…" She paused.

"What?" He knew it came out a little too loud.

"I want someone assigned to watch your house. We don't know what to expect."

Peter watched the forensic team finish dusting his kitchen. "All of this for a software program."

"All of this to stop your software program from being completed."

"But we're basically finished. They just don't know it yet. We removed all the bugs from the office on Friday, so they have no idea where we stand."

"And that may be why they did this. This is a risky move. If we find a connection to your brother's death through tampered bread, then there's no way to claim he died naturally from a heart attack. They must consider you a real threat. Peter, we need to contact everyone in your company right away. They could be targets, too."

> ❝ IF WE FIND A CONNECTION TO YOUR BROTHER'S DEATH THROUGH TAMPERED BREAD, THEN THERE'S NO WAY TO CLAIM HE DIED NATURALLY FROM A HEART ATTACK. ❞

"Unbelievable! We should start with the programmers, but they'd be hard targets to reach, unless Santomo can get into Checker's Pizza. I think they are all at the office."

The programmers had all gone home for a few hours' sleep, but only because Dean started an automated program to check the software for more hidden surprises. Even on Sunday morning, they were back for more. The seed-bomb attack had backfired worse than Santomo could have predicted. The geeks were motivated!

They took the news about Peter's 'incident' as a challenge. Peter had a sense that it was a big virtual reality game to them and they did not intend to lose it.

Monday morning finally rolled around. He made sure the staff was informed about the events of the weekend and insisted Dean and his team announce the hack they had found in the software and what

they had done to debug it. The other staff members were appropriately impressed.

They were scared, but they were staying on as part of the team. When Peter took a clear look at what was really going on, he realized that the biggest problem he faced was that once the software was truly finished, the company would need to quickly ramp-up the marketing process and look for follow-on products.

Peter was sitting alone at a table at the 14th Street Restaurant and couldn't stop thinking about the Saturday morning experience. His life  was truly insane. Here he was, coming within a hair's breadth of being murdered, a seminal event in anyone's life, and all he could think about was The Growth Curve Experience of seeing the patterns buried in the chaos of his early morning backyard symphony. Caught in the impact of the recall, he didn't notice Horace talking with the hostess and being directed over to his table.

"Good morning, Peter."

"Hi, Horace. Have a seat. I have two things to share with you that should blow your mind."

"One, I'm pretty sure someone tried to murder me on Sunday morning with poisoned whole wheat bread…. And – more importantly – I had a Growth Curve Experience. I now know what you were talking about."

Horace broke in, saying, "Whoa, slow down. You think someone tried to murder you?"

"Yes, indeed. But hey, all in a day's work, right?"

The amusement left Horace's eyes. "It makes me angry, personally and professionally. What the hell are they thinking? This is stupid and messy and wasteful. This is how business gets a bad name."

Peter said, "They're not going to win this battle. We'll deliver the product next week."

"Wow, that's terrific news, Peter. Now what is this about you having a Growth Curve Experience?"

"Well, I got blown out of bed 4:50 Saturday morning by the sunrise birds you told me about a week or so ago. I stood out on my deck for over an hour transfixed by everything going on. Then out of nowhere it struck me that this is what you were talking about: seeing the patterns through the chaos.

"Wow, were there ever patterns! Must have been hundreds all playing out at the same time. It was then that I understood what you were saying that the same thing is happening every day in a business.

"I understood how you could see through the chaos of a growing company and see the patterns that made the company what it was in that

> THE ONLY THING THAT WAS BRILLIANT WAS YOUR RECOGNITION OF SOMETHING THAT WAS HAPPENING UNDER YOUR NOSE ALL THIS TIME.
>
> CONGRATULATIONS. ONLY 1 PERCENT OF ALL THE BUSINESS LEADERS OUT IN THE WORLD TODAY COULD SAY THEY UNDERSTAND WHAT YOU JUST SHARED WITH ME.

moment. I couldn't believe it. I actually saw what you were talking about. It's brilliant!"

Horace slowly scratched his chin and said, "Well, the only thing that was brilliant was your recognition of something that was happening under your nose all this time. Congratulations. Only 1 percent of all the business leaders out in the world today could say they understand what you just shared with me. Keep driving to understand this work, Peter. Your inquiry and open mind will accelerate the process beyond your wildest imaginings."

Horace laughed, mirth in his eyes. "I knew I was right about you. So what's next?"

Peter answered, "I looked at my team and I believe that if I give them a chance, they'll come up with new product lines for the company to consider, as well as follow-on products for our current lines. I think the best defense is a good offense. I refuse to slow down regardless if Santomo, or whoever, interferes."

"OK, let's move this along. Peter, you need to bring your supervisory team together. I know, right now, it probably is very disconnected as teams go. They often are, in Stage 4 companies. This usually happens in Stage 5 companies but you're in circumstances that demand that we fast-forward the rules."

"It's important that you unify them right away as a working team. Set up an off-site meeting with all of them for one day this week. I'll come over and help you with the meeting. Let me know when and where. Also, make sure that you have finished processing the data from that assessment you gave your staff last week because we'll need it for the off-site. I also have two more CEOs for you to visit."

Peter looked at Horace and it was the first time that he realized just how tall Horace was. He had to be over 6'3". The bushy eyebrows, the steel-blue direct gaze and neatly cropped wavy silver hair all contributed to Horace's commanding presence.

The older man looked troubled. "It's hard enough growing a business and dealing with market forces. The people at this Santomo Company are out of their minds. I don't have a method to avoid being further terrorized by a competitor, short of calling the FBI. It's like a bad gangster movie!"

"Yeah, but apparently they're using real bullets."

Human Beings Challenge Us

As business leaders we, at times, are challenged by the irregularities of human behavior. We build evidence and subtle judgments about people that cut us off from the truth. We watch people make "dumb" mistakes. We observe lazy behavior. We see employees forget simple processes. We slowly begin to lose a measure of respect for the intelligence of those working around us. We begin to believe the statement that says, "The brains truly reside at the top." Eventually, we stop asking the brains at the bottom what they think. What is the cause chain of this phenomenon?

Beliefs foster **Filters** which foster **Patterns** which foster **Behavior**

"My staff at Juniper Galleries are a testament to the truth that ordinary people have an enormous capacity to generate wealth and satisfaction. If only 10 percent of the human brain is utilized then we have only just begun to realize the extraordinary productivity and satisfaction possible in the ordinary work community."
-Tracy Birch, lunch Feb 27

No One Can Convince You

Leveraging the ordinary path of genius "found on the shop floor" can be one of the most surprising revelations a CEO can have. No one can really convince you of this. It requires an open, curious mind willing to get out of the limiting box of its own making. It requires recognizing our own genius.

GROWTH

LEADERSHIP

MEETINGS

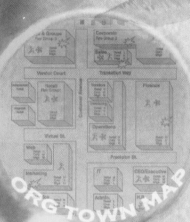

ORG TOWN MAP

COMMUNITY

Chapter 19

SHAPING CHANGE

"In an age when the speed, intensity, and complexity of change increase constantly and exponentially, the ability to shape change – rather than being its victim or spectators – depends on our competence and willingness to guide the purposeful evolution of our systems, our communities, and our society."
— **Bela H. Banathy**, *Designing Social Systems in a Changing World*

Standing out in the Chautauqua meadow staring straight up at the enormous granite Flatirons always gave Peter a fresh perspective. Climbers from all over the world were drawn to climb the famous rock faces. But every year there were accidents that took the lives of even the ardent enthusiasts. Being alone with the granite monsters pulled out the most reluctant courage in a person; the trick was not to lose your good judgment.

As Peter drove out of the Chautauqua parking lot, he reflected on his growing courage to let go of the command and control props he had relied on for years in favor of the elusive world of the bee-keeper. The trick was not to lose his good judgment, or he would end up like the occasional climber on the Flatirons.

Bear Creek Cards was located in Interlocken, a new industrial park off Highway 36, on the south

side of Boulder. The company had been around for years, so he assumed that it had only recently moved into this newer building to expand business. He was more right than he knew.

The CEO was a mercurial, reclusive ex-hippie named Corky Russell, who was something of a local legend. Like thousands of other young idealists, he had come to Colorado in the late '60s. Berkeley and Boulder were the meccas for people like Corky. Coming from the East Coast, Boulder had the convenience of being 1,500 miles closer than Berkeley.

Corky had lived in a commune and embraced the Free Love movement and drug culture with open arms. After two years of counterculture leisure, Corky couldn't stand the monotony or the poverty.

He had a talent for painting and saw an opportunity to sell fresh perspectives of Boulder's brightest to the parade of young tourists who longed for the illuminated lifestyle and freedom that Boulder represented in the early '70s. He started painting pithy, New Age greeting cards and began by selling them on Pearl Street, the main gathering place in town. The problem was, he couldn't make enough of the cards. The tourists bought everything he had in stock by noon every day.

> **CORKY'S RECLUSIVE NATURE HAD LED TO RUMORS OF HIS DEATH, BUT THEN HE WOULD SUDDENLY SHOW UP, LONG HAIR FLOWING, WITH TALES OF WORLD TRAVELING ADVENTURES IN TIBET OR SOUTH AMERICA.**

What followed in the intervening decades was the creation of a small but powerful 93-person enterprise that effectively challenged competitors hundreds of times its size. Indeed, there had always been rumors that Hallmark Cards was interested in taking over Bear Creek Cards, and of Corky doing top-secret contract work for his competitor.

Over the years, Corky's reclusive nature had led to rumors of his death, but then he would suddenly show up, long hair flowing, with tales of traveling adventures in Tibet or South America. He was such a fixture in local lore that when Horace mentioned him, Peter was thrilled he'd get to meet the elusive Corky Russell.

Peter was ushered into the executive office suite of Bear Creek Cards by a casually dressed girl who seemed disarmingly at ease. Peter asked her if she liked working at the company and she looked surprised. All she could say was that she had been waiting for this job for ten months and then ran out to answer the phone at the front desk.

The man himself came flying into the room with an assistant near Peter's age following close behind. Corky Russell was a solid, 190-pound, balding energetic man in his mid-50s. Dressed in designer jeans, an upscale T-shirt and an Armani jacket, he played the part of relaxed success.

"Hi, Peter. Corky Russell. Like the office? We just moved here a few months ago. Sure does beat the card table out on the corner of Pearl and Broadway, don't you think?"

"It's a real pleasure to meet you, Corky! I grew up in Boulder, so I've heard about you all my life."

"That's what keeps us in business. I hope you believed everything you heard?"

"I guess I believed most of it."

"Good! Most of it is myth, but a good myth is a public relations dream." As Corky continued, he surged with bravado and personal charisma. "I am a one-of-a-kind entrepreneur. I go where angels fear to tread and when I get there, I always ring the cash register."

Just at that point Corky's silent companion interjected, "Well, not always. We did take a huge hit on the Cascade venture and we are still paying on the 'Your Dharma' line of greeting cards."

Corky turned around and exclaimed, "My God, Peter, I forgot to introduce you to my son, Tom. He is the man in charge around here and, as you can see, the one who keeps me honest. And, yes, I guess we don't always ring the cash register, but we sure have been lucky over the years. At this point, I am just a figurehead who occasionally rocks the boat."

"Tom is the guy who runs the place. He is the one responsible for managing Bear Creek Cards through the last five years of rapid growth, keeping it all glued together, and making us great money every year. Hey, if I can trust him with my life climbing the Flatirons, I certainly can trust him to run the business."

Tom Russell had a clear-eyed, direct stare that took Peter by surprise. In the seconds he shook

Tom's hand, Peter felt Tom's grip go right up to but not beyond his own grip-strength. A handshake like that was proof that Tom Russell had nothing to prove to anyone.

In contrast to his father, Tom exuded a quiet, intelligent confidence. Peter suspected that he probably saved Corky's bacon out on the Flatirons more often than either one of them would care to acknowledge.

Corky started in, "OK, let's get down to business. Horace wants us to talk to you about Growth Community. I am going to warm you up with some of the basics, then Tom will introduce you to

the three primary building blocks of
Growth Community
1. **Leadership**
2. **Meetings**
3. **Organizational Town Map**

"Before I start, I have something to share with you according to the 'Zen of Business' by Corky Russell. Tom has heard me preach this over and over again. It is derived from over 28 years of working in and around this company. I am a simple guy, so I try to find the simple truth in things.

"The simple truth of business is made up of three things: cash, customers, and employees.

"That's it. No more, no less. Without any one of those three, your business is sunk.

> **WHEN YOU LOOK AT THE TYPICAL ORGANIZATIONAL CHART OF A COMPANY, ALL YOU SEE IS THE FOOD CHAIN OR POWER STRUCTURE OF THE ENTERPRISE.**

Everything else is secondary. When you have a clear line of sight at any given time to those three things, you have your head in the game. That's a pretty simple formula but, hey, Horace isn't the only one around here who has figured something out about business. Now let's talk about Growth Community."

Corky continued, "Peter, when you look at a typical organizational chart what do you see?"

Peter looked over at Tom as if this was a trick question. "I guess you see how the structure of the company is set up. Who reports to whom and the roles people hold."

Corky laughed, "Ha, another business school graduate. When you look at the typical organizational chart of a company, all you see is the food chain or power structure of the enterprise."

"Does it really tell you or anybody else the relationships and interdependencies between departments? Does it say anything about how the business works and interacts with the outside world? Does it tell you anything about which departments touch the customer? The truth? No, to all of the above. Honestly, Peter. Is it of any use to anyone?"

Corky didn't wait for Peter to answer and plowed ahead with his monologue. "A standard org chart is probably useful to someone out there who is looking to plug and play people like spare parts. We are not interested in that sort of thing around here. Let me tell you why."

"First, leadership and power in our company sit inside the people who work here. Yeah, sure, there are supervisors and managers who are responsible for getting their team across the finish line on time but, all in all, we infuse our people with a whole lot of responsibility and authority."

When someone hits the ball out of the park, everyone knows it, and when someone screws up or doesn't carry their load, everyone knows it.

"The people around here are accountable to themselves, the people they work with, and the company as a whole. Everyone is part of this community and watches over it. We have builders and protectors and connectors all working under one roof. Anyone who doesn't get on board with this doesn't last long."

Peter piped up, saying, "Sounds like this place is one big foxhole with everyone covering each other's backs."

"That is exactly what is going on here. Anyone who hasn't been here would probably think I'm full of hot air, spouting the latest fad out of *Harvard Business Review*. That just isn't the case. Go out and walk through our company on any given day. Talk to the people who work here. Ask them the hard questions. How do we confront things? How do we deal with conflict? Ask them how things get done around here. You'll see. This place runs from the ground up. It gets messy at times, but I wouldn't trade it for anything. And guess what? We have a waiting list of people who want to come and work here."

Corky stopped for a moment to catch his breath and check his watch. "I don't have a lot more time. I need to finish up so that Tom can share with you the key elements of Growth Community." He took a sip of water from the hiker's bottle he was carrying and then continued.

"Let's get back to our original discussion on org charts. Believe me, once we were able to get rid of the standard organization chart, things started to change around here. I may be a slow learner, but one thing hit me a couple of years after I started this company. I realized that a vital community

> "THIS GROWTH COMMUNITY EXISTS IN EVERY BUSINESS, WHETHER OR NOT THE OWNERS AND LEADERSHIP ACKNOWLEDGE IT. IT IS THE PRIMARY ECOSYSTEM OF AN ENTERPRISE. WITHOUT A HEALTHY ECOSYSTEM, THE BUSINESS EVENTUALLY DIES."

existed inside my business and I wasn't recognizing how interconnected it was to our success. Horace and I called it the Growth Community."

"This Growth Community exists in every business, whether or not the owners and leadership acknowledge it. It is the primary ecosystem of an enterprise. Without a healthy ecosystem, the business eventually dies."

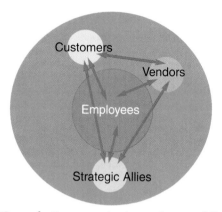

"A Growth Community is made up of four groups: an inside group and three outside groups. The Inside Group is made up of the employees. The Outside Groups are made up of the customers, the vendors, and the strategic allies or business partners of the firm.

"There is a continually evolving relationship among all four groups and it takes constant attention to keep all four in balance. Are you with me so far?"

"Yes, I am, Corky. This is refreshing. I never considered a business in terms of an ecosystem, much less an ecosystem made up of the groups you just named."

"Peter, your company relies on whatever form of culture you have to be the glue binding all four groups together. If the culture is not defined or intact, then the Growth Community doesn't ever gel. It stays disconnected and suffers." Peter began to say something, but Corky cut him off.

"Yes, I know, the 'preferred cultural style,' as Butler calls it, is the 'personality style' of the company, not the culture of the customers, vendors, and allies. The cultural personality style is demonstrated and expressed by the employees and leadership of a company."

"I am taking that idea one step further when we look at it as an invisible ambassador or bonding agent with the customers, the vendors, and the strategic allies. Ideally, when the intentional cultural personality is in the DNA structure of the employees, it ties all four groups together into a Growth Community."

Peter looked at Corky, shook his head, and said, "This sounds all very neat and tidy, Corky, but from my experience, establishing an intentional cultural style in a growing organization is very difficult. All the efforts I have ever taken to set the core values and establish a culture in a company have hit the wall of the company's invisible culture."

"You and I both know that the invisible culture is rarely a pretty sight. The 'under the rug' cultural norms and beliefs held by the staff about the leadership and about the company are tough to go up against. The combination of the company

history, entrenched employee beliefs, and the unfounded conclusions the staff hold as a result of being held in the dark by the leadership all contribute to the invisible culture. Any leader who doesn't think it exists is deluding herself. Don't you agree?"

Corky thought for a moment, then looked at Tom and said, "I think you should probably handle this question." Tom nodded in agreement.

Corky excused himself from the discussion, saying, "Well, Peter, I'm no fool. I know it's time to leave when the first hard question hits the board. I have a conference call that I need to take and there is no better spot for Tom to take over than on a question I wouldn't answer very well."

With that he shook Peter's hand, wished him good luck, and rushed out the door with the energy of a man half his age.

Peter stared into the backdraft of the open door, reflecting on how all legends, including the indomitable Corky Russell, inevitably reveal their clay feet.

Tom broke into Peter's reverie by picking up where Corky left off. "Peter, the invisible culture you are talking about never goes away, even in a healthy company. It is the shadow side of a Growth Community that keeps all leaders on their toes and accountable."

"A weak leader looking for employee approval is intimidated and pushed around by it. A strong leader looking out for the best interests of the enterprise takes responsibility for the mistakes of the company, listens to the murmurings of the invisible culture, yet persists in bringing to the organization a focus and direction as well as demonstrating on a day-to-day basis the intentional core values of the culture.

"And yes, I agree with you. Setting in place a culture based on a set of core values is difficult. The

> "SETTING IN PLACE A CULTURE BASED ON A SET OF CORE VALUES IS DIFFICULT. THE KEY IS LETTING IT EMERGE FROM THE WORK COMMUNITY RATHER THAN TRYING TO IMPRESS THE CULTURE AND VALUES ON THE COMPANY."

key is letting it emerge from the work community rather than trying to impress the culture and values on the company."

"Leadership's role in this is more of an art than a science. In the end-game, creating a value-driven culture is really about the leadership authentically demonstrating the values on a day-to-day basis. The staff will imprint and model leader behavior if it is for the best interests of the enterprise."

Tom motioned Peter to follow him out into the warehouse as he continued. "It just so happens that leadership is our first topic to discuss. Leadership is always a hot item because it is a reccurring challenge for most companies. What makes it even more challenging is the continual parade of trends and theories coming out of the management gurus that only skirt the real leadership issues in an entrepreneurial firm. Most leadership development programs only focus on the principles skill-building piece of Leadership.

"There are five other equally important pieces to entrepreneurial leadership that no one, and I mean no one, addresses. Leadership's job in the end game is all about getting results. My father drilled this into me since I was very young.

"You see, Peter, when push comes to shove, the average Leadership training doesn't get down into the trenches enough for an entrepreneurial leader. Getting results as a CEO in the entrepreneurial world takes a whole lot more than style and people skills.

"Don't get me wrong; they are supremely important, but they're not the whole package by any means. Because of the wide spectrum of issues that he or she oversees, the entrepreneurial leader needs to be hot-wired to the unique elements that drive performance, results, in an entrepreneurial environment. Horace and I call these the:

5 Elements of Growth Leadership Performance

1. **The CEO leader's profile — as measured by** his style and skill set — matching the profile of the enterprise's needs based on its stage of growth
2. **The disciplined process for making decisions**
3. **The continual upgrading of the enterprise profit design**
4. **Identifying and focusing the staff on the 3-5 correct profit drivers**
5. **Creating and applying powerful mechanisms that focus and change individual and group behavior**

"If you think about it, entrepreneurial leaders rarely adapt their leadership style and skills to the rapidly changing needs of their enterprises before it is too late. They are often confident decision makers but make terrible decisions – 65 percent of all leadership decisions are a bust."

"They are almost always innovators and idea people, but ironically it's rare that they innovate a sustainable, profit-driven profit design. They have tremendous energy and drive, but rarely identify and focus their company's energy on the correct drivers of their business. And they rarely have the tools to effectively focus and change the under-performing individual and group behavior of their enterprise."

Peter spoke up. "Wow. Now, that is really leadership in the trenches. I've never heard anyone sum it up so completely. You're right, the standard view of leadership just doesn't cut it with an entrepreneurial CEO. Most leadership development programs just barely cover profiling and improving your style and skills. They certainly don't even go into the other items."

> **" YOU SEE THE STARK REALITY OF THE TYPICAL ENTREPRENEURIAL CEO IS ONE OF DUCKING BULLETS ALL DAY LONG. "**

"That's right, Peter. You see the stark reality of the typical entrepreneurial CEO is one of ducking bullets all day long. Hey, the fact is, guys like us are lacking the proper tools, training, and resources to effectively lead entrepreneurial organizations. Why do you think so many small companies fail? And why do you think Horace spends so much time with us? He knows it all begins and ends with the CEO."

"Think about it. Ninety-three percent of the work force in this country work for guys like us. And 96 percent of all of our economy's innovations come from companies run by CEOs like us. But why is it then that within five years 85 percent of all companies started by entrepreneurial leaders are out of business? And the rest of the companies are barely squeezing out an 8 percent net at the end of the year?"

The two men turned the corner. Off to the side of a huge packing area was a group of seven people sitting in a circle, engaged in an impassioned discussion. Tom gently interrupted the discussion to ask permission if he and Peter could sit outside the circle and eavesdrop on the conversation. The facil-

itator looked at the group and made the thumbs up or thumbs down sign with his hand. Everyone flipped their thumbs up and in a ten-second period they were back in the heat of their debate. Peter leaned over to Tom and whispered, "Is this a Growth Circle?"

Tom smiled, "Ah, Horace told you about Growth Circles, did he? You weren't supposed to get introduced to Growth Circles until you came to Bear Creek Cards. Hmm…I'll have to talk with him about this. I must say it is rare when I ever have a chance to call Horace on the carpet, so I'll certainly enjoy this."

"At any rate, yes, this is a Growth Circle. I believe they are discussing whether or not two peer leader employees should be allowed to represent the staff at the weekly executive meeting. The entire company is voting on it this week. It is quite a hot issue. Each Growth Circle is debating the pros and cons and then voting as a group."

> **PETER WAS IMPRESSED AT WHAT A WELL-RUN MEETING IT WAS. THE FACILITATOR KNEW WHEN TO REFOCUS THE GROUP BUT NOT DOMINATE THE DISCUSSION. EVERYONE WAS SOLICITED TO GIVE HIS OR HER OPINION. THE ENERGY AND VOLTAGE WAS EXTRAORDINARY.**

Peter was impressed at what a well-run meeting it was. The facilitator knew when to refocus the group but not dominate the discussion. Everyone was solicited to give his or her opinion. The energy and *voltage* was extraordinary. Peter couldn't believe that these people really cared about the company more than they cared about their own interests. They seemed to be moving through a disciplined decision making process.

Before Peter knew it, they were voting on the issue. The facilitator again looked at everyone and gave them the thumbs up or thumbs down sign. Everyone tilted their thumbs down, voting against having the peer leaders in the executive meeting. The facilitator closed the process by summarizing that it been a unanimous vote against the issue, based on the fact that they believed they were better represented by the Growth Circles and the managers from their individual departments.

"That was a surprising outcome," Peter whispered to Tom.

"Yes, I thought so, too. Our employees are pretty mature in their thinking, and a whole lot wiser as a group than I ever will be. The core intelligence of this company still keeps blowing me away, and I have been intentionally working with it for over three years. When the Growth Community has powerful meetings like this, it becomes much easier to see and feel the core intelligence."

Tom continued, "This leads me to our next subject: Meetings. Most companies have terrible meetings. They are disorganized, too long, and generally boring. By the way, let's go and take a seat in the break room. When you are trying to create a Growth Community, you must have a dynamic meeting methodology. In order to do this you have to have a disciplined meeting template, a focused agenda, and a well-trained facilitator. Actually the key ingredients to our disciplined meeting template are simple."

Basic Meeting Template

- Everyone's opinion is respected
- Everyone arrives on time
- All staff latecomers pay $1 into a pool for being late, $5 for project managers and $20 for management latecomers
- There is a facilitator
- There is an agenda created by the facilitator before the meeting
- No one has the floor more than one minute straight unless allowed by the facilitator
- There is an appointed scribe who deposits the meeting notes in the company meeting database
- There is a timelined action list created at the end of each meeting with people's responsibilities clearly identified
- There is a timekeeper with a kitchen timer to keep the meetings on schedule
- There is an "agenda time allotment agreement" at the beginning of each meeting
- Meetings start on time and end on time
- Meeting notes are dispersed to everyone in the meeting by the end of the day

Peter exclaimed, "That's a great list. Do you have that written down? I could use that right away."

"Yes, I do, Peter. It is the same information that we give out at our new employee orientation. We also include a description of the three types of meetings we have here at Bear Creek Cards. They are the strategy meeting, the business meeting, and the community meeting."

"We are vigilant about keeping the meeting themes appropriate to the type of meeting that is being held. We found out the hard way that you absolutely must have all three types of meetings going on in your business or you lose the intensity of the Growth Community focus."

"There are three types of meetings here at Bear Creek Cards." As Tom talked, Peter took out his notebook and started writing.

Three Types of Meetings
1. **Strategy Meetings**
2. **Community Meetings**
3. **Business Meetings**

Three Types of Meetings
1. Strategy Meetings
2. Community Meetings
3. Business Meetings

Strategy Meetings

"These meetings are held with the management team once a month, or at least once a quarter, depending on the need. The company's Growth Map and Flash Sheet are present to track the firm's performance. These meetings are designed to generate, track, review, and realign the current strategic

> " EVERYTHING IS INTERCONNECTED IN A BUSINESS ECO-SYSTEM. WITHOUT A CLEAR INTENTION THE COMPANY'S STRATEGIES DON'T PROPERLY DRIVE THE DECISION-MAKING PROCESS AND WE ALREADY KNOW WHERE POOR DECISIONS TAKE US. "

focus of the company. Small company leaders very often lose sight of their compelling strategies in the meleé of day-to-day survival. Retaining that strategy-driven focus is hard, even for a company our size at 93 employees. You see, everything is interconnected in a business eco-system. Without a clear intention in this area, the company's strategies don't properly drive the decision-making process, and we already know where poor decisions take us.

Community Meetings

"There are two types of Community Meetings, the Growth Circle and the Town Meeting. These meetings are absolutely crucial to the health of the company. They should be designed to connect, inform, engage, and inspire the entire staff.

"The Growth Circle, as you have already discovered, is a powerful leadership mechanism that propagates and aligns the company culture, bridges the leadership-staff communication gap, keeps the staff informed, creates a feedback loop, generates a forum for brainstorming and innovation, perfects the company's ability to work in teams, builds camaraderie and provides an effective training tool."

"I can stand here and tell you that without the Growth Circles at Bear Creek Cards, it would have been a disaster over the last few years. They kept this place glued together when the chaos of growing through Stage 5 and into Stage 6 in less than 12 months was driving us to the edge."

"Our Growth Circles meet every week for 50 – 60 minutes. There are 6 – 10 people per Growth Circle, which lasts for three months and then we take a month off. During the three-month portion of the cycle, each Growth Circle chooses and completes a project that in some way advances the enterprise. The results from their project are presented to the entire company at a Town Meeting during the fourth month of the cycle."

"We have three cycles of Growth Circles in a year, and at the beginning of each cycle we change the mix of staff members to allow the staff a chance to get to know and work with everyone in the firm. At that time, we also select and train a new set of Growth Circle facilitators from the staff, which ends up being like a mini-leadership training."

"The cool thing about all this, Peter, is that after less than two years, 95 percent of your staff have facilitated a Growth Circle, they have learned how to effectively lead and work on a project team, they have gotten to know nearly everyone in the company, regardless of department barriers, they have helped initiate and orient new staff members into your culture, they have contributed to the company's innovation, they have been able to have a place to vent their concerns, and they have been trained to understand the tools of leadership. Nothing else touches the power of the Growth Circle mechanism in a dynamic business environment. This brings us to the Town Meeting."

"The Town Meeting is the one-and-a-half hours a month that everyone in the company gets together on the same page looking in the same direction. This is a well-planned, unifying event, with its main role being to review the company's performance based on agreed-upon goals and key health indicators.

"This is the time for the community as a whole to come together to discuss in an open forum any large issues facing the company. Every Town Meeting also has a section in its agenda where 1 – 3 departments, groups, and/or project teams make a presentation to the community about what they are working on. The Town Meeting is also the time when performance awards are given out and recognition of exemplary contributions by individuals and teams is made. The Town Meeting must be designed to generate and end on a high-voltage note, which is why we always end with recognition and awards."

Business Meetings

"There are many different types of business meetings, but we have narrowed it down to four at Bear Creek Cards:

Four Types of Business Meetings

1. One-on-one meeting
2. Project team meeting
3. Department team meeting
4. Management team meeting

> WE FOUND THAT EACH TYPE OF MEETING NEEDS A DISCIPLINED TEMPLATE TO FOLLOW AND EACH MEETING HAS CLEAR AGREEMENTS, ASSIGNMENTS, AND DEFINED GOALS.

"We found that each type of meeting needs a disciplined template to follow and each meeting has clear agreements, assignments, and defined goals. Everyone is held accountable to his or her agreements, assignments, and goals, right from the one-on-one up to the department and management meetings. When the meetings are run well, people perform well, and when people perform well, they tend to be happier. It is simple as that."

Peter stood up from the table where they were sitting and walked to the water fountain. Something was bothering him. How was it possible to implement all these great ideas without disrupting the important work occupying his employees' attention? What struck him most was the sheer enormity of training the staff to the competency level that produces results like those demonstrated right in front of him at Bear Creek Cards.

He saw Tom talking with one of his employees. The employee put a large 5' x 5' cardboard sheet on the table in front of Tom, pointing to blocks of styrofoam that were attached to the board. Peter strolled over to listen in on their conversation.

"Peter, this is Barry from our production department." Peter reached across the table to shake Barry's hand.

Tom continued, "Barry and I are talking about how one of our new production lines is confusing the floor staff. The staff is usually right, so we are trying to figure out how to correct the problem with this Organizational Town Map."

Organizational Town Map

> *WE ALSO USE THE ORG TOWN MAP TO PLAN OUT OUR PROCESSES AND THINK THROUGH SOME OF OUR PROCESS PROBLEMS.*

Peter's face twisted as he heard himself repeating the word. "Organizational town what?"

"It's an Organizational Town Map. We use these for a number of reasons. We use them as a meta frame of reference to explain how our business works to new employees, customers, partners, and vendors. It shows how all of our four Growth Community groups interconnect. We also use the Org Town Map to plan out our processes and think through some of our process problems."

Peter looked down at the board. There before him was a detailed foam core scale model of what appeared to be a small town with streets and houses and power lines. Each house had a name on the roof delineating what department or major function it represented in the business community and who worked in that department.

The main streets were given names like Customer Way, Vendor Boulevard and Partner Place. There were colored lines drawn in the streets showing connections that each building had to other buildings on the map. The streets showed the interdependency all the components had to each other. His first thought was, "Now, I have seen everything!"

Tom saw the look on Peter's face and started laughing. "Peter, I bet you are just waiting to see a model train coming around the corner. Right?"

"Well, come to think of it, I thought it might just finish off what appears to be a perfect Norman Rockwell scene. Tom, you have to be kidding. You use this to plan your major processes in the work community?"

"We sure do. There isn't a person in this building who couldn't show you how our major business processes integrate the work community by using this map. And you know what, Peter? This map is always changing as things change around here, and everyone has to keep up with the changes. Different Growth Circles take the responsibility on a monthly basis to keep different sections of the map current. Every quarter the primary Growth Circle in charge throws the map away and creates a fresh new 3D Org Town Map.

"Peter, you should know that a Growth Community is not a static thing. It is constantly processing through what Horace calls the Community Wheel.

"Here's how it works: moving around the wheel starting at 1 o'clock, you start in the acquaintance phase, getting familiar with the folks in the community, then you move to the communication phase, where you get better at communicating with each other, then you move into the trust phase, where you begin to trust the folks you are working with, then you move into the participating and commitment phase, where you are fully engaged, and finally you realize you have a community.

" A GROWTH COMMUNITY IS A PROCESS, A DYNAMIC STATE, NOT A DESTINATION. WHEN WE LOADED UP WITH A 45 PERCENT INCREASE OF EMPLOYEES OVER A PERIOD OF 12 MONTHS, WE WOULDN'T HAVE BEEN ABLE TO RETAIN OUR CULTURE IF WE DIDN'T HAVE THE GROWTH COMMUNITY MECHANISMS IN PLACE. "

"Any time you add new employees, the community wheel starts over, to some degree. Any time you take a major hit, such as Growth Trauma, you start the wheel all over. Any time there is a major shift or change in the cultural focus or direction of the company, you start the wheel all over. A Growth Community is a process, a dynamic state, not a destination.

"The ideal state called 'community' is a continually shifting target. Any time someone new is brought into a work community, there is a change. So when we loaded up with a 45 percent increase of employees over a period of 12 months, we wouldn't have been able to retain our culture if we didn't have the Growth Community mechanisms in place."

Peter stood up and made the standard time-out sign with his hands. "Tom, do you have any idea how much information you just downloaded to me? You couldn't mention the most valuable secret of business to me right now without making my brain scream."

Tom laughed. "Well, Peter, Horace told me to drill it home hard because you were a willing and attentive learner. Let's call it a day. I'm confident that you and I will be talking quite often in the next couple of weeks. Please don't hesitate to call if you have any questions or if you need to throw some ideas around with a fellow 'bullet dodger.' OK?"

Peter gave Tom a knowing nod as he put out his hand in appreciation for all the time and attention Tom had given him that afternoon.

Walking out through the front door of Bear Creek Cards, Peter looked around at the scenery of the Rocky Mountain Front Range. His mind was racing after all the information he had been given, and his thoughts quickly turned to his brother. What was Alan thinking?

There was no way he could have made Bolder Solutions work without some big changes on his part. Alan's company would have failed, and with it, the whole seed genome project and the hopes of feeding millions of people. The pressure Peter now felt wasn't the enormous pressure of the events surrounding his business and all the implications its success or failure implied. No, it was the pressure he felt inside to change himself, how he thought, how he considered and manifested the dream called Bolder Solutions. The only thing that had to change was Peter Logan, and everything else would follow.

© Gardiner Tucker

CHAPTER 19 — KEY POINTS

Three Primary Building Blocks of Growth Community:

1. Leadership

5 Elements of Growth Leadership Performance:

1. The CEO leader's profile (as measured by his style and skill set) match the profile of the enterprise's needs based on its stage of growth.
2. The disciplined process for making decisions
3. The continual upgrading of the enterprise profit design
4. Identifying and focusing the staff on the 3-to-5 correct profit drivers
5. Creating and applying powerful mechanisms that focus and change individual and group behavior

What an Entrepreneurial Leader Needs to Know:

- What aspects of his/her leadership style are working and what aspects are causing poor performance
- What his/her company's leadership requirements are, based on its current stage of growth, and how to adapt his/her style to those requirements
- How to know when he/she is making a poor decision and what to do about it
- What is his/her company's profit design? Does it really work and, if not, what to do about it
- What are the primary profit drivers for his/her business and how to get his/her staff focused on them
- How to focus and change individual and group behavior to improve enterprise performance

2. Meetings

Basic Meeting Template:

- Everyone's opinion is respected
- Everyone arrives on time
- All staff latecomers pay $1 into a pool for being late, $5 for project managers and $20 for management latecomers
- There is a facilitator
- There is an agenda created by the facilitator before the meeting
- No one has the floor more than one minute straight unless allowed by the facilitator
- There is an appointed scribe who deposits the meeting notes in the company meeting database
- There is a time-lined action list created at the end of each meeting, with people's responsibilities clearly identified
- There is a timekeeper with a kitchen timer to keep the meetings on schedule
- There is an "agenda time allotment agreement" at the beginning of each meeting
- Meetings start on time and end on time
- Meeting notes are dispersed to everyone in the meeting by the end of the day

Different Kinds of Meetings:

- Strategy Meetings
- Community Meetings
- Business Meetings

3. Org Town Map

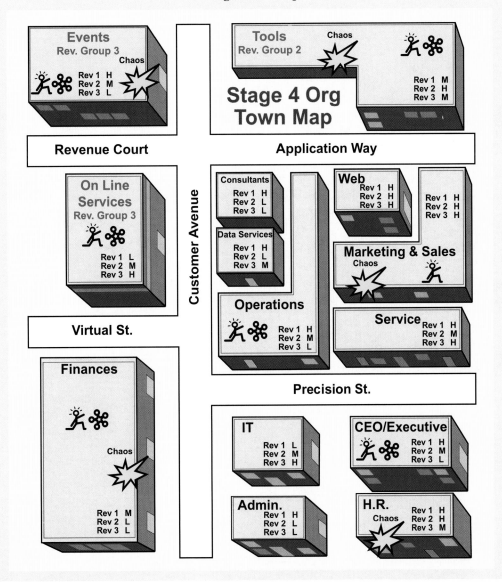

Chapter 20

CRACKING THE CODE

"The enlightening and revelatory characteristic of a good map derives from its encompassing vision, contained within a single consistent pictorial model. We obtain a vision of a place that we may never have seen, or divine a previously unseen pattern in things we thought we intimately knew."
— **William Owen,** *Mapping a Graphic Guide to Navigational Systems*

The 70-mile-an-hour reverie down Highway 36 into Boulder Valley was broken by Peter's cell phone reminding him that voice mail messages were backing up. There were eight messages. Two were from the office and six were from Jane. Dialing the office first, Peter asked for Dean, but Jeanie, the receptionist, told him that Dean had just gone for coffee with three of their top programmers.

Evidently, all three, including Maria, were offered 40 percent pay increases and a $10,000 cash bonus to move over to another development firm in Boulder. Then Jimmy got on the line to let Peter know that they were overextended on their line of credit and checks would start bouncing tomorrow if he didn't ask the bank for an increase to their credit line. All hell was breaking loose at Bolder Solutions.

Thinking Jane's calls would be respite from the stress guns at the office, he began listening to her

> **ASIDE FROM THE NEWS THAT THE POLICE DISCOVERED SOMEONE PLANTING A BUGGING DEVICE IN A TREE OUTSIDE HIS HOUSE, A FELLOW DETECTIVE ALSO FOUND HARD EVIDENCE THAT PETER WAS BEING TAILED BY A HIRED KILLER.**

messages. Each one was asking him to call her right away, and each message increased in its tone of urgency. Just before he pulled up to his next appointment he listened to the last call.

Her voice was shaking as she insisted that he call her. Aside from the news that the police discovered someone planting a bugging device in a tree outside his house, a fellow detective also found hard evidence that Peter was being tailed by a hired killer.

Peter pulled up next to a police cruiser parked outside Juniper Galleries on Pearl Street. He immediately dialed Jane's number, but it was busy. He left a voice mail and then called his bank officer. Again, he had to leave another message. Frustrated, he looked up to see a police officer approaching his car.

"Peter Logan?"

"Yes, I am Peter Logan. What's the problem, Officer?"

"Mr. Logan, Detective Jane Carnes assigned my partner and me to start a 24/7 protective watch over you. I'm afraid you're going to have to put up with our company until the department gets a better handle on the people trying to harm you."

"Officer? How did you find me here?"

"Detective Carnes called a guy named Horace. This guy Horace told her you were on your way to Juniper Galleries. So we drove right over here to wait for you."

"Well, thank goodness Ms. Carnes is resourceful."

"Yes, sir. She is that!"

"Gentlemen, I appreciate your help. Would it be suitable for me to continue my afternoon with my next appointment at Juniper Galleries?"

"Yes, sir. My partner will cover the back door and I will watch the front."

Peter opened the gallery front door, shaken by the sudden turn of events. Standing five feet from the entrance was a short, thin woman with streaked auburn hair, a bright red designer skirt that danced on her hips as she moved forward to introduce herself.

"Hi, I'm Tracy Birch. This must be the famous Peter Logan."

"Yes, it is, Tracy, police escort and all."

Tracy extended her hand to welcome Peter, adding, "Horace just called, Peter. He mentioned that you might be a little distracted by the current state of affairs, but that I was to reel you in and drill your focus into Growth Mapping."

Tracy laughed as she pulled Peter deeper into the gallery. "Peter, I know exactly how you feel. I have

> **I'VE HAD NEW GUINEA HEADHUNTERS CHASING ME, CROATIAN SNIPERS SHOOTING AT ME, RUSSIAN MAFIA LOOKING FOR ME, AND ONE OF THE HONG KONG TRIADS TRYING TO STEAL MY ART AND DUMP ME INTO THE SOUTH CHINA SEA.**

traveled all over the world looking for art, and believe me when I tell you I have experienced my share of tough spots. I've had New Guinea headhunters chasing me, Croatian snipers shooting at me, Russian mafia looking for me, and one of the Hong Kong Triads trying to steal my art and dump me into the South China Sea. On any given day, your number just might come up. It doesn't matter if it is a heart attack, a hit man, or a Mack truck. When it's your time, it's your time. Until that time, you got to keep pushing full speed ahead. Right?"

Peter laughed, saying, "Well, Tracy, putting death in those terms certainly does lighten things up a bit, now doesn't it? I'm intrigued with your confidence that you can shift my attention from being unduly concerned for my life to being absorbed in…what did you call it? Growth Mapping?"

Tracy looked silently at Peter for a long moment then turned a serious stare out the store front window. "Peter, I chose to be a businesswoman, not a scientist, not an art historian, not a teacher or a doctor for good reasons.

"Business provides me the greatest spectrum of exploration and personal growth for the kind of life that I want to lead. As such, I take business very seriously.

> " I HAVE OWNED THREE BUSINESSES. TWO OF THEM WENT BANKRUPT AND THIS ONE, JUNIPER GALLERIES, IS DEBT-FREE, RUNNING AT $43 MILLION A YEAR WITH 40 EMPLOYEES AND CONSISTENTLY BOOKING 21 PER-CENT PLUS NET PROFIT A YEAR. "

"My company isn't successful because of family money, or because I have a MBA from Harvard, or because I have great connections. I have none of them. As a matter of fact, I grew up in a poor family just outside Kansas City. I barely graduated from high school."

"When I turned 18, I took $200, a love for art, an unquenchable curiosity for seeing the world, and I hitchhiked to NYC. I have seen all the great art museums in the world. I have drunk tea in Beijing and sipped coffee along the Champs d'Elysees in Paris. Fifty-one countries and 22 years later, I have been rich once and I have been flat-broke more times than I care to think about. I have owned three businesses. Two of them went bankrupt and this one, Juniper Galleries, is debt-free, running at $43 million a year with 40 employees and consistently booking 21 percent plus net profit a year.

"My company is successful, Peter Logan, because my staff and I are cracking the code, the chaos, the obstacles we encounter every day with an intensity that is, frankly, extraordinarily stimulating. You see we love what we do here. Did we always love it? No. Did it take a long time to figure out how to make it all come together? Yes."

"I attribute our success at Juniper to three things: my staff, Growth Mapping, and our profit design. The single most important success tool we use here at Juniper is Growth Maps. We had great ideas and a very dedicated staff, but it wasn't until Horace introduced Growth Mapping to us that we really were able to create and sustain a level of focus that brought the bacon home. We live and breathe Growth Mapping around here, so Horace sent you to the right place to learn about it."

Peter stared at Tracy with disbelief. This woman had the rare, irrefutable confidence that is hard won everyday. She was a force of nature, ready and willing to take on the next challenge. Where did Horace find all these people?

After a long pause Peter picked up one of Juniper's brochures from the counter, stared at it, and said "Well, after a story like that, I'm ready for both barrels."

"Great! Then let's take a tour. If I were you, my first question would be, 'How in the name of heaven does Tracy Birch generate $43 million out of a storefront?'"

Peter smiled. "Actually, I was just wondering that!"

Tracy continued, "Good. Scalability of revenue groups in the standard fine art gallery profit design is practically non-existent in the art world. People have tried to create wider exposure by listing and showing photos of art on the Internet. For posters and prints it works all right, but people don't buy 'real art' that way. The purchase of a fine art piece is the result of an experience with the art. Fine art is rarely purchased because it is listed and/or displayed on someone's computer screen.

"You see, Peter, five years ago we realized that we were in the art experience business rather than the art distribution business. It was a huge revelation.

After doing our first Bucket Map we discovered that our top profit driver for Juniper was our ability to 'stage an art experience.' We have turned gallery design into a science. Let's take a walk around."

Tracy's gallery had a large volume of space that was created by high ceilings and 10,000 square feet of floor space. Yet, with all the space, the gallery still felt intimate and inviting. Peter had to admit that somehow the space slowed down his sense of time. He felt relaxed and at ease.

"Tracy, you have created a wonderful space here. How did you do it?"

"Thank you, Peter. If I told you I would be giving away our most prized trade secrets, but suffice it to say that we discovered a unique relationship between light, distance, color, and compression that, when combined according to our proprietary formulas, creates the optimum showcase for art."

"You see, if you came back to our gallery in two months, your experience of this space would be entirely different because it is likely that the art would be different and we would have changed the interior space to fit the art. We actually sculpt the space in the gallery. Every wall and ceiling panel is moveable. The lighting and wall colors can all be changed. Overnight. We can make our gallery small and intimate or wide-open and airy. In any given week, you can visit the gallery and not recognize the place from the last time you were here."

"Being able to accomplish this level of adaptability facilitates the type of art experiences that sell a

> **WE ACTUALLY SCULPT THE SPACE IN THE GALLERY. EVERY WALL AND CEILING PANEL IS MOVEABLE. THE LIGHTING AND WALL COLORS CAN ALL BE CHANGED. OVERNIGHT. WE CAN MAKE OUR GALLERY SMALL AND INTIMATE OR WIDE-OPEN AND AIRY.**

lot of art. What made us really successful was taking this space and building a virtual reality of it on the Internet. We simulated, through our proprietary formulas, the optimum display of any fine art in virtual reality."

"The incredibly lifelike conditions of our gallery onscreen are absolutely remarkable. Now, we can display more art because our virtual gallery has turned into 20 virtual galleries, plus, we have people coming to our site from all over the world to experience our art. As a result, our sales have skyrocketed."

Tracy took Peter over to the computer screen sitting on the sales counter and showed him the online virtual Juniper Gallery. He was shocked at how realistic and customized it was.

"Tracy, this must have cost millions to create this level of realism."

"Yes, it did, Peter. That is why my profit design is such an important factor in our success. We realized that in order to make this work, we needed

strategic alliances aligned with our revenue groups that had both capital and fine art inventory. I picked out the 20 best art galleries in the world, sold each of them a small piece of Juniper, and worked up agreements to display their fine art inside Juniper Galleries' Web site. So in one step we financed the Web site and found enough inventory to fill 20 Internet galleries."

Just as Tracy was about to further elaborate on Juniper's profit design, Kathy, her assistant, came over and politely interrupted her conversation with Peter.

"Excuse me, Tracy, you asked me to keep you on track in your meeting with Peter. By my reckoning you should be upstairs, deep into your discussion of Bucket Maps, by now."

"OK, Peter, let's take a hike upstairs. That's where all the action is anyway." As Tracy and Peter climbed the long wooden staircase to the second floor, Tracy introduced Peter to the principles of Growth Mapping.

"Peter, Growth Mapping is designed to fuse your enterprise with the future. Our Growth Maps are a combination of a blended left brain-right brain scorecard and a collaboration tool. They utilize the power of visual mapping to capture the attention and imagination of the staff. The maps you are about to see upstairs become the recurring frame of reference so critical to sustaining employee buy-in of our company strategies, goals, and initiatives."

"At Juniper Galleries, the purpose of **Growth Mapping** is:

1. To promote effective two-way Communication between the staff and leadership
2. To facilitate enterprise Involvement and Buy-in of the strategic initiatives, goals, and issues of a project, a department, as well as an entire organization
3. To assist the Tracking and Learning from the key daily indices connecting the performance of the enterprise with its strategic objectives
4. To secure the Alignment of responsibility and the key resources required to accomplish the desired strategies and goals
5. To support the Recognition of current performance as the fuel for higher performance in the future

" GROWTH MAPS BECOME THE RECURRING FRAME OF REFERENCE SO CRITICAL TO SUSTAINING EMPLOYEE BUY-IN OF OUR COMPANY STRATEGIES, GOALS, AND INITIATIVES. "

"We have found that after four years of extensive experimentation, there are three primary types of maps that we regularly use at Juniper Galleries."

Three Types of Growth Mapping
1. **Bucket Maps**
2. **Company Maps**
3. **Landscape Maps**

As Peter quickly jotted down notes, he asked, "Tracy, is this anything like the Balanced Score Card system?"

Tracy led Peter through the double-arch entryway to the second floor and turned to address his question. "Kaplin and Norton, the authors of the Balanced Score Card System, brilliantly introduced the double-feedback loop approach to translating strategy into action in managing large, complex organizations. They inspired Horace and me to develop the Growth Mapping system, which is more suitable to smaller, dynamic, and rapidly-changing companies. The Growth Mapping System has key indices mapping and feedback looping in it but it also has many other attributes."

Peter and Tracy stepped into an electric field of human activity as they passed into the large room. The afternoon light, pouring in through the high clerestory windows, framed the dozens of work centers filled with employees in small meetings or on the phones conducting business with buyers from all over the world. Peter heard a cacophony of human communication as he counted more than five different languages being spoken in the room.

Just as his mind was taken back to Horace's beehive analogy, a long, robotic telescoping arm, anchored at the center of the ceiling, swung five feet above their heads holding a 3'x 4' white foam core board. The board appeared to have some kind of relational process flowchart on it. The crane-like arm went past Peter and Tracy further into the room and released the board to a young woman who was gathering with four other employees in a meeting nook.

Peter looked at Tracy in awe and said, "Are you sure Scotty didn't just beam us up to the Enterprise?"

Tracy laughed and shook her head saying, "Peter, meet Rupert. Rupert is our automated Growth Map search and retrieval system robot. If you look over to the center of the east wall, you will notice our Growth Map storage system. Rupert is constantly delivering or retrieving Growth Maps to our employees all day long. You see we use a lot of Growth Maps here at Juniper. Horace's other companies use maybe 10 percent of the maps that we use here.

"We found that Growth Mapping became such a powerful management tool for us that we went from putting our Growth Maps on the walls or storing them in our work centers to organizing them as we organize and store our art in the vault downstairs. We employ the same type of robotic search and retrieval system in the basement whenever one

> " A BUCKET MAP IS DEFINED AS A CAUSAL WEIGHTING DIAGRAM THAT SHOWS YOU THE HIERARCHY OF IMPACT THAT KEY INTER-DEPENDENT ELEMENTS HAVE ON EACH OTHER WITHIN AN INTEGRATED SYSTEM. "

of our employees needs to bring a piece of art out to photograph it for the Internet, display it for a customer, or ship it somewhere."

Tracy continued by saying, "Let's go over and look at the map that Rupert just delivered to Nola. We call this type of map a Bucket Map. Bucket Maps are used to help all levels of our staff understand systems thinking.

A **Bucket Map** is defined as a causal weighting diagram that shows you the hierarchy of impact that key inter-

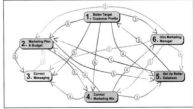

dependent elements have on each other within an integrated system.

"Systems thinking engages us to consider the relationship of the parts of our company as they are linked together in the whole. Systems thinking is crucial for our staff to capture a broader view or understanding of processes and core drivers in the business. You can't access the core intelligence of your work community if your staff gets stuck in the isolated view of the parts that so often happens in most small companies. Bucket Maps help us grasp the resources that contribute to the processes and drivers inside projects, departments, and inside a larger view of the company as a whole.

"All Bucket Maps have three things in common: They are relational, they are sequential, and they are value-weighted.

"The Bucket Map in front of us shows the weighted causal relationships between the key resources (the square buckets) and the end outcome, which in this case is the completion of one of our virtual Web sites."

Peter was taken aback at the maze of lines and arrows connecting the different buckets. As he studied the map, he could see which resources had critical roles by the number of arrows streaming in and out of them. He could also see by the numerical weighting process how the team identified a sequential flow.

By considering the relational, sequential, and value-weighting of all the resource buckets, he began to see how a project team could understand the interconnectedness among all the resource buckets inside the whole process.

Peter broke into Tracy's momentary silence and said, "Tracy, this map reminds me of the Town Map that Tom and Corky use over at Bear Creek Cards."

Tracy laughed. "Yes, the Town Map is a form of Bucket Map. Tom and I have had many discussions about the Town Map. He's a very creative guy. To think that he took the Bucket Map principles and

> **BUCKET MAPS FORCE OUR BRAINS TO THINK MORE GLOBALLY. BY UTILIZING BOTH SIDES OF THE BRAIN'S CAPABILITY WITH MAPS, WE ARE BETTER LEARNERS, BETTER THINKERS, AND BETTER PROBLEM SOLVERS.**

created a 3D version of it is terrific. A Town Map could be helpful in any kind of business environment for the staff to understand the larger processes and relationships in the Growth Community between the vendors, allies, customers, and staff.

"Peter, we use Bucket Maps to force our brains to think more globally. By utilizing both sides of the brain's capability with maps, we are better learners, better thinkers, and better problem solvers. We use Bucket Maps for everything from understanding process flow, to identifying key drivers, to teaching new staff how the company works, to thinking through complex, challenging problems.

"The Bucket Map, as an interactive collaborative tool, has become a very important part of our innovative thinking and analytical process here at Juniper."

Just as she finished her thought, Rupert, the Growth Map Robot, passed overhead with another map, but this one looked more like an eighteenth-century exploration map than a business diagram. The only reference to business Peter could see were the boxes in the four corners identifying the strengths, weaknesses, opportunities, and threats of the company.

As the robot released the map to a bearded man, Tracy said, "Rupert has great timing. Let's go over and talk with Isaac. He pretty much runs this place, the staff love him, and he knows more about our company and Growth Mapping than anyone here. By the way, he's also the inventor of Rupert, our robotic send-and-retrieve system."

A tall, black-haired man held the large foam core board as he greeted a handful of employees who were walking into the conference room. He waved to Tracy and Peter.

"Hi, Tracy. The managers and I are getting ready to make the changes to the Company Growth Map."

"Isaac, meet Peter Logan. He's a friend of Horace's and is here to learn about Growth Mapping. I know you're busy with the managers, but would you mind terribly giving Peter a quick overview on our use of Management Maps before you start your meeting? I need to run over across the street to finish setting up our new overseas account at Colorado Business Bank."

"Glad to meet you, Peter." Looking at Tracy, Isaac smiled and jokingly said, "But if Peter is half as dangerous as they say he is, then his story might be a whole lot more interesting than my explanation of Growth Maps."

Peter and Isaac shook hands as Tracy left for the bank.

Peter looked at the trim, well-tailored 50-ish gentleman who carried himself with a confidence born from years of selling expensive art in the finest galleries around the world. Isaac was the consummate expression of understatement, with the eyes of a seasoned businessman.

"Isaac, believe me when I say my story is more embarrassing than interesting. I'll bet you have 50 stories in your little finger for every one I have."

"Well, that's very kind of you, Peter. Life certainly has been engaging. Speaking of stories, that's a perfect segue into Management Maps."

"About two years ago, Tracy brought me here from Paris to run Juniper Galleries' move into virtual reality. It wasn't so much that I understood technology, because I don't, but more that I understood how to communicate with people to get things done. My venture into Growth Mapping started one day when Horace was here talking to Tracy and he mentioned that I might be able to coordinate the efforts of the company's multiple projects into one system of Project Maps. Well, that was the beginning of my relationship with Horace Bedford."

Isaac reached over to lean a number of maps face-up against the wall. "You see **Management Mapping**, one of three aspects to Growth Mapping, is comprised of three categories of maps: Enterprise Maps; Department Maps; and Project Maps. Admittedly, Peter, we are 'whole brain' enthusiasts around here and as a result, we have developed the art and science of business mapping to an extreme. Suffice it to say every map you see here today has survived a series of very tough practical tests to stay in the game. Above all else, each map must clarify the work, make the work easier, and provide insight for finding solutions in the work."

Isaac continued, "What you see here in front of you is a collection of three Enterprise Maps: Company Growth Map, Profit Design Map, and Stage of Growth X-Ray Map. They contain just about every piece of pertinent information that tells our staff and leadership team where we are, where we've been, and where we are going."

Pointing to the Company Growth Map, Isaac

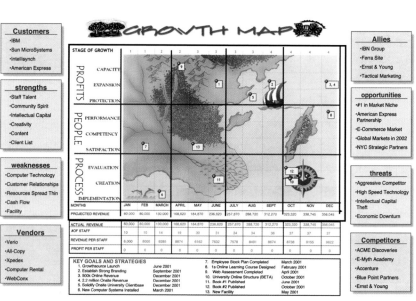

explained, "On this board, anyone in the company has access to our current strengths, weaknesses, opportunities, and threats, our goals, strategies and key initiatives, our customers, vendors, allies, competitors, and our important key indices projected out over 12 months and tracked monthly. This map also tells our current stage of growth, and what stage of growth we will be in according to our projections for the next 12 months, and much more.

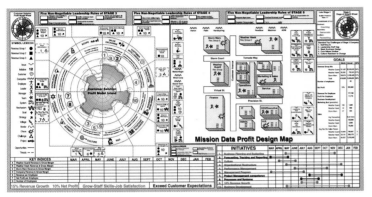

Moving over to the Profit Design Map, Isaac explained, "Milo loves this map. On this board the leadership team has access to the unique blend of 12 profit design components of our profit model, a two-dimensional version of our organizational town map, our key initiatives in relation to our profit model, our key constraints, our key indices tracking on a monthly basis, and much more."

Stepping over to the third and final map, the Stage of Growth X-Ray Map, Isaac explained, "This map is really more about our CEO organizing her thinking into a different view of the company by considering how compliant we are with the rules for our current stage of growth and to what degree

we are managing the hidden forces influencing the performance and health of the firm."

Peter squatted down to study the Company Growth Map. "Isaac, do all the maps contain this much information?"

"Yes and no, Peter. The Enterprise Maps don't change that often, maybe once a month. The Department Maps change dramatically every week, as do the Project Maps. These maps are feedback loops used to focus the staff around the important issues of the company."

"The key word here is loops. I say loops because this isn't a top-down information-

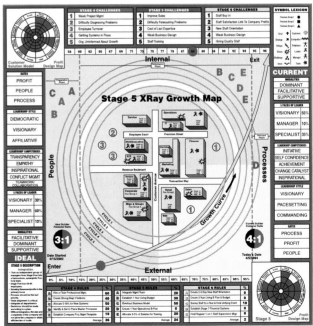

push, like you see in many outdated management systems. The Management Maps actually become the property of the staff. They own them and keep them current. They measure their team's or department's performance and communicate key concerns and new ideas to leadership. As you can see we take this very seriously and are disciplined about the on-going use of the maps."

"Peter, we both know that human beings need incentives to sustain profitable behavior patterns. It's not lost on us that we continually have to reinforce the use of the growth maps through our rewards systems. We never take our employees' interest in the performance of the company lightly. One day it can be going full-blast and the next the air could be out of our sails. We are constantly

"HUMAN BEINGS NEED INCENTIVES TO SUSTAIN PROFITABLE BEHAVIOR PATTERNS. WE NEVER TAKE OUR EMPLOYEES INTEREST IN THE PERFORMANCE OF THE COMPANY LIGHTLY. WE ARE CONSTANTLY FOCUSING THE ENTIRE COMPANY ON A PARTICULAR MAP AND ACKNOWLEDGE GREAT PERFORMANCE BY TRACKING WHAT OCCURS IN THE MAPPING SYSTEM."

focusing the entire company on a particular map and acknowledge great performance by tracking what occurs in the mapping system."

With that, Isaac handed Peter a small square cardboard sheet with printing on it.

"This should help you keep things in perspective. I use these cards all the time with the staff to help bridge their learning. I have all different kinds of them."

The cardboard sheet read, Management Maps provide:

- Communication between the staff and leadership
- Staff Buy-in and authorship of the strategic plan
- Flexible Planning that allows for tracking and learning from the key daily indices connecting the performance of the enterprise with its strategic objectives

Peter looked at Isaac and asked, "Why don't you just keep all the maps online? Wouldn't it be easier than handling all these boards? It seems like quite an ordeal."

"That's a good question, Peter. We experimented with going solely online, but it didn't work. You see, something happens when people meet together in a room. The magic just isn't there online. People need to see something physical that communicates and organizes the thinking in any particular session."

"But we do record and catalog the changes in the Growth Maps after every meeting. The meeting scribe has the responsibility of going into the network and making the changes and developments."

"We couldn't possibly keep for posterity all the Growth Maps that we use around here in the hard form, so we store the knowledge and experience with each map in our knowledge management system. We can pull up any project map we have used over the last three years. We also can search and filter for patterns in what works and what doesn't work by looking through the weekly department maps. We have essentially created a way of establishing organizational memory with the mapping system."

Isaac was briefly interrupted by an employee who needed approval on a large purchase order. Peter took the break to take in everything occurring around the large open room. He began to see how $43 million of revenue went through this business every year.

The room was a maze of intense chaotic activity. Everyone seemed to be running their own show. As he scanned the room, a flash of yellow caught his eye. Perched on the outside windowsill of a clerestory window was a small Western Meadowlark. Seeing the bird reminded him of the early morning backyard symphony he had experienced recently.

Then it struck him. This room was no different from the flocks of birds in his backyard. There were

patterns buried in the chaos that he wasn't seeing. As he realized this, he again scanned the room, looking for patterns. He began to decipher groups of people interacting and then he started distinguishing the selling voices from the administrative voices. The layers of activity became self-evident as he allowed himself to dwell in an inquiring mind instead of a reactive mind. This was definitely the work of a beekeeper.

Isaac broke into Peter's reverie by saying, "Hey, Peter, here comes Tracy. Perfect timing, because I have got to get back to my meeting. It was great talking with you. Be sure to say hello to Horace for me. Tracy will further elaborate on the last type of Growth Map, the Landscape Map. They're pretty neat and, coincidentally, they help build the continuity of cultural memory at Juniper."

Tracy arrived out of breath. She picked up the conversation right away by saying, "Never seem to be able to run up those darn stairs without getting winded. Been working at it for years. Did Isaac fill you in on the Management Maps?"

"Yes, he did. There seems to be so much to digest. I had no idea what Horace was leading me into by touring me through his circle of friends."

"Peter, he did the same to me a number of years ago. I frankly didn't know what piece to bite down on first. Do you know what he did to me?"

"No, what?"

"That old fox had me explain Growth Mapping to one of his new recruits before I ever implemented one Growth Map at Juniper. Can you believe that? He had me teaching this stuff before I had any clue about what I was talking about. It immediately shifted me from being a passive learner to being an active one. It got me out of the 'information collection' mode and into the 'make it happen' mode fast and I haven't looked back since."

"Well, I'm sure Horace has something similar in store for me. There's nothing restful about entrepreneurial learning."

"Speaking of which, Peter, we need to proceed on to Landscape Maps. The policeman downstairs mentioned that a female detective will be meeting you out front in ten minutes. OK, here's the thumbnail sketch on Landscape Maps."

"Landscape Maps serve one very important purpose at Juniper Galleries. They capture time: the past, the present, and the future in a snapshot image."

"OK, Tracy. Bear with me here. I don't mean to be rude. I'm sure that this is important, but I have a

pressing two-word question that pops into my head at times like this and I have to ask it. With all due respect, 'So what?' Why is graphically documenting what has happened, what is happening, and what will likely happen important in the context of all the responsibilities you currently have?"

"Good question, Peter. Frankly, on a day-to-day basis it isn't a high priority. But I live in two time warps: Short-Time and Long-Time.

"As an entrepreneur I spend most of my time in the Short-Time zone. I don't see much past the end of my nose, and stuff is flying so fast that it takes everything I have to keep up with it all. Horace calls this the Problem Modality. I am constantly putting out fires and dealing with problems.

"Once a month in our Town Meetings I'm forced to visit the Long-Time zone. Everything slows down. The entire company gets a chance to review what happened in the past month and what is currently happening. We even get around to discussing what is coming down the road. The Town Meeting forces all of us to slow down and smell the roses. The Landscape Map visually documents that meeting. We have an artist in-house who draws the meeting flow on this large sheet of butcher paper. At the end of the Town Meeting we all can see this incredible landscape drawing of people, events, ideas, goals, and numerous other things all depicting our journey for thirty days."

"What becomes useful from a business standpoint, Peter, is having the Landscape Maps reduced and framed. Follow me."

Tracy led Peter out through the door and onto the upstairs balcony overlooking the gallery space below. All along the walls were dozens of color drawings each with a nameplate defining a particular month and year.

"These are Landscape Maps?"

Tracy kept walking. "Yes, there are 36 maps representing three years of Landscape Maps. I can take you to any month in the last three years and tell you what was going on in the company in that month. As a matter of fact, everyone in the company can take you through a tour of these maps and tell you the company's history over the last three years. And I mean everyone, even the new employees who haven't been around long."

"You see, Peter, we think our company history — or what Isaac calls our company memory — is extremely important to us. We have our employees understand each one of these Landscape Maps so that they can in turn train other new employees about our history. We go to great lengths with this because a visual memory of our culture dramatically enhances our ability to learn from the past and respect all the efforts that went into making this company what it is today. If the Landscape Map does anything, it gives our employees a sense of continuity and respect for the enormous energy and focus all of us have contributed to this enterprise."

"Well, Peter, that's it for now. Just know all of this won't mean a hill of beans to you until you teach it to someone else and start using it yourself. Call me if you have any questions."

With that, Peter thanked Tracy and proceeded down the long wooden stairs to the first floor.

Pacing back and forth in the front entryway was a blond woman running out of patience. Jane drilled into him with steel eyes as he stepped into the lobby. "Welcome back to reality, Peter Logan."

It wasn't her words or her tone that bothered him. It was the baseball bat rolling around in her hands that he found disturbing.

1. Bucket Maps

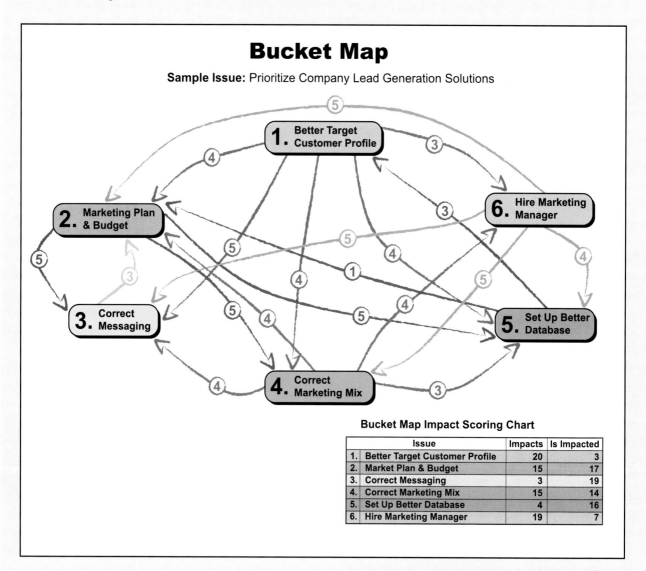

Bucket Map

Sample Issue: Prioritize Company Lead Generation Solutions

1. Better Target Customer Profile

2. Marketing Plan & Budget

3. Correct Messaging

4. Correct Marketing Mix

5. Set Up Better Database

6. Hire Marketing Manager

Bucket Map Impact Scoring Chart

	Issue	Impacts	Is Impacted
1.	Better Target Customer Profile	20	3
2.	Market Plan & Budget	15	17
3.	Correct Messaging	3	19
4.	Correct Marketing Mix	15	14
5.	Set Up Better Database	4	16
6.	Hire Marketing Manager	19	7

2. Management Maps
A. Company Growth Map

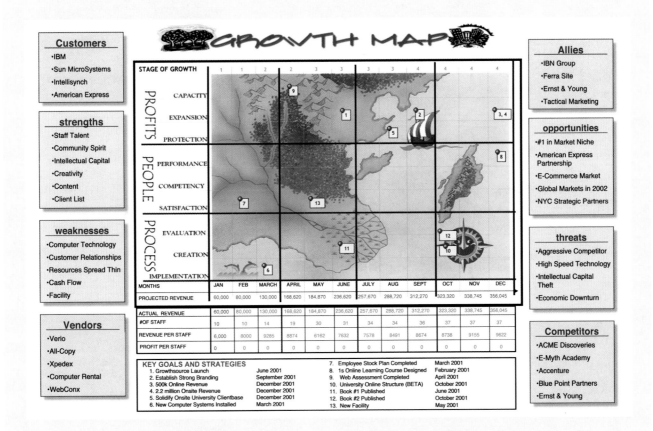

B. Profit Design Map

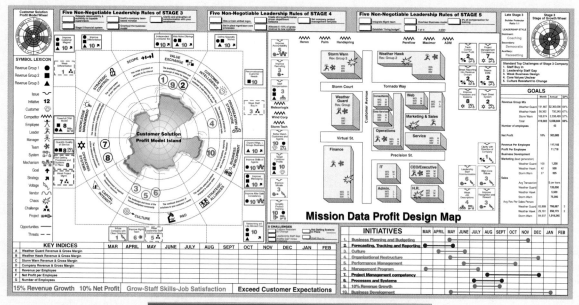

Mission Data Profit Design Map

C. Stage of Growth X-Ray Map

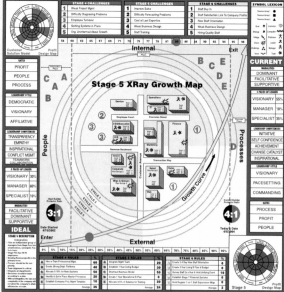

Stage 5 XRay Growth Map

D. Department Maps

Strengths		Weaknesses	
Description	**#Mos.**	**Description**	**#Mos.**
Experienced Sales Staff	4	Lack of Sales Assist	2
Great Sales Process	12	Too much paperwork	12
Hot Brochure	1	Weak Offers	2
Lead Generation System	3	Performance Bonuses	2

Opportunities		Threats	
Description	**#Mos.**	**Description**	**#Mos.**
Lead Industry in Sales	2	Stark cutting prices	5
Alliance with ARC	1	Staff Turnover	10
European Market	3	Too much paperwork	12
On Line Order Loading	3	System Crash	12

Strategic Initiatives & Goals	
Description	**Due**
1. European Campaign Plan	12/15/05
2. On Line Ordering	11/15/05
3. 400 K Sales Month	12/1/05
4. Adv. Sales Training	11/20/05
5. New Product Literature	12/1/05

Revenue	People	Process
		1 3
		4
		2 5

Key Monthly Indicators	Jan	Feb	Mar	Apr	May	Jun	Jul	Aug	Sep	Oct	Nov	Dec
Proposals	7	8	7	6	9	9	10	8	1	2		
Leads Generated	135	120	155	177	201	135	255	175	220	250		
Contracts Closed	3	4	3	5	4	5	6	4	5	5		

Top Goals for the Week — Week of: 10/5/2001

Silencers fixed	3 contracts closed
10 appointments	Dollars in 200K

Challenges & Issues

Item	# Weeks	Who
1. No Sales Assistant	8	Dan
2. Leads coming in late in week	1	Dan
3. Database down at critical times	3	Terry
4. Inventory of Brochures damaged	1	Dan
5. Silencers for phones don't work	2	Mike
6. Leads with no phone numbers	2	Terry
7. Compensation Plan stinks	8	Dan
8. Slow turn around on Proposal OK	5	John
9. Change the contract system for orders	9	Dan

Sales Department
Growth Map

Flash Sheet

Stage of Growth 4	Last	1	2	3	4	5	Goal
Leads Generated	250	55	65	35			260
Appointments	38	8	5	16			40
Proposals	12	2	3	4			15
Contracts Closed	5	1	1	3			6
Dollars per Contract	50K	20	75	55			50K
Volume	450K	20	01	65			560K
Sick Days	4	1	0	0			2
Vacation Days	4	1	2	1			4
Voltage	8	8	5	7			8

Stage of Growth / Month

Project Tracking

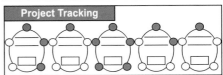

249

E. Project Maps

Project Map

Project Name:
Marketing & Sales Plan

Project Objective:
Write 10-12 page plan document
Get approval from E-Team
Recommend systems for tracking results
Design tactical operating roll out

Dan McGreggor
Project Mgr.

Milestones Wheel

Start __10/4__   Due __11/15__

Project Tasks:	Start	Due	Who	Gantt Chart 10/4	10/10	10/17	10/24	10/30	11/7	11/15
1. Competitor Survey	10/5	10/15	Terry	▬	▬					
2. Market Analysis	10/5	10/15	Dan	▬	▬					
3. Customer Survey	10/10	10/20	Greg		▬	▬				
4. Lead Lists Analysis	10/6	10/18	Dan		▬					
5. Target Market Assessment	10/10	10/17	Dan		▬					
6. Sales Process Upgrade	10/15	10/25	Terry			▬	▬			
7. Strategy Session	10/25	10/25	Dan					▬		
8. Goal Setting Session	10/25	10/25	Dan					▬		
9. Draft Copy of Plan	10/25	10/30	Janet					▬		
10. Systems Evaluation	10/26	11/5	Greg					▬		
11. Systems Research	11/5	11/8	Greg						▬	
12. Tactical Operating Plan	11/1	11/12	Dick						▬	
13. Budget Approval Mtg.	11/12	11/12	Dan							▬
14. Rewrite	11/12	11/14	Janet							▬
15. Completed Plan Presented	11/15	11/15	All							▬

Milestones and Milestone Tasks that are red lettered are completed.

Team Members	
Dick Carlson	Terry Swift
Janet Ball	Mary Stuart
Greg Fraser	Dan McGreggor

Milestones								
Description	**Date Complete**	**Milestone Tasks**						
1. Research	10/20	1	2	3	4	5	1	1
2. Process and Systems	11/8	6	10	11				
3. Planning Sessions	10/25	7	8					
4. Written Plans	11/14	9	12	14				
5. Presentation	11/15	13	15					

Resources Needed
40 hrs. Total Staff Time
$3,000 for data services

3. Landscape Maps

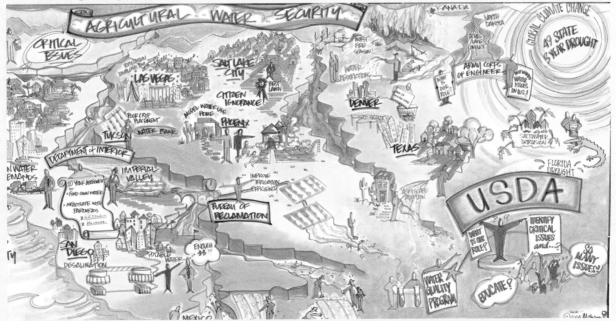

Map by Patti Dobrowolski, Senior Partner, Alchemy: The Art of Transforming Business

The Purpose of Growth Mapping Is:

1. To promote effective two-way **communication** between the staff and leadership
2. To facilitate enterprise **involvement** and **buy-in** of the strategic initiatives, goals, and issues of a project, a department, as well as an entire organization
3. To assist the **tracking** and **learning** from the key daily indices connecting the performance of the enterprise with its strategic objectives
4. To secure the **alignment** of responsibility and the key resources required to accomplish the desired strategies and goals
5. To support the **recognition** of current performance as the fuel for higher performance in the future

Management Maps Provide:

1. **Communication** between the staff and leadership
2. **Staff buy-in** and authorship of the strategic plan
3. **Flexible planning** that allows for tracking and learning from the key daily indices connecting the performance of the enterprise with its strategic objectives

GROWTH TRAUMA

CAUSES

SYMPTOMS

HEALING

GROWTH TRAUMA

"The pathology of organizational growth is rarely a pretty thing to observe or much less to be enmeshed in."
— **Horace Bedford**, *Journal*

"You are either very angry with me, or that baseball bat in your hands is something you won at the county fair."

> " YOU ARE EITHER VERY ANGRY WITH ME, OR THAT BASEBALL BAT IN YOUR HANDS IS SOMETHING YOU WON AT THE COUNTY FAIR. "

"Very funny. This baseball bat saved your life, pal. Would you like to know how?"

"I'm always game for a far-fetched tale."

"Well, there isn't much far-fetched about a 6'4" blond man driving a black Dodge pick-up hired to kill you, now is there? And there isn't much far-fetched about an off-duty detective driving up to a sports store 45 minutes ago to buy his kid a baseball glove, who discovers the black Dodge pickup parked out front. What's even more interesting is the fact that inside the sports store is a tall blond guy buying a baseball bat and glove for his kid, Toby Logan."

"Toby Logan? That's my nephew."

"Well, it just so happens that the off-duty detective overheard a conversation the blond guy was having with the counter clerk. You see Toby Logan, your nephew, is good friends with the detective's son. The detective put two and two together, called for back up, and arrested the guy right on the spot. The guy is being held in a jail cell until we can figure out who he is. With the new Homeland Security Act, you can now hold any suspected terrorist indefinitely. As you can imagine, we listed this character as a suspected terrorist until he tells us who hired him. Oh, and Peter? Guess what we found in this guy's truck?"

"Two tickets to *Cabaret*?"

"Such a sense of humor. No. We found recent floor plans to your house including the new addition you put on six months ago. We found pictures of your nephews, your sister-in-law, their house, your nephew's baseball team and a scope for a high-powered sniper rifle. A wonderful far-fetched collection, wouldn't you agree?"

"My God, Jane! The guy must have planned to be at my nephew's baseball game this afternoon. What do these people want?"

"What they want is to destroy your 'save the world' food project, and they don't seem to care how many people they hurt doing it."

"Well, they're too late. We're done with our side of things and Heritage is off and running."

The next day was troublesome. The ride to the off-site meeting made Peter nervous. He began to question why he was doing this. After hearing about the baseball bat story, Horace had ordered him to set up the meeting. Peter was not comfortable with anyone ordering him to do anything, plus he had no idea what Horace was up to and what the agenda for the day was to be. He had not seen Horace in action with anyone other than himself. Could he trust him with his managers? Would Horace dismantle in one meeting the little bit of trust and respect Peter had worked weeks to develop?

When Horace walked through the meeting room door everyone went dead quiet. Most of the managers were under 30 so their reaction to Horace was like watching an MTV video. Sean Connery meets Def Jam. Their looks ranged from disbelief to relief. The two worlds had few common points.

Horace immediately started the meeting. "Good morning, everyone. You don't know me. My name is Horace Bedford. I am 63 years old. I have been in business for over 42 years. I have owned and operated over a dozen successful organizations. I am a friend of Peter's who has volunteered to come in today and help out with this meeting.

"Let's get started. Peter, why don't you introduce me to everyone. Just give me first names and areas of responsibility."

Peter was shocked. Horace was running this meeting like it was boot camp. Jumping over the cliff, he started with Buck. "First person on your left, Horace, is Buck. He's our sales and marketing manager. Next is Jimmy, who is the company's CFO. Third are Tina, who runs production and her sister Gina, who is in charge of customer service Next is Shareesa, who is

> ❝ THE DAYS OF YOUR BEING CONCERNED ONLY ABOUT YOUR DEPARTMENT'S ISSUES ARE OVER. YOU MUST START COVERING THE BACKS OF YOUR TEAM MEMBERS. ❞

the head of human resources, and finally, directly to your right, is Dean, who is manager of research and development. This is the first formal meeting of this team. All other meetings have been one-on-ones with each manager."

Horace got right to the point. "Ladies and gentlemen, thank you for meeting today. As you may know,

Bolder Solutions currently has an extremely aggressive competitor trying to put you out of business. Your company's very survival over the next few months will depend on one thing: all seven of you must start working as a well-informed, fully integrated foxhole team. The days of your being concerned only about your department's issues are over. You must start covering the backs of your team members. You must start thinking and deciding and acting like you have worked together for years. The in-fighting, which I am certain exists, as it does in all Stage 4 companies, must stop."

Managerial Growth Circle

"You must continue your good work with the growth circles that Dean has already established and include a managerial growth circle now. By next week all of you will have created 8-10 key quantitative performance indices for your department. These indices will tell you and Peter about the health of your department and the company on a daily basis. Starting next Thursday, you will begin the daily tracking of those indices and hand them in to Peter at the end of every day. One of the programmers should be able to create a database on the network that will streamline report collection and reporting.

"These performance indices will be called the Flash Sheet and they will be aggregated into weekly totals or averages for you to review with each other at your weekly leadership meetings. Each of you will meet once a week with the staff in your department and review the prior week's department Flash Sheet. At that time, you will ask your staff for their ideas and suggestions, and you will ask them for the challenges and issues that are slowing the department down. All of this information will be noted on a large department growth map that Peter will be giving you next week. Any questions?"

The room was stunned. Buck was the first to speak up. "Horace, we don't really operate like this at Bolder Solutions. This is a little militaristic for us."

"Buck, it is Buck, right? Buck, ordinarily I would agree with you. We would work through the items I have mentioned and self-organize over a longer period, but you have a very real crisis on your hands. There are times when leadership must be demanding as it adjusts to the severity of the moment."

"Your leadership team has some serious catching up to do. You need to do it pretty quickly or you and your associates here will be out of business in 30 days. As a team, you need immediate focusing

> " YOUR LEADERSHIP TEAM HAS SOME SERIOUS CATCHING UP DO DO. WHEN WE'RE DONE, THIS TEAM WILL BE MAKING WELL-INFORMED DECISIONS AND EFFECTIVELY MOVING THE COMPANY THROUGH THIS CRISIS. "

and training. So I'm coming in, temporarily, as the bad guy and whipping everybody into shape. Just think of me as a coach before the season starts. When we're done, this team will be making well-informed decisions and effectively moving the company through this crisis."

"Now let's go through the agenda for today and set our timing. We'll need to spend a good part of the day going through the assessment data. You all will be generating a company growth map and a key goals and initiatives action list."

Peter was shocked as the day unfolded. Horace's drill instructor methods faded as the team's willing compliance became evident. Even Dean Baldridge took up the new team banner. Horace didn't allow anyone to not participate; everyone was held accountable and they seemed to revel in it. What looked like a total disaster at the beginning of the day turned into a resounding victory at the meeting's close. On top of it all, Peter came away looking brilliant for bringing in Horace.

As they were walking out the door, Peter leaned over and quietly mentioned to Horace, "I guess sometimes it comes in handy to be a watchmaker."

Horace looked at him and laughed. "Once in a while my bones just ache for the old days. I can't help it. See you tomorrow. I'm buying lunch."

The next afternoon Peter was amazed to see Horace holding a bona fide picnic basket. He felt his mirth burst into a hearty laugh. Horace shrugged good-naturedly and exposed the gourmet contents with flair. Peter reached for a thick sandwich on a Kaiser roll, eyeing the brownies fondly.

"Why does this sandwich taste so damn good?"

Horace chewed his own sandwich for a moment. "You're just happy to know this bread won't induce heart failure. I didn't get a chance to ask you yesterday what you thought of Corky, Tom, Tracy and Isaac?"

"I'm amazed at the collection of people you have collected around you. The word remarkable seems to fall short in describing them. I'm seriously thinking of sponsoring these folks to facilitate professional two-hour workshops at Bolder Solutions for my staff. Speaking of which, you made a remarkable impression on them yesterday."

"Well, it must be my winning personality. Even Dean Baldridge came around. You know, Peter, it is rare that you ever need to revert to the command and control approach like I did yesterday, except

> **IT IS RARE THAT YOU EVER NEED TO REVERT TO THE COMMAND AND CONTROL APPROACH LIKE I DID YESTERDAY, EXCEPT WHEN YOU HAVE A SERIOUS EMERGENCY WITH AN INEXPERIENCED TEAM.**

when you have a serious emergency with an inexperienced team." Then he became brisk and continued, "OK, I want to cover Growth Trauma, one of the nine components of the Growth Curve Solution, before you head back to your office."

"I thought we covered that last week?"

"Is it all starting to blur?"

"Yeah, a little."

Horace finished his sandwich. "Hang in there, Peter. There's more for you to know. The reason Growth Trauma is a separate part of this whole picture is that it impacts almost every company at some point. Growing companies are particularly susceptible, but even big companies experience it."

"Well, I know. My company is fairly traumatized by everything that's been going on."

"And now you have to decide what you'll do about it, so it helps to identify the causes accurately." Horace was thinking deeply as he stood up.

"There are three elements to consider when you look at Growth Trauma."

"The power of three?"

Horace smiled. "Yes, Peter, the power of three. If memory serves me, I hadn't gotten to that with you yet. Who told you?"

"C.J."

"Sounds like something she'd remember to tell you about. Anyway, here are the key

Three Elements of Growth Trauma:

1. **Causes**
2. **Symptoms**
3. **Methods of healing**

I'll start at the source, with the causes. Here's a list I put together for you." Horace handed Peter a sheet of paper.

Causes of Growth Trauma:

External Causes

- Market Forces
- Vendor Forces
- Customer Migration
- Shifts in Strategic Partners

Internal Causes

- Business as a Machine Model
- Imbalance of Builders and Protectors
- I'm Right, You're Wrong Syndrome
- Not Doing the Right Thing
- I Can Do It Better Myself Syndrome

3 Elements of Growth
Trauma:
1. Causes
2. Symptoms
3. Methods of Healing

Causes of Growth
Trauma:
External Causes:
Market forces
Vendor forces
Customer migration
Shifts in strategic
partners

Internal Causes:
Business as a machine
model
Imbalance of builders
and protectors
I'm right, you're wrong
syndrome
Not doing the right
thing
I can do it better
myself syndrome

"**Internal causes** are behavioral. The most damaging behavior in companies today is the pattern of ***clinging to the old machine model*** that views workers as cogs in a wheel, replaceable parts of the machine. Many companies still do this today, and they will find it increasingly more difficult to retain quality staff.

"Next cause is an ***imbalance of builders and protectors.*** A business needs both types of people. You need those who will build your company and those who protect it. But you have to remember that protectors act as brakes on the growth of the company. While you need some caution to keep you on track, too many protectors will stop growth, and too many builders will send the company over the cliff.

"Trauma can come in many shapes and sizes. It is best to lump trauma into internal causes and external causes. The **external causes** are usually event-driven. There are market forces, batched under a big umbrella; there are vendor forces, when you lose a big vendor and need to scramble to replace him; there's customer migration, where you lose a big customer or many big customers; and there are shifts in strategic alliances. You get accustomed to working with certain strategic partners and you lose them, for one reason or another. Any of these things can create trauma, but the causes are external.

"THE MOST DAMAGING BEHAVIOR IN COMPANIES TODAY IS THE PATTERN OF CLINGING TO THE OLD MACHINE MODEL THAT VIEWS WORKERS AS COGS IN A WHEEL, REPLACEABLE PARTS OF THE MACHINE."

"Every growth stage has its own optimal number of each type. At Stage 1, you need four builders to one protector. In Stage 3, you need three builders to one protector. By Stage 4, you're at a three-to-two ratio. When an imbalance occurs, companies usually tend toward expanding their staff, thinking that will help. It won't. It will, however, cost them a lot of money.

"Then there's the next cause, the *'I'm right, you're wrong' syndrome.* This happens when you have one or more people thinking their methods are always right. They storm around with their minds closed, refusing to listen to anyone else. This attitude stops communication between management and staff, and it can be very destructive.

"Moving along, the next cause of trauma is *'Not doing the right thing,'* which is difficult to quantify because it's about ethics. Everyone has a somewhat different take on ethical standards. Ethics stem from your company values. If you have someone in your organization who takes the easy route and skips past the ethical approach, as evidenced by the Enron scandal, it could seriously undermine the organization. It may take time, but ignoring or bypassing your ethics policy always comes back to haunt a company."

"The last cause is particularly germane to your situation. It's the *'I can do it better myself syndrome,'* which must have been your brother's approach. It's important to note he did it with the very best of intentions. He really did have answers for everything, until the time came when he just didn't have them any more. If he had lived, he would have been swamped by his inability to do everything himself. His actions caused significant Growth Trauma that you are only now uncovering. He would have had to find a better way to lead."

Peter stopped him. "It's funny. The staff had become painfully aware of what was happening, but they still depended on him for everything. They may have overcome it eventually, but it would have been tough. Apparently, things were starting to fray before he died."

Horace continued. "And sometimes the staff is aware before management is. It's human nature to think everything will somehow work out. But it also helps if management really understands what the symptoms of Growth Trauma look like. If they understand, they can take appropriate steps in time."

"What symptoms do you mean?"

"Here's a list to get you started."

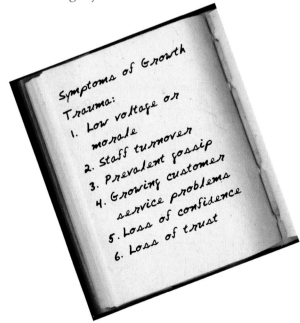

Symptoms of Growth Trauma:
1. Low voltage or morale
2. Staff turnover
3. Prevalent gossip
4. Growing customer service problems
5. Loss of confidence
6. Loss of trust

Symptoms of Growth Trauma

- Low *Voltage* or Morale
- Staff Turnover
- Prevalent Gossip
- Drop in Sales and Profits
- Growing Customer Service Problems
- Loss of Confidence and Trust

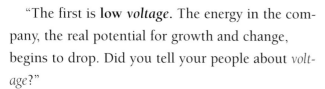

"The first is **low *voltage***. The energy in the company, the real potential for growth and change, begins to drop. Did you tell your people about *voltage*?"

"Actually, I told Dean Baldridge and let him tell them. He really connected to the electric-current analogy. I guess the staff really liked the concept; they've started using the term."

"Good! It will help. Just think of the atmosphere in the companies you've walked into in the last several days."

"Yeah, they were absolutely hopping with energy. And I couldn't help but feel the fun they all seemed to be having. They were still functioning at a highly professional level, but they were enjoying themselves."

"It's contagious, isn't it? OK, let me list some of the others.

"Staff turnover: If you have heavy turnover, you've got problems.

"Gossip. Gossip is probably the most glaring symptom of Growth Trauma: It means there's a lack of real communication so negative things begin to circulate, even if they're untrue.

"Then there's a drop in profits or a drop in sales. This doesn't just happen; it means something is going wrong.

"Growing customer service problems. If you suddenly have problems with a customer that you didn't have before, you need to look at it.

"Last, I'll list a loss of confidence and a loss of trust.

"A company doesn't necessarily have all these symptoms at once, but you probably always have one, or more of them, that require attention. If you see several rising up, you'll need to take a look at what is causing the trauma."

Peter noticed he was absorbing this material. Maybe it was all beginning to make sense. "OK, so tell me, doc, how do I heal the problems?"

"Here are four mechanisms to help **heal Growth Trauma**."

1. **Growth Circles**
2. **Positive Confrontation Model**
3. **Fostering a Community of Inquiry**
4. **Focused Activity**

"You've already taken a big step. In fact, it may have to do with why I'm pushing you. When you started the growth circles without hesitation, I knew you might have a real chance. The circles create a powerful force to help heal Growth Trauma."

"Another tool is to **create a positive confrontation model.** Human beings have disagreements, and they need a means to do so in helpful, constructive ways. Did you know that the personality styles of over 80 percent of the people in the work force are not built to be confrontational? That means people in general will not confront their problems with others. They will go around and commiserate with others instead of facing the person they have a problem with. It is just human nature. People aren't hard-wired to confront, so you have to train them to do it. This is especially true between management and staff.

"There are a few big ideas that we've been talking around, but have not specifically addressed. You must **foster a community of inquiry** rather than a community of opinion. This is not an easy task. Most companies fall into communities of opinion. What they get are judgments, arrogance, opinions, shortsightedness, closed minds, and professional egocentrism. Sounds wonderful, right?

"But the other path is a community of inquiry. Just like it sounds, it means that as a company style, people are curious about new ideas. They aren't threatened by disagreements; instead, they take the time to inquire about what's really going on.

"The Growth Circles are a big help in this area, because you've created a place for the staff to talk to each other. It's sometimes an adjustment for management to stop being opinionated, but it makes a huge difference."

Peter spoke up. "I gotta come clean. I think that was the very first mistake I made. I insisted the staff do things my way before they had a clue what my way was."

"Well, probably, but hold your thought. I want to come back to it."

"OK. Is there more to healing?"

"CIRCULATION AND CONSTRICTION ARE TWO AGE-OLD PRINCIPLES OF CHINESE MEDICINE THAT APTLY APPLY TO THE INTERNAL HEALTH OF AN ORGANIZATION....IT IS FOCUSED ACTIVITY THAT PROMOTES CIRCULATION IN THE ORGANISM OF THE COMPANY AND HELPS COMBAT CONSTRICTION."

"Circulation and constriction are two age-old principles of Chinese medicine that aptly apply to the internal health of an organization. If things are moving, the blood, the energy, the *voltage* of the company, is flowing, but if there is constriction, it all begins to slow down and eventually die. When a body is traumatized, it needs to get in motion, even if only gently at first, otherwise it atrophies. The same thing happens in a business. If you discover a trauma, you need to get the staff involved to work on the issue. Focused activity helps a lot.

It is movement, or in this case, focused activity that promotes circulation in the organism of the company and helps combat constriction, which is the precursor to chronic issues that likely will create serious consequences concerning the survival of the enterprise."

"I don't want to overstate the obvious, Horace, but I think we tend to ignore what's in our face."

"You're absolutely right! The function of recognizing how we see our company — which implies both our insights and our blind spots — defines how effectively we will deal with organizational trauma. If trauma conditions are not dealt with, the *voltage* in your staff will constrict and it will create a vulnerable condition, making your company susceptible to other traumas. It's like a human body that has a weakened immune system — it will be even more vulnerable to errant diseases that normally wouldn't be of concern."

"Now I want you to recall your experience about when you first arrived at Bolder Solutions and insisted on having things your way. Growth Trauma can hit an individual, a small action or project team, a group or a department, or the whole organization. Sometimes, it's a combination. But no matter how it hits, no matter how immediate the project or goal might be, it's vitally important to deal

with the trauma right away. Otherwise, it spreads like a virus."

Horace was silent, letting Peter think about his comments. He wanted Peter to figure out the point he was making. He only had to wait a couple of minutes.

"Of course! I've been too busy to see it. Thank you, Horace. Before I go back and put things right, I need to know when we can talk again."

"Tomorrow. I'll call you in the morning. I think it's time you come to my office."

As soon as he walked into Bolder Solutions, he went straight to Dean Baldridge. Even Dean was amused by his energy. Dean agreed to gather everybody together at three o'clock.

Peter was waiting for them as they seated themselves in the bullpen.

"Sometimes we can get so consumed by a situation, we forget what caused the situation in the first place. First, you are all free to go for the day if you choose. Second, those who would like to do so are invited to stay and have a discussion, a discussion that we've needed to have since I first got here."

Dean spoke up. "What do you want to talk about, Boss?"

"My brother: what he meant to you, what his loss has meant to all of us. I want to talk about Alan Logan."

CHAPTER 21 — KEY POINTS
Growth Trauma

Causes of Growth Trauma:

External Causes
- Market Forces
- Vendor Forces
- Customer Migration
- Shifts in Strategic Partners

Internal Causes
- Business as a Machine Model
- Imbalance of Builders and Protectors
- I'm Right, You're Wrong Syndrome
- Not Doing the Right Thing
- I Can Do It Better Myself Syndrome

Symptoms of Growth Trauma:
- Low *Voltage* or Morale
- Staff Turnover
- Prevalent Gossip
- Drop in Sales and Profits
- Growing Customer Service Problems
- Loss of Confidence and Trust

Healing Growth Trauma
1. Growth Circles
2. Positive Confrontation Model
3. Fostering a Community of Inquiry
4. Focused Activity

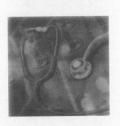

FOCUSING BEHAVIOR

GROWTH MECHANISMS

MECHANISMS

PEOPLE MECHANISMS

CHANGING BEHAVIOR

PROFIT MECHANISMS

Chapter 22
FOCUSING AND CHANGING BEHAVIOR

"Leaders, almost by definition, are people who change minds...a mind change most often results from a slow, almost unidentifiable shift of viewpoint rather than by virtue of any single argument or sudden epiphany."
— **Howard Gardner,** *Changing Minds*

Like a lone survivor looking up from an empty battlefield, a large sealed card lay on his desk, greeting him in the morning sun. Peter hesitated to open it, knowing full well, after the session last night, what it might be.

His hands, as though disconnected from his own volition, moved ahead through his reluctance to unseal the envelope. Fully opened, the card (with 42 signatures etched across the inner face) held the profound sympathy for Alan's passing as though it were a huge ancient oak witnessing the tragedy of yet another battle unfolding under the broad reach of its branches. A deep and final wave of grief rolled up through his last attempts at containment. Then Peter's head gently fell into his two open hands resting on the desk.

Thirty minutes or three hundred minutes could have passed. It was impossible to measure the time spent lost, alone in his thoughts about Alan. All Peter knew was that something had lifted, and the small things of his day seemed to once again feel important.

> "ALL PETER KNEW WAS THAT SOMETHING HAD LIFTED, AND THE SMALL THINGS OF HIS DAY SEEMED TO ONCE AGAIN FEEL IMPORTANT."

Kate sealed the final moments of his reverie by gently knocking on his door and poking her head into Peter's office. "Boss, I have two things for you: You got a message fifteen minutes ago from Horace instructing you to meet him in an hour over at his company, BGT, and you have Grace McGregor waiting for you in the reception area.

Whispering under his breath, Peter grumbled, "Perfect. Just what I need, another tirade from her."

Sensing Peter's reluctance, Kate promised to interrupt him in ten minutes with an "important diversion," if Peter needed it, to cut the meeting short.

"Yes, Ms. McGregor?"

Stopping in the doorway of his office, Grace McGregor stood frozen in an open stance, prepared for the worst. "I guess this is my time to eat crow. I want to acknowledge that I owe you a huge apology, Peter. So here it is. I'm sorry I misjudged you." She blurted it out, and then stopped talking. He thought maybe she was done. But just before he could speak, she continued.

"Apologizing is the hardest thing in the world

> **APOLOGIZING IS THE HARDEST THING IN THE WORLD FOR ME TO DO, SO I HAD TO JUST SAY IT. I WAS WRONG, AND I STAND CORRECTED.**

for me to do, so I had to just say it. I was wrong, and I stand corrected."

This was not what he expected.

She went on. "I was very fond of your brother and his family. I believed in Alan and what he was trying to do."

Peter found himself slightly embarrassed. He couldn't help but wonder if she were serious or simply baiting him. No, she was sincere.

"Well, thanks for letting me know. What made you change your mind?"

"A couple of things. I wasn't kidding when I told you I had access to information. I found out about the attempt on your life. I know now that you weren't part of Santomo's plan. At first, it was hard for me to accept that it was a mere coincidence you worked for them. Then a close mentor of mine suggested I reconsider my unfounded, ill-advised accusation of you."

"You have a good advisor."

"Yes, I do. So do you. His name is Horace Bedford."

Peter's interest perked at the mention of Horace's name. Grace continued earnestly, "Look, I know this is a surprise. So let me just say this: I want to help you, Peter. Santomo should not get away with what they've done to you and your family. I think there is a way to make them pay. Think about it. When you are ready, I have a plan that will definitely stop them in their tracks. If you're interested, please call me. I left my number with your assistant." Grace waved her right hand slightly in the air indicating she was departing and disappeared from view.

The seven-foot walnut front door was the only opening into BGT, Horace's three-story concrete office building. What was it with these guys and plain architecture? The door handle, a customized stainless steel pull-type, tugged open easily for a door so large and heavy. It occurred to Peter that despite its plain exterior, the place was well-built. Clearly, an artisan had hung the huge door.

Entering onto simple but elegant marble flooring, Peter walked through the lobby up to a curved granite reception desk behind which a young man sat staring intently at a large, flat-screen monitor. He looked up. "Hello. Welcome to BGT. May I help you?"

"I have an appointment with Horace Bedford."

"Oh, you must be Peter Logan. Let me tell him you're here." He started to rise, then stopped. "Have you ever been here before?"

"No. This is the first time."

The receptionist smiled. "Then you really should take a look." He pointed to the opening that led into the rest of the office.

The stone faced waterfall behind the reception desk hid Peter's view, so he moved to his left to see what the young man was pointing at. The reception area gave way to a vast open arena with numerous waterfalls and a vaulted ceiling rising up three stories. It was an extraordinary sight! The working area was a series of three terraced tiers, with some parts of the open room utilizing all three levels, some areas using two and some only the main floor level.

There were hanging gardens and plantings everywhere. Large skylights managed to light the entire space. There must have been 30 or 40 people at desks, in various meeting areas, and moving among the three levels by an intricate array of bridges and walkways.

> "THE MOST STRIKING FEATURE OF THE HUGE AREA IN FRONT OF HIM WAS THE FLEET OF SMALL, BRIGHTLY COLORED MINIATURE BLIMPS MOVING THROUGH THE OPEN AIR."

But the most striking feature of the huge area in front of him was the fleet of small, brightly colored miniature blimps moving through the open air. Some of them towed banners touting weekly goals; some carried supplies; some seemed headed toward a specific desk. It was unlike anything Peter had ever seen before.

While he was attempting to take it all in, a three-foot long gold dirigible flew by, heading for the highest tier. As he followed it with his eyes, the receptionist piped in, saying, "The flying dirigible system was Horace's idea. He calls it a communication delivery mechanism that forces us to slow down and to think outside the boundaries of e-mail and the phone to connect with each other. Horace wanted to fill the three-dimensional space we work in with something whimsical as well as useful. They really are quite cool. If we have to, we pick up a phone. But we try to use the tiny blimps to carry messages most of the time. They all have a patented helium flotation system that gets refueled once a week and computer-driven guidance systems, so we can program them to go wherever we want."

"In this case, the gold one you were looking at is hunting for Horace. He moves around a lot, so he's got a special pager that puts out a homing beacon. See, he's talking to that group up on the top level. When the blimp arrives, it will beep at him until he deals with it. Everyone has a transmitter on their belt so the dirigibles can find them."

Peter watched as the familiar face looked up, read something on a small display underneath the dirigible, and looked down, right at him. He smiled broadly, and made a big production of motioning Peter up to his area.

As Peter made his way up the walkways and bridges, he couldn't help but feel the electricity in the office. This was *voltage*! These people were charged up.

By the time he made his way to Horace, the small group had left, and he was standing by him-self. "Now you know what I do. I spend my days watching over a circus. What do you think?"

"It's great! Did you design it?"

"Not a chance. It's all based on an idea that I'd come up with, and many of these people added to it. We hired a local hotshot designer/builder to make it happen. We were looking for a stimulating environment. Gets your attention, doesn't it?"

"Are you kidding? I want to move my whole company in here."

Horace laughed. "Yeah, we get that a lot. Why don't we meet in my office?"

Peter followed him across one of the bridges to an office that seemed to be suspended high in the corner of the big open space. Just to the right of the door to Horace's office was a large brass plaque that stated a quote from Plutarch: "The Mind is not a vessel to be filled but a fire to be ignited." Peter looked over to Horace and said, "Sure does feel like my mind has been stuffed to the brim over the last week or so."

Horace laughed and responded. "Peter, that's just the kindling you needed to ignite the bonfire."

"Very funny. Well, any time you want to throw a match in there, I'm ready."

The walls didn't quite extend up to the ceiling, so it felt like a high balcony overlooking the main space. Still, the moment they crossed into the office, they were enveloped in silence. Horace read his mind.

"It's eerie, isn't it? We had a sound design engineer come in and figure out how to do it. Somehow between the materials and the layout, this little corner is really quiet. I feel like I walk into a refuge when I enter here."

"So when do you tell me what you do here?"

Horace smiled. "Well, like I told you last week, I'm not in the railroad business. But you know what? One of our companies might be."

"Companies?"

"Peter, over the last thirty years, I've been involved in several industries. My biggest successes

> **I'VE MADE ENOUGH MONEY TO FUND THE CASH PURCHASE OF A COUPLE OF FORTUNE 500 COMPANIES, WITH MONEY LEFT OVER TO LIVE LIKE A KING FOR THE REST OF MY LIFE. I GUESS YOU COULD SAY THAT I HAVE BEEN VERY FORTUNATE.**

came in building three companies: an aerospace-electronics company, a medical-instrument company, and a telecommunications company. I've made enough money to fund the cash purchase of a couple of Fortune 500 companies, with money left over to live like a king for the rest of my life. I guess you could say that I have been very fortunate. I had the energy to work hard, and I've employed some of the most creative and brilliant people in the world."

"My interest has always been in the area of growing a company. Once an enterprise was up and running and making money, I'd start looking for a new challenge. After my venture in telecommunications, I started thinking about how a company grows, and how I might articulate a methodology that could be taught to others. So I founded BGT, Bedford Growth Technology. I wanted a place where we could study the problems and find solutions."

Peter interrupted him. "That's what all these people are doing?"

"Yes, but it gets better. Under the umbrella of BGT, I have created a foundation to go more deeply into the question of how a company grows. I wanted a place where we could research and test new methods and practices of growth in emerging entrepreneurial enterprises. But the ultimate goal is to find ways to train people in the principles we discover or develop. What you see here is mostly the activity of the foundation. It's called the Bedford Emerging Growth Foundation."

"One of the first things we did was to form an alliance with the university. The young man you met downstairs is an intern, smart as a whip. I have no doubt that when his internship is finished, he's going to start a business of his own. After his time with us is concluded, he will have an extraordinary foundation in the methodology we've developed."

"Why didn't you tell me all this before?"

"Like you said, you didn't have a frame of reference. Besides, it was much more fun to keep you in suspense."

"I'm just glad to know you have a roof over your head."

"Here's the plan for today. I want to tell you about another chunk of the Growth Curve Solution matrix called **Growth Mechanisms**. Then tomorrow, if you have time, there's somebody you really need to meet, OK?"

"I'll make time."

"Good. So can I assume that, even with all the life and death drama spinning around you for the last few weeks, you are beginning to make sense of the Nine Fundamentals of The Growth Curve Solution?"

> " I MUST BE CRAZY TO SPEND ALL THE TIME THAT I DO VISITING THESE BUSINESS FRIENDS OF YOURS WHEN SO MANY OTHER ISSUES ARE MORE PRESSING. "

Peter said, "Funny that you mention it. Jane asked me the other day if I had a screw loose in my brain. She can't understand why I am so determined to understand these new business methodologies of yours in spite of the relentless attacks on my business and my personal life. She may be right, I must be crazy to spend all the time that I do visiting these business friends of yours when so many other issues are more pressing."

Peter continued, "All I can tell you is that I feel like I'm caught in some kind of business-knowledge tractor beam that is downloading dozens of years of business education and experience into me in just two weeks. So am I making sense of all this material? Yes, I am. And yes, even though I have only been introduced to six of the fundamentals, it has become apparent to me how they are all interconnected. It's hard to talk about one without overlapping into another."

"Right! And this next fundamental is no exception. Today, we are going to talk about **Growth Mechanisms**. It's incredibly important for entrepreneurs to understand this material, but like you, they need to get all the pieces before they can see the whole. Once you have a language to talk about the mechanisms of growth, then you will have a powerful tool to shape and focus your company."

"Now let me clear up something right at the start. Mechanisms are different from systems in that mechanisms are used to shape and focus individual, group, and organizational behavior. Systems are used to address the complexity of activity and processes."

Peter clarified his understanding by repeating what Horace said. "So let me get this right. Systems address the complexity of processes and mechanisms shape and focus human behavior."

"Yes. The need for constant adjustment and fine-tuning of workplace performance makes the recognition, development, and implementation of successful mechanisms one of the most important skills a leader can exercise in a growing enterprise. All successful change initiatives institute mechanisms that promote new beliefs, attitudes, and behavior. At the end of the day, all enduring transformation, innovation, and performance enhancement is a result of Growth Mechanisms being introduced and utilized in the workplace. As a way of understanding Mechanisms you need to think of them in three categories: Growth, People and Profit. To distinguish among categories it is helpful to understand that within each category there are three mechanism qualities." Horace wrote on a piece of paper the list of mechanism qualities:

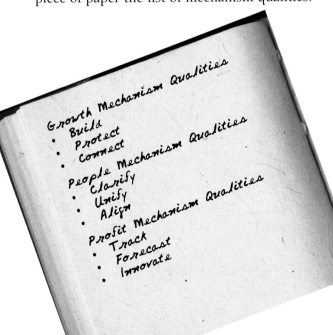

Growth Mechanism Qualities

- Build
- Protect
- Connect

People Mechanism Qualities

- Clarify
- Unify
- Align

Profit Mechanism Qualities

- Track
- Forecast
- Innovate

"To complicate the discussion, any mechanism is not going to exclusively have only one of these nine qualities. It will have a mix of any number of them. An enterprise mechanism may be heavily weighted as something that builds, but it will also function, to some degree, as a mechanism that forecasts and clarifies. Organizing how you think about mechanisms allows you to be more effective designing, developing, and implementing them in the workplace."

"For purposes of our conversation here, there are 12 Master Mechanisms that shape and focus the individual, group, and organizational profit behavior of an enterprise. They have been proven to be highly effective, but I want to reinforce the idea that the mechanisms you create yourself can be equally effective. The 12 Master Enterprise

Mechanisms I have found from my research are:

12 Master Enterprise Mechanisms

1. Flash Sheet/Dash Board
2. Management Growth Maps
3. Decision Making Template
4. Town Meeting
5. One-on-One Meeting
6. Bucket Maps
7. Profit Net Program
8. Meeting Template
9. Customer Reconnaissance Model
10. Recognition and Reward Model
11. Hiring and Orientation Model
12. Growth Circles

Horace further elaborated by saying, "The formula for developing anyone of the above mechanisms, or for that matter any mechanism that you come up with, is simple."

Mechanism Development Formula

- Identify the specific need for a mechanism.
- Determine a very clear purpose or solution your desired mechanism will fulfill.
- Inquire from those who will be affected by the mechanism what it is that they suggest.
- Test and challenge all your assumptions about what this mechanism must accomplish.
- Measure both the possible positive and negative impact of implementing such a mechanism.
- Verify that your new mechanism is in alignment with your company's strategies, goals, and values.
- Enroll a pilot group of willing peer leaders to test the new mechanism in the workplace before you implement it with the entire staff.

"When you're considering implementing a

Master Mechanism Qualities Grid / 12 Master Mechanisms	Growth Mechanism Qualities			People Mechanism Qualities			Profit Mechanism Qualities		
	Build	Protect	Connect	Clarify	Unify	Align	Track	Forecast	Innovate
Flash Sheet/Dash Board	X	X		X		X	X	X	
Management Growth Maps	X	X	X	X		X	X		
Decision Making Template	X	X	X	X	X	X			X
Town Meeting	X	X	X	X	X	X	X		X
One-on-One Meeting	X	X	X	X	X	X			
Bucket Maps	X	X	X	X		X			X
Profit Net Program	X	X		X		X		X	X
Meeting Template	X	X	X	X	X	X	X		X
Customer Reconnaissance Model	X	X		X			X	X	X
Recognition and Reward Model	X	X	X		X	X			X
Hiring and Orientation Model	X	X		X		X	X		
Growth Circles	X	X	X	X	X	X			X

mechanism in your company, it helps to think of mechanisms in three groups, according to their complexity. Some are simple and easy to implement. Some are complex and difficult to implement. For purposes of identification, we call them mini, maxi, and mammoth mechanisms.

"The most effective ones are probably the mini

> **" IF YOU COME UP WITH QUICK SOLUTIONS THAT CAN BE ADOPTED AND IMPLEMENTED EASILY THROUGHOUT THE ORGANIZATION, YOU QUICKLY IMPACT YOUR ENTERPRISE. "**

mechanisms. If you come up with quick solutions that can be adopted and implemented easily throughout the organization, you quickly impact your enterprise. Just follow the formula I just gave you to design, develop, and implement them."

Horace thought for a moment. "For example: Let's take the growth circles. They are by definition a Master Growth Mechanism. And they help illustrate a point. To some companies they are a mini mechanism, quick to implement and understand. To others, they may become a mammoth mechanism because of the resistance encountered in their implementation. In your case, you managed to replace this phrase. But look at the impact the growth circles have already had."

Peter stopped him. "In fairness, I think I was

desperate and so were my people. But we did jump into the concept."

Horace looked pleased. "That's very good. Things change and evolve. How about the Strategic Growth Map you saw over at the art gallery?"

Peter quickly responded, "I was so caught up in Tracy's enthusiasm that I mistakenly thought the idea would be easy to adopt. But after reviewing it in my mind, I think it's so complex it would be in the top category. What was that called?"

"Mammoth. I would agree with you, Peter. It's a very good tool, but it requires a degree of persistence and consistent repetition in meetings in order to have it take hold in the workplace."

Horace was up on his feet again. "That's the point. All of this has to be flexible. It's designed to let you look at your business and make choices based on real-time information. There's one other thing to take into consideration. You've already heard a little about levels of acceptance, right?"

Peter had to stop him. "Hang on a second! Yes, I have heard about the three levels of acceptance, but the practical side of me is screaming, 'Why?' Why is this important? What does this do for my staff? I know they need to learn this stuff, and I saw that Tracy's group actually had learned it. But so what? I just flashed on your concept of 'bubble-up growth,' and I'm wondering why they need to know this information?"

Horace stared at him for a moment. Finally, he chuckled. "That's part of a gap we keep looking to cross. We have to make sure the entrepreneurs understand all of it, and then we have to help them see why the whole staff needs to understand it, too. You have to know two things:

"First, when we talk about transitioning from a

> WHEN WE TALK ABOUT TRANSITIONING FROM A TOP-DOWN GROWTH MODEL TO A BUBBLE-UP GROWTH MODEL, WE ARE DESCRIBING A SIZEABLE PARADIGM SHIFT FOR NOT ONLY THE LEADERSHIP BUT ALSO THE STAFF OF A COMPANY.

top-down growth model to a bubble-up growth model, we are describing a sizeable paradigm shift for not only the leadership but also the staff of a company."

"Second, your staff still needs a structure for observing, evaluating, and understanding what's going on in their organization. Remember, I told you that the matrix of The Growth Curve Solution would tell you five things: 1) what's happening right now, 2) what brought you here, 3) how to predict what's likely to occur, 4) what needs to be done, and 5) what's the next best step to take."

"So you're saying that all this information helps them become real, conscious contributors to the bubble-up growth model?"

"Yep. They have to understand it because, ultimately, they have to make it happen. I heard someone coin a term that goes something like this, 'They have to know it to grow it.' It's a bit corny, but it does sum it all up. The staff has to understand and talk the language if they are going to make it happen. "

Peter digested this for a second. "OK, I'll need to think about that for awhile. I think you were going to say something about acceptance?"

"Yes. And in keeping with your question, let me start by reiterating that all this data is interconnected. So getting your people to speak in terms of Growth Mechanisms and how they impact the company is very important. You will notice that each time you, or they, identify, create, and implement a growth mechanism, it will go through the three stages of acceptance. It will begin as untested, and if it survives the initial resistance found in every organization, it will move into the unchallenged stage where people will comply, and then it will become an unconscious part of your working world."

"If everything is accepted as well and as quickly as the growth circles, it won't be a problem. But I suspect they won't all be quite so easy."

Horace laughed out loud. "Not a chance!"

"How do I identify other mechanisms?"

"First, you need to be clear about how you want the organization to perform. You and your management team need to evaluate on a larger scale what type of corporate behavior you want to facilitate.

Take C.J., for example. She wanted to facilitate her staff integrating, mingling, and talking with  each other more. She chose a mechanism that ended up being a great in-house restaurant with Sammy as its head chef. It ended up having mammoth qualities because it took a while for the staff to buy in to the idea of staying at work for lunch. Eventually the experiment proved successful by bringing people together to break bread who wouldn't ordinarily have much of an opportunity to talk to each other. This mechanism changed people's behavior in a positive way."

"Another growth mechanism example is your new Flash Sheet that the Bolder Solution's management staff is using. It helps to measure the daily life pulses surging through your company. The Flash Sheet is probably one of the most important mechanisms that a company can utilize. The real impact of the Flash Sheet happens when it evolves from a measurement tool to a growth mechanism."

There was a tap at his door and the college kid was standing there. "Excuse me, Horace. Do you want to take a phone call from Edward Johnston?"

"Tell him I'll call him right back, Lonny."

As the young man left, Horace thought a moment. "That's one of our best Growth Mechanisms, the alliance with the university. We constantly have new students rolling through here as interns. The permanent staff rotate to give the constant flow of new people their orientation to what we do. It is formally called our Hiring and Orientation Mechanism. Everyone regularly gets a chance to transfer our core values, culture, vision, and mission to someone new, thus reactivating their own conviction. We use this as a mechanism to reinforce who we are. Do you see what I mean? Very often the need for mechanisms is obvious, but companies don't take the creative steps to make them a reality. A big part of success with a growth mechanism is getting it accepted at the unconscious level."

Peter was still thinking about Bolder Solutions. "Remember your speech to the managers at the off-site about getting their departments in shape?"

"Sure."

"Well, the managers really took your speech to heart. Our Flash Sheet system is almost up and running on the network and each manager is religiously holding weekly department meetings around the department Growth Maps. The staff initially complained that they didn't have time for weekly meetings. They said the same thing about the Growth Circle meetings.

"What they didn't have time for were meetings that wasted their time. That's not the case with either the growth circles or the weekly department meetings. These few simple steps have so radically improved the way we run the company."

Horace picked up the conversation. "This also illustrates the levels of acceptance. Your staff was sitting in the untested stage because the concepts hadn't been introduced to your company yet. You'll usually have to pass through a few rough spots before you get to the unchallenged stage. Any time you introduce something new to your company it takes time. It is just the way human beings operate. If you encourage the staff's feedback and stay with the new mechanisms, eventually you'll get to the unconscious stage."

Peter exclaimed, "Whatever it takes! It certainly doesn't happen overnight."

Looking over at Peter, Horace continued, "That's  why acceptance is a whole piece of this puzzle all by itself. You said you hoped that someday you'd meet the guy who helped me. Well, that's what I'd like you to do tomorrow. His company is out by you in Gunbarrel. I'd like you to hear about acceptance from him. In its own way, acceptance is the key to all this. If I hadn't gotten everybody to buy in here, any innovative concept simply wouldn't get put into operation."

"When can I meet him?"

"I'll call you and let you know what time."

"Excellent!"

"There's something else. Now that you're about ready to deliver the software, Elijah will need some help with acceptance as well. You'll have a motivated group of people who need the software, but it's still a new way for them to do things. What you'll learn tomorrow will help you in your business, and it will help in selling a customer on your product, because you'll able to tell him that you can insure its acceptance."

"Given the events of the last few days, I think Elijah will welcome all the help he can get." Peter stopped. "I almost forgot, Horace. Do you know a woman named Grace McGregor?"

Horace laughed. "I wondered if you were going to ask about Gracie."

"Gracie? I can't imagine anyone calling her Gracie."

"I wouldn't advise it. She tolerates it from me, but I don't think she lets many people get away with it."

"So?"

Horace seemed to reflect a moment. "I've known Grace for a long time. She is the most tenacious individual I've ever known. I had no idea she was involved with your brother's company. She happened to mention you in passing, and I told her I knew you. So she told me about her recent conversations with you. I've worked with her, Peter. She's a remarkably bright woman and very, very good at her job. Fostering a strategic alliance with her would be to your advantage."

Peter sighed. "She says she wants to help us. She thinks she can put some pressure on Santomo."

"She told me the same thing. She didn't want to say how, but I wouldn't count her out."

"Did she tell you she accused me of being involved in Alan's death?"

"Yeah, she mentioned it." He laughed again. "All I will tell you is this. You want her as an ally, not an enemy."

Chapter 22 — Key Points
Mechanisms

Growth Qualities That:
- Build
- Protect
- Connect

People Qualities That:
- Clarify
- Unify
- Align

Profit Qualities That:
- Track
- Forecast
- Innovate

The formula for developing a mechanism is simple:

- Identify the specific need for a mechanism.
- Determine a very clear purpose or solution your desired mechanism will fulfill.
- Inquire from those who will be affected by the mechanism what it is that they suggest.
- Test and challenge all your assumptions about what this mechanism must accomplish.
- Measure both the possible positive and negative impacts of implementing such a mechanism.
- Verify that your new mechanism is in alignment with your company's strategies, goals, and values.
- Enroll a pilot group of willing peer leaders to test the new mechanism in the workplace before you implement it with the entire staff.

12 Master Mechanisms that shape and focus the individual, group, and organizational profit behavior of an enterprise:

1. Flash Sheet/Dash Board
2. Management Growth Maps
3. Decision Making Template
4. Town Meeting
5. One-on-One Meeting
6. Bucket Maps
7. Profit Net Program
8. Meeting Template
9. Customer Reconnaissance Model
10. Recognition and Reward Model
11. Hiring and Orientation Model
12. Growth Circles

"PARAMEDIC WAGONS, POLICE CARS, HELICOPTERS, AND HAZ-MAT TEAMS CONVERGED ON THE CRIME SCENE LIKE HUNGRY PIRANHAS. REPORTS OF A TERRIBLE DISEASE ONSLAUGHT, FEARS OF CONTAGION, AND RUMORS OF BAD PIZZA RIFLED THROUGH THE REPORTER'S STORY."

Chapter 23
MESSAGE IN THE SHADOW

"Wisdom is knowing what to do next. Skill is knowing how to do it and virtue is doing it."
— **David Starr Jordan**

Paramedic wagons, police cars, helicopters, and haz-mat teams converged on the crime scene like hungry piranhas. The drama playing out on the TV newscast was born from a bad movie, and the pretty young reporter relating the story was barely able to contain her own palpable fear. Unfounded reports of a terrible disease onslaught, fears of contagion, and the rumors of bad pizza rifled through the reporter's story. Taking a quick moment to listen to her headset she interrupted her own report to say, "OK, we have confirmation. All but one person employed in the building was affected. The only survivor is in quarantine. We'll give you more information as it comes in."

Kate was at his door. "Your police friend is on the phone."

Peter picked up the phone and punched the line button. "Jane?"

"Are you listening to the news?" No hello, no nothing.

"No, I'm working. Why, what's going on?"

She yelled "in a minute" to someone nearby.

"Look, find a TV and watch what's going on. I'll call you back." And she was gone.

He went to the conference room television but he saw that it had been dragged into the bullpen area. The whole office was migrating toward it. As Peter watched the unfolding scene on the news, he had a fleeting moment of horror as he recalled making some silly comment about Santomo controlling Checker's Pizza. But the reporter said the illness had started at an architectural firm. What could possibly have happened?

And then Jane called again. "Sorry I had to dump you. This is quickly getting out of hand. Have you been watching?"

"Yeah, what's going on? Have people died?"

"No, no one has died. Yet. TV commentators are calling the one employee who was not affected a survivor. Great! We've kept a lid on some of this, but it's not going to last. Listen to me, Peter. This Santomo, or whoever, is after you."

"What does this have to do with me? That was an architectural office."

"Yeah. But what they haven't reported is that it was a mistake: It was a Checker's Pizza order that made everyone sick, and it should have been delivered to Heritage Genomics."

Peter felt sick. "Does Heritage know?"

> IT WAS A CHECKER'S PIZZA ORDER THAT MADE EVERYONE SICK, AND IT SHOULD HAVE BEEN DELIVERED TO HERITAGE GENOMICS.

"They did after the reporters showed up. The press was tipped to go to the Heritage offices. Their building is under guard now, but they're terrified. This is really scary, Peter. We don't know if it's a contagious outbreak, much less if anyone is going to die from the poisoning."

"Have you talked to Elijah about that?"

"He says what the docs say — it's likely not contagious or the non-affected woman would have come down with the symptoms as well. But we have to wait and see if those who actually did eat the pizza survive."

Something nagged at Peter. "Wait a minute. You said the press was tipped to go to Heritage? Why?"

"Glad to see you're paying attention. Don't you get it? Someone not only expected this to happen at Elijah's company, they also wanted the press to know about it. The fact that the reporters were sent to the wrong address makes it clear that this had been staged."

He thought for a moment. "We can't let them win, Jane."

"It gets better or worse, depending on what it all means. The reason I had to cut you off a few minutes ago was that a woman's body was found in a fatal car crash not far from here. Her description matches the description of the female cook who vanished from Checker's. Ironically, it appears to have been an accident with a bread truck and she was the only casualty. She had a cache of weapons in the car. Maybe we got lucky with this one. You know they often work in teams of two."

"Teams of two? Two what?"

"Two assassins."

"Did she have a connection to this?"

"We just don't know. We'll run her prints. If she is a professional killer for hire, her prints may or may not be available. Here's the thing. It might be over."

"Over? Why?"

"If she and her blond boy friend are pros, and if they are involved, as I suspect, his arrest and her unforeseen death have created an unexpected link closer to the source of this biochemical terrorism. Whoever is behind this is playing a very dark game.

If those victimized people survive, it will be by design. The perpetrators have staged all this mayhem for effect and they've made their point. And now with the press involved, they cannot afford another accident or screw-up. They may be through endangering you."

"But you can't know for sure?"

"No."

> **LAB TESTS SHOWED IT TO BE A CATALYST THAT ACTIVATED A GENETIC TIME BOMB IN DOUGH.**

In the days to come, the contents in a small aerosol can retrieved from the crash vehicle would reveal an unknown oily substance. Lab tests showed it to be a catalyst that activated a genetic time bomb in dough. The public would be informed that a bad batch of dough was the problem, contaminated with bug spray by a part-time employee who had an unfortunate mental problem. There would be no further outbreaks.

Lab experiments on the bits of crust retrieved from the architectural office and samples of the

dough bought from the store would demonstrate that the catalyst had turned simple pizzas into ingenious weapons. Furthermore, a fingerprint found on the small aerosol can

would be identified as belonging to the crash victim, a professional assassin who worked on all continents. Tracing a trail to Santomo would be highly improbable; however, the pizza mix-up and car crash would rattle them.

Back at the office, Peter stared at the phone number scribbled in his brother's handwriting. Grace McGregor made him feel wary, but this last stunt by Santomo could not go unchallenged. What could she possibly do? He picked up the phone and punched in the number.

"I was hoping to hear from you."

"Grace, I talked to Horace and he speaks very highly of you."

"And of you, too."

"Do you really think you can make Santomo pay for what they've done?"

"Yes. I think I can make them stop what they're doing."

"Really?" Peter hesitated. "Have you listened to the news today?"

"Of course."

"Did you hear about those people who ingested poisoned food?"

"Yes. Terrible."

"Have your extensive connections told you anything about it?"

"No, but I haven't tried to learn anything. Why?"

"Because it's Santomo. Santomo is behind it."

He told her about the afternoon's events, leaving out the details Jane had asked him not to disclose. Grace listened intently.

"My God! They're crazy."

"So tell me. What's your idea to stop them?"

"Blackmail."

"I beg your pardon?"

"Remember I told you I have access to information most people don't have?"

"Sure."

"Tell me what you know about Daniel Tayakanagi?"

"Tayakanagi? Truthfully, not much. I thought I was going to meet him the week they fired me. He was essentially a phantom, and I've only seen pictures of him. I do think he ran the show."

 HE IS WILLING TO GO TO WAR IN ORDER TO WIN IN BUSINESS. BUT THE ONE TRUE THING HE CAN'T STAND IS PUBLICITY. ,,

"True. The piece of the puzzle that stays out of public domain is that he is a true paranoid. He is willing to go to war in order to win in business. But the one true thing he can't stand is publicity. It is his one real weakness."

Peter spoke up. "What does that do for us?"

"I propose to create a publicity campaign to tell the world that Tayakanagi is responsible for all

that's happened. He has lawyers, but he will avoid the public spotlight at any cost."

"But if we start a campaign, we could be hit with a defamation of character suit."

"Yes. But only if we actually use the publicity."

Peter was confused. "I'm not following you."

"I believe we can blackmail him with just the threat of exposure. Anybody else would look us in the eye and say, take your best shot. But no one, no one, has ever tested Tayakanagi in legal proceedings because they think they couldn't win. I think he'll balk."

"Exactly what are you going to accuse him of?"

"Murdering your brother, attempting to murder you, creating lethal weapons out of tampered food products, attempting to murder people in the architectural office, even though they were not the intended victims."

"We can't prove any of it."

"We don't have to. The scrutiny of Santomo and the constant surveillance of him by press zealots will crumple his carefully-guarded wall of privacy."

"Will that stop him?"

"We will insist that he gets out of the genetic-agricultural business. I know Horace has been telling you about his methods of growing a business, and I assume he's told you about trauma, right?"

"Yep."

"Imagine the kind of trauma that can happen in a giant corporation, one that is essentially the extension of a single individual's flawed personality. We threaten that individual with exposure as a suspected murderer. Not only will this create a corporate crisis for him at Santomo, it will force him into making a rash decision."

" **THE THREAT OF BEING PUBLICLY HUMILIATED AND ITS ENSUING TRAUMA WILL ABSOLUTELY BE THE MAIN CONSIDERATION IN HIS DECISION MAKING.** "

"The threat of being publicly humiliated and its ensuing trauma will absolutely be the main consideration in his decision making. A rational response would be expected from most people, but he is not rational. His attorneys will be handicapped by his paranoia. So what I am telling you is that I can buy you some time."

Peter's mind was racing.

"Wait a second! That might do it. If we stop them for a year, even nine or ten months, we give Elijah Brown's group a chance to get ahead."

"That's true."

The silence hung on the line for a moment.

"Horace was right, you are a force to be reckoned with. Thank you, Grace!" Peter surprised himself.

"It is my pleasure, Peter. I'm going to start on this right now. The quickest way to get a response is to send a press release to Tayakanagi's secretary with an official request for comment. The address is also a closely-guarded secret, but…"

"It's just more of the information you have access to."

She laughed wickedly. "Fasten your seat belt, Peter. Whether this works or not, they will respond quickly. I'm going to make certain that Tayakanagi himself is singled out."

Elijah Brown was subdued when Peter spoke with him.

"So much for me being too high-profile for them. I eat with the staff. I most certainly would have had a slice of pizza. I think they knew that, just like they seemed to know everything else."

"Are you taking extra precautions?"

"Oh, yes. But I think it is unnecessary."

"Why?"

"Peter, they have too much exposure at this point. They have one of their operatives in jail and one dead. They may have wanted you and me out of the way to advance their objectives, but ultimately they wanted to make a point. They were proving something. I think the whole exercise was a test. And I would say it succeeded beyond their wildest dreams."

Peter was trying to catch up. "In what way was it a test?"

> ❝IT WAS A WEAPON, PETER. SURE, THEY MISSED THEIR TARGET, BUT THEY HAVE PROVED THE EFFECTIVENESS OF USING THE FOOD SUPPLY AS A WEAPON.❞

"It was a weapon, Peter. Sure, they missed their target, but they have proved the effectiveness of using the food supply as a weapon. We've lagged behind them every step of the way because we assumed they wanted to control the supply. They just wanted to manipulate it. We have been fighting the wrong war. Oh, we will finish our work, and your software will help, but they are already capable of producing a bio-weapon. Maybe, just maybe, our work will help some bright young scientist think of a way to fight them."

He paused for a moment. "Look, this is pure speculation on my part. They may want it all. They may still want our processes. I just don't know."

Peter was stunned. It all fit. It was everything Jane had concluded and more. In the last month he had lived behind every learning curve that confronted him. This was just the latest. "I don't know what to say, Elijah."

"There is another reality we have to consider. They may have stopped us in a roundabout way.

The press will eventually piece it all together. We will be labeled as the real target, and we may be painted as bio-terrorists. Why else would some unnamed group want to stop us? My only hope is that the real environmental organizations will step up to the plate and explain what it is we are trying to accomplish."

"You're not going to quit, are you?"

Elijah laughed. "Do I sound that sorry for myself? No, if anything, this all just strengthens my resolve. But the next few months are going to be an interesting ride."

"If it's any consolation, my team says they're ready to deliver. Do you want to wait a few days?"

"I do not, but my people might. They are having a hard time with this. They cannot believe they were almost killed. Let's set up a presentation for Friday so they can hear everything, and then they will have the weekend to prepare for the changes."

"That's fine. We'll do a full court press on the software. And I might have some solutions that will help them accept the new process."

"That would be extremely helpful."

"Santomo may have won this round, Elijah, but then again, maybe not. Let's see what happens."

Jane called him at home. "My life was much simpler before you came back to town."

"What have you found out?"

"We've had some interesting visitors in Boulder. The crash victim was a known professional killer. She went by the alias 'The Keeper' and her sidekick cut a deal with the FBI and was swept out of town last night to parts unknown."

"Have you spoken to Elijah?"

"No, I still want to find out a few things. How is he?"

Peter told her about his conversation with the scientist. "Horace said that Elijah was the smartest man he's ever met. I think I have to agree."

She was silent for a moment. When she spoke, she sounded tired. "Well, none of what he suggests surprises me. I stopped being surprised when I saw those people this afternoon. Everyone who ate the

> ❝ SO THEY WERE TOYING WITH US? THEY JUST WANTED TO SHOW US THEY COULD DO THIS VILE THING TO PROVE THAT WE ARE ALL VULNERABLE? ❞

pizza has recovered. I mean they are weirdly better. They were so dangerously ill earlier and now the doctors are saying that they seem to have completely recovered. Which is OK, but there is absolutely no explanation for their medical turnaround. The patients are staying overnight in the hospital, but it seems the danger has passed."

"So they were toying with us? They just wanted to show us they could do this vile thing to prove

that we are all vulnerable?"

They were silent for a moment. He knew he should tell Jane about Grace and their plan to take on Santomo, but he suddenly wondered about the legal implications for Jane if she were to know. Besides, the events of the last few days had him thinking about his new detective friend in a more personal way.

"Look, I know this isn't the best time, but you and I need a 'time out' together. What do you say we get away from this crazy nightmare, even if it is just for one evening?"

"Are you going to make me an offer I can't refuse?"

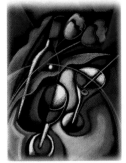

"Yes, I am. How about dinner Saturday at the Flagstaff House?" This was the finest restaurant in the area and had a phenomenal view of Boulder Valley, plus an extensive wine list.

"I think that's a pretty good start. Anything else will just have to be left up to fate. Would you agree?"

Peter laughed softly. "Yes, ma'am!"

ACCEPTANCE

SEEING WITH CLARITY

Chapter 24

RELEASING RESISTANCE

"Let us consider a boat made of wooden planks and some of the planks begin to rot and have to be replaced. There comes a time when not one of the original planks is left. The boat still looks like the original craft but in material terms it has totally changed. Ask yourself: Is it still the same boat?"
— Antoine Danchin, *The Delphic Boat*

The intermittent looks of fear, determination, confusion, and humor that were etched across the landscape of faces throughout the office left Peter concerned but at the same time encouraged. Yes, they were all shell-shocked. Who wouldn't be? But there was something else going on. They were surviving and rising to the occasion.

> ## FOR ALL THEIR IDIOSYNCRASIES AND THEIR PECULIAR HABITS THEY WERE TOUGH...A TRUE WORK COMMUNITY.

Peter started the morning by moving from desk to desk, talking and laughing with each employee, connecting with the people who shared the foxhole with him called Bolder Solutions. He was proud of them. For all their idiosyncrasies and their peculiar habits, they were tough. They were a true work community coming into its own sense of strength and purpose.

Peter's cell phone rang inside his coat pocket and as he put the handset up to his ear he heard

Horace's resonant voice greeting him. "I've got to hand it to you, Peter. When I met you in the park a few weeks ago, I had no idea you would be such a survivor. I must say I am impressed. The events of the past few weeks would have been challenging to the most seasoned leader."

"Thanks, Horace. I appreciate the vote of confidence. In the middle of it all, I just accepted the events for what they were, however strange that may have been, and moved myself forward. I am sure, in hindsight, I will wonder how I made it through it all in one piece. Regardless, I am ready to keep moving on with your Growth Curve Solution tour. Based on our conversation yesterday, am I correct to assume that you have one more person for me to visit?"

"Yes, I do, Peter. His name is Michael Collins, and his company is called the Dublin Corporation."

"What do they do?"

"I'll let Michael tell you himself."

The Dublin Corporation was located in an industrial park close to Bolder Solutions so the drive over took less than two minutes. As Peter walked into the spacious front entry he expected to find brightly colored dirigibles floating through the air, but none were to be seen. Instead he found himself staring at an enormous landscape painting that grabbed his attention from across the entry. It was reminiscent of the Hudson River School paintings of 200 years ago. The raw power of nature, the dramatic light, the grandeur and expansive landscape portrayed in the piece transported Peter to a different time and place. The sound of steps walking onto the stone-tiled entry behind him interrupted his reverie.

> ❝ THE RAW POWER OF NATURE, THE DRAMATIC LIGHT, THE GRANDEUR AND EXPANSIVE LANDSCAPE, TRANSPORTED PETER TO A DIFFERENT TIME AND PLACE. ❞

A man in his mid-fifties walking with a youthful gait engaged Peter, saying, "That painting you are looking at is one of my favorites. It reminds me of a saying the mountain men of the early 1800s had when speaking of the enormity of nature. Believe it or not, these men were often out in the wild regions of the West for months, even years, at a stretch, without human contact. They coined the phrase, 'facing the elephant,' when referring to the overwhelming realization, the bone-crunching fear, that nature could snuff out their life at any moment. 'Facing the elephant' meant facing your deepest fear and vulnerability, coming to terms with it, and releasing the native resistance to surrendering to forces larger than yourself. The men who couldn't come to terms with this fear either returned to civilization or died. For many it was a life-changing experience, a deep coming to terms with or moving into harmony with nature. It signaled the release of the illusion that they could control the entirety of their world. Ironically, it meant that in order to survive they had to yield, to surrender to its flow."

Looking over at him, the man offered Peter his hand in greeting and continued by saying, "Hi, I'm Michael Collins. You must be Peter. Horace has told me all about you. And from what I hear, you have really had your hands full recently over at Bolder Solutions."

Peter shook Michael's hand, nodding, "It's a pleasure to meet you as well, Michael. In light of your comment, you might say I have been facing my own elephant over the last few weeks and I am not so sure I passed the test."

Michael smiled and added, "From everything that I hear, the fact that you are standing here in my office is evidence enough that you went to the edge and survived."

"Well, Michael, that may be the truth today but will it be the truth tomorrow? I guess time will tell."

> **"DEEPLY ACCEPTING 'THE WAY THINGS ARE' IN ANY GIVEN MOMENT OPENS THE GATE TO A RARE SORT OF PERSONAL FREEDOM, A LEVEL OF CLARITY THAT FEW PEOPLE EVER ENCOUNTER."**

Glancing up at the painting, Michael mused, "Deeply accepting 'the way things are' in any given moment opens the gate to a rare sort of personal freedom, a level of clarity that few people ever achieve."

Trying to slow his descent into what appeared to be a particularly personal topic, Peter moved to shift the focus of the conversation. "So, Michael, Horace has you as the last person on the Growth Curve Solution tour. Where do you and I proceed from here?"

Grinning with appreciation for Peter's sidestep, Michael responded, "Well, Peter, you and I have the good fortune to discuss the important role that acceptance plays in the Growth Curve Solution. In light of that, we would be best served by continuing the conversation from which you just so adeptly extracted yourself."

"Was I that transparent?"

"Let's just say that your 'duck and weave' move told me more than you will ever know. The interesting thing is that you

aren't alone. Every one of the business owners you spoke with over the last couple of weeks essentially acted the same way when they confronted the topic of 'acceptance' at the end of their Growth Curve Solution introduction. It is not lost on me that all of you operate in a very concrete world. Discussing a concept such as 'acceptance' in the context of business is either too 'woo-woo,' seemingly irrelevant, or as in your case, too revealing of your core vulnerabilities."

"You see, Peter, business leaders, by their nature, and I include myself, are hard-wired to believe they must control their world. If they don't then any number of factors can or will implode and put them out of business. In short, the misguided belief that control keeps their business alive is buried in their DNA. Ask yourself — is this true about you?"

"Absolutely, Michael. I am hard-wired to control every moving part of my business. It seems to be a family trait. My brother was challenged by it as well. Since it is evident that I can run but I can't hide from this discussion, I might as well hit this one straight on. You might say it is an integral part of my business survival mechanisms. It is so deeply embedded in me that regardless of Horace's inroads with embracing the beekeeper mindset, I am a long way off from total immersion. Considering the Causal Chain of Behavior:

BELIEFS *forge* **MENTAL FILTERS**
which forge **PATTERNS**
which forge BEHAVIORS

I am so entrenched in a belief about the necessity for 'control' that I could be a hopeless case for 'conversion.'"

"Strange as this may sound, Peter, ironically, some of the best candidates for beekeeper conversion are the business leaders with the strongest wills and the greatest inclination to control. Horace and I left 'acceptance' as the last piece of the Growth Curve Solution puzzle for three good reasons. It is the hardest component to embrace for the average practical business leader. It is also the

> " IRONICALLY, SOME OF THE BEST CANDIDATES FOR BEEKEEPER CONVERSION ARE THE BUSINESS LEADERS WITH THE STRONGEST WILLS AND THE GREATEST INCLINATION TO CONTROL. "

hardest to teach. It is best understood only in the context of beliefs about business provided by the other Growth Curve Solution components."

Planted squarely in front of this enormous painting and caught in the tractor beam of Michael's intensity, Peter seriously wondered where all this would take him. At the end of the day, how in the name of heaven would he ever find a practical application to the topic of this last stop on Horace's tour? Trust in Horace and a healthy curiosity for the unknown fueled his continuing interest.

"So let me get this right. Are you the source of all Horace's theories?"

Half-shocked and half-amused, Michael laughed,

"Did he tell you that?" He shook his head. "Horace is an enigma. He would have the world believe that I was the force behind the Growth Curve Solution, but in fact I was just a small contributor. He is the brains behind this whole venture. Did he, by chance, tell you what we do here?"

"No, in fact he refused. He said he wanted you to tell me yourself."

Michael laughed. "OK. The short answer is that we are business consultants and growth trainers. And after twenty years of listening to and advising CEOs of growth companies all over North America, we realized that we were seeing the same problems over and over, regardless of industry. There were some simple truths that were always present in every company that we visited. And then I met Horace. Between us, we further developed the Growth Curve Solution and its parts. Now, when we advise a company, we do it in the context of the matrix of the Growth Curve Solution."

"Your customers must appreciate that."

"That's very kind of you to say, but the truth is it takes forward-thinking people to engage our ideas. It is not surprising that only 15 percent of all small business CEOs make time to reflect on their businesses in any meaningful way. Those who are open and choose to work with us are curious, smart, and very committed. Most business leaders who work

with us struggle with our ideas at the onset. We are presenting a radical approach to sustaining and growing a healthy enterprise. It all starts with one major step."

"Acceptance?"

"Exactly. You see, Peter, Horace and I firmly believe that the world of business leadership is still in its infancy. The underlying mission of every business leader is to discover how to release the spirit of their organization. In this case, learning how to harness the awesome power of an emerging small enterprise continues to lie beyond the reach of many executive leaders."

> **THE GREATEST OBSTACLES ARE THE LEADER'S OWN FIXED VIEWPOINTS, THEIR STRONG OPINIONS, AND THEIR PROCLIVITY TO NOT EASILY RELEASE CONTROL TO OTHERS.**

"It is our belief that one of the first steps to releasing the spirit of any company is through the leader's willingness to look at himself and his company through a lens of neutrality. Accepting the whole of the enterprise for what it is sounds simple but is, in reality, a daunting task. The greatest obstacles are the leader's own fixed viewpoints, strong opinions, and proclivity to not easily release control to others.

"Here is a definition to get us started on the right track: Acceptance is the state of non-resistance to what is. This implies that the individual has somehow been able to momentarily suspend preconceived judgments, strongly held beliefs about the subject being perceived. In that moment we would say that the object of perception is being accepted for simply what it is, not what it could be or what it shouldn't be, just what it is."

Peter started rolling his eyes back in his head and Michael caught him before he could say anything. "Yes, I know this is not your standard business fare. But sooner or later every continuously successful business leader, including you Peter, faces the unavoidable truth about his own state of consciousness as the root cause, the formative source of 'all' experiences in his daily reality. This is a core building block to understanding the reflective nature of our operating businesses."

"Michael, I must say that since I met Horace, I certainly have gotten more than my share of business philosophy. It seems you guys look at business through some kind of heightened awareness lens. I have never encountered anything like it. If you weren't so successful with your businesses, I'd be inclined to think all of it was a bit over the top."

"That's a good point, Peter. The practical nature of a business leader is such that the rubber must meet the road of everyday business life and be measured in improved performance or he won't give it the time of day."

> " TRUE ACCEPTANCE, IN ANY GIVEN MOMENT, IS THE SUSPENSION OF RESISTANCE TO THE THING BEING PERCEIVED. "

Michael continued, "True acceptance, in any given moment, is the suspension of resistance to the thing being perceived. Why is this important to a business leader? The law of reverse effort states that whatever you resist will persist. So if you are having a challenging issue, in theory, that issue will persist as long as you continue to resist it. Our goal is always to see the deeper causal chain behind things. We want to see underneath the surface of an issue to its core cause.

"OK. Now let's take it one step further. Allowing a state of acceptance to any persisting issue releases your resistance to it. When you personally release your native resistance to something and subsequently release the evidence you have built up for or against it, you actually free yourself up to seeing it on a wholly different level. You allow yourself a rather remarkable level of supernatural clarity to actually see it and all that is contributing to its issue-ness. This is really very powerful."

Peter walked over to a chair to the right of the painting and sat down, his hands holding either side of his head as though a migraine headache was wrapping itself around his brain. Michael followed suit and sat in the adjoining chair. "Allright, Michael, let me see if I'm getting this straight. Are you saying that if I am willing to personally let go of my opinions, judgments and considerations about a perplexing issue, I will strangely be able to see into this issue with a greater degree of clarity? And will I then be able to 'see' the real cause of this issue, which up to now was hidden from me, and make a more informed decision in addressing it?"

"Yes, Peter, that is exactly what I am saying."

"Well, Michael, if that is true, then give me the pill or whatever it is that you are smoking that lets me get to that level of mental clarity on demand. That sounds phenomenal. Sign me up for the program because there is no way I have the wherewithal to get there on my own. I am just too stuck in making conclusions, in building evidence,

and in forming opinions about the world around me."

"That is where you are mistaken, Peter. There is no pill. There is no special magic formula that gets you there. You get there on your own, and it is easier than you are imagining."

"Remember that the primary benefit of acceptance is that it allows you to see with a greater degree of clarity the hidden forces influencing your ability to lead, your company's ability to perform, and your company's ability to master change. Some people are able to internally suspend their fixed viewpoints and naturally move into acceptance, while others require a more methodical approach."

> " REMEMBER THAT THE PRIMARY BENEFIT OF ACCEPTANCE IS THAT IT ALLOWS YOU TO SEE WITH A GREATER DEGREE OF CLARITY THE HIDDEN FORCES INFLUENCING YOUR ABILITY TO LEAD, YOUR COMPANY'S ABILITY TO PERFORM, AND YOUR COMPANY'S ABILITY TO MASTER CHANGE. "

"The methodical approach is comprised of three elements. They are:

1. **Taking a true inventory** of the 10 hidden agents that impact your leadership effectiveness and your company's performance.
2. **Being totally accountable** for both your

advancing and damaging contributions to the issue.

3. **Agree to suspend all related fixed viewpoints** for a short and predetermined period of time.

"Michael, as with all formulas, they are only as good as the person practicing them. How can you guarantee me that this will work?"

"I can't guarantee that this will work for you, Peter. It has worked for many leaders before you, and it very likely will work for you if you apply yourself. In financial terms, once perfected, this method of getting greater insight into yourself and your business through the process of acceptance could make or save you millions of dollars. Peter, as I mentioned earlier, there are a total of 10 hidden agents influencing leadership effectiveness and enterprise performance."

Michael handed Peter a booklet entitled *The 10 Hidden Agents* that he had been holding for the duration of their discussion. Michael continued by saying, "We're going to talk about the Hidden Agents, but I thought familiarizing yourself with this booklet when you get back to your office would be a helpful step in getting a handle on the acceptance process." Here they are in greater detail.

THE 10 HIDDEN AGENTS

THE HIDDEN AGENTS

5 Hidden Agents Impacting Leadership Effectiveness

1. **Leader Hidden Agent: Leadership Style**

   Description: Leadership style is the mechanism that quantifies how a leader links to the "feel of the company." In the last 10 years, significant business research has proven skeptics wrong about the impact of human climate on business performance. It has been noted that the link between the enhanced human climate of an organization and a company's ultimate business performance represents a 20-30 percent advantage in terms of multiples for both revenue per employee and profit per employee. The enterprise growth specialists at Dublin concur with this research and take it one step further by stating that every stage of growth demands a different "feel for the company." As such, if the leader intends to maximize performance outcomes, it is proven that he must 1) understand his leadership style 2) adjust his style so that it resonates with the style required by his company's stage of growth.

   Why is this valuable? First, being aware of one's leadership style is paramount to intentionally managing your link to the company's human environment. Second, maximizing and adjusting your leadership style to best fit the needs of the company in its current stage of growth allows for a powerful tool to improve financial performance by up to 20-30 percent or more.

2. Leader Hidden Agent: Modality

Description: Modality measures the degree of "direct or indirect influence" a leader applies to manifest the company's goals. This influence is expressed as a "mode of involvement" (dominant, facilitative or supportive) utilized by the leader in his daily interface with the company.

Why is it valuable? The misalignment of a leader's modality with the requirements of a company's stage of growth can be disastrous if left unaddressed for any period of time. Through awareness of one's modality and its careful intentional adjustment (if necessary), a leader applies the correct degree of direct or indirect influence to secure the performance behavior necessary to reach the company's goals.

3. Leader Hidden Agent: 3 Faces of the Leader

Description: The three faces of the leader measures the blend (by percentage) of three primary leadership roles (visionary, manager,

specialist) that an enterprise leader adopts as he directs the affairs of his company. Research tells us that there is an ideal blend of the three leadership roles for each stage of growth. It is the leader's ability to reshape his own blend of these three leadership roles (in an effort to meet his company's needs in its current stage of growth) that distinguishes the leader's degree of effectiveness.

Why is this valuable? As an enterprise leader, there is nothing more valuable than to have a high degree of clarity about what you need to deliver to your company to make it successful. Adjusting your blend of the three leadership roles to fit your company's current needs will give you an added advantage in realizing your goals.

4. Leader Hidden Agent: Leadership Competencies

Description: Using a set of 18 core leadership competencies is a key benchmark Dublin employs to determine leadership capacity in individuals and in organizations. Developing a leadership competency model at your company is an important starting point. Leadership operates at its best when it creates resonance. Based on Dublin's research, the leadership competencies that best serve a company are determined by the company's stage of growth.

Why is this valuable? Intentionally developing leadership competencies that are based in self-awareness, self-management, social awareness, and relationship management help define leadership effectiveness. Research points to the fact that effective leaders exhibit half a dozen or so competencies. Combined with the application of those competencies based on the company's stage of growth, these competencies further enhance leadership effectiveness in growing small-to mid-size organizations.

5. **Leader Hidden Agent: Learning Style**

Description: It is an undisputed fact that the "leadership package" of a CEO or executive leader is the currency that he trades with to make or break a growing company. Within the "leadership package" lies a little known contributor to leadership effectiveness — learning style. A leader's learning style (concrete, model, trial and error, or reflective) defines the speed, the depth, the risk tolerance and the flexibility of how he thinks. Since how we think and how we see our organization fundamentally influences what we do with our organizations, learning style is a huge influence on the thinking of a leader and thus a huge influence on a leader's choices.

Why is this valuable? Leveraging our current learning style enhances our ability to make better decisions. Understanding and adapting other learning styles as they become more effective in certain situations accelerates our ability to recognize the truth of any situation and narrow the optimum choices at our doorstep.

5 Hidden Agents Impacting Enterprise Performance

1. **Company Hidden Agent: Builder/Protector Ratio**

Description: The Builder/Protector Ratio measures the intensity and the balance between the state of confidence and the state of caution inherent in the psyche of an organization, a department, a team, or an individual.

Why is it valuable? It improves your insight into your company's mental health by:
1. Allowing you to measure the company's ability to meet and overcome its challenges.
2. Communicating the company's willingness to perceive and take advantage of the opportunities in its path.
3. Measuring the strength of the company's immune defense system, which acts as a barrier against low moral and poor performance.

4. Assessing the company's willingness to advance itself through change.

5. Telegraphing the company's belief in its future.

6. Communicating the company's trust in its leaders.

2. Company Hidden Agent: 5 Challenges

Description: There are 27 challenges that consistently surface in small to medium size enterprises. Of these 27 challenges there are 5 unique challenges that commonly stand out for each stage of growth. By calibrating a company's current challenges with the full spectrum of challenges that surface for the different stages of growth, a deeper understanding of the causes of the company's current challenges can be revealed and addressed.

Why is this valuable? By looking deeply into the origin of your company's challenges, you avail yourself of a more informed view to make better decisions and set the correct priorities to move your company through its challenges and then forward confidently into the future.

3. Company Hidden Agent: 5 Strengths

Description: There are 27 strengths that consistently surface in small to medium size enterprises. Of these 27 strengths there are 5 unique strengths that commonly stand out for each stage of growth. By calibrating a company's current strengths with the full spectrum of strengths that surface for the different stages of growth, we can clarify and address the causes of the company's current challenges.

Why is this valuable? By looking deeply into your company's current strengths in the light of what strengths your company requires in its current stage of growth, you avail yourself of the truth of your company's behavior and ultimately its performance.

4. Company Hidden Agent: 5 Non-Negotiable Rules

Description: Every natural system, whether it is a hardwood forest or a commercial business, succeeds by aligning itself to fundamental natural laws that establish order and balance. Based on nine years of growth company research, 35 fundamental laws or rules exist for emerging enterprise growth. It has been proven that out of these 35 rules there are 5 non-negotiable rules for each stage of growth and the effective completion of these 5 rules improves the likelihood for continuing survival and financial success.

Why is this valuable? The rules for continuing survival and financial success exist, whether or not a leader is aware of them. Every enterprise leader must adhere to the 5 Non-Negotiable Rules for both their company's previous stage of growth and its current stage of growth or pay the price in the form of low productivity, poor financial performance, and/or the possible demise of the organization.

5. **Company Hidden Agent: Cycles of Maturity**

Description: Time and duration affect the vibrancy and behavior of every living system, including businesses. It is of particular interest that when combined with the knowledge about an enterprise's stages of growth, understanding the cycles that manifest within each stage of growth becomes very important. Each of those cycles has unique characteristics that influence the behavior and performance of an enterprise.

Why is this valuable? By gaining a deeper understanding of your company's stage of growth, as well as its cycle of maturity inside that stage of growth, you are given a powerful tool for leveraging the resources and tools available to you in your company's current position.

The deep continuous sound interrupting their discussion seemed to emanate from every direction in the office. As though emerging out of a parallel reality, Peter shook off the intensity of his focus and silently looked to Michael for an explanation of the sound's origin.

"Peter, that sound is coming from a large Chinese temple gong at the entrance to our conference room at the back of our office. I picked the gong up two years ago while I was working with one of our clients in Asia. Everyone in the company decided that we needed a better way of acknowledging our accomplishments. So the various teams ring the gong when they have a victory to celebrate. My guess is that our sales team closed the new client contract they have been working on for the last few days."

"Michael, that was pretty interesting how the sound from that Chinese gong so effectively framed our discussion on acceptance. You do realize that

> **" I WONDER JUST HOW MANY BUSINESS LEADERS WOULD BE WILLING TO SUSTAIN SUCH A LEVEL OF INTENSE FOCUS IN AN EFFORT TO UNDERSTAND THEIR BUSINESSES IN A DEEPER WAY? "**

there are few people quite as intense as you and Horace. I wonder just how many business leaders would be willing to sustain such a level of intense focus in an effort to understand their businesses in a deeper way?"

Michael nodded his head as though this was a continually perplexing problem he faced. "Just as long as the intensity bears some sort of fruit in the practical world, a small percentage of them will pay the price. Follow me, Peter. Let's go and sit down in my office. I'll tell you how the 10 Hidden Agents bear fruit in the practical world."

Walking back through the company to Michael's office revealed the energy, activity, and the feel of a vibrant small village. The concentrated clusters of activity zones as represented by office groupings, meeting rooms, and team cubicles defined the spaces of connection. Everywhere chairs, couches and tables were interspersed in the open environment, providing ad hoc meeting zones for small groups. The intensity of Michael's staff could only have been the result of everyone working on meeting a deadline.

"Michael, the *voltage* in this place is off the charts. This is one very intense place. What's going on? Are you all trying to meet a deadline for a client?"

"Actually, Peter, this is pretty normal. Some of our teams may be working to meet project deadlines, but this level of activity and focus is standard fare for us. We have 33 people working here at the present. So we are just moving into a flood zone on our way from Stage 3 into Stage 4. So we certainly are flooded with activity. But I must say that we still have some tough Stage 3 challenges that we need to get past before we can say we are a Stage 4 company."

Pointing over to the staircase to their left, Michael said, "Our office environment is a little dif-

> " WE HAVE 33 PEOPLE WORKING HERE AT THE PRESENT. SO WE ARE JUST MOVING INTO A FLOOD ZONE ON OUR WAY FROM STAGE 3 INTO STAGE 4. "

ferent. We have five staircases in the office like the one you see there to the left. We could get by with two, but I wanted people to have an ease of access to each other. Look behind you."

Peter turned around to see a large polished brass pole descending from a hole in the ceiling of the

second level and anchored on the solid walnut flooring of the first level.

"It's a firehouse pole. You'd be surprised how often people find a reason to come down that pole to the first floor."

"What made you install it?"

"I thought it would be fun. There are specific tools that help the process, like growth language, but there are also intangible tools like fun and quirkiness that are priceless. The firehouse pole was more successful than I ever hoped."

Michael ushered Peter into his office and closed the door behind him. Not surprising to Peter was

> **" IF OUR IDEAS ARE TO TAKE HOLD, WE HAVE TO ANCHOR THEM IN CONCRETE REALITY. "**

the unusual look of Michael's workplace. It had a huge circular Asian rug on which Michael's granite desk was amply positioned with two high-back chairs in front of it. Peter noticed that one whole wall had architectural drawings taped up over what appeared to be framed antique prints. The office

was a disaster, cluttered with notebooks, growth maps, and spreadsheets going every which way.

Michael urged Peter to grab a seat and continued, "In concluding our discussion around the 10 Hidden Agents, I wanted to add one more thing. Very similar to how the firehouse pole works in our office, if our ideas are to take hold, we have to anchor them in concrete reality. The 10 Hidden Agents are tied to the practical world of running and managing a business through the help of Growth Guard. Growth Guard is a predictive indexing tool that aggregates the information from the 10 Hidden Agents and tells the story of both a leader's and a company's state of health. It is similar to an MRI for a small business. It interprets the impact that each Hidden Agent has on both the leader's effectiveness and on the company's performance based on the company's stage of growth."

Peter interrupted Michael by saying, "Let me get this right. You are integrating the ten factors that you call the 10 Hidden Agents, you are weaving them into a meaningful context, and you are coming out showing a leader how his effectiveness is being influenced and what is influencing the company's performance?"

"Exactly, Peter. This gives the enterprise leader an informed view of both his leadership and the company's performance. Once that is framed and the leader releases his resistance to the information and accepts it for what it is, the portal opens up. The beekeeper steps forward into what we call a defining moment of truth. This is where they move from engineering their company's performance to facilitating it. The heightened clarity to see deeper into the enterprise workings reveals the company's causal chain. The leader can finally see the crystal-clear causes of the company's challenges and can move forward with confidence to address them. Seeing the workings of your company in this light is really quite profound."

> **SEEING THE WORKINGS OF YOUR COMPANY IN THIS LIGHT IS QUITE PROFOUND.**

With that, there was a loud tap at Michael's office door and a familiar voice boomed into the room. "You two haven't been talking about me, have you?"

Startled by the interruption, both men laughed. Michael jokingly said, "Horace, you're all I ever talk about."

"Peter, Michael hasn't been telling you it was all my idea, has he?"

Peter glanced from Michael to Horace. "Well, as a matter of fact…"

Michael looked amused. Holding his well-used leather journal, Horace paced while he spoke. "If it weren't for Michael, we wouldn't have gotten this far."

Michael had heard it before. "Yeah, right, Horace. I'm not going to argue with you."

Horace looked at Peter. "Heard enough yet?"

"Enough? I could write a book on what I've heard from just today's conversation."

"There's more."

"More?"

Michael picked it up. "Peter, I saw you looking at my walls when you came in. Those architectural elevations aren't just decoration; they are for a project Horace and I are doing together."

"Are you building a new office?"

"Much more than that. We are building an academy."

Horace walked over to the wall. "After all the help Michael's methods have been to me, I wanted to help him do something more permanent. We are building a Growth Curve Academy. It's almost completed. And we both hope you'll come join us for a session."

Peter smiled. "So the last few weeks have been your sales pitch?"

Michael chuckled. "I certainly hope not. We can't count on all of our future students being in mortal danger."

"What do you have in mind?"

Horace stepped in again. "Total Immersion. You've managed to glean a huge amount of information, perhaps more than any student to date, because of the added pressure. But what if we'd met two weeks earlier? You might not have been so focused. Or what if we'd met just today? You'd be so sidetracked by everything else that you might not even talk to me."

He continued, "No, we've needed a place for growth entrepreneurs to learn this methodology. And it can't take forever. Most of them have been through business schools, and they know a lot. We can't ask them to stop being CEOs for two years or even two months."

Michael picked it up. "But we can ask them for five days. Five days of their undivided attention in a multi-million-dollar state-of-the-art facility. Five

> "WE'RE FOMENTING A REVOLUTION HERE, PETER.
> WE WANT COMPANIES TO LAST CENTURIES."

days of a combination of growth boot camp and Disney World. Five days where they eat, sleep, play, work, and learn The Growth Curve Solution for twelve hours a day. We're fomenting a revolution here, Peter. We want companies to last centuries."

Peter was looking at the drawings on the wall. "I guess it's impractical to send people on the same

journey you've sent me on. It would take forever."

Horace said, "We do want them to take the journey, but not all over town. We can teach these methods in such a way that people will walk out with an absolute belief in themselves and their ability to really see their company from an illuminated perspective."

There was a moment of quiet. Finally Peter said, "Well, sign me up. What I've learned so far has changed the way I look at my company. Not withstanding another seed bomb or tainted pizza delivery, I would guess both of you have more surprises up your sleeve."

CHAPTER 24 — KEY POINTS

Causal Chain of Behavior

BELIEFS *forge* **MENTAL FILTERS**
which forge **PATTERNS**
which forge **BEHAVIORS**

Acceptance

This methodical approach to acceptance is comprised of three elements. They are:

1. **Taking a true inventory** of the ten hidden agents that impact your leadership effectiveness and your company's performance.
2. **Being totally accountable** for both your advancing and damaging contributions to the issue.
3. **Agree to suspend all related fixed viewpoints** for a short and predetermined period of time.

• •

THE HIDDEN AGENTS

5 Hidden Agents Impacting Leadership Effectiveness

1. **Leader Hidden Agent: Leadership Style**
   Description: Leadership style is the mechanism that quantifies how a leader links to the "feel of the company."

2. **Leader Hidden Agent: Modality**
   Description: Modality measures the degree of "direct or indirect influence" a leader applies to manifest the company's goals and is measured by the leader's mode of involvement (dominant, facilitative, or supportive).

3. **Leader Hidden Agent: 3 Faces of the Leader**
   Description: The three faces of a leader measures the blend (by percentage) of three primary leadership roles (visionary, manager, specialist) that an enterprise leader adopts as he directs the affairs of his company.

4. **Leader Hidden Agent: Leadership Competencies**
   Description: Using a set of 18 core leadership competencies to determine leadership capacity in individuals and in organizations.

5. **Leader Hidden Agent: Learning Style**
   Description: A leader's learning style (concrete, model, trial and error, or reflective) defines the speed, the depth, the risk tolerance, and the flexibility of how he thinks.

5 Hidden Agents Impacting Enterprise Performance

1. Company Hidden Agent: Builder/Protector Ratio

Description: The Builder/Protector Ratio measures the intensity and the balance between the state of confidence and the state of caution inherent in the psyche of an organization, a department, a team, or an individual.

2. Company Hidden Agent: 5 Challenges

Description: By calibrating a company's current challenges with the full spectrum of challenges that surface for the different stages of growth, a deeper understanding of the causes of the company's current challenges can be revealed and addressed.

3. Company Hidden Agent: 5 Strengths

Description: There are 27 strengths that consistently surface in small-to-medium size enterprises. There are 5 unique strengths that commonly stand out for each stage of growth. We clarify and address the causes of the company's current challenges by leveraging their current strengths.

4. Company Hidden Agent: 5 Non-Negotiable Rules

Description: 35 fundamental laws or rules exist for emerging enterprise growth. Out of these 35 rules there are 5 non-negotiable rules for each stage of growth and the effective completion of these 5 rules improves the likelihood for continuing survival and financial success.

5. Company Hidden Agent: Cycles of Maturity

Description: Time and duration affect the vibrancy and behavior of every living system, including businesses. Each cycle of maturity has unique characteristics that influence the behavior and performance of an enterprise.

I am starting to realize that the profitability of a company is a symptom of enterprise health, not the cause of it. I am beginning to see that to look at the true inner workings of a commercial enterprise, you must see past the secondary effects of performance. My bet is that if you learn how to read the underlying patterns demonstrated on a daily basis in the company, you can tell the origin of the company's performance, as well as its financial health. - Peter Logan, May 25

Weeding out the bad apples:

The best way of filtering out the employees who do not resonate with the vision, mission, and values of the firm is through an effective, well-defined organizational culture. A healthy culture requires that the values, mission, and vision of the organization are really understood and demonstrated. Trust and commitment become the currency of the day. Most employees will do the right thing. Yet, someone who may not really be interested in enhancing the idea of community and teamwork sticks out and quickly finds his or her way out the door.

Seven laws to leverage the core intelligence of a company:

1. You believe your employees' perspectives can improve your company's performance.
2. You ask for your employees' anonymous opinion in a structured, intentional manner.
3. You inform your employees of what you heard them say.
4. You consistently reinforce, recognize, and reward employee buy-in.
5. You employ the "best of the best" input from your employees in designing your company's "go-forward" plan.
6. You always prepare the internal and external resources required to support expansion prior to adding capacity.
7. You recognize that the shared agreements with your employees around company values, vision, mission, and the strategic direction of the enterprise precede the company's alignment and improved performance.

> WE THOUGHT THAT THIS PLACE NEEDED A SYMBOL THAT REPRESENTED SUCCESS AND HIGH ENERGY IN THE OFFICE ENVIRONMENT.

Chapter 25

UNFINISHED BUSINESS

"The leader's unending responsibility must be to remove every detour, every barrier, to ensure that vision is clear, and then real. The leader must create an atmosphere in the organization where people feel not only free to, but obliged to, demand clarity and purpose from their leaders."
— **Jack Welch,** *Jack Welch and the GE Way*

Peter had been irrevocably changed by everything that had happened and by everything he had learned. He was in the middle of a great leap of faith, and he wasn't sure where he was going to land.

In a few short weeks he had lost a job, lost a brother, taken over the reins of a company, met a man who changed his life, had his life threatened, nearly lost a company, and started dating a detective. Now things seemed to be getting on track quite well, and that too was a surprise.

As Peter drove the short distance back to his office, he felt like he was outside of himself. He didn't feel bad, just strange. It was as if he were detached, watching himself drive and think and plan. Yep, it had been an interesting couple of weeks.

As he pulled into the parking lot, he remembered that his staff had been discussing the events of the last few days. He wondered how they were doing, and if they had finished their talks. As he opened

the front door, it was the laughter that caught him off guard.

As he walked through the front entrance, Peter noticed the new Chinese dragon kite hanging from the ceiling, winding its way along the hallway and back into the large staff office space. It was a huge, long, red surge of energy electrifying the office. Peter looked over at the receptionist for clarity about its origin, but all she did was wink at him indicating that everything was OK.

Kate saw him first. "Hey, Boss!" Now even she was calling him "Boss."

"Hi, Kate. Hello, everyone. Hey! What's with the fire-breather?" as he pointed up towards the dragon.

The staff grouped in the front entry started smiling enthusiastically. Kate spoke up first. "We thought that this place needed a symbol that represented success and high energy in the office environment, so the Fujimori sisters said the best thing would be to hang the dragon. We weren't sure that you would like it, but all of us thought it was very cool."

He couldn't resist. "No, It's great. I love it. Now, what were you all laughing about?"

And the place erupted into laughter again. Kate said, "All of it! Absolutely all of it!"

Dean said, "Come on, Boss, you gotta admit it's all unbelievable and hysterically weird. Computer hackers, bugged phones. This is a movie plot."

Maria chimed in, "We had a seed bomb! We had seeds blown all over the place. I was picking seeds out of my clothes all weekend."

"And poisoned pizza?" It was Jimmy Valentine. "Isn't it enough to deal with the indigestion from eating one?"

Peter began to laugh, too. And then he remembered where he'd experienced this underlying feel-

> " NOW THAT THEY WERE READY TO MOVE PAST THE INITIAL DEVELOPMENT OF THE SOFTWARE FOR HERITAGE GENOMICS, IT WAS TIME TO TALK ABOUT A NEW MARKETPLACE FOR BOLDER SOLUTIONS — KNOWLEDGE MANAGEMENT. "

ing of camaraderie before. He'd sensed it at O'Connor Electronics and all the other companies he'd recently visited. His staff was starting to grow within themselves.

It was time to tell them about Horace and Michael and the Growth Curve. There was a lot of work to do. It was also time to chart the course for their future. Aside from developing newer versions of their original products, there was an enormous market for knowledge management tools. Now that they were ready to move past the initial development of the software for Heritage Genomics, it was time to talk about a new marketplace for Bolder Solutions. Knowledge management was going to be that marketplace.

Thursday morning found Peter sitting in his office reviewing the plans his sales and design people had come up with. He knew there would have to be adjustments to the plans, but he was impressed that they had all been able to sit in the same room and reach a partial agreement. He looked up to find Kate staring at him.

"You have a visitor. He looks familiar, but his name doesn't ring a bell. It's Robert Oberlander."

R.O. himself stepped around the corner and into Peter's office. He didn't say a word until Kate closed the door.

"We have a matter to discuss."

"Uh-huh."

"Your friend, Ms. McGregor, is spreading defamatory and libelous rumors about Santomo."

"No. She's threatening to spread information about your boss, Daniel Tayakanagi."

"She is treading on dangerous ground. I'm here to ask you to persuade her to desist."

"Why should I?"

"Because you will personally be destroyed by the fallout."

"Only because you failed to eliminate me a few weeks ago."

Oberlander caught himself. "I have no idea what you're talking about."

Peter was surprised at how little he was enjoying this. "Let's cut to the chase, Bob. Daniel's terrified, and he sent you here as his errand boy. If you were in any position to be a tough guy, you wouldn't have flown here unannounced to chat with me. I'm betting you flew in the company jet so no one saw you, and that there's a big black car out front waiting to whisk you back to the airport. How am I doing?"

Oberlander remained mute.

"Here's what I want, Bob. I want Santomo to get out of the genetic-agriculture business. I want a public announcement by next Friday stating that they have either sold the company or disbanded it, and that they have no intention of ever going into agri-genetics again. And if any of you try any more nonsense here in Colorado, we'll hound Tayakanagi so hard he'll have a *Sixty Minutes* crew on his doorstep."

Oberlander sighed. "As much as I hate Daniel Tayakanagi, what you're asking is preposterous. I would crush you like a snail."

"You'd try, Bob, you'd try. But you're just a puppet on a string. When you take over Santomo, hopefully you'll play by different rules. But Tayakanagi is paranoid, and that gives us a trump card that we're playing now. If we proceed with this attack campaign, it will create such a public outcry that the authorities, including the Feds, will have to consider these charges. On the other hand, you, and more importantly, Daniel, can stay out of court if you agree to our demands to cease operation. At least for the time being, that is."

Oberlander smiled. "If I'd known you had a killer instinct, I'd have kept you in the company. You played this well, Peter, if not a little naively."

"I'm not naïve, Bob. I know that inside of a year Santomo may sneak back into the business, but with all the screw-ups and tragic accidents befalling you, you guys are beginning to look vulnerable and, quite honestly, inept. Tayakanagi is over the edge and may even turn on you. Here's a hot tip: Stay away from whole wheat."

"Funny. But know this, Peter. Daniel's fear is only worth so much. If you attempt to use that information, we will come after you whether or not he likes it."

> **PETER EXPLAINED THE GROWTH CIRCLE IDEA TO ELIJAH, AND THE SCIENTIST AGREED TO START THE GATHERINGS IMMEDIATELY SO HIS PEOPLE COULD DISCUSS THE SOFTWARE, AS WELL AS ADDRESS THE RECENT DANGERS THEY WERE EXPERIENCING....**

"Is that a threat?"

"As clear a threat as I can make under the circumstances. Don't cross us again."

"Have a nice flight back, Bob. Give my regards to Daniel."

Oberlander got up to leave and seemed to reconsider. "Do the police have this information? And please don't be coy; we know about you and Detective Carnes."

"To be perfectly honest with you, I don't know everything they've got. If they have the evidence, they will proceed with the case. Count on it."

"Well, until we meet again, Mr. Logan."

"Yeah, hasta la vista, Bob."

And he was gone.

On Friday, Peter and Dean visited Elijah's company and gave a presentation about the new software.

He had given Dean an outline of what he had learned about Acceptance, and they had come up with a simple strategy to get the researchers started. Dean was able to give them some details on how the software would speed up their work.

Peter explained the Growth Circle idea to Elijah, and the scientist agreed to start the gatherings immediately so his people could discuss the software, as well as address the recent dangers they were experiencing as a result of being part of Heritage. He also got Elijah to identify a few people who would likely be champions for the new program.

The staff was motivated by the information they received. Peter and Dean both knew they would be seeing a lot more of these people in the months ahead. But by the staff acknowledging that Acceptance was a process and that they would need some assistance, the normal resistance to a new product was diminished.

Jane called late Friday afternoon.

"I don't know if we'll get much more information, Peter. We'll try to follow the money found in the assassin's bank account, but they didn't leave a lot to chance."

"Well, are you ready for tomorrow night?"

"The question is, Peter Logan, are you ready for tomorrow night?"

Sunlight streaming through the boxwood tree was the perfect backdrop for a busy day and his  first real date with Jane. The combination of a 30-mile bike ride, two Little League baseball games, and ice cream cones at Ben and Jerry's with his nephews spun his day in a whirlwind.

Now, standing at the front porch of a woman who had not only been unraveling the mystery behind his brother's death but also keeping him alive for the last few weeks was understandably strange. Yet the last three and half weeks had been nothing but strange, so why should this evening be any different?

As the door opened, he stood there stunned, as a beautiful woman greeted him dressed in a black silk robe, tied at the waist. "Hi, Peter. I'm running a few minutes late. Come on in."

He tried not to stare, but she apparently had just gotten out of the shower and was wearing nothing underneath her robe. This was definitely not the detective he saw in the office. This was the woman who would be his date for the evening.

He entered the hallway and noticed the artwork arranged on the wall, then turned to her as she closed the door.

"Great place. It's…"

But when he looked at her, the words dissolved in his mouth. She leaned back against the door-frame, smiling sweetly, slowly untying the knot of her robe.

"Mr. Logan, I believe we have some unfinished business."

> CREDIBILITY IS THE FOUNDATION OF LEADERSHIP. WHEN IT COMES TO DECIDING WHETHER A LEADER IS BELIEVABLE, PEOPLE FIRST LISTEN TO WORDS, THEN THEY WATCH THE ACTIONS. — KOUZES AND POSNER

Chapter 26

FULL CIRCLE

"I was stuck because I had a problem I didn't think I had — a problem I couldn't see. I could see matters only from my own closed perspective, and I was deeply resistant to any suggestion that the truth was otherwise. So I was in a box — cut off, closed up, blind."
— **The Arbinger Institute**, *Leadership and Self-Deception*

The phone was ringing at 8:50 Monday morning when Peter walked into the office.

"Good morning, Peter. Horace here! By my reckoning, I am your first call for the morning, so let's cut to the chase. Please forgive the speakerphone. I'm here with Michael. We've been chatting about you and your business. Now that you're done with the Growth Curve Tour, we thought it might be a good opportunity to chat with you about a few ideas we have for you and Bolder Solutions."

"Gentlemen, it's Monday morning, my plate is clear, and I'm all ears."

"Excellent. We are wondering if you have time to meet with us this evening, say at eight o'clock?" It was Michael speaking.

Peter tried to think about his evening, but it was hours away. "You know, I have no idea what I'm supposed to be doing tonight, but I'll be there. Your office, Michael?"

Horace again. "Actually, meet us at 1655 Spruce Street. I have a surprise for you."

"Fine with me. So far your surprises have actually been very cool, so I'll see you tonight."

Eight o'clock came quickly, but the last thing Peter expected was to be standing in front of a construction site staring up at a hand-painted sign with the numbers "1655" tied loosely to a tree. The nearly-completed, three-story stone, glass, and steel building occupied two city lots commanding the neighborhood in a gentle but firm manner. Its architecture was reminiscent of Boulder's late 19th century formality, with an added contemporary flair. The massive stone base supporting the structure gave it a feeling of strength and durability, while the confident rooflines and generous use of glass expressed a fresh awareness of personal freedom.

As Peter found his eyes drawn to the elegant entry, the door opened and out walked Horace Bedford. Horace actually looked like this building, or rather the building looked like Horace: self-assured, gracious, intelligent, and consummately present in the moment. As Horace glided down the stone steps, avoiding the occasional pile of construction debris, Peter suddenly realized what this building was. It was the new Growth Curve Academy.

"Hello, Peter. Thanks for coming."

"This building is very impressive, Horace. Is it the new home for your Growth Curve Academy?"

Horace came closer and leaned against the large elm tree framing the east end of the building. "Yes, it is, Peter. This building, and more importantly the Growth Curve Academy, has been a dream in the making for over five years. I thought you might appreciate seeing it tonight. But before we go inside, I want to let you know that my sources at the FBI tell me that they have run into a dead end on finding the people behind your brother's death. They have strong indications that Santomo was behind not only hiring the two contract assassins, but was also secretly experimenting with bio-molecular reorganization in certain strains of wheat DNA. Unfortunately, at this point, they still have no concrete proof to put the people responsible behind bars."

"Thank you. I hadn't heard back from the FBI and didn't expect to hear anything from them until next week. Detective Carnes, the Boulder police detective assigned to the case, said the FBI indicated that the bio-engineering behind the enzyme imbalance in my brother's blood was still so new that they were not able to find experts knowledgeable enough to give them any substantive answers."

Horace continued, "I also talked with Elija today and he has set up the 'open source' community for the plant genome database that your company created. He has already seen inquiries from as far away as Siberia, Kenya, and Australia. When people get wind of the free DNA gene pool information for the Heritage Seed food plants, it will change the lives of millions. Good work, Peter."

> " WHEN PEOPLE GET WIND OF THE FREE DNA GENE POOL INFORMATION FOR THE HERITAGE SEED FOOD PLANTS, IT WILL CHANGE THE LIVES OF MILLIONS. "

"Honestly, Horace, Elija was the brains behind this whole project. He deserves all the credit. We just gave him the engine to process his research. The world should be thanking him for the next ten generations."

"Speaking about generations, how is your young management team coming along over at Bolder Solutions? My guess is that with your new input and their sustained voltage, you could see your little company turned around in three to six months."

Peter nodded in agreement. "Horace, the only thing I am concerned about is being able to implement, or apply, all the knowledge I have collected over the last few weeks. It is actually quite daunting."

"Peter, the key to organizing your thinking around this new knowledge is setting it in the correct hierarchy of order. When it comes to a business, there are three levels of thinking. They are:

Design Mindset — This includes visioning, values, profit design, goals, and strategy.

Planning Mindset — This includes developing growth maps, business and project plans, and understanding how to organize the work of an enterprise.

Execution Mindset — This includes employing mechanisms, actually executing the plan, and finally managing the company's action items in a timely manner.

Most business operators get caught in the very practical world of the Execution Mindset, and find themselves swamped by the never-ending challenge of getting things done. The irony is that they rarely find the time to design their business and then plan how to effectively manifest their design. Peter, if

> " MOST BUSINESS OPERATORS GET CAUGHT IN THE VERY PRACTICAL WORLD OF THE EXECUTION MINDSET, AND FIND THEMSELVES SWAMPED BY THE NEVER-ENDING CHALLENGE OF GETTING THINGS DONE. THE IRONY IS THAT THEY RARELY FIND THE TIME TO DESIGN THEIR BUSINESS AND THEN PLAN HOW TO EFFECTIVELY MANIFEST THEIR DESIGN. "

you go through all your notes from the last couple of weeks and sort them based on these three mindsets, it will be easier to access the knowledge when you need it."

"Horace, how long did it take people like CJ and Butler to integrate this information into their businesses?"

Horace laughed and said, "Well, CJ and I are still debating on some of the basics, and it has been over three years since we started working together. Butler was a very quick study and had fewer strong opinions about how things should look. So, as a result, he actually integrated the Growth Curve tools and mechanisms within six months. Both CJ and Butler have done a wonderful job of releasing the spirit in their organizations."

Horace continued, "Peter, my guess is that you have three to six months of hard work ahead of you to set the foundation in place at Bolder Solutions. Remember that the people you met during your tour are available to help you if you have any questions. They are an incredible resource for you to use. Speaking of which, I have a little surprise for you. Let's go inside."

The two men crossed over into the spacious circular foyer. The construction scaffolding scattered throughout the room reached up to touch the 12-foot cove ceiling. Walking around the worker's tools, Horace led Peter into a large conference room to the left of the entry. Horace was a man on a mission as he pulled back the drop cloths protecting the fine maple wainscoting. Pressing the wood every two feet or so, he finally found what he was looking for. "Ah, the secret button." With that a portion of the wall slid open, revealing an elevator. He pressed another button and the doors parted silently. "I have always loved secret elevators. This is the first time I have been able to try it out." Pointing Peter toward the elevator, Horace beckoned, "Shall we? I would take you via the main stairs, but this is far more exciting."

Peter didn't know what to expect. Knowing Horace, the elevator could go anywhere: up, down, or sideways. As they started to rise to the second floor, Horace looked at Peter saying, "Peter, tonight is a pivotal time for more than one reason, and I want you to know how much I appreciate your interest and focus on the Growth Curve material that has been presented to you over the past few weeks."

"Horace, it has been a fascinating, yet frightening, journey and frankly I should thank you. My life has changed forever due to our meeting. I don't know how I can possibly repay you."

"Well, this evening will be an opportunity for you to see even more clearly what we are up to. I hope you enjoy yourself."

With that the elevator doors opened. Facing Peter was a nearly finished private library/office. There were club chairs placed in a circle that looked a bit out of place next to stacks of sheet rock and molding. A large, highly polished table, placed off to the side of the room, was set with an elaborate assortment of food and refreshments.

There were also people.

It took Peter a second to realize that he had met most of the people in the room. They were all looking at him, smiling. Michael stood up and approached. "Thanks for coming, Peter. I think you know almost everyone here, Milo, C. J., Corky, Butler, Tom, Tracy, and of course you've met Horace's daughter, Grace."

Peter's brain was exploding. Grace was Horace's daughter? How could that be?

Horace read the confusion on Peter's face and interrupted him saying, "Peter, Grace uses her name from her previous marriage. She's divorced now and decided that McGregor fits her better than Bedford."

Grace piped in, "Hi Peter. We're all glad you could come." She was beaming at him.

Horace continued. "Now that everyone has arrived, I'd like to open our little evening with a toast." Everyone picked up a glass from the table. "I would like to toast our new associate and friend, Peter Logan, for demonstrating an indomitable spirit under extremely adverse conditions and showing genuine curiosity in learning more about leading and growing an entrepreneurial enterprise. Peter, you have been an inspiration to us all."

Everyone cheered in unison, "Here, here, to Peter."

Peter was surprised, humbled, and generally appreciative for all the goodwill expressed by the group. "Thank you Horace, and everyone. You are all very kind. I must admit that I have learned more in the past few weeks about growing and sustaining a business than I have in the last ten years, and I have all of you to thank. So here is another toast. This time it is to all of you." Peter lifted his glass and nodded to everyone in the room.

Horace put his glass down and addressed the group. "Please, everyone, sit down. Peter, as you know from one of our first conversations, I have a deep interest in facilitating a major shift in how entrepreneurial companies become sustainable growth enterprises. All of us here believe that the entrepreneurial workplace community is the next critical testing ground for the emergence of a new breed of passionate, intentional character-driven leaders. We believe that our society, our environment, and our planet are rapidly approaching a dangerous crossroads where innovative solutions will be needed to meet what might appear to be insurmountable problems. We believe that it will take thousands, even millions, of people, like the people in this room, to make the difference."

" IN FACT, PETER, OUR VISION IS TO LIBERATE THREE MILLION GROWING ENTERPRISES FROM THE THINKING, THE STRUCTURE, AND THE PATTERNS THAT CONFINE HUMAN CREATIVITY, HUMAN POTENTIAL, AND THE EXTRAORDINARY FINANCIAL PERFORMANCE WHICH IS THE BIRTH RITE OF ALL EMERGING ENTERPRISES. "

"In fact, Peter, our vision is to liberate three million growing enterprises from the thinking, the structures, and the patterns that confine human creativity, human potential, and the extraordinary financial performance which is the birth rite of all emerging enterprises. With that in mind, Peter, we would like to invite you to join us as a new member of our Growth Curve Leadership Group."

Peter felt like he'd just stepped into an Ayn Rand novel populated by strong principled characters with a mission to save the world. He was a bit taken back by the passion in Horace's voice. How could he, Peter, possibly help "save the world" when he could barely keep his own company alive?

Horace continued. "Now, more than ever, the implications of our work are huge. The people you see here, the people you've been meeting with, are committed to:

- Intentionally improving the understanding and authoring of individual and enterprise growth;
- Supporting entrepreneurial CEOs in our community as they process their challenges and share their victories;
- Creating a community of enterprise leaders committed to respecting the dignity of the individual, the underlying principles of the Growth Curve Solution, the core intelligence of an entrepreneurial enterprise, and the satisfaction of intentionally growing a sustainable, profitable business;
- Envisioning, realizing, and demonstrating the art of "living well."

"The reason each one of these people is part of the team is that they picked up a thread of The Growth Curve Solution and found a way to add to it. Our methodology, like a growing company, is a living thing. It evolves. But it won't get very far if Michael and I are the only ones creating it. We need people like you, with a forward vision who can understand what we're trying to do, to make this knowledge grow and impact businesses."

Peter listened.

Michael spoke, "Peter, when you were able to absorb the large quantity of information that we threw at you in the last few weeks and contribute your own perspectives, we knew you were the kind of person to join our group."

Peter replied, "I don't know what to say. I am intrigued. But how can I help?"

Up until now C. J. had been quiet. "Peter, we are carving out an incredible future here that rattles the imagination."

Tracy, dressed in art-gallery black, added, "A group like this needs brains and creativity to fuel it. Peter, you have both."

Peter realized he was being asked to join a group of remarkable people, even though he barely knew them or much less understood the full extent of their vision. "How can I possibly say no? What do I have to do?"

Horace said, "This is probably as good a time as any. Peter, everyone in this room owns a piece of the Growth Curve Academy and the building we are meeting in. When we decide to invite someone to join our group, we ask them to become a full and equal partner by buying an undivided sh: the enterprise and the building. If you decide to join us, you will pay the same price that all of us paid, and if you ever want to sell your share, you can only sell it back to the enterprise at your purchase price. Any financial gain you may realize while you are a partner will occur only when distributions are paid out from the net profit of the company. If you require financing to purchase your share, I will be more than happy to facilitate that for you."

Corky spoke up, "Peter, you might be wondering, what's in this for you?' It's really very simple.

- *You get a chance to invest your money in something that may, or may not, give you an extraordinary financial return.*
- *You have an opportunity to hang out with some very cool, smart, successful people.*
- *You have an opportunity to freely contribute hours to further the Academy even when it seems you are already heavily committed.*
- *You have the great privilege to facilitate other small business leaders as they move through a process that, literally, unleashes the spirit in their enterprises.*

Corky grinned as he finished this litany of "opportunities," and then continued. "Based on your recent tour, my guess is that your imagination can easily embrace how many lives will be impacted if we are even only partially successful."

Milo spoke next. "You may also be asking yourself how can one little group in Boulder, Colorado, impact the entire planet? Again, it is very simple. We are going to start a virus. Not a bad virus, but a powerful word-of-mouth virus that has the potential to seed every city, town, and hamlet with groups like us based on the fundamentals of the Growth Curve Solution."

Peter interrupted to ask, "How are you going to make this project work? It sounds like you intend to give a whole bunch of time and energy away free."

Tracy exclaimed. "Exactly my thoughts when I first heard about the Academy from Horace. I just couldn't see how this group's mission would succeed. Then Horace introduced me to Zeno, and it all became crystal clear. Have you met Zeno yet?"

Peter looked confused as he glanced at Horace. "Not that I am aware of."

Horace stood up and announced, "Actually, Peter, you haven't met Zeno, and this is an excellent time to take a break and do just that. Most of you haven't seen the new additions to Studio A, so this will interest you as well. Pointing toward the door, Horace played the role of the gracious host. "Shall we, ladies and gentlemen?" Leading everyone across the large second floor landing to Studio A, he slowed down just enough to pull up beside Peter so that he could personally escort him through the studio's doors.

Horace leaned over to attract Peter's attention.

> ❝ PETER, WHAT YOU ARE ABOUT TO EXPERIENCE IS A REVOLUTION THAT'S BEEN IN THE MAKING FOR THE PAST NINE YEARS. WITH ZENO'S HELP, WE WILL CHANGE THE FACE OF BUSINESS AS MOST PEOPLE KNOW IT TODAY. ❞

"Peter, what you are about to experience is a revolution that's been in the making for the past nine years. With Zeno's help, we will change the face of business as most people know it today."

Ever the cynic, Peter mused to himself that whoever this Zeno was, he certainly must be eccentric, and probably very smart. By all appearances, Horace's confidence in the abilities of this mystery man was off the charts. With that, the solid wood, double doors automatically slid into the walls to reveal a 36-foot circular room. A slightly raised, 12-

foot round dais was centered under a jet-black doomed ceiling. A thin young man with horned rimmed glasses waited patiently on the dais. "Welcome. You must be Peter."

Peter's mouth opened in surprise, and before he could stop himself he blurted out, "You're not Zeno, are you?"

The young man laughed and replied, "Oh my God! No, I'm not Zeno. My name is Archer. I work with Zeno. Actually, I am a member of a special team which has been working with Zeno for the past few years."

Horace was enjoying this a little more than he expected. "Archer, let's get to the point and introduce Peter to Zeno."

Archer motioned Peter up onto the dais. Thinking he was in for some sort of "rite of passage" prank, Peter prepared himself for the worst. Everyone from the group stood around the platform smiling as Peter stepped up beside Archer. The young technician pulled out an electric remote from his pocket, touched a few buttons, and three sets of wires and a helmet dropped slowly from the ceiling. He motioned Peter to the center of the dais and said, "Peter, I need to put this equipment on you so bear with me. I'll put the helmet on first, and then I will hook up each of your hands and legs."

Tracy was the first to speak, "This is when it gets very exciting."

Peter's knee-jerk response was, "For who, you or me? Can anyone tell me what this is all about before this young fellow straps me in for good?" Everyone laughed. The joke was lost on Peter.

Visions of the inquisition and other macabre thoughts flew through Peter's mind as Archer silently hooked up the equipment. Horace interrupted his thoughts by saying, "Peter, let's just say

> " VISIONS OF THE INQUISITION AND OTHER MACABRE THOUGHTS FLEW THROUGH PETER'S MIND AS ARCHER SILENTLY ATTACHED THE EQUIPMENT....ARCHER COMPLETED HIS WORK AND PETER WAS HOOKED UP, LOOKING A LOT LIKE A CHARACTER IN A NEW-AGE FRANKENSTEIN MOVIE. "

that you are one of only 20 people who has ever met Zeno."

As Horace finished, Archer completed his work and Peter was hooked up, looking a lot like a character in a new-age Frankenstein movie. Then Archer shut the helmet visor and Peter's world changed forever.

Inside the helmet a bright world surrounded Peter, and he found himself standing at the front entry of a large, classic building similar to the ancient Greek Parthenon. Standing outside the building off to the left was a distinguished, bearded man in his mid-forties who held Peter's gaze in an all-knowing way. The man approached Peter and introduced himself.

"Good evening, Peter. My name is Zeno, and you are entering the virtual Growth Curve Academy. You can speak to me and you can move freely. The mobile floor underneath you, in the physical world, will adjust to your movements. The responses made by your hands, head, arms, and legs are all connected to the virtual reality you are currently experiencing. Dissimilar to a movie theater, this virtual world totally surrounds you. You are really in it, not just observing it. I only ask that you not move too suddenly. Just relax as though you were actually physically here. In a manner of speaking, you are having a physical experience, but we can talk about that later. I will be guiding you through a short introduction to the Growth Curve Experience, which will barely scratch the surface of what we are preparing for business leaders like yourself in the future. Please follow me."

As Peter followed Zeno into the building, he felt as if he were actually walking. A strange sense of movement flowed through his legs. He was almost convinced that he was really in this virtual reality. As he moved through the foyer, he noticed the huge stone floor with a classical colonnade forming a walkway around the room's empty center. He was surprised to see very purpose-ful-looking

people briskly walking through the room. An odd thought spun through his mind. He wanted to ask Zeno if these people were real, but just as he was beginning to form the words, Zeno spoke up. "Peter, you are probably wondering if these people are real, or for that matter, if I am real. All I can tell you is that the computer program running this virtual reality has been designed to replicate your world in the finest detail. So, I will let you decide if it is real or not."

Zeno continued. "The Growth Curve Academy is charged with the mission of training thousands, even millions, of small business leaders. In order to accomplish this mission, we had to find a delivery method that totally immersed the participant in the learning experience, so that a very deep level of transference occurred. We also needed to be able to do this at a distance. In short, we needed to create a simulated reality that we could control at the Academy and still allow business leaders across the country, or eventually around the world, to access the information at their leisure. This is or will be the Application Service Provider model of the future."

> **HE WAS SURPRISED TO SEE VERY PURPOSEFUL-LOOKING PEOPLE BRISKLY WALKING THROUGH THE ROOM....HE WANTED TO ASK ZENO IF THESE PEOPLE WERE REAL.**

Zeno continued. "Let me give you a quick sample of the power of this simulation. Push that button in front of you that says 'Growth Language.'"

Peter complied, and suddenly CJ appeared next to Zeno smiling. "Hi, Peter. I am here to explain the three elements of Growth Language to you. They are the 3 Gates of Growth, the Stages of Growth, and Growth Patterns. Follow me. I want to introduce you to some of my staff." Peter followed the virtual-reality CJ through a door that appeared out of thin air into her office at O'Conner Electronics. Everything at CJ's office was as he remembered it. Zeno suddenly appeared in CJ's office and instructed Peter to touch the button with the word

"Disengage" on it. Immediately Peter was back at the Academy.

"Peter, we have a module with each of the Growth Curve Academy partners instructing at their place of business. Now, look down and you will see a button that says 'Simulate' right after the 'Growth Language' button. If you push that button it will run you through five levels of simulated Growth Language experiences with real-life scenarios to interface with, giving you an opportunity to address the given challenges with appropriate solutions. We have simulations for each element of the Growth Curve Solution. All in all, it would take someone a solid week to go through all of our programming. That is if they passed every level of simulation. So far, only Horace and Michael have passed every level successfully. There are others, like Butler and Tracy, who are close. Since we do not have the luxury of time tonight I will disengage the Academy Program now. Thank you, Peter, for your apt attention and I look forward to seeing you at the Academy again in the near future." Suddenly Peter's helmet went black and he was instructed to lift the visor.

Horace was standing right in front of him. "Welcome back, Peter. Rather amazing, wouldn't you agree?"

Peter gazed around the room. The silent, knowing faces all told the same story — that the experience Peter just had was his initiation, and not until he had gone to meet Zeno was he really ready to join the group. All Peter could manage to say was "Oh my God! You guys are really into some very cool stuff. Where do I sign up?"

Everyone laughed and applauded as they came up to welcome Peter and shake his hand. For the rest of the evening Peter ate, laughed, and talked with this incredible band of leaders. The good will and camaraderie expressed among them all lifted Peter's understanding of friendship to a new height.

As the evening came to an end, Horace stepped to the center of the group to make a few final comments. "Everyone, I wanted to let you know that the official open house of the Growth Curve Academy is slated for 60 days from tonight. I will be out of town until the day before the opening. Grace will be watching over the construction and the affairs of the Academy. Please direct any questions to her while I am away."

CJ piped up and asked, "Horace, where are you going?"

"CJ, let's just say that I need to see an old friend about some unfinished business. Oh and by the way, Peter, I have an Academy welcome present for you. Please wait until you get home to open it."

As Peter walked out of the Academy building his head was spinning. Just when he thought he was beginning to piece it all together, Horace threw him

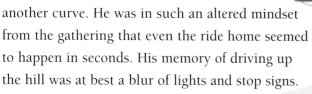

another curve. He was in such an altered mindset from the gathering that even the ride home seemed to happen in seconds. His memory of driving up the hill was at best a blur of lights and stop signs.

Standing in his dining room, Peter opened the present from Horace. As the thick colored paper fell away and Peter slowly lifted the top off the box, he felt both awe and surprise. He looked down at Horace's leather journal sitting in the box. Inside the journal Horace had left a short note. It said, "Peter, take this journal and use it as you see fit. Maybe there is some value buried in my musings that will help you over the next three to six months. As you see, there are numerous blank pages begging to be filled. I encourage you to continue my work and include your own revelations. Until I see you again, best of luck at releasing the spirit of your organization." Signed, "Horace"

Looking out his front window onto the hardened granite face of the famous Flat Irons, Peter could only wonder what was coming next.

Sources

BOOKS:

A Pattern Language by Christopher Alexander. New York, New York: Oxford University Press, 1977

A Simpler Way by Margaret Wheatley and Myron Kellner Rogers. San Francisco, California: Berrett-Koehler Publishers, Inc. 1996

Faster Company by Patrick Kelly. New York, New York: John Wiley & Sons, Inc., 1998

Finding and Keeping Great Employees by Jim Harris and Joan Bannick. New York, New York: Amacom, AMA Publishers, 1999

Good to Great by Jim Collins. New York, New York: Harper Business, Harper Collins Publishers, 2001

Hiring: How to Find and Keep the Best People by Richard S. Deems, Ph.D. Career Press, 1998

Leadership and Self-Deception by Arbinger Institute. San Francisco, California: Berrett-Koehler Publishers, Inc., 2002

Leadership and the New Science: Discovering Order in a Chaotic World by Margaret Wheatley and Myron Kellner Rogers. San Francisco, California: Berrett-Koehler Publishers, Inc., Revised 1999

Learning to Read the Signs by F. Byron Nahser. Boston, Massachusetts: Butterworth-Heinemann, 1997

Primal Leadership: Realizing the Power of Emotional Intelligence by Daniel Goleman, Richard Boyatzis and Annie McKee. Boston, Massachusetts: Harvard Business School Publishing, 2002

Profit Patterns by Adrian Slywotzky and David Morrison. New York, New York: Random House, 1999

Sacred Geometry by Robert Lawlor. New York, New York: Thames and Hudson, Inc., 1992

Seeing Systems by Barry Oshry. San Francisco, California: Berrett-Koehler Publishers, Inc., 1995

Surfing the Edge of Chaos by Richard Pascale, Mark Millman and Linda Gioja. New York, New York: Crown Business, 2000

The Circle of Innovation: You Can't Shrink Your Way to Greatness by Tom Peters. New York, New York: Alfred A. Knopf, 1997

The Delphic Boat: What Genomes Tell Us by Antoine Danchin. Cambridge, Massachusetts: Harvard University Press, 2002

The E-Myth Revisited by Michael Gerber. New York, New York: Harper Business, 1995

The Great Game of Business by Jack Stack with Bo Burlingham. New York, New York: Doubleday, division of Bantam Doubleday Dell Publishing Group, Inc., 1994

The Healthy Company by Robert H. Rosen, Ph.D. with Lisa Berger. New York, New York: Jeremy P. Tarcher, Putnam Company, 1991

The Living Company by Aries De Guise. Boston, Massachusetts: Harvard Business School Publishing, 1997

The McGraw-Hill Guide to Managing Growth in Your Emerging Business: Guidelines for Transforming Your Small Business into and Exceptional Enterprise by Stephen C. Harper. New York, New York: McGraw-Hill, 1994

The Profit Zone by Adrian Slywotzky and David Morrison. New York, New York: New York Times Books, Random House, 1997

The Seven Mysteries of Life by Guy Murchie. Boston, Massachusetts: Houghton Mifflin Company, 1978

The Timeless Way of Building by Christopher Alexander. New York, New York: Oxford University Press, 1979

The White Roots of Peace: The Iroquois Book of Life by Paul Wallace. Revised: Santa Fe, New Mexico: Clear Light Publishers, 1994

Value-Creating Growth by Thomas L. Doorley III and John M. Donovan. San Francisco, California: Jossey-Bass Publishers, 1999

Waking the Tiger by Peter Levine. Berkeley, California: North Atlantic Books, 1997

Zapp! The Lightening of Empowerment: How to Improve Productivity, Quality, and Employee Satisfaction by William Byham and Jeff Cox. New York, New York: Ballentine Publishing Group, Revised Edition 1998

AUDIOTAPES:

Focusing Your Unique Ability by Dan Sullivan. Toronto, Ontario: The Strategic Coach Inc. 1995-97

INDEX

1. **5 Challenges** — Of the 27 challenges that consistently surface in small-to-medium-size enterprises, there are 5 unique challenges that commonly stand out for each stage of growth. By calibrating a company's current challenges with the full spectrum of challenges that surface for the different stages of growth, a deeper understanding of the causes of the company's current challenges can be revealed and addressed. (pp. 299, 306)

2. **5 Strengths** — Of the 27 strengths that consistently surface in small-to-medium-size enterprises there are 5 unique strengths that commonly stand out for each stage of growth. By calibrating a company's current strengths with the full spectrum of strengths that surface for the different stages of growth, a deeper understanding of the causes of the company's current strengths can be revealed and addressed. (pp. 299, 306)

3. **Acceptance** — A powerful methodology that facilitates the willingness in the CEO of a company to release resistance to the issues causing low performance and see underneath the surface to the real causes. (pp. 84, 89, 133, 138, 196, 197, 273, 274, 276, 291, 292, 294-296, 300, 305, 312)

4. **Adjacent Business** — All revenue that is generated from a blend or the related spin-off from the core business. Healthy companies generate between 20-30 percent of their revenue from their adjacent business. (p. 158)

5. **Advancing Patterns** — These patterns are, by their nature, advancing to the company's goals, strategies, plans, values and the work community as a whole. (pp. 133, 134, 138)

6. **Blended Gross Margins** — The percentage of revenue that blended gross profit represents on any aggregate sale of products and/or services.

7. **Blended Gross Profit** — The profit you make from the combination of a number of transactions. The actual dollar amount that is left from a multiple product or service sale(s) after you have subtracted your cost of goods (direct labor + direct materials + allocated overhead) from the sales revenue you have received.

8. **Bread-and-Butter Revenue** — Any sale that helps your company reach its monthly revenue goal.

9. **Builder/Protector Ratio** — The Builder/Protector Ratio measures the intensity and the balance between the state of confidence and the state of caution inherent in the psyche of an organization, a

department, a team or an individual. (pp. 119-125, 147, 48, 298, 306)

10. **Bulldozer Margins** — A gross margin on a product or service that lands between 35 percent and 50 percent gross margin. (pp. 111, 148)

11. **Business Development** — The function of targeting, capturing and caring for the customer. (pp. 160, 161, 165, 168, 184)

12. **Capital Intensity** — The measurement and management of the required financial resources. (pp. 160, 166, 167. 168. 184)

13. **Champion Revenue** — Any sale that represents 50 percent or more of your company's quarterly revenue goal.

14. **Community** — People go to work, in part, to belong. Community is the organizing of a company's vision, mission, goals, strategies and objectives that engage and empower employees to help them contribute to the success of a company. It's the second rung on the staff satisfaction hierarchy and must be met before moving on to Performance. (pp. 15, 40, 79, 83-89, 101, 113, 122, 135, 139, 147-149, 168, 192, 199, 213-217, 220, 221, 224-226, 238, 289, 307, 316, 329)

15. **Core Business** — All revenue generated by activities of the primary and unique abilities of the company. Healthy companies generate 60 percent or more of their revenue base in their core business.

16. **Culture** — The landscape and focus of the human workplace community as defined by a blend of four enterprise cultural styles: a) Innovation Culture; b) Spirit-Driven Culture; c) Customer Service Culture; d) Operational Excellence Culture. (pp. 160, 164, 168, 184, 191, 193-196, 216, 217, 245, 307)

17. **Customer Charter** — The unwritten agreement you have with your customers to solve their problems and/or deliver that which pleases them. (pp. 182, 185)

18. **Customer Intelligence** — The informed awareness of who the customer is and what they want. (pp. 158, 160, 165, 168, 184)

19. **Cycles of Maturity** — Time and duration affect the vibrancy and behavior of every living system, including businesses. Each of the 5 cycles of maturity have unique characteristics that influence the behavior and performance of an enterprise in any stage of growth. (pp. 300, 306)

20. **Destructive Patterns** — These patterns are, by their nature, destructive to the company's goals, strategies, plans, values and the work community as a whole. (pp. 133, 134, 138)

21. **Dispersion Patterns** — These patterns are, by their nature, more scattered and often are outward focused. Gossip is a good example of a dispersion pattern. (p. 134)

22. **Edge Business** — All revenue that is generated by the new and untested lines of a business that may or may not prove to be valuable in the future. Healthy companies generate 5-15% of their revenue from their edge business. (pp. 158, 172, 173)

23. **Empire Revenue** — Any sale that represents 30 percent or more of your company's annual revenue goal.

24. **Enterprise Growth Knowledge** — An important model or foundation for how blending the principles of nature, complexity and growth intelligence produce greater performance and innovation in commercial enterprises. Turns the understanding of organizational growth from that of "business as a machine" to one of "business as a living, intelligent organism." (pp. 92, 93, 103)

25. **Five Non-Negotiable Rules** — 35 fundamental laws or rules exist for emerging enterprise growth. Out of these 35 rules there are five non-negotiable rules for each stage of growth and the effective completion of these five rules improves the likelihood for continuing survival and financial success. (pp. 299, 300, 306)

26. **Flood Zone** — This is the transition zone where there is a flood of activity to such an extent that there is never enough staff to handle all the work. (pp. 121-124, 129, 301)

27. **Galactic Margins** — A gross margin on a product or service that lands between 50 and 75+ percent. (pp. 111, 131, 147, 148)

28. **Gross Margin** — The percentage of revenue that your gross profit represents on any product or service. (p. 162)

29. **Gross Profit** — The profit you make from any transaction, the actual dollar amount that is left after you have subtracted your cost of goods (direct labor + direct materials + allocated overhead) on any product or service from the sales price of that product or service. (pp. 161, 162, 168, 175, 179)

30. **Growth Circle** — A regular structured gathering of 5-10 employees that supports the health, the communication and the harmony of the workplace community. It can act as an effective vehicle to: train employees, brainstorm, make decisions, provide new staff orientation, manage projects, assess, and provide a channel for employees to vent their concerns. (pp. 46, 49, 219, 220, 222, 223, 225, 255, 276, 312)

31. **Growth Community** — Redesigns how we think about and create the modern work community so that it better serves both the company's vision, strategic goals, objectives and culture and also correctly addresses the interests, needs and requirements of the staff. (pp. 213-217, 220, 221, 224-227, 238)

32. **Growth Curve** — The fine line that a company navigates between chaos and equilibrium in any stage of growth, the path of balance between chaos and equilibrium that arc through every stage of growth. (pp. 49, 53, 129, 147, 303, 310, 317, 318, 329)

33. **Growth Mapping** — A dynamic new method of communicating, tracking and enterprise planning through the use of 'visual maps' that is accessible by the entire organization. It facilitates 'bottom-up' engagement, strategic authoring and buy-in by the entire staff. (pp. 232, 233, 235-237, 239, 240, 244, 251)

34. **Growth Mechanisms** — Reveals the important role of key infrastructure mechanisms that facilitate the application of the Growth Curve Solution in a business enterprise at any stage of growth. (pp. 270, 271, 274, 275)

35. **Growth Trauma** — Is a unique methodology that reveals the causes, symptoms and cures for trauma in the workplace. (pp. 84, 89, 147, 225, 257-263, 329)

36. **Knowledge Management** — The manner in which you leverage, gather and store your company's unique knowledge. (pp. 160, 164, 168, 184, 243, 310)

37. **Language of Enterprise Growth** — Creates the everyday language of growth that is required for deep change in the organization and explains the three elements of growth (stages, gates, patterns).

38. **Leadership Competencies** — A set of 18 core leadership competencies, based on the work of Daniel Goleman, to help determine leadership capacity in individuals and in organizations. (pp. 297, 298, 305)

39. **Leadership Style** — The mechanism that quantifies how a leader links to the "feel of the company". (pp. 218, 227, 296, 297, 305)

40. **Learning** — People go to work to be stimulated and to personally grow in their job and careers. Learning is the fourth rung on the staff satisfaction hierarchy and must be met before moving on to Meaning. (pp. 13-15, 28, 34, 98, 192, 199, 236, 242, 244, 251)

41. **Learning Style** — The four learning styles (concrete, model, trial and error, or reflective) define the speed, the depth, the risk tolerance and the flexibility of how a leader thinks. (pp. 298, 305)

42. **Linear Patterns** — These patterns are focused on the end result. They are sequentially driven and build on each other. (pp. 133, 134, 138)

43. **Material** — At the base of the staff satisfaction hierarchy. People go to work to make a living and to work in an engaging and enjoyable work environment. This need must be met before moving on to Community. (pp. 192, 199)

44. **Maxi Mechanism** — A mechanism that impacts an entire department.

45. **Meaning** — People go to work because they want to contribute to their world. This is the highest rung on the staff satisfaction hierarchy. (pp. 192, 199)

46. **Mechanism** — A process, method or tool that changes and/or focuses the behavior/activity of an individual, team, department or organization. (pp. 13, 85, 87, 174, 222, 223, 271-275, 279, 305)

47. **Mini Mechanism** — A mechanism that impacts a small work team. (p. 273)

48. **Minnow Sales Prospect** — A sales prospect that if sold would be equivalent to one day's sales quota or more for a sales rep.

49. **Modality** — Measures the degree of "direct or indirect influence" a leader applies to manifest the company's goals and is measured by the leader's mode of involvement (dominant, facilitative or supportive). (pp. 81, 87, 120, 244, 297, 305)

50. **Money You Keep** — The net profit of a company. (p. 156)

51. **Money You Make** — The gross profit of a company. (p. 156)

52. **Mosaic Patterns** — These patterns concentrate on a process, are inward focused, collaborative and contributory. (pp. 133, 134, 138)

53. **Mountain Mechanism** — A mechanism that impacts multiple departments and/or the entire company.

54. **Neutral Patterns** — These patterns neither advance nor detract from the goals, strategies, plans, values and the work community as a whole. (pp. 133, 134, 138)

55. **New Profit Model** — The New Profit Model provides a powerful new perspective on the sustainability and advancement of enterprise profit as it is a) critically tied to the design of the business, b) dependent on the profit net or profit competency of the entire staff and, c) reliant on the continued loyalty of the customer base. (pp. 83, 88, 151, 156, 160, 173, 180, 181, 183, 184)

56. **Operating Systems** — The support structure for critical enterprise processes. (pp. 160, 166, 168, 184)

57. **Organization Structure** — The organizing of people to successfully complete tasks. (pp. 160, 165, 166, 168, 184)

58. **People Gate** — All issues and concerns that center on and affect the people of a company. (pp. 115, 122, 124, 125)

59. **Performance Phase** — Upon entering a stage of growth and having proceeded through a period of planning, a healthy company will spend 70 percent of its time in the stage of growth executing the company's plan. (pp. 129, 130, 138)

60. **Performance** — The third rung on the staff satisfaction hierarchy. People go to work to achieve and perform and to be rewarded for their performance. Must be met before moving on to Learning. (pp. 40, 41, 84, 86, 89, 116, 179, 192, 236, 241, 242, 251, 255, 271, 296, 297, 300, 302, 303, 306)

61. **Preparation Phase** — Upon entering a stage of growth a healthy company will spend 20 percent of its time in that stage of growth in planning and preparation activities. (p. 129)

62. **Pressure Phase** — As a company nears the end of a stage of growth it will enter into a transition period of extreme pressure. A healthy company will spend 10 percent of its time during a stage of growth challenged by this pressure phase prior to moving into the next stage of growth. (p. 129)

63. **Process Gate** — All issues and concerns that center on and affect the processes and procedures of an enterprise. (pp. 115, 123)

64. **Profit Net** — The profit net is a combination of mechanisms that train and engage your staff to know 1) how the company makes and keeps money; 2) how every activity should be no more than three steps away from the Profit Zone; and 3) the factors contributing to the company's profitability. (pp. 83, 88, 156, 164, 174, 178-180, 184, 185)

65. **Profit Sequences** — The profit sequences are the three step combinations that result in profitability for the enterprise. Any activity an employee or staff member engages should not be any more than three steps from the profit zone. (pp. 174, 177, 178, 185)

66. **Profit Zone** — A relentless, precise and intense mindset held by the staff to make and keep money for the organization. (pp. 177-179, 185, 329)

67. **R&D** — The continual discovery of solutions to your customer's needs. (p. 166, 184)

68. **Revenue/Profit Gate** — All issues and concerns that center on and affect the revenue generation and profitability of an enterprise. (pp. 115, 122, 124)

69. **Scooter Margins** — A gross margin on a product or service that lands between 20% and 35% gross

margin. (pp. 111, 131, 147, 148)

70. **Scope** — The range of products or services to be offered. (pp. 160, 163, 168, 184, 197)

71. **Staff Satisfaction** — Reveals the core requirements of staff satisfaction and shows the deep connection between staff satisfaction and enterprise profitability at every stage of growth. (pp. 55, 72, 76, 83, 88, 151, 188-193, 198, 199, 329)

72. **Stage 1** — Start Up Stage of Growth, 1-10 employees (pp. 121, 126, 159, 258)

73. **Stage 2** — Ramp Up Stage of Growth, 11-19 employees (pp. 98, 120-123)

74. **Stage 3** — Delegation Stage of Growth, 20-34 employees (pp. 71, 98, 121-123, 126, 258, 301)

75. **Stage 4** — Professional Stage of Growth, 35-57 employees (pp. 120, 123, 124, 126, 208, 255, 258, 301)

76. **Stage 5** — Integration Stage of Growth, 58-96 employees (pp. 121, 124, 159, 208, 222)

77. **Stage 6** — Strategic Stage of Growth, 97-160 employees (pp. 121, 124, 125, 192, 222)

78. **Stage 7** — Visionary Stage of Growth, 161-350+ employees (pp. 120, 125)

79. **Strategic Alliances** — The specific external partners engaged to expand sales. (pp. 124, 125, 160, 166, 184, 235, 258)

80. **Strategic Control** — The unique attractive power of your offerings. (pp. 160, 162, 163, 168, 184)

81. **Three Faces of the Leader** — Measures the blend (by percentage) of three primary leadership roles (visionary, manager, specialist) that an enterprise leader adopts as they direct the affairs of their company. (pp. 297, 305)

82. **Trout Sales Prospect** — A sales prospect that if sold would be equivalent to one week's sales quota or more for a sales rep.

83. **Unchallenged Patterns** — Patterns which have become familiar to the staff and the work community so the staff no longer resists them. There is still a need to reinforce this type of pattern until it has been accepted at a deeper level. (pp. 133, 138)

84. **Unconscious Patterns** — These patterns are no longer consciously considered by the staff and now operate freely at an unconscious level. (pp. 133-135, 137, 138)

85. **Untested Patterns** — New patterns that have been introduced to a group which have not been tested by the group. In most cases, the staff resists these patterns until they become more familiar with them. (pp. 133, 138)

86. **Values Bridge** — The values bridge is a set of commonly agreed upon values shaping direction and behavior in the daily work environment and are the practiced base of cultural norms in a principle-driven organization.   (pp. 191, 192, 197, 199)

87. **Value Exchange** — The profitable organization and exchange of value for money. (pp. 160, 161, 165, 166, 168, 184)

88. **Voltage** — The energy in the workplace that reflects the level of enthusiasm and the intensity of focus as expressed by the people working in that work environment. (pp. 39-41, 43, 56, 59, 66, 67, 71, 139, 145, 147, 148, 177, 185, 190-193, 220, 259, 260-263, 268, 301)

89. **Whale Sales Prospect** — A sales prospect that if sold would be equivalent to one month's sales quota or more for a sales rep.

90. **Wind Tunnel** — The transition zone where the management methods and tools that worked in the past unfortunately no longer work. As such, leadership must discover new management methods and tools to address the challenges of the company. (pp. 122, 124, 125, 129)

APPENDIX

From the notebook of Horace Bedford...

The 9 Fundamentals of the Growth Curve Solution

1. Provide a dynamic new method of planning that is accessible by the whole organization and allows contribution and strategic authoring by the entire staff.

2. Redesign how we think about and create the modern work community so that it not only better serves the company's vision, strategy, and goals, but also correctly addresses the interests, needs, and requirements of the staff.

3. Create a language of growth that: a) explains how companies grow, and b) gives a vocabulary of growth that everyone in the organization can use to communicate about the company's growth.

4. Provide a powerful new perspective on the importance of profitability in regard to the growth process and how it is: a) tied to the design of the business, b) dependent on everyone in the enterprise being in the profit zone, and c) reliant on the continued loyalty of the customer base.

5. Turn the understanding of organizational growth from one of being "business as a machine" to one of being "business as a living, intelligent organism."

6. Reveal the core requirements to staff satisfaction, and show the deep connection between staff satisfaction and enterprise profitability at every stage of growth.

7. Reveal the causes, symptoms, and cures for Growth Trauma.

8. Create key mechanisms that facilitate the application of the Growth Curve Solution in a business enterprise at any given stage of growth.

9. Introduce a method that facilitates the willingness of the CEO to release resistance to the company's current challenges in order to see below the surface of those challenges to the real causes of the company's issues.

James Fischer

As a successful entrepreneur, consultant, business manager, trainer, CEO coach, educator, author, and speaker, James contributes an unusual breadth of experience and insight into the key challenges confronting every enterprise growth leader today. Based on his experience working with over 650 CEOs and their companies, in 35 different industries, James has created a comprehensive methodology for understanding and managing entrepreneurial growth. His research and development of the 7 Stages of Enterprise Growth is a proven model for predicting how growth will impact small firms with up to 350+ employees. Based on the 7 Stages as an Enterprise Development Model, James consults and trains enterprise CEOs to adapt to the requirements of change in their growing company, focus their resources on the right thing at the right time, and effectively predict the needs of their company 6 to 12 months in the future.

Apply the Growth Curve Solution to Your Own Company

You have just witnessed Peter's unique journey into Horace Bedford's world of entrepreneurial growth and profitability. Now it's time for you to discover how all this information applies to you and your company.

Go to www.origininstitute.com

Take a "FREE" Growth Curve Entrepreneurial Assessment and receive a powerful report giving you useful insights on:
- How to leverage your company's current stage of growth
- How to better understand how to leverage your unique leadership potential
- How to improve your company's financial performance

Receive a monthly "FREE" Entrepreneur E-Zine that will give you:
- Powerful management tools, methods and insights for your growing company
- Unique insight into your company's stage of growth
- Stories from other CEOs growing their companies on the Growth Curve

Participate in the growing community of entrepreneurial CEOs, Executives, and Advisors that will:
- Connect you to your peers and their fresh ideas, innovative tools, and proven methods to better manage and grow your enterprises
- Give you specific help with your company's unique challenges
- Give you a sounding board to help you think about and see your company in a new, more advancing perspective

Create a Profit-Driven, People-Centered, Growth-Smart Company

Go to www.origininstitute.com and learn how to:

1. Create a Powerful New Profit Design for your company
2. Infuse a Proven Entrepreneurial Decision-Making method into your company that can save or make you hundreds of thousands of dollars a year
3. Explore your Stage of Growth X-Ray by illuminating the 10 Hidden Agents influencing every level of your company's performance

Origin Institute • 877-282-6959 • 4450 Arapahoe Avenue • Suite 100 • Boulder, CO 80303

Growth Curve Press
proudly presents

Harvesting Clarity:
12 Revelations of an Enterprise Leader

James Fischer

See the following page for a preview of "Harvesting Clarity"

GROWTH CURVE
PRESS

4450 Arapahoe Avenue, Suite 100
Boulder, CO 80303
303-546-7939
www.growthcurvepress.com

PROLOGUE

The marker was the remains of an old fishing boat beached during the storm of '38. Nothing else could distinguish the visual sameness of dunes and sand as far as the eye could see. If memory served him right, there was no place quite like this anywhere along the sixty miles of slender Fire Island white sand. Nowhere else could you look in both directions and not see a single dwelling. Nowhere was the Atlantic so remarkably clean as to reveal schools of fish swimming through the waves as they broke along the shore.

This was the place, fifty-five years ago, where two boys sealed a lifetime pact to always remain the best of friends. Right at the tip of the old fishing boat bow they had engraved their names and the spiral sign of their secret club. With the dune grass softly bending around his legs, Horace Bedford rubbed his fingers over the faint outline of the carved names and wondered what had gone wrong.

"This place hasn't changed much, has it, my old friend?" The voice behind Horace startled him out of his reverie. He spun around to meet the intruder, and found the black feral eyes of his fiercest adversary staring back at him.

Smiling through his surprise, Horace exclaimed, "The infamous Daniel Tayakanagi. Well, we meet again. I must say the contrast of seeing your face framed by the sweetest waves the Atlantic has to offer is one of the true contradictions of nature. By the way, were you man enough to come alone or did you hide your handlers behind the dunes?"

Unruffled, Tayakanagi stood firm in the sand with a rock-hard face chiseled by decades of ruthless negotiations. "I am not here to spar with you, Horace Bedford. I am here to bargain for your daughter's life."

To be continued...

341